HIPPOLYTE DREYFUS-BARNEY

HIPPOLYTE DREYFUS-BARNEY

DISCIPLE OF ‘ABDU’L-BAHÁ

By
Yann Ballanger
In collaboration with Parivash Ardei-Amini
Translated from the original French

BAHÁ’Í PUBLISHING
EVANSTON, ILLINOIS

Bahá'í Publishing
1233 Central St., Evanston, IL 60202

 Published 2025
Printed in the United States of America ∞
28 27 26 25 1 2 3 4

Library of Congress Cataloging-in-Publication Data

Names: Ballanger, Yann, author. | Amini, Parivash Ardei, author.
Title: Hippolyte Dreyfus-Barney : disciple of ʻAbdu'l-Bahá / by Yann Ballanger ; in collaboration with Parivash Ardei Amini.
Description: Evanston, IL : Bahá'í Publishing, 2025. | Translation of: Hippolyte Dreyfus-Barney : premier bahá'í français. | Includes bibliographical references and indexes. | Translated from the original French.
Identifiers: LCCN 2024056287 | ISBN 9781618512598 (paperback) | ISBN 9781618512604 (epub)
Subjects: LCSH: Dreyfus, Hippolyte, 1873–1928. | Bahais—France—Biography. | Bahai Faith—France—History.
Classification: LCC BP395.D74 B35 2025 | DDC 297.9/30944—dc23/eng/20250130
LC record available at https://lccn.loc.gov/2024056287

Cover design by Carlos Esparza
Book design by Patrick Falso

To all who have dedicated their lives
to applying the teachings of Bahá'u'lláh
in their efforts to build a better world.
May Hippolyte Dreyfus-Barney's extraordinary life
and unwavering commitment continue to inspire
generations to come.

Contents

Foreword

The history of the Bahá'í Faith is replete with the true-life stories of courage, devotion, dedication and sacrifice of the early followers of Bahá'u'lláh, tales of steadfastness and service to humanity that will surely inspire people from all over the world for generations to come. The firmament of Bahá'í history is brilliantly lit up by the many shining lights among those early believers whose life stories qualify them to be remembered as heroes and heroines. We can all remember, for example, the unique sacrifices of the early Persian believers and martyrs during the Heroic Age[1] or the epic determination with which Western believers arose in response to answer the Guardian's calls to go pioneering and propagate the Faith during the Ten Year Crusade. Among all these extraordinary souls from the first century of the Faith is a towering figure whom Shoghi Effendi designated, along with eighteen others, a Disciple of 'Abdu'l-Bahá and a Herald of the Covenant: Hippolyte Dreyfus-Barney.[2]

For many of the followers of Bahá'u'lláh, Hippolyte Dreyfus-Barney is at once a very well-known name and yet a deeply unknown figure in the history of the Faith. He was famous for being the first French Bahá'í in France and a pioneer in spreading the Cause in Europe through his translations of the Holy Writings of Bahá'u'lláh. However, as recent research has brought to light the details of his life, we have discovered that Hippolyte Dreyfus was undeniably much more than that: it is now an established fact that he was a tireless worker, a fearless traveler, an unyielding defender of the Cause, a spirit sanctified by his love for the Master and the Guardian. We now know that the services he rendered to the Faith are as innumerable as they are historically significant. This book will strive to do justice to his stellar record of selfless service and tireless devotion, his erudition, and his unremitting personal endeavors in the protection and advancement of the Cause of God as revealed by Bahá'u'lláh.

Often, the life of such a hero who has left an indelible mark in the annals of the Faith is characterized by an alternation of crisis and victory, of highs and lows, and is marked by occasional periods of "down-time." Remarkably, what strikes any keen observer of Hippolyte's life is the constancy and stability of his unremitting service, and the high level of intensity with which he dedicated, from the day he decided to embrace the Faith, even his minutest moments to serving it. And in this unflagging endeavor, he persevered, staunchly and steadfastly, until his last breath.

Some episodes of his life are reminiscent of the most colorful adventure novels, such as when he found himself face to face with tribesmen armed with spears in the middle of the Vietnamese jungle or when he was forced to escape from Tsing-Tao,[3] then a German colony in China, at the outbreak of the First World War. Sometimes his story resembles a mystical tale in which, with his heart aglow with love for his Beloved, he engages, without the slightest hesitation, in the most difficult missions. And, when one reads the text of his conference papers or any of his many literary works, the reader finds himself projected into the presence of a brilliant intellectual capable of conversing with flawless eloquence on the most complex subjects.

In his clear grasp of the fundamental truths of Bahá'u'lláh's Writings as elucidated to him by 'Abdu'l-Bahá, his beloved Master, and in his certitude and steadfastness, Hippolyte was acknowledged by his fellow believers as a preeminent expounder of the Cause of God as revealed by Bahá'u'lláh. His mastery of the Persian and Arabic languages enabled him to translate some major works among the Holy Writings of Bahá'u'lláh into French, in a manner that drew the scholarly admiration of French Orientalists of his time.

It is hoped that this book will provide readers with a fuller appreciation of the valiant and historical role played by Hippolyte Dreyfus in the introduction and consolidation of the Bahá'í Faith in the West and the East, as well as throw light on the extraordinary spirit of sacrifice and devotion that animated him throughout his life.

For those readers who live in France, or who are francophone readers, the authors earnestly hope that many will become so inspired by Hippolyte's life of service that they will each aspire to become one of his worthy successors. We hope these inspired souls will succeed in giving a second breath to the flame of love that Hippolyte strove so hard to light in Paris, that they may hold up a torch to shine a light on a revelation that is destined to spread an eternal splendor over the intellectual and spiritual life of our beloved native land.

Yann Ballanger
November 21, 2024

Foreword to the English Edition

Hippolyte Dreyfus is generally known as the first person of French nationality to have embraced the Faith of Bahá'u'lláh in France. His is a life story that deserves our avid attention. His life and his record of service are truly worthy of praise and grateful remembrance, as acknowledged by Shoghi Effendi in his 1929 tribute to Hippolyte Dreyfus, certainly one of the most emotion-filled and lengthy which he has written. However, until recently, only a relatively small number of people anywhere in the world would have heard of the illustrious and exemplary life of Hippolyte Dreyfus, a marvelous figure who actively promoted the Cause of Bahá'u'lláh during the early years of the Bahá'í Faith in the West.

In 2021, a book about Hippolyte Dreyfus was published, at long last, in French. The author was hopeful that his labor of love would bring spiritual illumination to the hearts and minds of the people of France and all the francophone countries of the world. However, my dearly loved friend, the author of this book, realized that Hippolyte Dreyfus had been conceptually restricted to being known as the first French Bahá'í, which is a very, very limited understanding when we now take into consideration his amazing service and outstanding achievements. It is our most cherished hope that the friends will remember him as serving not only France but also the Bahá'í world and the whole of humanity. Hippolyte Dreyfus was posthumously named a Disciple of 'Abdu'l-Bahá by Shoghi Effendi; he was sent all around the world to teach the Cause and to represent the Faith on behalf of the Master, and, later, the Guardian; he was also one of the rare Bahá'í persons who, despite being neither American nor Persian, was invited as a keynote speaker at conferences or Spiritual Assembly meetings in North America. Hippolyte Dreyfus was sought after by virtue of his close association with 'Abdu'l-Bahá, who directly expounded the Faith to him, and also because of his sure grasp of the fundamental tenets of the Faith.

What is truly admirable about the way Hippolyte Dreyfus lived his life immediately after he embraced the Bahá'í Faith is that he promptly arose to promote the Word of God, gave up a lucrative career as a lawyer to master the Persian and Arabic languages, and became an erudite scholar and eminent translator of Bahá'u'lláh's Writings. He began to serve humanity by his unremitting endeavors to serve the Cause through selfless devotion and obedience to the Head of the Faith, 'Abdu'l-Bahá. Eventually, after the passing of the Master, Hippolyte served Shoghi Effendi, the Guardian of the Cause, with equal distinction and unflagging devotion until the end of his own life. We are only now just beginning to get a clearer insight into the vast range and profound depth of Hippolyte's contribution to the effort to spread the teachings of Bahá'u'lláh not only to the people of France but also to the rest of the world.

As a matter of historical fact, many important documents pertaining to the life of Hippolyte Dreyfus came to light only in the last two or three years, and these have enabled the author to complete the writing of this book with new stories, anecdotes, and accounts that were not available at the time of the publication of the first edition of the book in French. It was only after recent extensive research, broad-ranging investigation, and deep analysis by the author of this timely and precious book that we can now begin to do justice to the life and works of this admirable early believer. The enormous research endeavor of an intrepid team of collaborators, researchers, and translators who assisted the author must also be acknowledged in order to do justice to their labor of love and give credit where it is due.

In the years and decades ahead for the entire human family, the people of the world will have to learn how to worship together and serve humanity together. Throughout his life of service, Hippolyte strove to share with others Bahá'u'lláh's message that summoned all people to work for unity and peace. The urgency of this message has only intensified in the intervening years since the glorious period of his high endeavors.

Disunity is a major characteristic of the times in which we live. The Universal House of Justice, the head of the Bahá'í Faith, has written, "Does not disunity fuel the crises and conflicts that afflict the world? Does it not exacerbate the pain and hardship experienced by so many?"[1] As humanity enters a new epoch in its search for ways to overcome the existential threats posed by global issues, it is earnestly to be hoped that all people of goodwill will study the life of Hippolyte Dreyfus-Barney to discover the inspiration of his world-embracing vision—and thereby recognise the spirit of the age in which we live.

Bahá'u'lláh has written that "the purpose for which mortal men have, from utter nothingness, stepped into the realm of being, is that they may work for the betterment of the world and live together in concord and harmony."[2] He has revealed spiritual teachings that make this goal possible. Building a society that consciously pursues this collective purpose is the work of not only this generation, but of many generations to come, and Bahá'u'lláh's followers welcome all who labor alongside them in this undertaking. Living together "in concord and harmony" means learning how to raise up vibrant, outward-looking communities, learning how to bring about spiritual and material progress, and learning how to contribute to the discourses that influence the direction of that progress.[3]

The entire life of Hippolyte Dreyfus-Barney was consecrated to these sacred purposes from the early years following his embrace of the Faith of Bahá'u'lláh. Hippolyte would, if he were with us today, welcome all who wish to labor alongside him to work for the betterment of the world. The Universal House of Justice has written, "At a time when the urgency of attaining higher levels of unity, founded on the incontestable truth of humanity's oneness, is becoming apparent to larger and larger numbers, society stands in need of clear voices that can articulate the spiritual principles that underlie such an aspiration."[4] This book offers one such "clear voice" emanating from France in the early 1900s to disseminate the spiritual principles that are now reverberating throughout the world in a vast array of languages.

Today, as the spiritual descendants of the early followers of Bahá'u'lláh arise, galvanized by the Universal House of Justice to follow the example of 'Abdu'l-Bahá and implement his Tablets of the Divine Plan, as they reach out to their fellow human beings in a worldwide endeavor to carry forward an ever-advancing civilization, may they derive inspiration from the newly documented exertions of Hippolyte Dreyfus-Barney, to whose life of selfless service the Guardian has paid such a glowing tribute.

It is hoped that every reader of this book will be moved to investigate the timely urgency of the message of Bahá'u'lláh that Hippolyte strove to share with such pure-hearted, powerful, and revitalizing love.

William Hui
Singapore, 5 January 2022

Author's Note

Like many biographies, this book does not claim to be complete, as the documentary record from certain periods of Hippolyte's life remain to be discovered and analyzed: the present account is offered simply as a humble and modest attempt to carry forward the precious work done by Armindo Pedro, Pascale Louvet, and Eric Louvet titled *Hippolyte Dreyfus: Apostle of 'Abdu'l-Bahá.*[1] Future historians will surely be able to enrich the literature on his life in light of new documents currently being collected and classified at the Bahá'í World Center and in the national archives of various Bahá'í communities.

In writing this biography on the life of Hippolyte Dreyfus-Barney, we have essentially relied on the documents made available to us by the Archives of the Bahá'í National Center in France, which include the private archives of Laura Clifford Dreyfus-Barney, Hippolyte's wife.[2] A veritable gold mine for the researcher, the materials available at the Archives of the Bahá'í National Center in Paris contain documents that have allowed us to acquire a global vision of the life and activities of Hippolyte Dreyfus. Above all, as these materials include a plenitude of personal documents that belonged to Hippolyte or his relatives, such as letters, postcards, passports, manuscripts, and travel diaries, these resources have been extremely useful for cross-checking the information already published and bringing into clearer resolution the personality of Hippolyte Dreyfus. This foundational research work was then enriched by, on the one hand, the many biographies and autobiographical accounts written in English and/or Persian by his contemporaries, and, on the other hand, by all the Bahá'í periodicals from the turn of the century such as the *Bahai News, Star of the West,* and the *Bahá'í World,* all of which are available online.[3]

One word of caution to the reader about the quality of the translations. We have attempted to translate certain letters and telegrams, sent by 'Abdu'l-Bahá to Hippolyte, from Persian into English in order to make the narrative more vivid and to allow the reader to get a glimpse of the unique relationship between the Master and Hippolyte. While these provisional translations can in no way be considered as the original words of the Master, they have been approved by the Bahá'í World Center for this publication. We also ask the reader for utmost clemency with regard to the overall accuracy of our translations: as the majority of the available resources are in French or Persian, we have endeavored to convey their meaning as faithfully as possible, but we invite the reader, if necessary, to seek out the original texts, which are referred to in the endnotes.

Additionally, some of the information presented in this book is based on "pilgrims' notes," which are the recollections of others of the words of 'Abdu'l-Bahá. Such recollections should not be regarded as 'Abdu'l-Bahá's actual words. Shoghi Effendi on numerous occasions cautioned against attributing too great an importance to "pilgrims' " or the personal impression of 'Abdu'l-Bahá's words from an individual believer: "It was chiefly in view of the misleading nature of the reports of the informal conversations of 'Abdu'l-Bahá with visiting pilgrims, that I have insistently urged the believers of the West to regard such statements as merely personal impressions of the sayings of their Master, and to quote and consider as authentic only such translations as are based upon the authenticated text of His recorded utterances in the original tongue."[4]

Further guidance regarding the use of "pilgrims' notes" can be found in a letter dated October 2, 1935, written on behalf of Shoghi Effendi to the National Spiritual Assembly of the United States and Canada: "He would also urge you to attach no importance to the stories told about 'Abdu'l-Bahá or to those attributed to Him by the Friends. These should be regarded in the same light as the notes and impressions of visiting pilgrims. They need not be suppressed, but they also should not be given prominence or official recognition."

Finally, for the convenience of the reader, we have added a glossary of names of believers. Additionally, we have added a glossary of important Bahá'í terms—which may be new and unfamiliar to a reader—that appear throughout the work. We have chosen not to include the content of these glossaries in the body of the text, as we wish to avoid overloading an already heavily annotated work.

Acknowledgments

We would like to express from the bottom of our hearts our gratitude to the National Spiritual Assembly of the Bahá'ís in France for offering us the unique opportunity to work on the biography of Hippolyte Dreyfus-Barney and, above all, for their continued availability, support, and encouragement through the National Bahá'í Library and the Bahá'í Archive Center, both of which operate under their auspices. Two friends have particularly contributed to the preparation, writing, and verification of this book: Ms. Zineb Malouche and Mr. Jan Teofil Jasion. We would like to offer them our deep gratitude for the professionalism, the generosity, and the constancy of their support. Their individual deeds of selflessness in this joint labor of love is gratefully acknowledged.

We would also like to extend our warmest thanks to all the friends who have assisted us during the writing of this book, including various National Spiritual Assemblies and the Archives Department of the Bahá'í World Center in Haifa. We are particularly indebted to William from Singapore; Tom from Macao; Jelle from the Netherlands; Gisbert from Germany; and Armindo, Frédéric, and Laurent from France; all of whom, with their valuable advice, their translation assistance, and their expertise made our task much easier.

Finally, a special thank you must be addressed to Alliah for the countless hours she has spent meticulously reading and rereading every sentence of this work. She has our deep gratitude for the patience and dedication she has shown over the past few months—an amazing effort that only a mother's love can offer. Our profound and heartfelt thanks go to her.

1 / Early Years

Hippolyte Isidore Dreyfus is born on April 12, 1873 at 2:15am in the eighth arrondissement of Paris, 11 rue Rovigo, into a wealthy Jewish French family.[1] His father, Georges Arthur Lucien Dreyfus (1840–1911), is a stockbroker; his mother, Léa Marie Sophie Inès Cardozo (1848–1913), looks after the family home. They will have a second child, a daughter, Yvonne (1875–1941), with whom Hippolyte will have a particularly close and affectionate relationship.

The Dreyfus family is known in Parisian cultural circles for the musical evenings they organize at which amateurs, connoisseurs, and artists gather to express and experience their love of music. Art is omnipresent in young Hippolyte's childhood: his uncle, Gustave Louis Dreyfus (1837–1914) is a great traveler—he worked in Egypt for the construction of the Suez Canal—and a recognized art collector; his first cousin, Carle Dreyfus (1875–1952), will become the curator of the art department at the Louvre Museum. Very early on, Hippolyte develops a passion for classical music that he will retain for the rest of his life. His sister-in-law, Natalie Barney, remembers his love of the music of Wagner and Claude Debussy: ". . . he entered a concert hall alone, listened to the piece for which he had come, and went out quietly without waiting for the rest."[2]

At this time, better known as the Belle Époque, Europe is going through a tremendous transformation: it is marked by significant social, economic, technological, and political progress, and Paris, where artists and intellectuals from all over the world converge, radiates their philosophical, spiritual, and political values as the preeminent center of European culture. However, the social environment of the time is complex, the rise of intolerance and anti-Semitism is increasingly strong and is exacerbated by the case of Captain Alfred Dreyfus, who, it might be noted, is not related to Hippolyte by blood.[3] In this very particular context of the complex times in which he lived, Hippolyte nevertheless has a happy childhood during which he develops his own distinctive qualities: a great openness of mind, an artistic sensitivity, and a pronounced taste for intellectual activities. So it was that "he grew up strong in appreciation of life and all that it has to offer."[4]

In 1886, Hippolyte completes his grammar school studies. In 1890, he passes his Bachelor of Arts at the Lycée Condorcet in Paris.[5] He then attends the Faculty of Law of the School of Political Sciences: he earns a Bachelor of the Law degree in 1892 and becomes a law graduate in 1893.

Class photo at the *Lycée Condorcet.* 2nd row, 5th from left to right: Hippolyte.

At the age of twenty, Hippolyte performs his military service in Rouen in the 74th infantry regiment for one year, instead of the required three years, in order, as the law allows, to be able to continue his studies. In 1894, he is admitted to the Bar of the Paris Court of Appeal and becomes a doctor of the law in 1898 after successfully defending his thesis on "The rights of succession of the surviving spouse in French law and in the principal foreign statutes."[6] Finally, he becomes secretary to François Thévenet,[7] one of the most eminent lawyers at the Court and former Minister of Justice and Religious Affairs in the French government.

Hippolyte (center) as a young lawyer

Building on his academic and professional successes, Hippolyte is also attracted by questions of social justice and devotes his time to offering aid and assistance to the most unfortunate in his community, to whom he tirelessly tries to provide support and comfort.[8] In fact, he has been a very active member of the Visitors' Society,[9] a home-based social assistance center for the neediest members of society, since its foundation.[10] He is noted for his "ideal of justice and goodness," his “sense of collaboration,” his “great generosity,” and his ardent desire “to direct his life differently from others.”[11]

Hippolyte (center) as a young lawyer

2 / First Encounter with the Bahá'í Faith

At the dawn of the twentieth century, Hippolyte is a dynamic young man who divides his life between his work with influential lawyers, personal involvement in voluntary social service, and prestigious evenings within Parisian cultural, intellectual, and artistic circles. He considers himself "an agnostic who believed [believes] that life and character are above dogma and creed."[1] However, like many skeptics, he feels that there is "something else"[2] that he cannot identify, so he decides "to explore the occult sciences, but they disappointed [disappoint] him because he could [can] not find what he was [is] looking for."[3]

In 1901, this sincere and ardent thirst to search for the truth is eventually confirmed. During a musical evening organized by his family, he meets Margaret Sanderson and her daughters, Sybil and Edith, with whom he has been acquainted for several years. Margaret Sanderson is close to her uncle Gustave Dreyfus, and her daughters studied piano with Jules Massenet,[4] a close friend of the Dreyfus family.

During the evening, Hippolyte is stunned by the transformation he notices in his friend Edith: she exudes a new confidence, a mixture of joy and certainty that he has never seen previously in her. He questions her, and she confides in him her secret: she recently met friends who were returning from 'Akká[5] in Palestine where they met a fantastic character who preaches a new faith that aims at the unity of religions and humanity. Intrigued, Hippolyte asks for more information. Edith then offers him an invitation to meet the one who entrusted her with this message, an American residing in Paris: May Bolles. Enchanted by the idea, he agrees.

At the beginning of the twentieth century, the Bahá'í community in France is composed of only a dozen members who are mainly orbiting around May Bolles, one of the first American believers. She lives in Paris where her brother, Randolph Bolles (1871–1939), continues his studies at the École des beaux-arts.[6] In 1898, she was part of the first group of Western pilgrims to visit the Holy Land in order to attain the presence of 'Abdu'l-Bahá.[7]

'Abdu'l-Bahá was the eldest son of Bahá'u'lláh, the Founder of the Bahá'í Faith. He was named 'Abbás (Lion) when He was born to Mírzá Husayn-'Alí Núrí (later called Bahá'u'lláh) and His wife Ásíyih Khánum. Bahá'u'lláh Himself, during His lifetime, had encouraged all His followers to refer to 'Abbás Effendi as "the Master." In His Kitáb-i-'Ahd (Book of the Covenant), Bahá'u'lláh appointed 'Abdu'l-Bahá as the Center of the Covenant, to Whom all believers were to turn upon the passing of the Prophet-Founder of the Faith. All the early believers, and especially the Western pilgrims who engaged in journeys of pilgrimage to 'Akká, were drawn to Bahá'u'lláh's resting place, the sacred spot that was the focal point of the nascent faith community. These pilgrims were also overwhelmed with the joy of attaining the presence of their beloved Master, who welcomed them with immense love and patiently nurtured them in their understanding of the new Revelation.

On her return to Paris, May Bolles succeeded in establishing the first Bahá'í center on the European continent, thanks to her constant efforts carried out in accordance with the instructions of 'Abdu'l-Bahá; thus, the Bahá'ís living in Paris at that time regard her more or less as their spiritual guide.[8] Among this group of early believers who responded joyfully to the teachings of the Blessed Beauty,[9] as enunciated by his humble servant May Bolles, we find several characters who will make a mark and leave an imprint of their lives in the history of the Faith: Edith MacKaye, Laura Barney, Thomas Breakwell, Marion Jack, Charles Mason Remey, and Sydney Sprague.

During the summer of 1901, Hippolyte travels, as promised, to the small apartment occupied by May Bolles that was located on Avenue de Iéna and placed at her disposal by her friend, Ms. Edith Jackson. Let us leave it to May Bolles to tell us about this first meeting, a meeting that will totally change the course of Hippolyte's life:

> The Beloved sent that month the destined one to shed the light of Baha in France through the marvellous translations into French of a number of revealed books of Baha'u'llah. Never shall I forget the overpowering impression of grace and power in the person of Hippolyte Dreyfus the first time he came to see me.
>
> He said, "I have come to learn what it is you have done to produce so remarkable a change in Edith Sanderson. She is not the same, she has found joy, serenity, and a deep purpose in life"—and with his charming smile—"how did you do it?" He asked to know the tenets of a Faith which had, he said, transformed a friend of his. With fervour, simplicity, and, conscious of my utter ignorance in the face of such a scholar, putting my full trust in Bahá'u'lláh, as the Master had bidden me in Acca ['Akká] to do—I told him all I knew! He listened with courteous attention, deep interest at times, searching questions, and overall, a light veil of humour and slight scepticism.
>
> When he rose to go, he took my hand warmly and cordially and told me that it was no doubt interesting, that he did not recognize its historic importance, that he was touched by the ardour of my faith, but he did not believe in any force outside, or beyond natural forces, and that he had never in his life experienced anything that would lead him to believe in Divine or spiritual influences. Then he left, saying he would come again some time.
>
> Within 8 or 10 days he returned, amazed and disturbed. It appeared he had been having a series of somewhat strange experiences governed by laws, or conditions, which he could not explain by natural forces, although he argued with himself

for an hour or more, seeking to prove their natural phenomenon. Frankly, I was amused and delighted, having many times been an eyewitness of the mighty, mysterious workings of Baha'u'llah, and I knew that this great soul was in the toils!"[10]

Portrait of Hippolyte

Following these conversations, Hippolyte realizes that his rational mind cannot explain everything. His skepticism weakens, and at the same time, an intense and irresistible attraction to the Faith matures in his heart. He then begins to read about the Faith and studies everything he can find on the Bábí and Bahá'í movements and prepares for himself a bibliography[11] of some thirty works and articles published in French, English, German and Persian, among which are the publications of famous orientalists of that time such as Clément Huart,[12] Count Joseph Arthur de Gobineau,[13] A. L. M. Nicolas,[14] and Joseph Ernest Renan.[15]

3 / Recognition of the Divine Message

Irresistibly drawn to the Faith, Hippolyte decides to begin corresponding with 'Abdu'l-Bahá. Very shortly afterwards, he declares to the Master his Faith in Bahá'u'lláh in a letter dated April 22, 1902. In this letter, written in French and sent from Paris, Hippolyte supplicates 'Abdu'l-Bahá to count him as one of His disciples, to illumine his eyes with beholding His divine presence, to enlighten his understanding with the light of faith, to cause him to enter His Sacred Threshold, to aid him to resign himself to the Will of God, to strengthen him to teach the Cause, to assist him to deliver his loved ones from waywardness and ignorance, to guide him to the knowledge of God, and to bestow upon him everlasting life through the love of God.[1]

On June 22, 1902, Hippolyte receives a reply from 'Abdu'l-Bahá in which He accepts his declaration of faith. Here is an extract:

> He is God.
> O thou who hast sought the light of divine guidance! I perused thy missive abounding in eloquence and wisdom, which affirmed thy belief in the oneness of God and bore witness unto His divine singleness. It was a testament unto thine enkindled heart, thy purity of soul and the intensity of thy love for His Beauty. [. . .] I beseech God to brighten thy face with the light of His knowledge, to cause thee to proclaim the evidences of His Kingdom for all nations and to enable thee to remain wholly

> devoted to Him; that thou mayest strive to scatter abroad the divine fragrances, guide the wayward, awaken the heedless and heal the blind and the deaf with the spirit of wisdom, becoming a promoter of the heavenly mysteries, a servant of the Cause of God in His Vineyard.[2]

Within the same year, Hippolyte sends another letter to the Master to obtain permission to go to the Holy Land and meet Him in 'Akká, the place of His imprisonment.[3] It should be noted that at that time it was common practice to write directly to 'Abdu'l-Bahá to ask Him questions, declare one's Faith, or seek permission to go on pilgrimage.

Waiting for a response from Palestine, Hippolyte continues his investigation of the Faith. He reads a lot: his assiduous and constant reading of the Writings from the first hours of his encounter with the Faith is a practice that would remain habitual throughout his life.[4] As Laura Barney later confided: "His constant reading of Bahá'u'lláh's works in this language, and later on in Arabic, gave him an unusual insight into the teachings and mission of this great Manifestation."[5]

At the same time, Hippolyte mingles with the nascent Parisian Bahá'í community that continues to grow around May Bolles. This small and fervent group of believers gathers to study the Writings, and it is spiritually animated by the continuous flow of Tablets,[6] written or dictated by 'Abdu'l-Bahá, from the Holy Land. It soon receives the invaluable blessing of being able to welcome into its ranks the great scholar of the Faith, Mírzá Abu'l-Faḍl-i-Gulpáygáni (1844–1914) who, accompanied by his translators Anton Haddad (1862–1924) and Ali-Kuli Khan (1879–1966), arrived at the request of the Master to deepen and encourage the friends for several months.[7] In 1902, the believers receive a new letter from 'Abdu'l-Bahá in which He expresses His great affection for the friends of Paris. He praises the believers for their spiritual qualities, urges them to be kind and merciful to everyone they meet, and asks God to shower blessings and praise on each of them. [8]

Early Bahá'í community in Paris, circa 1902.
Bottom row, from left to right: Ms. Edith MacKaye, Ms. Holzbecker, Ms. Edith Sanderson, Mr. Sigurd Russell, Mr. Thomas Breakwell, Ms. May Bolles, Mrs. Hanet, Ms. Watson. Back row, from left to right: Ms. Bignardi, Mr. Herbert W. Hopper, Ms. Florence Robinson, Hippolyte, Ms. Berthalin Lexow, Mr. Mason Remey, unidentified, Mrs. Marie-Louise MacKaye, Mrs. Bignardi, Ms. Stephanie Hauvais, Mr. Sydney Sprague.

The long-awaited pilgrimage finally takes place in December 1902: Hippolyte, accompanied by his friend Edith Sanderson, leaves for 'Akká, where they are joined by another friend and believer, Lua Getsinger (1871–1916), who was already present at their arrival.

During the three weeks of their stay, from morning to evening, Hippolyte immerses himself in the Master's teachings and the principles of the Cause. Their philosophical, intellectual, and spiritual discussions continue even at lunch and dinner, during which, afire with the spiritual food delivered by 'Abdu'l-Bahá, Hippolyte dutifully takes many notes. The words that can certainly best describe the effect produced by these days spent with the Master are those of Shoghi Effendi, who writes of their having experienced "a spiritual communion" with 'Abdu'l-Bahá.[9]

The Master's translator during this stay, Youness Afroukhteh, testifies to the impression that Hippolyte made on him:

> Dreyfus's knowledge of the Faith, considering his recent conversion to it, was remarkable. His time spent acquiring further knowledge and discussions of philosophical and spiritual subjects continued at the lunch or dinner table. The discussions were obviously in French and he frequently took notes. [. . .] He had become totally enkindled and attracted, longed to be of service to the Faith, and even yearned to sacrifice his life and gain a martyr's death. 'Abdu'l-Bahá granted that request, but only within the context of the spirit of the word." That is to say, he could devote himself fully to the service of the Faith until the end of his life.[10]

During his stay, the Dreyfus affair makes headlines. One evening, during dinner, 'Abdu'l-Bahá asks Hippolyte if he is related to the famous Alfred Dreyfus;[11] he answers in the negative. 'Abdu'l-Bahá then reportedly tells him: "That Dreyfus found renown in the world of politics. I desire for you even greater fame in service to the Faith of God."[12]

Strong ties are forged between Hippolyte and Youness Afroukhteh, and a sincere and respectful friendship—a bond that will last their whole life—is born in 'Akká. On another day, over dinner, Hippolyte confides to his new friend that an embarrassing encounter took place between himself and the Master:

> One day at the dinner table he [Hippolyte] said, "Today I inadvertently played the role of Adam and was terribly embarrassed." Not understanding the meaning of this statement, I translated the words. The Master said, "Tell him there is no shame. Because of my great love for him, I wished to behold the entirety of his physical being." Later, I asked him [Mr. Dreyfus] about this. He said, "Don't tell anyone, but today I turned into Adam." I asked again, and he replied, "Don't ask! I am afraid I

> may be driven out of paradise. You see, I always lock the bathroom door when I bathe. This time I neglected to make sure that the door was locked. When the Master knocked on the bathroom door and called my name, without thinking I asked Him to come in. He opened the door while I was naked. I was terribly embarrassed: I realized I had done what Adam did![13]

After almost a month spent with 'Abdu'l-Bahá, Hippolyte's stay at the Holy Land comes to an end. In a letter he sends to his sister Yvonne on 1 February 1903, Hippolyte explains the reasons for his departure, describes the complicated conditions of his trip to the Holy Land, and shares his immediate plans:

> Sunday night. I suddenly decided to leave, on the news that an Austrian boat was going to pass through Haifa this morning, and I left the Master in the night. I do not need to tell you the sadness of the separation. I shall take the train tomorrow to Jerusalem, where I will stay 5 or 6 days until there is a boat to Alexandria. But right now, all the services are disorganized, and when I get there, I will probably have a few more days of quarantine. In any case, I intend to be able to embark for Marseille around the 13th. So, I will be there on the 18th. I hope you are all well, and while waiting to see you again I send you all my love.[14]

The impact of these days spent with the Master in the Holy Land is immense; as a journalist of *Le Temps* will recount a few years later: "his interviews with 'Abdu'l-Bahá ended up attaching him to the Bahá'í Cause."[15] Back in France, Hippolyte is completely transformed. Convinced of the social and universal values of the Faith, he decides to devote the rest of his life to the study of Eastern civilizations and the spread of Bahá'í teachings.[16] Joining action to his thought, he enrolls in the religious section of the *École pratique des hautes études*[17] in Paris and begins training with recognized orientalists such as Hartwig Derenbourg[18] and Clément Huart.[19] His goals are clear: first, he wants to master the Persian and Arabic languages so that he can converse directly with 'Abdu'l-Bahá; secondly, he wants to be able to read the original texts of the Writings of the Báb and Bahá'u'lláh and offer translations to French-speaking audiences.[20]

'Abdu'l-Bahá is also extremely touched by Hippolyte, in whom He detects remarkable abilities. In a letter, the Master likens Hippolyte to a unique bird among other birds in Paradise. He predicts that soon Hippolyte will produce melodies that will amaze other souls around him and that God will enable him to diffuse heavenly breezes in the regions he visits.[21]

Hippolyte will receive many letters from 'Abdu'l-Bahá throughout his life, in which He expresses to him how much He appreciates him. In one letter, the Master tells him, "O thou sincere herald! Wert thou to know how much affection this Servant of God doth feel for thee, thou wouldst assuredly fly forth in such ecstasy and bliss that thou wouldst bring delight to all."[22]

During the early years of his conversion, the Master writes to him very frequently to encourage him to become aware of his unique spiritual potential and begin to serve the Cause. In one of His first letters, 'Abdu'l-Bahá thus exhorts him: "Render thanks unto God that He hath caused thee to enter this Kingdom and graciously confirmed thee therein. Erelong, divine bestowals shall encompass thee and the gates of His bountiful favours shall be opened in thy face, astonishing even thee. Rest thou not for a moment and pause not for breath. Be thou like unto a candle that burneth night and day, a bird that warbleth its song to the gathered assemblies. Be ever ablaze with the flame and heat of the love of God so that thou mayest, with the confirmations of the Lord of Hosts, breathe spiritual life into the hearts and become an Ark of salvation."[23]

This stream of encouragement flows continuously. In another letter from the same period, 'Abdu'l-Bahá confirms him in his endeavors and confides in him His hopes for Paris:

> My hope is that thou shalt, day by day, burn with ever greater love, be ever more illumined and so devote thyself to service to

the Cause of God that thou mayest become the envy of the world of humanity, a commander of the cohorts of eternal life. [. . .]

Paris hath through the efforts of the friends gained a certain capacity. Were all to strive as thou hast done to raise the Word of God and disseminate the divine fragrances, that city would in a short time become world-renowned and that country like unto Paradise itself. [. . .]

In the coming winter season ye must all, with eloquent tongues and pure intent, with lofty resolve and heavenly strength, with sweet melodies, enraptured souls, joyful spirits and hearts filled with the Holy Spirit of the Kingdom, arise to spread the divine fragrances. Then ye shall find the gates of confirmation thrown wide open.[24]

4 / Arising to Serve the Cause

In 1902, the news from Persia about the persecutions against the Bahá'ís and the atrocities suffered by the Bahá'ís intensifies. Having heard of the coming of the shah of Persia to Paris, 'Abdu'l-Bahá asks Lua Getsinger to go to France to prepare a petition with Mariam Haney (1872–1965) and present it to His Majesty, Muẓaffari'd-Dín Sháh.[1] This petition, written on behalf of the Bahá'ís of Paris, includes three requests: an audience with the shah, protection of the Bahá'ís in Persia, and permission for 'Abdu'l-Bahá to leave the walls of 'Akká.[2] It would eventually become clear that this third appeal, added to the first two requests, is a personal initiative of Lua Getsinger.

Hippolyte, always ready to perform "the most difficult tasks,"[3] plays a leading role in this mission. First, thanks to his linguistic skills and legal training, he translates the petition from English into French. Then he uses his network of high-level relationships to attempt to obtain an audience with the shah. At this time, Hippolyte is close to Azíz'u'lláh Azízí, a Persian Bahá'í who has access to the court of the shah. Azízí, faced with Hippolyte's vigorous insistence, proceeds with the necessary arrangements and organizes a preliminary meeting with the prime minister of Persia.[4] Finally, Hippolyte accompanies Lua Getsinger to the *Hôtel du Palais de l'Elysée* for her to hand the petition to the shah.

On the day of the meeting, the prime minister refuses to receive them, arguing that his son is sick and that, therefore, he does not have time to see them. Lua offers to return the next day if his son has recovered, to which the prime minister agrees. In the evening, the Bahá'í community of Paris gathers for a prayer vigil. They pray for the recovery of the prime minister's son and an opportunity for the envoys of the Master to meet with the shah.

The next morning, the good news arrives: the prime minister's son has recovered. Lua and Hippolyte once again go to the hotel; this time, the prime minister receives them and promises to deliver the petition to the shah. Lua and Hippolyte are fully resolved to gain an audience with the shah, however, and the two friends calmly and firmly insist on meeting the shah personally, to hand over their request to him, and to gain from him the commitment that everything will be done to protect their friends in Persia.[5]

The prime minister acquiesces, and Lua and Hippolyte present themselves that same day at the large reception hall of the Elysée Palace Hotel, where the shah can be found with his entourage of one hundred and fifty Persians. From this audience, Azíz'u'lláh Azízí reports the following dialogue between the shah and Hippolyte:

> After touching on various subjects at the outset, Mon. [Monsieur] Dreyfus stated: "It is a pity that my brothers, under the kingship of so just and beneficent a monarch as yourself, should endure such persecution and torture even to the point of death." The Shah reacted with some nervousness and asked, "Who are your brothers in Iran?" Mon. Dreyfus made mention of the Bahá'ís. Of course, the Shah already knew he was speaking of the Iranian Bahá'ís and asked if Mon. Dreyfus was himself a Bahá'í. He affirmed that he was, and the entire encounter ranged over many other important subjects which greatly impressed the Shah. The King had given his word to Mon. Dreyfus that, upon his return back to Iran, he would look into the matter, and moreover, Mon. Dreyfus could be assured that the matter would be given personal consideration.[6]

The fearlessness, firmness, eloquence, and courage evinced by Hippolyte during this interview make a deep impression on Lua

Getsinger. A few days later, she writes to May Bolles: "Oh May, you will never know what a great blessing and help Mr. Dreyfus has been to me! (. . .) You can't imagine how he has grown—and how wonderful he is!"[7]

Early Bahá'í community in Paris, circa 1903. Lua Getsinger is sitting, third from left. Hippolyte is standing, fourth from left.

Following further persecution of the Bahá'ís in Persia, notably in the cities of Yazd and Iṣfahán, a second petition is prepared by Lua Getsinger in 1903. It highlights the atrocities inflicted, describes the harrowing history of some of the martyrs, and calls for the restoration of order and justice. It is signed by many Bahá'ís such as Hippolyte, Edith Sanderson, Lucien and Inés Dreyfus,[8] Yvonne Meyer-May,[9] and Rosa and George Winterburn. The petition is then delivered through official diplomatic channels to the shah.[10] As a result of these petitions and the rise of a new prime minister, persecution of the Bahá'ís gradually subsides.[11]

This period is very difficult for 'Abdu'l-Bahá, who suffers, along with His family, from the continual intrigues of the Covenant-breakers[12] led by Mírzá Muḥammad-'Alí, His half-brother. The latter conspires with the Ottoman authorities, spreads rumors among the population, disseminates false accusations among believers, and mounts multiple attempts to stop the construction of the mausoleum of the Báb on Mount Carmel.[13]

Strongly affected by the news of the sufferings that overwhelm the Master and propelled by their boundless love and devotion to ‘Abdu’l-Bahá, the friends from Paris decide to act. They are determined to free ‘Abdu’l-Bahá from the yoke of His oppressors. Their bravery is reported to us by Youness Afroukhteh, who describes the friends as being willing to “sacrifice their possessions, even their lives” to see the gates of the prison city of ‘Akká open.[14] Hippolyte and Edith Jackson, assisted in their efforts by Lua Getsinger, Edith Sanderson, Ellen Goin, Edith MacKaye, and several other believers, organize a fundraiser and manage to raise a large sum of money.[15] Their goal is to travel to Constantinople, the capital of the Ottoman Empire; to meet Káẓim Páshá, the *vali*[16] of Beirut; and to petition him for the Master’s release while hoping that the money raised will be an additional motivator for him to see reason.

When news of this initiative reaches ‘Abdu’l-Bahá, He promptly sends them a telegram to tell them to immediately stop their action. He knows that the Covenant-breakers will seize upon any such move as an opportunity to complain to the Ottoman authorities and plot an intensification of persecutions against the Bahá’ís. The friends decide to obey the Master’s orders and remain in Paris, and they take no such action.[17]

5 / Early Stirrings of the Cause in Paris

The years following Hippolyte's return from the Holy Land are also marked by the ardor with which he embarks on deepening his understanding of the Faith and spreading the Cause to the French-speaking public.

In Paris, the community life of the first believers is becoming more and more structured: regular meetings are set up to study the writings, Edith Sanderson organizes musical evenings with her family at which friends have the opportunity to share the message of Bahá'u'lláh, and the studio of Frank Edwin Scott gradually becomes a gathering place, the Bahá'í center where believers, spiritual seekers, and Bahá'í pilgrims passing through Paris have a venue at which to gather and meet with like-minded people. It is also during this period that, as direct witnesses of the transformative power of the new revelation on Hippolyte and irresistibly attracted by a faith of which he speaks to them with such ardor and rapture, Hippolyte's mother, his father, and his sister Yvonne begin to sympathize with the Cause, and eventually declare their faith in Bahá'u'lláh.[1]

Around 1904, Youness Afroukhteh arrives in France; he spends a few days in Marseille, then leaves for Paris. Sent by 'Abdu'l-Bahá to consolidate the community and deepen the knowledge of the believers, Youness spends several weeks in the capital where, day and night, he meets friends, well-wishers and seekers. He notes, "At that time, the fire of the love of God had only recently been ignited and the light of faith and devotion had illuminated the hearts of only a handful of

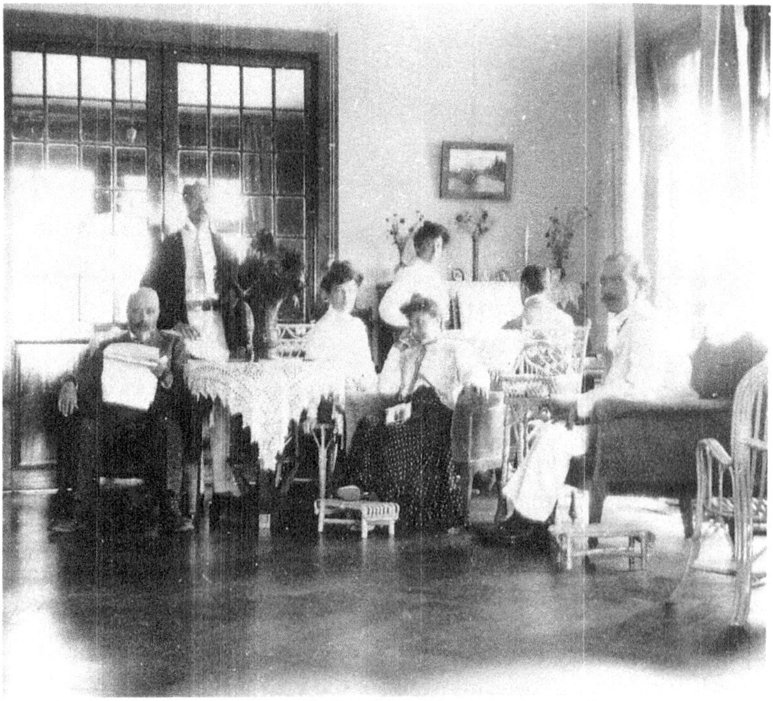

The Dreyfus Family. Sitting, from left to right: Hippolyte's father, his sister Yvonne, and his mother. Hippolyte is standing between his father and his sister.

individuals. The centre and essence of this fire and attraction was the revered person of Hippolyte Dreyfus [. . .] and the Bahá'í population of the city was around fifty or sixty souls. In addition to this, some ten or twenty others had begun to investigate the principles of the Faith; some of them were sympathetic, others critical, and a few confused and perplexed."[2]

Youness also meets Hippolyte's close associate, Mírzá Habíbu'lláh Chirazí,[3] who impressed him greatly as being a person whose "nights and days were spent in service to the Cause and in assisting Monsieur Dreyfus to proclaim the teachings to the inhabitants of Paris."[4]

When Youness has free time, Hippolyte accompanies him on his walks in Paris. One of their most memorable outings is a visit to Thomas Breakwell's grave. Youness relates:

Early Bahá'í community in Paris, circa 1902. Bottom row, from left to right: Valentine and Jacques May—Hippolyte's niece and nephew—and Mr. Sacy's three daughters. Middle row: Lucien and Inès Dreyfus (Hippolyte's parents), Mrs. Yvonne Mayer-May (Hippolyte's sister), Ms. Harvey, Ms. Edith Sanderson, Mrs. Georgine d'Ange d'Astre, unidentified, Mrs. Madeleine Jenny Sacy, unidentified. Top row: Mr. Engleman, Mr. Edwin Scott, Mr. Christophe, Mrs. Josephine Scott, Dr. Sally, unidentified, Hippolyte, unidentified, Ms. Marion Jack, Ms. Prebble, Mr. Paul Meyer-May (Hippolyte's brother-in-law), Mr. Sydney Sprague.

When I was in Paris in the company of Monsieur Dreyfus, he told many stories about Breakwell. "When this young man was in hospital," he related, "all the doctors, nurses and patients were overwhelmed by the intensity of his devotion and spiritual attraction, for he invited all to the divine Kingdom. Some were perplexed and moved, but some of the patients made spiteful and taunting remarks. Armed with only a few words of English, they sneered at him, pointing their fingers at him, and repeating the words, "You are dying, you are dying!" to which he responded, laughing, "I am not dying, I am going to the Kingdom of the heavenly Father. There, I will intercede for you." In short, at his death all the nurses wept, and thus he left an enduring memory in the hearts of those who knew him in that hospital. One day, Mr. Dreyfus and I visited his grave, and since I did not have the text of his Tablet of Visitation with me, I repeated three times, "O Breakwell, O my dear one!"[5]

On March 1, 1904, Hippolyte gives his first lecture at the *École des hautes études sociales* in Paris: "Le Babisme et le Béhaïsme" [Bábism and Behaism].[6] This speech is part of a series of seven presentations given by speakers of various faiths and religions; these talks are not aimed at scholars or academics but at the general public, at people wishing to better understand the social role played by religions.

From the first sentences of his speech, Hippolyte firmly asserts that the Bahá'í Faith is a "new religion," not a "superstition nor of some tribal religion, nor one of those new faiths founded by the force of dollars in an ephemeral glory by some American prophet," but "a true religion, with principles so elevated, with views so broad, that it turns to nothing less than to uniting all existing religions under the same banner, by freeing them from all the worn-out shackles of dogmas and rites."[7]

He then presents the history of the "reform of the Báb": this is an opportunity for him to clarify the historical context surrounding the appearance of the founding Prophet of the Bábí Faith and to denounce the false ideas and rumors that have spread in certain writings, incorrectly regarded as historical. He proceeds to demonstrate how this religion, "confined at first within Iranian boundaries," eventually heralded "a universal religion," the Bahá'í Faith. He describes how the Faith took root "in the most diverse classes of society, creating among all of its believers the ties of a union and an affection whose parallels can be found nowhere in history, except in the early days of Christianity," and this, despite "the terrible persecutions that it had to endure" during its short, dramatic, and turbulent history. Finally, based on what he saw, heard, and experienced during his pilgrimage to the Holy Land and during his meetings with 'Abdu'l-Bahá, he expounds on certain exceptional features of the Bahá'í Faith, thus demonstrating its unique, progressive, universal, and independent character.[8]

The text of the speech is published the following year in *Religions et sociétés* under the same title "Le Babisme et le Béhaïsme" [Bábism and Behaism]" and receives a relatively large press coverage.[9] Henri Mazel,[10] in *Mercure de France,*[11] analyzing progress within religions, writes: "Mr. Hippolyte Dreyfus [. . .] sees in Persian Bábism the birth of a new Islamism, that is quite tolerant and progressive; it is [due] to the progress of Bábism and its derivative, Behaism, that Persia would have gained its current relative prosperity. Once again, the importance of the religious element at the social level would manifest itself."[12]

Jean Réville,[13] in *Revue de l'histoire des religions,*[14] says that Mr. Hippolyte Dreyfus ends the volume with an article on the Bábí Faith and the Bahá'í Faith. Mr. Réville is very considerate towards the new universalist religion born in Persia.[15] In *Revue critique d'histoire et de la literature,*[16] the author mentions the "enthusiastic narrative of a movement where one finds the idols of the day, solidarity, tolerance, pacifism, a religion emptied of any religious element."[17]

In addition to the traditional media, the Christian press also announces the release of this publication. In *Revue chrétienne,*[18] the author mentions that the series of lectures ended with Mr. Dreyfus's presentation "on the history and doctrines of Bábism and Behaism, which, according to the author, contributed powerfully to the civilization of Asia Minor and Persia, where they originated."[19] In *Revue du clergé français,*[20] the critic notes the enthusiasm of "Hippolyte Dreyfus, who seems to speak well of Bábism and especially of Baha'ism as a fervent neophyte" in an exposé [referring to Hippolyte's speech] whose intellectual flavors he [the critic] had 'personally tasted.'"[21]

The text of this conference was also translated into English by Rosa Winterburn under the title "Babism and Bahaism,"[22] and then into German[23] by Margarette Platte in 1909.

The community in Paris becomes more and more structured and begins to organize events to spread the Cause to the general public. However, literature on the Faith, which would allow believers to deepen their understanding, remains very scant. May Bolles reminds us of this very particular context: "At that time translations of the Baha'i teachings in any language were so meagre that the greatest proof of their power lay in the dauntless faith and courage of the early followers. As with the Disciples of Christ, so was it with these early believers by their faith and ardour, their devotion and enthusiasm, they became magnets attracting others to their ranks. Thenceforth Mr. Dreyfus-Barney set himself the task of mastering the Persian language and studying the writings of Baha'u'llah in the original, translating these teachings, so fundamental to the needs of the age, into French."[24]

In the early 1900s, the letters exchanged between believers from all over the world, especially from those who are on pilgrimage or who reside in the Holy Land, are very important in fostering and maintaining the devotion of the members of the nascent community. An individual embodying this ardent love that binds the first believers—Lua Getsinger—writes Hippolyte a letter most probably penned around 1903–1904 while she is staying with the Holy Family:

> My dear, your several letters have arrived, and I regret to say it has been impossible for me to reply sooner. [. . .] But I have not for a single hour forgotten you—nor have I failed to mention your talk in the Holy and Sacred Presence of our Master and at the Blessed Tomb. [. . .]
>
> Oh, my dear, I remembered you and begged God in His great and infinite Mercy to bless and keep you under the great pavilion of His Protection and tender Love! [. . .] Thus again, dear, I remembered you and asked God to let that day be the dawn of a new peace, a new power, and a new & fuller hope within your noble heart! Thus, you see, although you did not receive my letter you have had something better from me, my tenderest thoughts and most sincere prayers! [. . .]
>
> Our Beloved Lord just this moment came into my room and asked what I was doing. I replied that I was writing to our brother Mr. Dreyfus—do you have a message to send him? Yes,

> He answered come with Me, I will give it to you. I went to His room and He gave me the enclosed tablet for you which He had just written, and being enclosed makes my letter its humble servant, and worthy of sending to you! I hope I may ever have such beautiful messages to send you, and that God will ever thus bountifully bless and remember you! Your box of things as well as the two bathtubs—have arrived and have been distributed! All were pleased with your memories and send their thanks.[25]

In the early 1900s, the Dreyfus family owns a second house in Switzerland, on Mont Pèlerin, near the town of Vevey, in the canton of Vaud. More than just a holiday home, it is a place open to loved ones and friends attracted by the Faith. But, above all, it is a refuge for Hippolyte, a haven where he can isolate himself, study, write, and translate, especially with his collaborator from the first hour: Mírzá Habíbu'lláh. This house is known to the friends as *Daro's-Salam,* "Abode of Peace" in Arabic.

Family house in Switzerland

Hippolyte in the countryside

Thus, it is in this house that Hippolyte, in collaboration with Mírzá Habíbu'lláh, finalizes his first translation into French of the Holy Writings. At the end of 1904, he publishes The Book of Certitude (Kitab-el-Ikan),[26] one of the major theological works revealed by Bahá'u'lláh. This book is considered today to be the first translation of the Writings of Bahá'u'lláh to be published in Europe and the first available to the general public in French. In *God Passes By,* Shoghi Effendi presents the Book of Certitude as follows:

> Within a compass of two hundred pages it proclaims unequivocally the existence and oneness of a personal God, unknowable, inaccessible, the source of all Revelation, eternal, omniscient,

Hippolyte in the countryside

omnipresent and almighty; asserts the relativity of religious truth and the continuity of Divine Revelation; affirms the unity of the Prophets, the universality of their Message, the identity of their fundamental teachings, the sanctity of their scriptures, and the twofold character of their stations; denounces the blindness and perversity of the divines and doctors of every age; cites and elucidates the allegorical passages of the New Testament, the abstruse verses of the Qur'án, and the cryptic Muḥammadan traditions which have bred those age-long misunderstandings, doubts and animosities that have sundered and kept apart the followers of the world's leading religious systems; enumerates the essential prerequisites for the attainment by every true seeker of

> the object of his quest; demonstrates the validity, the sublimity, and significance of the Báb’s Revelation; acclaims the heroism and detachment of His disciples; foreshadows, and prophesies the world-wide triumph of the Revelation promised to the people of the Bayán; upholds the purity and innocence of the Virgin Mary; glorifies the Imáms of the Faith of Muḥammad; celebrates the martyrdom, and lauds the spiritual sovereignty, of the Imam Ḥusayn; unfolds the meaning of such symbolic terms as *“Return,” “Resurrection,” “Seal of the Prophets”* and *“Day of Judgment”;* adumbrates and distinguishes between the three stages of Divine Revelation; and expatiates, in glowing terms, upon the glories and wonders of the *“City of God,”* renewed, at fixed intervals, by the dispensation of Providence, for the guidance, the benefit and salvation of all mankind. Well may it be claimed that of all the books revealed by the Author of the Bahá’í Revelation, this Book alone, by sweeping away the age-long barriers that have so insurmountably separated the great religions of the world, has laid down a broad and unassailable foundation for the complete and permanent reconciliation of their followers.[27]

In his introduction, and similar to his speech at the *École des hautes études sociales,* Hippolyte explicitly states that the Bahá’í Faith should not be confused with the Bábí Faith, nor should it be considered a sect or a reform movement of Islam, but that it is an independent and universal religion: “‘If Bábism could have been considered as a purely local religious reform movement, as one of the many Muslim sects that abound in the East, and especially in Persia where the Shi’ite religion and Sufi philosophy lend themselves more than any other to metaphysical speculation, the same is not true of Behaism, which, by the height of its principles, and the liberality of its doctrine, has the full scope of a universal religion.’”[28]

Then he introduces Bahá’u’lláh and clarifies in eloquent terms His rank: He is “The Glory of God,” “Him whom God shall make manifest,” “The One whose coming had been so emphatically foretold by the Báb," "who was to establish the definitive Religion of which the Báb had been the herald," "the Great Manifestation of God promised in the Books for the last days."[29]

Finally, he describes the historical context surrounding the revelation of the Book of Certitude and briefly comments on its content and style. He concludes, "The work, while it employs a mystical symbolism characteristic of the then prevailing forms of Islamic thought, is conceived in a poetic and energetic style, which sometimes is so permeated with the vehement expression of an anticlericalism that one would think it was inspired in another realm. He has acquired a considerable reputation throughout the Muslim world. We thought that he also deserves to be known to those in our country who are interested in the intellectual movements of the East."[30]

This first publication, Hippolyte's first effort to spread the Faith to the general public, seems to receive a good reception from critics. Jacques Brieu[31] writes in *Mercure de France:* "The *Book of Certitude* is of a very high mysticism. It is very rich in poetic expressions and images. In this book there is much energy, gentleness, and kindness; but sometimes there are also violent accents against priests. It deserves to be read; not only by occultists, but also by all those who are interested in the movement of religious ideas in the East."[32]

In *Bibliothèque universelle,*[33] the critic refers to the Book of Certitude as an "extremely interesting little volume [. . .] full of poetry and theological science [. . .] suffused with a broad and invigorating breath." He also points out "the excellent translation rendered by Mr. Dreyfus which reveals all the dialectical power and all the symbolic richness [of the original]."[34]

Clément Huart, in *Revue de l'histoire des religions,* describes the book as "a most useful contribution to the history of the origins of the Baha'ism."[35] Although he regrets the problems of consistency in the transcription of Persian words and the lack of explanatory notes that could have made the symbolic language of Bahá'u'lláh more understandable to the uninitiated reader, he commends the translators who "did well to enable us to read one of Behâ's[36] principal works in its entirety." At the end of his article, he contradicts Hippolyte on his vision that the Bahá'í Faith can become an independent religion because Huart personally considers that "without cult ceremonies, without rites, without literature other than vague mystical preaching, it is a theosophy." This last observation will be the subject of long and cordial exchanges between the two men during the years that follow.

After reading this article, Hippolyte sends Clément Huart a letter of thanks. The latter addresses him a very encouraging response in October in which it is also learned that the Bahá'í community in Paris is considering—already at the time—the project to build a Mashriqu'l-Adhkár.[37] Mr. Huart writes:

> Dear Sir, upon returning to Paris, I find the kind letter that you kindly addressed to me on the occasion of a small critical article published in the *Revue de l'Histoire des religions.* I am very interested in your attempts to introduce the sacred books of the Bahá'ís into French literature, and as I would like to share this interest with the readers of this special review, I naturally, while pointing out the good sides of your work, wanted to point out to them certain details that could have misled their judgment. [. . .] The opening of a Behá'í mosque in Paris would really be a very interesting thing, and I would not be the last to visit it: Isqabat[38] cannot be forever the Mecca of the new religion, to which I wish many followers without counting on myself to be a part.[39]

6 / In the Heart of Asia

In 1904, Hippolyte receives a new letter from 'Abdu'l-Bahá in which He confides to him the joy and gladness brought by the letters sent to Him by the friends from Paris, and how happy He is to see the progress of the Faith in France. He invites Hippolyte to come to see Him for the second time, in the spring, and then to go to Hindustan so that—referencing the Persian poet Hafez—similar to the parrots of India revelling in sweets, Hippolyte will praise and glorify the Abhá Beauty[1] among the local people.[2]

The Master's invitation is clear: He asks Hippolyte to go to India and Burma[3] to guide the communities and encourage them in their development. Of course, the Master, as Hippolyte's friend Sydney Sprague reminds us, "never commands, or compels obedience, he only sweetly suggests, and his followers have found that to follow his suggestions will surely lead them in the right way."[4]

'Abdu'l-Bahá tells Hippolyte that he will have to rejoin Sydney in Burma since he, Sydney, is already in the Holy Land and is about to leave for India. The two friends will thus become the first two Western Bahá'ís to travel to the "Far East" to "bring the good news that believers in Europe and the United States are one in their love and unity with the eastern brethren" and become witnesses to the fulfilment of this magnificent prophecy of Bahá'u'lláh, "The East and West shall embrace as lovers."[5]

On March 10, 1905, Hippolyte embarks on the *Victoria* in Marseille. He stops at Port Said, passes through Jaffa and Haifa, where he briefly meets some Persian believers, and arrives at ‘Akká on March 17. He remains there for five days and is honored to be in the presence of the Master almost every day, either for conversations that extend throughout the day, or for dinner when ‘Abdu’l-Bahá is back at His home. The most significant event of his stay is certainly March 21: he spends the day and night in Bahjí,[6] where the community of believers celebrates Naw-Rúz, the Bahá’í new year.

He also spends time with Mírzá Abu’l-Faḍl, the famous Bahá’í scholar and Apostle of Bahá’u’lláh[7] whom he had previously met in Paris in 1901, and other Persian believers such as Ḥusayn Yazdí, Siyyid Assadu’lláh-i-Qumí, and Muḥammad-Riḍá, with whom he visits Haifa and Mount Carmel several times. Finally, he embarks on March 24 aboard the SS *Amphitrita* to reach Port Said, where the boats depart for the Far East. While waiting for the SS *Himalaya* to begin his journey to the Indies, Hippolyte shares with Yvonne all the excitement he experiences in having been given the mission entrusted to him by the Master, as well as his happiness in meeting the friends from Egypt:

> My dear, a quick word before leaving Port Said where I spent three charming days. There was the whole Woodcock[8] family, an American painter, student of Benjamin Constant:[9] they will come to Paris in May, and I hope you will see them. You will like them very much. Moreover, Ahmed Yazdi and the others are so kind! I got a cap, and here I am, ready to face the tropical heat. My boat arrives today and tomorrow morning we will enter the Canal. The crossing lasts 16 hours. I will try to finish my mission in the Indies for the month of June. Love to the children and Paul. Lots of love to you also from your dear Hippolyte.[10]

On March 28, he boards the SS *Himalaya* to sail towards the Suez, then to Aden at the southern tip of the Arabian Peninsula where he boards another ship, the *Peninsular*. After five days of sea crossing, he finally arrives in Bombay[11] on April 7 at 9:00 am.

In 1905, India and Burma are under British colonial rule and are part of the British Raj, more commonly known as "British India" or the "Indian Empire." The Faith appeared in India as early as during the lifetime of the Báb, and Bahá'u'lláh had sent Persian believers to India, including the famous teacher Jamál Effendi, who found great receptivity and formed the first groups of believers.[12] The first Burmese community was later established in Rangoon[13] by the famous Siyyid Muṣṭafá Rúmí in 1878. It was during this period that an entire village of more than eight hundred people—Daidanaw—converted to the Faith, becoming the first Bahá'í village outside Persia.[14]

Hippolyte spends four extremely busy weeks in Bombay. First, he multiplies his personal contacts: he meets important figures of society such as the French, Persian, and Russian consuls and ambassadors, as well as local political and intellectual figures such as Behramji Malabari[15] and Navroji Dorabji Khandalevala.[16] He makes two speeches before the Theosophical Society[17] and has a long interview with the president of the Franco-Persian circle. He notes in his travelogue that he has very pleasant conversations about the Faith with people he meets during his travels, such as Indians and Persians, who are happy to be able to speak in Persian with a European. He also takes the opportunity to immerse himself in Indian spiritual and religious culture: he visits temples and attends Hindu processions.

He visits the city's Bahá'í center several times to meet and encourage the friends, as the Master had asked of him. At the time, the Bombay community regularly held three meetings a week: on Tuesday, Thursday, and Sunday. The Tuesday meeting is reserved for representatives of the institutions of the Faith; the other two meetings usually host from eighty to one hundred believers, which corresponds only to a part of the total number of believers in the city. Many of them own and operate shops and do not ordinarily have the opportunity to close their shops in time in order to attend the sessions. Women have a separate meeting, and there is a school for the children.[18]

At meetings in the center, the text of revealed Tablets is chanted, and then, in general, one of the believers speaks on a given theme. On Sundays, seekers, well-wishers, and curious inquirers participating in the meetings have the opportunity to ask their questions, to which believers strive to provide answers as best they can.[19] Sydney Sprague recalls in his memoirs that becoming a Bahá'í in India often required great sacrifices: loss of friends, money, or status by reason of prejudice and social ostracism, but, despite this, there was great solidarity among believers, a phenomenon all the more magnificent since "these groups are composed of men of different castes and creeds who were but yesterday strangers, if not actual enemies—such, for instance, as the Zoroastrians and Mohammedans."[20]

On April 21, Hippolyte celebrates the most important of the Bahá'í festivals with the local community, the feast of Riḍván.[21] During the evening, he reads to the believers a poignant message, signed by the Chicago Bahá'ís, that he had just received from the United States and that was filled with love, brotherhood, and encouragement.

The next day, he writes an answer on behalf of the Bombay community in which he describes, with his characteristic humility, the state of extreme joy and exultation in which he finds himself:

> As I am currently passing through Bombay, the believers of this city have entrusted me with the great honour of expressing their thanks to you, and to tell you the precious value they attach to your memory. [. . .]
>
> Steeped in the teachings of the Blessed Perfection,[22] you have understood that today it is our duty to help our Lord 'Abdu'l-Bahá to unite the various nations in bonds of affection and solidarity that nothing can shake, and your initiative will certainly have the best effect in all the cities of this glorious East. In recent years, India especially, the land of ancient religions, always open to spirituality, seems to have attracted the special attention of our Lord and deserves his solicitude. He sent his most learned apostles there, next to whom the signatory of this letter is in a very modest posture. It is felt that nowhere more than here, where people from different nations, who live in close proximity to each other while practicing their own respective

creeds, some of whom have understood that behind all these religions there lies a single truth which all strive to attain, and nowhere does the Light of Bahá seem to me to be called upon more urgently than here to dispel the darkness of doubts and superstitions. [. . .]

Therefore, my dear brothers, be sure that your letter has gone straight to the hearts of all the friends, they wish it to be the signal of a new habit that will make our spiritual brotherhood manifest. [. . .] May Bahá'u'lláh always guide your steps!

On behalf of the Bahá'ís of Bombay—[signed by] Hippolyte Dreyfus.[23]

On May 2, Hippolyte leaves Bombay to reach Calcutta[24] via Nagpur by train. He stays there for the remaining four days to meet the believers. On May 7, he boards the steamer *Bangala* and arrives at Rangoon in the late afternoon of May 9. Accompanied by Siyyid Mihdí, a Persian pioneer, he divides his time between meetings with believers, interviews with the Persian consul, and visits to the breathtaking sites of Shwedagon[25] and Lake Royal. Meetings at the Bahá'í center are also particularly moving: the room is mostly too small to accommodate the flood of participants who hasten to that venue to see the two Western Bahá'ís. Believers arrive from all classes of society, from different religious backgrounds—Buddhists, Muslims, Hindus, Christians, Jews, Zoroastrians. Many have received a higher education, and some are lawyers, doctors, or employees of the British government.[26]

On May 5, while he has been in Rangoon for a few days, Hippolyte writes about all the joy he feels at being in Burma on a postcard depicting the Shwedagon pagoda. He sends the postcard to Yvonne: My dear Yvonne, here I am in Rangoon for two days. You cannot imagine the welcome from the friends here! And the enchantment of this country! These flowers, these lakes, these trees, and these monuments! It is like being in Japan! I am leaving on Saturday for Rangoon[27] where Sprague cannot wait to leave to come back here with me as it seems that it is very hot there![28]

Rangoon, Burma, 1905. Sitting, second from left: Mírzá Maḥram. Third from left: Jinab-i-Adíb. Fourth from left: Muṣṭafá Rúmí. Standing, third from left: Sydney Sprague. Fourth from left: Hippolyte.

On May 13, he arrives in Mandalay, where he meets his dear friend Sydney Sprague. At that time, the Mandalay community has about a hundred believers, making it one of the largest Bahá'í communities outside of the Middle East. Unlike Rangoon, the believers, predominantly local, mostly come from much more modest classes: they are mostly weavers, and few speak English. They meet twice a week, in the house of the Burmese widow who provides lodgings for Hippolyte and his friend.[29]

During his stay, Hippolyte stays with the widow of a believer, Mrs. Mong Taw. In the account of his journey, Sydney tells how Hippolyte, a great gentleman, is disturbed by the fact that he has not managed to meet their hostess since his arrival:

> With all that sense of politeness which Frenchmen possess, he insisted that he must see his hostess to thank her for her hospitality. But the widow could never be found. The most attractive

> and well-cooked meals were sent to us from somewhere, and everything was kept in perfect order, but the widow remained invisible. [Dreyfus], began to think she was some mysterious being who had no earthly existence; when, the day before our departure, some friends brought her to see [us. She] seemed much embarrassed, and on [Dreyfus] thanking her profusely she said: "But I have done nothing at all; you would do the same for me if I came to see you."[30]

The two friends stay for about a week in Mandalay. Each day, a meeting is held at the Bahá'í center; the meetings usually begin with chanting of revealed Tablets, then one of the believers gives a small speech in Burmese. At the end, Hippolyte or Sydney address the congregation of believers with the help of an interpreter. Meetings usually end with tea and cake, and the children hand out a handful of roses and jasmine to each participant.[31]

Mandalay, Burma, 1905. In the center, fourth row, second from left: Hippolyte. Third row, first from left: Sydney Sprague.

The day of their departure from Mandalay is magical: a meeting is organized in their honor, and all the rooms of the house that welcomes them are full to overflowing. Sydney tells us:

> After [Dreyfus] and I bade a few words of farewell, an aged Burman [Burmese], the oldest Bahai in Mandalay, arose, and with a voice that shook with emotion, made a most touching and beautiful speech. He told us what our coming had meant to all of them. How much they appreciated our visit, and he spoke of the barrier that had always existed between the East and the West, which was partly their fault as well as the fault of the English who governed them. He thanked God that he had lived to see the day when, through the manifestation of Bahá'u'llah, their hearts in the Orient, in faraway Mandalay, had been united by so wonderful a love to the hearts of their Western brothers in Europe and America.
>
> By this time, although it was after midnight, the whole assembly, men, women, and children, insisted on coming with us to the steam train. Some mistake had been made in ordering the carriages for us, and there were none to be found. "We will all walk," they cried—the distance was over two miles. We started off, a curious and picturesque procession. The light of a full moon made it almost as clear as day, and the bright silk robes of the Burmans shimmered and waved in the breeze, and it seemed as though some ethereal army of pink and white was being blown gently down the road. The effect was startling in its beauty. Before we had gone halfway some bullock carts caught up with us, and we finished the journey in these.
>
> On reaching the riverbank, they all grouped themselves around us to say goodbye. The solemnity and the beauty of that scene was indescribable. What a picture it was! The red fezzes and the long white robes of the Mohammedans, the pink and yellow silks of the Burmans, the little children in their bright dresses, the women with their big white combs and wreaths of jasmine in their hair, standing under the waving palm trees

> flooded by the glory of the full moon. Again, some kind words were uttered, and the tears were streaming down everyone's faces as we said goodbye. I said to my friend [Dreyfus], "Would that all the people of the world could see this; there would be no need of teachers to prove the truth of the Bahai Cause, for this is its proof. Where such love exists, there is God." To think that a group of Buddhists and Mohammedans should weep at the departure of a Christian and a Jew [Sydney and Hippolyte's previous religions] from their midst![32]

After three days of sailing on the Irrawaddy,[33] they arrive in Pyay and take a train to Rangoon. The two weeks in the capital are animated by a large number of conferences attended by very diverse audiences: Christians, Hindus, local believers, etc. . . . One of the talks given by Hippolyte is thus organized in a hall rented by a person of Jewish faith and another one is given before an audience of Christians strongly attracted by the beauty and nobility of the message they had heard during one of his previous conferences.[34]

Rangoon, Burma, 1905. Sitting, second row, second from left to right: Muṣṭafá Rúmí, Mírzá Maḥram, Jinab-i-Adíb, Hippolyte, Sydney Sprague.

In his memoirs, Sydney notes that these public speeches give rise to several articles on the Faith, published in various Indian languages and in various newspapers of the Indian Empire.[35] From Burma, the two friends are especially struck by the fact that the Cause has managed to bring together, once again, under one roof and "in a true spirit of love and brotherhood," believers from such different religions: Buddhists, Muslims, Hindus, Christians, Jews, and Zoroastrians.

For their departure, the believers organize a picnic in a beautiful garden on the outskirts of the city. They take this opportunity to show the two friends a magnificent white marble sarcophagus that has been prepared to accommodate the remains of the Báb. As the situation in the Holy Land was still very difficult due to unceasing attacks from Covenant-breakers, they were advised not to send it for the moment and to keep it in a safe place in Rangoon.[36]

After Burma, Hippolyte plans to travel to northern India for several weeks to continue his work of teaching and of encouraging the friends, then to Karachi and finally to Persia.[37] On June 8, after several days at sea, he is back in Calcutta; the conditions are extremely trying, as an oppressive heat wave, compounded by a terrible drought, has fallen on northern India. After a few days, Hippolyte decides to travel to the North, and he goes to Benares[38] in the hope of escaping the harassing heat. He visits the Theosophical Society center, located in a nearby town, then travels to the Ganges, but the weather conditions worsen and make his teaching work unbearable. He eventually decides to move up the date of his return journey home. He leaves on the 15th for Karachi, makes stops in the cities of Lucknow, Agra, and New Delhi and finally arrives in Bombay on June 21. The next day, he sails via Aden for Port Said, which he reaches after fourteen days at sea. From there, he takes another vessel and arrives in Marseille on July 9.[39]

On his return to France, a rather funny anecdote is reported to us by May Bolles. When Hippolyte hands the negatives of his photos to be developed by the photographer, the latter informs him that some photos are not authentic and that they have been artificially retouched. Hippolyte asks him the reason, to which the photographer answers: "The people in these groups are of such mixed caste that they could never be brought together without killing one another. Therefore, it is evident that these pictures are not genuine." In response, Hippolyte explains that these groups of people who formerly had been in the utmost enmity and hatred were now united in the bonds of love and brotherhood through the power of Bahá'u'lláh and His teachings.[40]

7 / A Man of Letters

Back in Paris, Hippolyte receives a new letter from 'Abdu'l-Bahá in which the Master congratulates him on his trip to India where he successfully was able to spread "the teachings," establish "the divine principles and instructions," and "sow the seed of the love of God." "The results of this trip," the Master says, "although they are already visible, will be even more glorious thereafter." This Tablet ends on this exhortation: "It is incumbent upon thee now to strive to spread the divine fragrances in Paris and to bring the loved ones of God together, showing them the utmost kindness and affection, that from the unity and harmony of the friends the flame of the love of God may be kindled, setting all hearts ablaze like candles."[1]

This first trip to the Bahá'í communities in Asia and the reception of this Tablet further strengthens Hippolyte in his faith. Feeling exultant because he has received the encouragement of the Master Whom he loved so much, and driven by his desire to always do more for the Cause, in which he sees the solution to the problems of this world, he decides in 1905 to leave the Paris Bar association and devote himself fully to the writing and translation of the Holy Writings. On October 26, 1905, he receives a letter of acceptance of his resignation from the Bar.[2] From then on, Hippolyte no longer presents himself as a lawyer but as a "man of letters"; this is evidenced by the designation on his passports of the following years.[3]

With this new professional identity, Hippolyte begins a prolific correspondence with the great orientalists of the time. These exchanges allow him to deepen his knowledge of the Arab and Persian worlds, to spread the Faith that, for the time being, remains little studied due to an obvious lack of literature, and, above all, to restore certain historical truths. Indeed, on the one hand, the false accusations against the Bahá'ís propagated by the Persian and Ottoman governments, in order to justify their persecutions, are intensifying, and on the other hand, the treacherous statements regarding the ranks of Bahá'u'lláh and 'Abdu'l-Bahá spread by Covenant-breakers, in order to sow trouble among the believers, are becoming more frequent and violent.

One of the first orientalists with whom Hippolyte establishes a regular and productive correspondence is the French diplomat and admirer of the Báb, A. L. M. Nicolas. The latter was the official interpreter of the French legation in Persia and is now, in or around 1906, the consul general of France in Tabriz.[4] He has the distinction of being born in Persia, and, as he himself confides, he spoke Persian and Russian even before mastering the French language. At the end of the nineteenth century, he had read *Religions and Philosophies in Central Asia*[5] by Arthur de Gobineau, and, intrigued by the doctrine of the Báb, decided to study the Bábí Faith.[6] He then embarked on the translation into French of the Bábí literature in order to propagate its teachings.

The two men will maintain a lifelong correspondence that will last over twenty-five years and will lead them to meet several times in France and in Persia. However, the first exchanges between Nicolas and the first French Bahá'í are not going to be easy. The major reason is the confusion—widespread at the time—that surrounds the ranks of the Báb, Bahá'u'lláh, and 'Abdu'l-Bahá. The main grievance A. L. M. Nicolas has is the denigration he feels has been shown toward the Báb. Through his eloquent and erudite letters, Hippolyte will succeed, little by little, year after year, with kindness and great firmness, in dispelling the misunderstanding and clarifying the unique stations of Bahá'u'lláh and the Báb and the concept of the Covenant.

This correspondence with A. L. M. Nicolas is very important. In several letters He writes to Hippolyte, 'Abdu'l-Bahá emphasizes how maintaining constant correspondence with Mr. Nicolas, who is in

Persia, is indispensable, as the supporters of Mírzá Yaḥyá[7] are sowing doubts and rumors.[8]

A major turning point in the relationship between the two men takes place during their meeting in Persia. On his return to Paris, Hippolyte helps his friend—who is experiencing great difficulties in his communication with his Parisian publisher and the printers—by reaching out to them. Their respective families begin to appreciate each other and send each other gifts for different occasions.

While residing in Persia during the bloody persecutions perpetrated against the Bábí and Bahá'í communities, A. L. M. Nicolas, a horrified observer, recounts to Hippolyte the abuses he witnessed. For example, in the following letter dated 1907, he recounts:

> My dear friend, there was in Tauris[9] a Behahi [Bahá'í] named Kerbelabi Sadiq, by his trade a dealer in attar,[10] and who exercised his profession peacefully. However, every time he went to his shop quite distant from his house, he met [. . .] Hassan, a Muslim baker and fanatic who violently insulted him and his religion. The calm of Kerbelabi Sadiq ended up enraging the Muslim group who, last Thursday, April 25, warned a baqqal[11] neighbour of the Behahi that he should close his shop if he wanted to avoid a bloody scene. The latter obeyed and disappeared. So around 7 o'clock, [. . .] Hassan, along with his wife's brother Khalil, his own brother and his servant came to Sadiq's shop, which at that time sold tobacco to a customer. The insults rained down and as Sadiq begged his insulters to leave him in peace, they dragged him out of his shop and began beating him. One of them grabbed a stool [and knocked him out]. Sadiq fell, and they butchered his face with their heels. The unfortunate man was picked up in agony and died only the following Saturday as a result of the ill-treatment he had suffered. [. . .] The believers in Tauris are in desolation. They addressed [the authorities] of Tauris who did not want to compromise themselves. The governor replied that it did not concern him. Believe me, my dear friend, your devotee.[12]

Another prominent orientalist with whom Hippolyte maintains regular exchanges is the British scholar and orientalist Edward Granville Browne (1862–1926). A professor at Cambridge University, Browne was also influenced at an early age by Gobineau's famous *Religions and philosophies in Central Asia;* his reading prompted him to explore the Bábí Faith, the Bahá'í Faith, and to travel several times to Persia. He has a unique position in history because he is the only Westerner to have met Bahá'u'lláh in person in the Holy Land when the latter, in the last years of His life, was residing at Bahjí.[13]

The extremely cordial exchanges between Hippolyte and Professor Browne are mainly concentrated around the authentication of texts and the identification of authors of Tablets that both men receive from Persia or the Holy Land. Sometimes in English, sometimes in French, these letters are occasionally peppered with Persian or Arabic words, when the equivalents in their respective mother tongues, French and English respectively, are not able to convey in a fair and precise way the original meaning of their words. The two confreres become very close over the years, to the point of organizing meetings in the presence of their respective wives and families.

The relationship between the two men is also very important in the eyes of 'Abdu'l-Bahá, Who asks Hippolyte in several of His letters to meet and maintain a continuous correspondence with Professor Browne. The Master encouraged Hippolyte to express himself with kindness, gentleness, sincerity, and firmness to accompany Professor Browne in his exploration of the Faith.[14]

In 1911, 'Abdu'l-Bahá confides His concerns about the accuracy of Professor Browne's understanding of the Faith, because Browne is, at that time, concurrently also in communication with some Covenant-breakers residing in England:

> A brief missive was penned to Mr. Browne, and copies of several letters for him are being sent to thee. Deliver them as soon as possible. [. . .] He will certainly pass through Paris on his way to Persia. It is essential that thou, together with the handmaiden of Bahá,[15] endeavour to meet with him. This matter is import-

> ant. Exert thy utmost to reach him, as the followers of Yahya have him in their thrall and flatter him relentlessly. This hapless man hath fallen for their empty adulation, through which they secured his support. God willing, thou mayest be able to guide him so that he may at the very least act with fairness, and refrain from reckless endorsement of their cause.[16]

In his efforts to spread the Faith and the Writings, Hippolyte also engages in regular correspondences with other renowned orientalists and historians such as Salomon Reinach,[17] who will later testify to Hippolyte's considerable contribution "to the history of oriental religions,"[18] Edgar Blochet[19] to whom Hippolyte hands over Writings of the Faith, including an original copy of the Kitáb-i-Aqdas,[20] and Clément Huart, who will greatly appreciate Hippolyte for his efforts "to introduce into French literature the sacred books of the Bahá'í Faith."[21]

8 / The Hidden Words

On his return from India, and in accordance with the advice of 'Abdu'l-Bahá, Hippolyte resumes his teaching work and again focuses on spreading the Faith in France. In 1905, he publishes a translation of The Hidden Words[1] with Ernest Leroux, in collaboration with Mírzá Habíbu'lláh. In addition to the Persian section of The Hidden Words, the book includes a translation of The Most Holy Tablet, The Tablet of Wisdom, and The Seven Valleys.

The Hidden Words were revealed by Bahá'u'lláh in 1858 while He was pacing, wrapped in His meditations, along the banks of the Tigris River in Iraq. This work summarizes the basic essence of certain spiritual truths contained in all the religions of the past in abbreviated and pithy form. There are two sections, one is written in Arabic, the second in Persian. Hippolyte and Mírzá Habíbu'lláh offer in their published work a translation of the Persian section but not the Arabic one. In their short preface, the translators present The Hidden Words as "a series of precepts and exhortations, of transcendent morality rendered in a language whose translation can unfortunately give only a very inadequate impression of the original meaning."[2]

Alongside The Hidden Words, Hippolyte and Mírzá Habíbu'lláh give access to three other main works of Bahá'u'lláh—The Most Holy Tablet, The Tablet of Wisdom, and The Seven Valleys. The Lawḥ-i-Aqdas, also known as The Most Holy Tablet or The Tablet to the Christians, was addressed to a believer of Christian background. In this Tablet, Bahá'u'lláh proclaims His station by referring to passages from the Bible. The Lawḥ-i-Ḥikmat, or The Tablet of Wisdom, was revealed by Bahá’u’lláh to Áqá Muḥammad, known as Nabíl-i-Akbar. In this Tablet, Bahá’u’lláh redefines the fundamentals of true philosophy. Several philosophers of ancient Greece are mentioned, such as Hippocrates, Socrates, Plato, and Aristotle. The Seven Valleys was written around 1860 in Baghdad by Bahá’u’lláh in response to the questions asked by Shaykh Muhyi’d-Dín, a judge known for being a fervent follower of Sufism. The Seven Valleys is often considered Bahá’u’lláh’s most mystical work. In it He describes, in highly poetic language, the path of the soul on a spiritual journey. During this journey, the soul passes through different stages as it draws closer to God.

Several specialized journals welcome the release of this book. In the *Journal des débats politiques et littéraires,*[3] the critic writes, “These pamphlets or epistles, as remarkable for the nobility of ideas as for the elevation of form, contain the very essence of the ethics of the new religion, of the new revelation, which promises happiness to humanity reconciled in the same faith and freed from the old dogmas. This very curious collection deserves the reader’s interest even more since Baha’ism, coming from the East, has, it is assured, already made so many proselytes in America, in London and even in Paris.”[4]

Sébastien Voirol[5] publishes an exciting article in *Mercure de France.* Having just returned from the Holy Land where he met the Master, he paints an edifying portrait of the history of the Cause, from the time of the Báb to that of ‘Abdu’l-Bahá, and of the precepts of the Bahá’í Faith. In this twenty-page article, he cites Hippolyte Dreyfus’ and Mírzá Habíbu’lláh’s translation of The Hidden Words and commends the relevance of the work done by the translators for having chosen to present, in the same volume, The Seven Valleys, The Most Holy Tablet, and The Tablet of Wisdom:

> The main attribute of the modern Behai [Bahá’í], which the distinguished orientalist Mr. Hippolyte Dreyfus so remarkably brought out in a recent publication called “the Hidden Words in Persian” [. . .] is the skill with which according to the belief of the one to whom he addresses his discourse, he will employ dif-

> ferent arguments. To a Muslim he will speak of the disappearance of Imam Mahdi and the arrival of the Ka'im [Qa'im]; to a Jew or a Christian he will recall the apocalyptic writings of the Bible and the New Testament, the prophecies of Christ relating to his return; with a free thinker he will stand on the scientific ground; always showing that Béha-oullah [Bahá'u'lláh] is the Promised one, the one whose doctrines, when put into practice, will ensure the well-being of humanity reconciled in one and the same faith. This religion of brotherhood, solidarity, and peace, as a whole, could be compared to the one professed with some brilliance by the writer already named, the great Tolstoy, during his lifetime. According to more than one scholar, Bábism will one day become more powerful than Christianity is today."[6]

Clément Huart, in *Revue de l'histoire des religions,* also welcomes this new work in a very positive way, although, in the same vein that he expressed in his critique of the translation of The Book of Certitude, he regrets the lack of explanatory notes that could have better guided the reader in his understanding, and he also points out a number of inaccuracies in the translation. He nevertheless concludes, "Despite these slight flaws, the small volume that enriches the collection of Bábí and Béhaï books offered for the admiration of European readers is not bad. The translators certainly succeeded fully in translating, into French, the enthusiasm that animated the editor. [. . .] Mysticism, on the contrary, belongs to all times and all countries; as long as there are enlightened ones in the world, there will be readers and even admirers for the effusions of divine love among the Bábís, the heirs of the great Persian mystics, of the thirteenth and fifteenth centuries."[7]

There is a similar resonance expressed in the *Critical review of history and literature.* The reviewer also regrets the lack of explanatory notes that could have allowed readers to have "the full measure of the texts" and notes some translation problems. Nevertheless, he ends his article in a beautiful way: "The collection of the four small treatises for which Messrs. Dreyfus and Mirza Habib'ullah have just given us the translation, deserves to be welcomed with favour [. . .] [although] there are inadequacies of little gravity that do not detract from the interest of this little book, let us welcome it as a new document and not without value for the history of a great religious movement, called perhaps to infuse a new sap into the aged trunk of Islam."[8]

9 / In the Cradle of the Faith

Around 1906, Hippolyte receives a new letter from 'Abdu'l-Bahá inviting him this time to travel to Persia, the birthplace of the Faith, to meet and encourage the communities of believers scattered throughout the country.

This proposed expedition to Persia has been bouncing around in Hippolyte's head for quite some time. Back in August 1905, A. L. M. Nicolas confided in him his disappointment upon learning that Hippolyte could not come to Persia: "Dear Mr. Dreyfus, I deeply regret that you did not come to Tehran this year, and I convey to you the regrets of the Bábí community, whom I had informed of your visit, and who were thirsty to see you. I had informed the whole league, and now you are making us realize ours was a false leap of joy: you will not be forgiven until you are in Tehran and staying in my house."[1]

On May 19, 1906, Hippolyte, animated by his unalterable sense of service and immediate obedience, qualities so characteristic of the first heroes of the Faith and its early believers, boards the famous *Orient Express*[2] train to travel to Constantinople,[3] the gateway to the countries of Central Asia and the Middle East. He arrives in Constantinople on the evening of May 23, where he meets his two future travel companions, Emmanuelle Lachenay and Laura Barney. They embark the next day on the *Imperial Nicholas II* and reach Odessa,[4] where they remain stranded for almost a week: the city is severely immobilised by a violent maritime strike, fueled by a large-scale popular uprising that forces the authorities to declare the city as being under siege.

As soon as the situation allows, they take a train to Baku,[5] which they reach after three days. They spend the day in the neighborhood of Bibi-Heybat, where they meet believers; the Baku community has the second largest number of believers in the region, after Ashgabat. The next day, they cross the Caspian Sea, and after being stuck for several days in Krasnovodsk[6] due to the floods ravaging the city, they finally reach their first goal, Ashgabat, on June 8, late in the evening.

Ashgabat is, at that time, the place where the Faith is developing most rapidly, at which the number of believers exceeds a thousand, and where, for the first time in the history of the Faith, a pattern of community life, with its institutions, places of worship, schools, medical facilities, and cemetery, is being established.[7]

In Ashgabat, the three travelers spend most of their time on the site of the first *Mashriqu'l-Adhkár,*[8] whose construction began in 1902 and will eventually be completed in 1908. On the site, the large hall for prayer meetings is almost ready; it is there that the local community meet regularly.[9] Accompanied by Áqá Ḥusayn 'Alí Ahmadov, one of the most influential Bahá'ís in the local community, Hippolyte and his two companions are fortunate to be able to observe and experience, each day, the exceptional devotion that animates the community, to deepen their understanding of this unique institution that is the *Mashriqu'l-Adhkár,* and are to be given the rare privilege of witnessing the earliest efforts at translating into reality some aspects of Bahá'u'lláh's vision at the level of community life. Laura Barney reminisces about their first day:

> The Mashriqu'l-Adhkár, this majestic monument, [. . .] it is not a monument of stone, and contains no pulpit. There is no leadership there, it is governed by a community of love and devotion to one another. Here, I had my first meeting, and the men were all seated, and as I came in with Mr. Dreyfus, they arose and greeted us with love and affection.

After I had returned their greetings, I gave them the news from Acca ['Akká], which they were longing for. The meeting was one of deep sincerity and emotion. This temple was built by the people for the love of Bahá'u'lláh to bring about the harmony of the different races, religions, and mentalities of mankind.

After the meeting we drove to the top of the mountain, near the temple, and from there we had a magnificent view of the vast plains. A wonderful vision indeed of peace and tranquillity. Here nature voiced a hope for the future generation to be kind and generous.[10]

They eventually leave Ashgabat on the evening of June 12, to visit the believers in the cities of Mary, Bukhara, and Samarkand. Although the community is much smaller, the town of Mary is also a very active center of the Faith in the region.[11] The more modest Samarkand community is also one of the centers of activity in the region: it had the privilege of having among its members, for several years, the well-known Mírzá Abu'l-Faḍl. Laura recounts, "Samarkand was once a great city but is now in ruins. [. . .] There are many homes here that are filled with Baha'is. Joy was radiant in their faces and hearts."[12] The travelers return to Ashgabat on June 17 and spend the next day with the believers at the site of the Ma<u>sh</u>riqu'l-A<u>dh</u>kár.

Back in Ashgabat, Hippolyte takes time to send a letter to Yvonne to share his impressions and his enthusiasm, and as always, he does so in all humility:

My darling Yvonne,

On my way back to Echqabad [Ashgabat] that night, I found your letter of June 6th written after a word from James. This is the first line that has come to me from Paris since I left, I fear that the other letters will no longer reach me: the newspapers have talked too much about me; the police must have had my letters intercepted and it is only after having seen [their] innoc-

Ashgabat, 1906. Second row, standing in the center: Hippolyte. First row, sitting fifth from left to right: Hand of the Cause Hájí Amin, Laura Clifford-Barney, Emmanuelle Lachenay, Hájí Mírzá Muḥammad-Taqí, Vakílu'd-dawlih, "Kabir-i-Afnan," main architect of the Mashriqu'l-Adhkár and Apostle of Bahá'u'lláh.

uous character that the censor has decided to allow them to be delivered. Which is lovely! (. . .)

I think you will have received my letters and cards from Samarkand. Our journey has been wonderful. Scheykh [Shaykh] Mohamed Ali and Agha Mechedi Yousof,[13] 2 believers from here accompanied us; and in Merv, in Bokhara where we stopped for a while, the believers came to wish us in crowds *Allaho Abha!* In Samarkand, the same warm welcome. We stayed 2 1/2 days excited by the warm reception shown by the friends, the beauty of the monuments from the time of Tamerlane,[14] the refreshing beauty of the gardens!

Believers from Kokend,[15] Tashkend,[16] Israelites from Tashkend with the chief rabbi had left to receive us but floods delayed them by 2 days on the way so much that it was only 20 minutes before the departure of the train that they could see me. Some left, others got on the train to Bokhara and then alighted to return to their homes.

You understand that I am the very first [Western believer to visit them], [and] that my popularity is ridiculous and unjustified, but I tell you all of this so that you know the enthusiasm of the believers. Our stay in Samarkand, by the way, could not have gone on without scandal, as foreigners do not easily enter Russian Turkestan, and I will tell you when I return about my interview with the chief of police. We returned here last night and tonight we leave for Persia. (. . .)

Your Hippolyte.[17]

On June 19, Hippolyte, Laura, and Mrs. Lachenay resume their travel to reach Persia. This trip is a new historical moment in the annals of the Faith, as the three fellow travelers are poised to become the first Western Bahá'ís to visit the native land of the Báb and Bahá'u'lláh.[18] They pass through Krasnovodsk, Baku, Lankaran, and finally arrive in Persia on June 23 in Bandar-e Anzali where they immediately report to the *rais*[19] of the city to explain the purpose of their trip. They then go to the town of Rasht where they participate in a dawn prayers meeting with the local believers.

The situation of the Bahá'ís in Persia is terribly precarious, and persecutions are raging. Between 1903 and 1906, violent unrest was stirred up in many cities such as Rasht, Malayer, Hamadan, Isfahan, and Yazd, where the mobs, enraged and excited by the mullahs' instigation, attacked, persecuted, and tortured a large number of Bahá'ís. Many believers thus drank the cup of martyrdom in many excruciating forms of suffering, only because they had embraced a religion which, on the face of it, appeared different to that of their compatriots.[20]

On June 25, the three companions arrive in Qazvin, and stay with a believer named Ḥakím Báchí. The day is, as usual, very busy. After meeting with the local community, they attend a women's meeting at the home of Shaykh Káẓim Samandar, and end their day with a prayer meeting with believers at the home of a certain Ḥájí Ismá'í.

Laura recalls, "Our joy cannot be overestimated over the crowds that met us on our arrival at the different places we went to."[21] At midnight, they are back on their way to Tehran.

They stay in Tehran for almost two weeks. During their stay in the capital, Azíz'u'lláh Azízí, whom Hippolyte has known since 1902, serves as their guide and helps to organize their days. Their friend's first concern is to find acceptable accommodation, but the conditions of sanitation in Tehran are appalling, with hotels and restaurants no longer functioning. Their arrival in 1906 coincides indeed with the beginning of the Persian constitutional revolution against the rule of the Qájár dynasty. Tehran is under martial law: the city seems peaceful, but soldiers are to be found everywhere in the streets. Finally, Azízí ends up finding "dirty and poorly kept" rooms, rented by a Romanian entrepreneur above a sewing workshop. To his great surprise, not only are Hippolyte and his companions satisfied, but they also do not seem at all concerned about the housing. Above all, they express their eagerness to finally be able to go meet their Persian friends.[22]

Their stay in Tehran is divided between meetings with Persian authorities, ministers, and princes—with whom they tirelessly plead the cause of the Faith, with the hope of succeeding in reducing the persecutions and sufferings of the believers—and visits to the French, Belgian and Ottoman consuls, as well as Hippolyte's friend, A. L. M. Nicolas. It is important here to pause and mention one of the main roles of Hippolyte Dreyfus-Barney: very early on, he became one of the first diplomats of the Bahá'í community and the Master's most trusted Western envoy. Throughout all his life, whether he was in France or traveling in America, Asia, or Northern Africa, Hippolyte would have interactions with government representatives, princes, kings, diplomats, and leaders of thought from many parts of the world. Hippolyte would, on those occasions, represent the emerging Bahá'í community and act on behalf of 'Abdu'l-Bahá and subsequently on behalf of Shoghi Effendi. He always endeavored to expand the growing reputation of the Faith in the higher circles of society, to plead for justice for Bahá'ís, and also to denounce the

Persia, 1906. Second row, in the middle: Hippolyte.
Last row in the back: Laura Clifford-Barney and Emmanuelle Lachenay.

horrible persecutions, unwarranted arrests, false imprisonments, beatings, and tortures faced by its members, especially in Persia. This task, which today would probably be called "external affairs," was of the utmost importance at that time in the growth of the Bahá'í Faith. Some of Hippolyte's contacts would later open doors for the Bahá'í community to engage with significant organizations such as the League of Nations, help to make its voice heard in Persia and Northern Africa when important legal issues would arise, and also to "prepare the ground" for future Bahá'í teachers who would seek to enter or settle in foreign lands.

The rest of the time, prayer meetings and consultations are held with the members of the community. The pace is intense, and they have at least two or three appointments every day. Laura recalls, "After all the meetings, we were constantly informed by messengers inviting us to additional meetings, saying there were many thousands who were anxious to meet us, but our time was in a sense limited and we regretted our inability to stay on."[23]

Very special moments, Hippolyte notes in his travel diary, occur when he finds himself several times in the presence of the Hands of the Cause: Mullá 'Alí-Akbar Shahmírzádí (also known as Ḥájí Ákhúnd) and Ḥaji Mírzá Ḥasan-i-Adíb.

Persia, 1906. First from left: Ḥájí Amin. Third from left, Emmanuella Lachenay. Fourth and fifth from right: Laura Clifford-Barney, Hippolyte.

At the invitation of students, the three travelers also meet Ṣadru's-Ṣudur, a great scholar and founder in 1904 of the first Bahá'í teacher training school. In his classes, young students explore the sacred texts and the principles of Faith. The meetings are an opportunity for Hippolyte and his companions to ask questions on different themes, whether spiritual, religious, or theological. The exultation that emanates from these gatherings brings indescribable joy to the participants, both for our three travelers and for the Persian friends, who have the blessing of being witnesses to the realization of one of Bahá'u'lláh's prophecies: friends from the East and the West, sharing the same vision of love for the world, are, before their very own eyes, gathered in an atmosphere of deep brotherhood.[24] Following her return, Laura will eventually deliver a report to 'Abdu'l-Bahá in which she sets out the contents of their interviews;[25] this work is known as "the logical proofs of the new religion, as explained by Ṣadru's-Ṣudur." The Master, very satisfied, will reveal in response a Tablet to congratulate Ṣadru's-Ṣudur.[26]

Persia, 1906. First row, from left to right: Hippolyte, Ṣadru's-Ṣudur, Emmanuelle Lachenay, Laura Clifford-Barney.

In Tehran, the three companions are in a state of joy and gladness such as only spiritual confirmations can produce. Laura Barney takes advantage of one of their rare moments of rest to write a letter to her mother in which she confides how the believers are "wonderfully sincere and kind" and that they are among "the most important people of Persia."[27]

The friends take the opportunity to visit the Tarbiyat School, the famous Bahá'í school for boys, founded by the Hand of the Cause Ḥaji Mírzá Ḥasan-i-Adíb. During this meeting, Hippolyte, Laura, and Ḥaji Mírzá Ḥasan-i-Adíb consult together to select Western teachers who could potentially come and teach there.

They also travel several times to Shemiran,[28] north of Tehran, for two main reasons. First, they want to meet with Hippolyte's friend A. L. M. Nicolas, who owns a residence there. Next, two places of importance for Bahá'ís are found in Shemiran: the second house where Bahá'u'lláh's family used to take refuge during the months of intense summer heat, and, at the gates of the district, the residence rented by Bahá'u'lláh in which 'Abdu'l-Bahá, Mírzá Mihdí, and Bahíyyih Khánum were born.

When he is in Shemiran, Hippolyte writes a letter to his mother to tell her about the events of the last few days. Here is an extract:

> My dear Mother,
>
> I received your letter of June 20th. I am worried from what you write that some of my letters have been lost, as I have always written to you very regularly. But with Russia, you must be ready for anything. Since my last letter, I have spent 3 days in town. Reception of the French Minister who we went to wait for at the gates of the city in a beautiful garden belonging to the Shah and from where with great pomp after the sorbets and the tea, the procession formed to enter Tehran in clouds of dust. He is very friendly and is very interested in what I tell him. Many meetings in different corners of the city. Since the political situation here is a little troubled (the Shah is constantly receiving attacks), we must act with great caution. The [participants in] meetings cannot be more than 19, nor can meetings be held twice in a row at the same place. Yesterday we had one with the Zoroastrian believers in a superb park, and in the evening, in the moonlight, [held] another on a roof in the Jewish quarter, I was to meet more modest believers, shopkeepers, you can imagine their joy. There are maybe 90,000 Baha'is here and all of them would like to see us, but as you know it is impossible. (. . .) I am playing a little bit with the authorities at the moment because of my trip to Isfahan: also, I'm still here for 2

> or 3 days then I'll go down to the city to leave probably around the 14th for Isfahan. (. . .)
> I received a nice autographed tablet![29]
> Love to all,
> Your Hippolyte[30]

Two or three days after sending this letter, Hippolyte is back in Tehran to prepare his trip to Isfahan. He takes up his pen to share with his mother an unlikely incident that shows that divine assistance surrounds everyone who shares the message:

> I saw the Minister of Foreign Affairs in Chimran [Shemiran] who was most kind and offered me a letter for Zell us Sultan,[31] the brother of the Shah and governor of Isfahan. On the way out of his house, I met the Shah who was taking a car ride. When he saw me, he signed for me to stop and waved for me to come over; he spoke to me at length in French and asked me to send him an account of my journey. He will receive our translations; it will be better! These two almost unexpected interviews took place the day after I received a Tablet from the Master promising me success in this journey. Think how happy these little incidents make the believers![32]

Toward the end of their stay in the capital, Azízí rents, from his friend Jalálu'd-Dawlih, one of the sons of Ẓillu's Sulṭán,[33] a beautiful garden on the outskirts of Tehran, in the Jalálíyyih district,[34] in order to organize a party for his new friends. He invites many believers, including most of the Hands of the Cause residing in Tehran. A speech is made about the services rendered to the Faith by Hippolyte and his companions, and is followed by a time of rejoicing during which they mingle, discuss issues, and socialize. Hippolyte takes full advantage of the opportunity to forge strong bonds with some of the Persian believers whose kindness and friendship he feels quite strongly.[35] Thanks to his knowledge of the Persian language, which he now speaks and writes fluently, he forms friendships with

Hippolyte and Laura Clifford-Barney, Persia.

individuals who will always remain faithful to him.[36] One of the best examples is his friendship, which continues to grow, with Azíz'u'lláh Azízí. When the latter goes to Paris the following year, he will spend as much time as possible with Hippolyte. Azíz'u'lláh Azízí writes:

> After receiving a Tablet from 'Abdu'l-Baha for the second time, I made my departure for Europe on business, and set out also for pilgrimage to the Holy Land. I carried with me a very worthy gift for my western friend, Mon. Dreyfus. When I presented it to him, he was very surprised and asked what it was for? I replied "Don't you know we are Persians? It is customary among Persians to offer gifts and this is acceptable to Baha'u'llah. Doing this for a friend like you is not too much at all." So, he accepted the gift, and this strengthened the bond of friendship between us. Consequently, we were corresponding all the time and were constantly in touch. Whenever he intended to travel, he would let me know and I would inform him likewise. In short, whenever I would go to Europe, I would make certain to meet him every time.[37]

Persia, 1906. First row, fifth from left, to right: Emmanuelle Lachenay, Laura Clifford-Barney, Hippolyte.

On July 10, the three travelers set off again, this time to Isfahan. On the way, they stop in the cities of Qom, Kashan, and Khalid Abad where meetings with believers are held. Laura remembers in particular, "We had wonderful meetings at Kashan, one particularly at midnight. At 11:30, we walked through strange streets and arrived to meet these eager loving people."[38]

They arrive in Isfahan on the evening of the 13th. They meet Mírzá Asadu'lláh Khán-i-Vizír and Fátihu'l-Mulk, two political figures of the city, who welcome them warmly.[39] As in Tehran, they fervently plead the cause of the believers to foreign consuls and princes residing in the city. Armed with unwavering courage and confidence, they meet several times with Ẓillu's Sulṭán who, as mentioned in a previous chapter, was the governor of the province and was known for being the originator of the persecutions of the Bahá'ís in Isfahan. From his first days in Isfahan, Hippolyte left us a unique testimony reported in a letter written once again to his mother:

Allaho Abha[40]
My dear mother,

I am afraid that the news from Russia and Persia are not made to give you much joy and I would like this letter, albeit very late, to come to reassure you about the happy way in which our journey continues. Besides, the telegram I sent upon my arrival here should have informed you that we left Tehran during the time of the troubles. You may have read in the newspapers that a few mullahs were killed and that the bazaars have been closed.

All this . . . only forces us to be very careful. I am delighted with Isfahan where we also have a house made available to us by a rich Parsi but that we do not stay in, preferring to be here in Julfa,[41] on the other side of the Souk. The air is exquisite, barely warm in the day, and the nights on the roofs are exquisitely cool. The water is abundant; the flowers have disappeared a little but succulent fruits replace them. The friends’ welcome is always enthusiastic! And the monuments! At least those spared by the squandering of Zellus Sultan [Ẓillu’s Sulṭán] erect under the sun their blue domes, their piercing minarets.

The great event of our stay was the visit to the Djummah[42] Mosque and the Iman Djummah (it was the first time that Europeans entered his house) and the welcome of Zellus Sultan, the tyrant of Isfahan! Before yesterday, a word from the Minister of Foreign Affairs told me that he would receive us to meet with him, 2 hours before sunset. So, we left for his garden, certainly the most beautiful in Persia, and we found him in front of a small tent in a neglected rather unceremonious white canvas. Tea, sorbets, fruit, walk in the park, then he apologized for the lack of his welcome and announced that he would send cars to pick us up again the next day, show the ladies around the Enderoun[43] and introduce me to his sons.

Indeed, the next day at 5 o’clock, 3 cars harnessed 4 horses in [illegible], with valets in uniform who came to take us to the great stir of Julfa. His doctor, a Frenchman, Dr Sorel, in full dress as a major accompanied the Persian general and was invited with us; you saw the astonishment of the Isfahans [Isfahanis] when they saw the Baha'is pass by faranguis[44] in this ceremony! At the palace everything was to suit: the uniformed servants were all outside, the guard returned the honours and the great eunuch Aga Bachi, with his key ring in hand, standing waiting for us. First, we went up to the apartments where Zellus Sultan was waiting for us. Then, after tea, he drove the ladies into his harem while I had sorbets with the princes and Dr Sorel, then other cars took us for a drive around his park and brought us to the edge of a pool where we sat with him until dark. Finally, to each, he gave his photograph with his signature. We return with the same ceremony in our same travel cars. The funny thing is that he is a fierce enemy of the believers and when he finds out who we are, he will be furious! (. . .)

Finally, tomorrow we leave at sunset for Tehran. We will arrive the next morning Insh'allah in Kachan[45] where we will rest a little during the day if the believers allow us. Then the next day in Koum[46] and after that, Tehran. I hope to find a lot of letters and good news from all my darlings. Excuse the rambling of this one but we do not have time to write because in the day we are travelling, and in the evening the mosquitoes do not allow us to stay near the lamps.

Lots of love,
Hippolyte[47]

They also visit several holy places: the palace of Manúchihr Khán in Chihil Sutún, where the Báb found refuge in 1846–47 and whose host became a devoted follower; the house of the Imám-Jum'ih, where the Báb stayed for some time; and the house of Mírzá Asadu'lláh Vazír, where the remains of the Báb were kept for a few days before being transported to 'Akká.[48] In Isfahan, the friends intend to extend their journey to the south, then the east, and eventually to India, but the instability in this part of the country [Persia] makes it impossible to travel further.[49] On July 21, they decide to return to Tehran and again pass through Kashan and Qom. They arrive on July 25 and, as was its practice during their first visit to the capital, Hippolyte, sometimes alone, sometimes accompanied by his two fellow travelers, attends multiple gatherings with believers, visits A. L. M. Nicolas, and holds meetings with the local authorities. He notes, in his travelogue, a meeting with the Holy Family—probably members of the Báb's family, some of whom are still residing in Tehran at the time.

Persia, 1906. From left to right: Laura Clifford-Barney (second from left), Hippolyte (third from left), Ṣadru's-Ṣudur (eighth from left).

The meetings in Persia between A. L. M. Nicolas and Hippolyte strengthen the friendship between the two men and allow them to have face to face conversations to clarify, in consultation with the Persian Bahá'ís, the positions of the Bahá'í Faith on the rank and station of the Báb. A few months after Hippolyte's return to France in early 1907, A. L. M. Nicolas writes to him: "Needless to say that the Béhaïs are angels to have a consul of their faith."[50] Then in April, he will share with Hippolyte his happiness at receiving a photo from the Bahá'í group in Paris: "[he] gave me the group photograph where you are behind Miss Sanderson, with your father on the outside right. Which means that you are in my office with your family."[51]

The situation in the country, and in Tehran, is increasingly precarious. Hippolyte therefore makes preparations for the return journey, and they plan to travel through northern Persia. To his brother-in-law, Paul Meyer-May, who, worried about what he was reading in the French press, asks him for news of the situation in Persia, Hippolyte writes, "You probably already know the details of our trip to Isfahan. I arrived back here in the middle of revolution, the newspapers will have taught you the exodus of the Mullas in Qoum, the people who fled to the legation of England (about 7000 rabbits who turned this park into one of the most game in the capital), the fall of Atabek,[52] the disarray of the government. I believe it will not be long before England has finally sorted things out in its own way."[53]

A few days later, he also confides in Yvonne: "Here you probably know the situation from the newspapers: it's a revolution. It has been 15 days since all shops were closed. There are still 7000 refugees at the legation of England, the Mullahs locked up in Qum who have already obtained the fall of Atabek increase their claims: we want a Duma, and no one knows how it will end. In any case . . . believers every day see new prophecies of these events in the writings of the Master and Baha'u'llah."[54]

On August 9, they set out for northern Persia, destination Tabriz. They make several stops in small cities and towns along the way, notably in Qazvin—where they visit the holy places associated with

Ṭáhirih—Zanjan, Aghmazar, Jemalabad, and Turkmenshay, and arrive in Tabriz on August 18 in the late afternoon. Tabriz has a unique place in the history of the Faith: it is the city where the Báb was imprisoned, the city of His "trial," the city where He publicly announced that He was the Qa'im,[55] and the city where He was martyred in 1850. Laura Barney testifies: "You can imagine what our feelings were on the sacred ground, what imagery can bring to a realization the difficulties and trials of the Báb and His blessed people."[56]

When Hippolyte and his companions arrive in Tabriz, the believers formally inform the prince of the city, who invites the three travelers for an interview. The prince is very pleased to see the photograph taken by Hippolyte with the believers of Ashgabat a few weeks earlier.

Their time is once again divided between visits to local authorities, consular personalities (of France and Great Britain), and meetings with believers. As Hippolyte describes in the following letter addressed to his friend A. L. M. Nicolas on August 22, most of these meetings have been made possible through letters of introduction issued by the latter:

> My dearest Nicolas,
>
> If I had to wait until the opportunity presented itself for me to lock myself in a proper office to write you a few lines, the inordinate delay would entitle you to find my apparent negligence unforgivable and to tarnish my reputation with all the contempt my seeming ingratitude would deserve. Therefore, I have chosen to hastily write you a few lines without further ado between the numerous visits of the friends coming to our little house in the Armenian district.
>
> Our trip went very well: 16 hours to Qazvin, 19 hours to Zanjan, and 6 days to arrive here. Your gracious referrals opened many doors for me, particularly those at the French consulate where Mr Rettel cordially welcomed me. His support helped to secure meetings with the Kargozar[57] and the Valiahd.[58] We plan to stay here 4 or 5 more days and then leave [Persia] for sweet

> Russia. (. . .) I should be in Paris at the end of September where I hope I will hear from you and your mother. I hope she did not suffer too much from the discomfort she had the day before I left for Persia. I am still very profoundly grateful, believe me my dearest friend, for all you did for me in the last few months, and I hope that you will give me the chance to express my appreciation by calling upon me without any hesitation, if I can at all be of some service, when I am back in Paris.[59]

Several gatherings are organized by the community to honor the visitors: each time the rooms are too small to accommodate all the believers, who come in droves.[60] They visit several historical sites, including the infamous courtyard where the Báb was executed. Laura Barney recounts this unique moment: "We visited many historical places (to the Baha'is) among them the Court of the Lord of the Age where the martyrdom of the Bab had taken place. It was empty and our party was alone there. Coming to our minds was the picture of the wonderful figure of the Báb, suspended on the wall, being made a target of, and shot to death for his beliefs."[61]

They also spend a day in the adjacent village of Milan, the scene of violent persecution that decimated almost the entire local Bábí community in the 1850s.

The three fellow travelers then leave for Maku. They pass through Marand, Khuy, and Qarah Zia od Din where they meet with the believers and finally arrive at their destination on August 29 late in the evening. After crossing the countryside, desert, cities, and villages, they reach the middle of the remote mountains of the Azerbaijan province. They spend a day on the site of the fortress in which the Báb was imprisoned in extremely dramatic conditions, for nine months, from the summer of 1847 to the spring of 1848. Maku is also the place of confinement at which the Báb was most prolific in the stream of His revelation writing, for it was here that He revealed the Bayán in Persian, and The Seven Proofs, among the best known of His works. Laura Barney said, "This very desolate grim prison place, houses of stone, made us realize what men who lived here tried to do to the Bab in the time of persecution."[62]

It is after this last day of prayer and meditation, at this most important site, that the friends decide to leave Persia. On the way back, Hippolyte stops for several days in Tbilisi, where he tirelessly meets with believers. In Batumi, at the western end of Georgia, he takes a boat to Constantinople, where he also meets with believers. Finally, on September 14, he takes the *Orient Express* alone to return to Switzerland, to Vevey, where he arrives on September 17.

10 / Intensification of Teaching Efforts

Back in Paris, Hippolyte receives a letter from 'Abdu'l-Bahá in which the Master reveals how much this mission has brought Him joy:

> The beloved ones of God have written from all those parts of Persia thou didst visit on thy journey, expressing their joy and delight in meeting thee and conveying gratitude for all that thou hast said and done. They complained, however, of the shortness of thy stay and of thy hasty departure! In those provinces thou wert unable to visit, the friends were greatly saddened for they all wanted to meet thee. The friends in the villages of Ádhirbayján, Saysán, Khalkhál, Mamaqán, Urúmíyyih, Maráqih, and other places eagerly awaited thee and had prepared for thy arrival. Alas, the time was insufficient, through no fault of thine.[1]

Also, in this same Tablet, 'Abdu'l-Bahá invites Hippolyte to refocus on the teaching of the Faith in Paris. He advises him to organize devotional meetings and spiritual gatherings, to strengthen hearts, to share the glad tidings with other souls, and to generate greater enthusiasm among the Bahá'ís. He expresses the hope that, similar to young, tender plants receiving the rain and breezes of the sweet and pure fragrances of God, each of the friends may grow spiritually.[2]

In accordance with 'Abdu'l-Bahá's call, Hippolyte resumes his writing work. In 1906, in collaboration with Mírzá Habíbu'lláh, he publishes a new translation of Bahá'u'lláh's writings titled *Les Préceptes du Béhaïsme*[3] *(The Precepts of Behaism)*. This volume includes the Tablets revealed by Bahá'u'lláh titled Ornaments,[4] Words of Paradise,[5] Splendors,[6] Effulgences,[7] and the Tablet to the Chief.[8]

In the introduction, Hippolyte justifies the publication of this new collection by alluding to the appeal of Eastern spiritual thought and the interest that the previous translations have generated: "The many articles in the press and in the special magazines that have welcomed the publication of the *Book of Certitude* and the *Hidden Words* in Persian, testify to the interest that the public on the one hand, and the scientific criticism on the other, bear in Behaism, this universalist religious movement, which, once again, is coming to us from the East, at a time when the old dogmatic formulas are close to disappearing under the victorious push of reason and science."[9]

He then devotes several pages to clarifying the characteristics of the Faith that seemed to be equated by many orientalists to Hurufism.[10] Finally, Hippolyte explains to readers why he chose to translate these five Tablets:

> The booklet we are publishing today contains, under titles reminiscent of the brilliance and gilding of the Eastern sun, some of the texts, or poems should we say, that we have heard "chanted" most often in the meetings in India. They are by no means "homilies," and yet they seem to us just as accessible to the non-orientalist reader, as they were attractive to the Behais [Bahá'ís] of Rangoon or Bombay. What characterizes these compositions, in fact, is their practical scope. It is the way in which, in a few words, Beha-Ullah [Bahá'u'lláh] exposes the essential principles that must lead societies toward peace. The conditions of a good government, the role of religion in the education of men, the legitimacy of the fortune acquired by labour, the relations of different peoples among themselves, the role of the press—these questions arise in all countries, and always solicit the thoughts of philosophers. Without being able to fix a precise date on these writings, it is easy to see that

> they are all after the arrival [of Bahá'u'lláh] at Saint-Jean d'Acre ['Akká] in 1868.[11]

In these Tablets revealed after the Kitáb-i-Aqdas, Bahá'u'lláh explains, among other things, the nature of the Divine Manifestations. Additionally, He calls on the Bábís to recognize Him as "Him Who Will Be Made Manifest,"[12] extols the importance of good character and moral values such as honesty, wisdom, moderation, and tolerance, and He presents some of the fundamental principles of His Revelation, such as the obligation to provide for the moral education of all children, the adoption of an international language to bring understanding and promote unity among people, the prohibition of asceticism and withdrawal from the world to live in seclusion, the obligation to participate in the progress of society, and the importance for followers of all religions to consort with each other in a spirit of friendship, fellowship, and communion. These Tablets have a fundamental place in the literature of the Bahá'í Faith. 'Abdu'l-Bahá, in His encouragement to the believers, says:

> To thank Him [God] for this, make ye a mighty effort, and choose for yourself a noble goal. Through the power of faith, obey ye the teachings of God, and let all your actions conform to His laws. Read ye The Hidden Words, ponder the inner meanings thereof, and act in accordance therewith. Read, with close attention, the Tablets of Ṭarázát (Ornaments), Kalimát (Words of Paradise), Tajallíyyát (Effulgences), Ishráqát (Splendours), and Bishárát (Glad Tidings), and rise up as ye are bidden in the heavenly teachings. Thus, may each one of you be even as a candle casting its light, the centre of attraction wherever people come together; and from you, as from a bed of flowers, may sweet scents be shed.[13]

In *Revue de l'histoire des religions,* Huart devotes several pages to the review of this work. At first, he shares his excitement: "Finally! We will therefore find out what this doctrine of Behaism, intended to revolutionize the world of religious thought, to lead societies toward peace, to spread brotherhood in the world, is." His criticism is then quite sarcastic or perhaps simply cynical, especially against Bahá'u'lláh's exhortations for His followers to strive to attain to good character and a virtuous life: "All this is very beautiful, and part of universal morality; one need not believe, to practice these virtues, that Béha [Bahá'u'lláh] is a reflection of the splendour of the unattainable Being." Nevertheless, he agrees with this appeal or exhortation "if this belief can bring back to good a multitude of corrupt and dissolute Asians, as it did in Persia, according to well-informed witnesses, all the better!" He concludes his article by thanking "Mr. Dreyfus and his guide in the arcana of Béhaïe phraseology, that is Mirza Habib'ul-lah Chirázi, for having made available to the French public, curious and interesting exhortations."[14]

Also, in 1906, the Bahá'í Faith, thanks to Hippolyte's efforts, enters for the first time[15] in the French encyclopaedia *Le Nouveau Larousse illustré: dictionnaire universel encyclopédique.*[16] In just over five hundred words, Hippolyte presents the origins of the Faith, its fundamental principles, and the three Central Figures of the Bahá'í Faith, who are the Báb, Bahá'u'lláh, and 'Abdu'l-Bahá. Hippolyte thus achieves another victory for the spread of the Faith on French territory: this becomes clear when we appreciate the fact that the Larousse is at the time the standard reference book to which the majority of French people turn when they are looking for information.

The relevance of this masterly synopsis of the Faith is also appreciated by the Bahá'í community outside of France. When the members of the committee for the publication of Bahá'í literature in the United States decide, in 1909, to publish a very large English compilation of the Master's writings, known as the *Tablets of Abdul-Baha Abbas,*[17] they refer the neophyte reader to the definition of the Faith (translated into English) written by Hippolyte Dreyfus for the *Larousse.*

Tireless in his efforts, Hippolyte decides to take full advantage of his historic journey into the cradle of Faith, and he decides to write a ten-page article titled *The Béhaïs and the current movement in Persia.*[18] In this article, which is published the following year in *Revue du monde musulman,*[19] Hippolyte endeavors to reestablish the truth about the role played by the Bahá'ís during the Persian constitutional revolution. To achieve this goal, he draws on his personal experiences in Persia, where he witnessed popular uprisings, and on the fundamental principles of the Faith as taught by Bahá'u'lláh. His demonstration is unequivocal: "That Behaism, as an organization, (if one assumes that the purely moral bond that exists between its followers can be called an organization), that the leaders of the new religion ordered, prepared or directed the July revolution: obviously not."[20]

His argument is simple and straightforward: "[. . .] the principles of their religion, the very instructions they [the Bahá'ís] were constantly receiving from St. John of Acre[21] even in the absence of the most basic wisdom, would have prevented them from doing so."[22]

The article establishes the fundamentally peaceful character of the Bahá'í Faith and recalls the Master's "precise instructions, renewed at every opportunity"[23] regarding obedience to the civil authorities and goodwill towards the shah for whom Bahá'ís are sincere well-wishers purely by virtue of their Faith. It then depicts the social context of Persia from 1905–06 and, in the light of the then recent historical facts, demonstrates the origin of the trouble. However, he does not deny that: "among the 30,000 Béhaïs [Bahá'ís] in the population of Tehran, including all those who are permeated with liberal and progressive ideas, some have [in ignorance of the teachings] joined the protest movements."[24]

Finally, he recognizes that the spread of progressive ideas of the Faith, such as openness to a world-embracing vision, learning foreign languages, and education for all surely played a role in the emancipation of a society plagued by superstitions and corruption: "This fact alone is significant; and for those who know Persia, it indicates, more than anything else, the tremendous change that has taken place in the country since the new ideas [the Revelations of the Báb and Bahá'u'lláh] were introduced there."[25]

The publication of this detailed and factual article is very timely. In the same period of time, in January 1907, when the French press publishes the news of the death of Muẓaffari'd-Dín S͟háh, who just passed away of a heart attack, several journalists wrongly write that his father, Náṣiri'd-Dín Sháh, had been assassinated by some followers of the Bábí Faith. This is the occasion for Hippolyte to reach out to prominent French newspapers and set the historical record straight. Let's mention here one article featured in *Le Temps:*

> We said yesterday that Nasr-eddine [Nasiri'd-Din Shah] was assassinated by a Babí merchant. One of our readers, M. H. Dreyfus, who just came back from Persia, wrote us the following:
>
> > The murderer, a man called Moulla Riza [Mirza Reza Kermani], was a disciple of the famous activist Jemaleddine Afghani [Jamal al-Din al-Afghani], and had no relation with the Babís.
> >
> > The Babís, and especially . . . the Béhaïs [Bahá'ís], their successors, . . . care first and foremost to avoid political turmoil, and only wish to improve the moral and social condition of the country.[26]

Hippolyte's actions to spread the Cause take various forms. In addition to his translation work and lectures, Hippolyte also enjoys sharing his Faith in more intimate, more personal conversations. As Laura describes so well: "Though ready of speech and eloquent, he preferred talking of the Bahá'í Message to individuals and to small groups rather than addressing large audiences."[27]

One of these most memorable encounters is certainly his meeting with Lady Blomfield. In 1907, Sara Louisa, who will later be known after her marriage as Lady Blomfield, hears about the Faith for the first time in London through Bertha Herbert.[28] Knowing that her very interested friend is about to leave for Paris with her daughter, Mrs. Herbert offers to arrange an appointment with two of her friends who would know more: Ethel Rosenberg, the second person of the British Isles to declare as a Bahá'í, and Hippolyte Dreyfus. At this time, Ethel Rosenberg and Hippolyte are very close in their service to the Cause, and these two tireless workers are considered each to be the other's counterpart in their respective countries.[29] Lady Blomfield tells us, "The appointment was made. We were introduced to Ethel Rosenberg and Mr. Hippolyte Dreyfus. These two friends of 'Abbas Effendi[30] told me a lot about the sacred task of the Great One, Bahá'u'lláh."[31]

Robert Weinberg writes of this meeting, "Dreyfus was a brilliant intellectual who tempered his intelligence with gentle, compassionate humour and infinite patience. His grasp of the Bahá'í teachings among Europeans was second to none. Ethel Rosenberg, while perhaps not so personable as Dreyfus, shared with Lady Blomfield a strong foundation in the New Testament, was a stickler of accuracy, devoted to the Movement and more than at home with the British upper classes. Laura Barney also made a profound impact on Lady Blomfield, who would come to love and greatly admire her as an outstanding Bahá'í."[32]

In the following years, Lady Blomfield and Hippolyte develop a great friendship, nourished by their common love for the Master and their joint efforts to spread the Faith.

At the end of the year, on December 15, 1907, Hippolyte gives a new lecture, which he simply calls "Le Béhaïsme [Behaism]," at the headquarters of the Theosophical Society in Paris. As in his previous public talks, he applies himself from the very beginning to clarifying the nature of the Bahá'í Faith and asserts that it is "a true universal religion in the highest sense of the word, and whose aspirations synthesize what is most noble in our minds, a vast movement toward the religious unity of all mankind." His presentation is divided into three distinct parts: he first describes the history of a movement "local in the beginning, which has become universal," he then presents the "religious spirit" and the "social ideas" that animate the Faith, and, finally, he shares with the assembly one of the Writings of Bahá'u'lláh that he has recently translated: The Seven Valleys.[33]

In his presentation of Faith, Hippolyte emphasizes the unity of God and of the different world religions, and he clarifies the concept of God's Manifestations as a way to access divine knowledge: "One can compare God to the sun, the spirit emanating from it to its rays, and the manifestation of God to a mirror, said Béha-Oullah [Bahá'u'lláh]. The more polished the mirror, the sharper its surface and the more heat and light it will distribute so that the most perfect mirrors will seem to reflect all of the heat and light from the sun."[34]

When he discusses the social principles of Faith, he emphasizes that every individual has a duty to practice a trade and to engage in the life of society: "Religion [. . .] must [. . .] be practiced in all acts of life rather than merely in the performance of certain rituals of worship. Every man must have an occupation or profession, and the legitimation of wealth by science[35] is one of the main principles of his teaching."[36]

A large part of his speech is also devoted to the respect that must be accorded to governments: it is an opportunity for Hippolyte to share with the audience his travels to India, Burma, Persia, and the Holy Land. In each location, the Bahá'í communities are organized around the divine principles revealed by Bahá'u'lláh, but always with respect for the legal framework of the country (and obedience to the laws of the land) in which they reside.

His presentation concludes with a reading of his own translation of The Seven Valleys, a mystical work in which Bahá'u'lláh "sets out the steps that must be followed by the seeker who wishes to come to the knowledge of God. He must cross a number of 'valleys' where different trials await him."[37]

The text of his speech was published in early 1908 in the *Annales Théosophiques,* a quarterly collection of lectures and works that were presented in the French theosophical centers by prominent figures of the main spiritualist groups and the Theosophical Society.

11 / Spreading the Faith Across his Native Land

In 1908 Hippolyte continues his efforts to spread the Faith to the French-speaking public with the same dexterity, enthusiasm, and joy as when he was traveling and teaching the Cause abroad. On May 23, as part of the annual series of lectures of the Lyon Section of the Mission laïque francaise[1] (French Secular Mission), he delivers a talk titled "A new religion: Behaism."[2] This conference in the city of Lyon is one of the first direct presentations of the Bahá'í Faith recorded in France outside Paris.[3]

From 15 May, the secretary of the Lyon Section announces in the *Lyon Universitaire*[4] the participation of Hippolyte:

> Soon, Mr. Hippolyte Dreyfus will make known to Lyon circles a new religion, "Behaism." [. . .] In a very remarkable lecture that he once gave at the *École des hautes études sociales,* Mr. Hippolyte Dreyfus, the first person to do so in France, traced the very recent origins of this religious movement, its history, that of its martyrs and analysed its pacifist aspirations. Devoting his free time, and I would say almost all his activity, to know and make known this religion, to translate the manuscripts of its prophets and founders, to travel to Asia to study and penetrate the new doctrine by being there among its devoted adherents, he acquired a very thorough experience of Behaism. [. . .] In the *"Documents of Progress"* of last March, Mr.

> H. Dreyfus summarized in these terms what characterizes the Béhaïe religion: "Recognizing the validity of earlier religions in the principles brought by their founders, Behaism invites men to appeasement and union, for moral and social progress. No more rites, no more clergy, no more dogmas that we impose; the knowledge of God, human brotherhood are our goal, our reason enlightened by the teachings of the prophet is our guide. Thus must fall the hitherto impassable barriers raised by previous religions; thus will disappear the prejudices of race and caste, continuous obstacles to progress." [. . .] Behaism is developing in Asia Minor, India, Russia, Egypt, and in Turkey. It already has many followers in Europe and in America. The prophet's manuscripts are now translated into English and French; the French translation has just been published by the publisher Leroux, by the care of Mr. H. Dreyfus. Behaism therefore presents itself with a certain urgency to contemporary scientific curiosity. [. . .] The "French Secular Mission," which is developing its action in Asia Minor, Persia and the Far East, must carefully study the Behaï movement. The members of the Lyon Committee are therefore invited to the conference of Mr. H. Dreyfus. But this conference is also of interest to all those who, free thinkers or believers, are attached to the study of religious movements.[5]

The assembly is chaired by Mr. Édouard Herriot,[6] mayor of Lyon and president of the Lyon Section of the French Secular Mission. The presence of Mr. Édouard Herriot, an important figure in French politics, gives a lot of weight to Hippolyte's public speech and attracts a large audience.

In his introduction, Hippolyte adapts his speech to his new audience: to the theosophists, he speaks of the unity of religions; to the members of the French Secular Mission, he chooses to speak of liberalism as well as the values of respect and of tolerance shared by the Faith and by his listeners. True to the tenor of his previous public talks, he presents the Bahá'í Faith as a new religion and makes it explicitly clear that the Bahá'í Faith is not a body of superstitious beliefs, or a cult, or a form of tribal worship: "A universal undertaking of human reconciliation in the field of beliefs that hitherto had divided more than united, of a religion without cults, without dogmas, without priestly hierarchy, and which addresses all classes of humanity, resolved to freeing themselves from ancient superstitions."[7]

This address follows the logic he has successfully adhered to in his previous lectures: the presentation of the Persian context and the history of the Faith; the evolution of the Bábí Faith into a universal religion, namely the Bahá'í Faith; and finally, the enunciation of its ethical and social principles, which he describes as being "perfectly adapted to modern civilization."[8] The originality of his argument resides, this time, in the importance he places upon the task of explaining why the term religion has lost its true meaning and the time he spends redefining and reframing the concept of true religion. He insists that the Bahá'í Faith, as a religion, is neither based upon superstition nor propagated by means of manipulation but is perfectly compatible with liberalism and science: "In France, the country of Voltaire and the Revolution, which has had so much trouble breaking free from the shackles of a state religion, and where the struggle against clerical interference in the affairs of politics never seems to end, there has always been more or less an attempt to confuse religion and catechism, and the beliefs of different peoples have often been included in the same distrust or indifference. Only recently has it been realized that faith and science are not so irreconcilable."[9]

In his presentation of the fundamental principles of Faith, he focuses his discourse on the importance of unity between men and moral values, then gradually demonstrates how these principles define true religion:

> The essential idea of Behaism is that, far from proclaiming itself the sole holder of the truth, and considering as heretics the followers of older beliefs, it claims instead to unite them all in a common ideal, at once sociological, ethical and religious. For it asserts that no faith, no religion, no philosophy has a chance of

> subsisting, unless it contains in it a parcel of the great truth that makes all things live. Therefore, in every religion, both in Greek Paganism and in Buddhism or Christianity, there is a common basis that, freed from the complications of dogmas and rites that the corruption of the centuries has ended up adding to them, must serve to unify all men in the love of God and his brethren.[10]

Furthermore, he explains that the purpose of religion as taught by Bahá'u'lláh is to "show men that their happiness and their progress depend on abandoning the superstitions of the past, and putting into practice the doctrines of love and solidarity that constitute the essence of all religions."[11] Finally, it sets forth certain principles of Faith, such as the independent search for truth, the importance of moral education, the equality between men and women, and the characterisation of work performed in a spirit of service as an act of worship. "Religion is not exercised [. . .] in the ceremonies of a cult, but in the continuous activity of our life," he concludes.[12]

In the last part of his speech, Hippolyte endeavors to demonstrate the transformative power of the Bahá'í religion by looking back on his experiences in the Holy Land, in Burma, and in India, where he had the privilege of witnessing how the believers actually put into practice the principles of tolerance, love, and solidarity within communities where people of different nationalities, castes, social backgrounds, and beliefs meet with the greatest mutual respect and collaborate in unity of purpose, thought, and action.

After Hippolyte's presentation ends, Mr. Herriot takes the floor again, thanks him, and notes "that it would often be desirable for the béhaï ideas of fraternity and social solidarity to penetrate a little the peoples who like to call themselves the most civilized."[13]

The next day, the *Lyon Républicain,*[14] a newspaper which had reached a circulation of 100,000 copies before the war, publishes a long article on the lecture given by Hippolyte. The journalist recounts the history of the Faith and its principles and mentions Mr. Herriot's final assessments. The article ends with these words from Hippolyte:

"Behaism presents itself to you as the reconciliation of free thought with the religions."[15] The texts of all the lectures would eventually be published at the end of the year in a collection with a preface written by Édouard Herriot.[16]

In the same year, Hippolyte travels to the Holy Land for the third time. The main objective of this trip is to verify and validate with 'Abdu'l-Bahá his understanding and his translation of *Some Answered Questions,*[17] as he hopes to be able to publish it in French and Persian in the same year. This book contains the Master's answers to questions posed by Laura Barney on religious, philosophical, and scientific topics that she compiled during her many trips to the Holy Land between 1904 and 1906. Initially, these were simple notes taken in Persian during informal discussions, during meals, or when the Master had free time between appointments or activities. Realizing the great value of these conversations, 'Abdu'l-Bahá reviewed and, where necessary, revised the contents, then commissioned Laura, who spoke Persian very well, to translate them into English and make them available to the general public. In her introduction, Laura Barney writes:

> This book presents only certain aspects of the Bahá'í Faith, which is universal in its message and has for each questioner the answer suited to his special development and needs.
>
> In my case the teachings were made simple, to correspond to my rudimentary knowledge, and are therefore in no way complete and exhaustive, as the Table of Contents may suggest—the Table of Contents having been added merely to indicate the subjects thereof. But I believe that what has been so valuable to me may be of use to others, since all men, notwithstanding their differences, are united in their search for reality; and I have therefore asked 'Abdu'l-Bahá's permission to publish these talks.[18]

To this work, which is entirely written by Laura Barney, Hippolyte adds in the French version only one note in the introduction: "We would make it a scruple to add anything to the preceding lines and forming the introduction to the English edition of this work: better than any commentary, they show with what grateful zeal the elements of this book were collected, and what its value is. We hope that our translation will enable all those who cannot go to St. Jean d'Acre ['Akká] to appreciate, in turn, the great truths that emerge from the oral teaching of 'Abdu'l-Bahá."[19]

A key work of the Bahá'í Faith, *Some Answered Questions* is positively received during its release in France. We may quote the following words by Mr. Hartwig Derenbourg:

> The book that I offer you will be the breviary of the Parisian Béhaï community, whose importance is constantly growing and whose followers belong to the most cultured classes of French society. [. . .] It is for current and future adherents that Mr. Dreyfus translated into French the Persian text of these edifying confidences, drawn from the very source by Miss Barney. He will soon, with his special competence, publish it. The goal of the scrupulous reproduction and above all the faithful translation would be achieved, if they succeeded in the conversion of our Company or at least some of its members to Behaism.[20]

Another important event takes place in the year 1908: Hippolyte travels to Stuttgart in the autumn to support the teaching activities of the German friends. During a large public gathering organized by the local community, Hippolyte, Sydney Sprague, and Mr. Eckstein, a German believer, take turns speaking in their respective languages—French, English, and German. "The meeting was well attended by well-educated people. The principle of Bahá'u'lláh concerning the need for a universal language in order to establish world contact was well brought out. All three speakers gave eloquent talks on the Baha'i Faith," the article in *The Bahá'í World* reads.[21] After their talks, the three friends take turns answering questions from the audience gathered in large numbers for the occasion.

12 / Crafting a Masterpiece

The following year, in 1909, Hippolyte publishes one of his most important works, *Essai sur le Béhaïsme: Son histoire, sa portée sociale*[1] (first translated as *Essay on Baha'ism: Its history and social scope,* and eventually published in English under the title *Universal Religion: Baha'ism*). It is the first introduction to the Bahá'í Faith to be published in Europe, and it focuses on the Faith's history, teachings, and vision for society.

In the foreword, Hippolyte humbly presents this essay as a complement to *Some Answered Questions,* which he describes as the first book to have "contributed to placing within the reach of the public the teaching of the new religion [. . .] till now, in fact, limited only to the Orientalists." He then explains to readers the purpose and origins of this new book: "It seemed to us interesting to show what position such an important movement has in history, to examine, independently of any philosophical system, and solely from the point of view of social institutions briefly sketched, what could be its [potential] influence on modern civilization."[2]

The book is divided into two separate parts. As his title suggests, Hippolyte first traces the history of the Faith, and then explains its social scope. The first part is divided into thirteen small chapters of a few pages each: (1) Science and Religion, (2) Necessity of a Renewal of Religion, (3) Baha'ism—its Character, (4) The Great Prophets, (5) Babism, (6) The Exile of the Babis, (7) Bahá'u'lláh, (8) Baghdád, (9) The declaration of "Rizwan," (10) Constantinople, (11) Adrianople, (12) 'Akká, (13) 'Abdu'l-Bahá. The second part has seven chapters: (1) The True Religion, (2) Baha'ism and the State, (3) Universal Peace, (4) Baha'ism and Society, (5) Baha'ism and the Individual, (6) Patriotism, (7) Work.

In his historical presentation of the Faith, Hippolyte emphasizes the importance of adopting a scientific approach in the exploration of religious truth. He recounts the reasons that led to the appearance of the various Prophets and thus demonstrates the need for a renewal of religion throughout the ages. Having outlined the general historical context, he continues his narrative by formulating a new and very strong concept: "Baha'ism [The Bahá'í Faith] is not a new religion; it is Religion renewed." This is the first time that Hippolyte expresses the idea—as revealed by Bahá'u'lláh—that there is only one religion, which is revealed gradually to humanity by different Messengers Who each successively bring a broader, more advanced Revelation. This new Revelation is more adapted to the time in which They appear, and, in this sense, the Faith revealed by Bahá'u'lláh is the most recent form of God's religion, "eternal in the past, eternal in the future."[3]

Finally, he presents the Central Figures of the Faith—the Báb, Bahá'u'lláh, and 'Abdu'l-Bahá—in a much more clearly synthesised and direct way than the approach he had used in his earlier lectures.

In the part of the book devoted to the link between the Bahá'í Faith and society, Hippolyte redefines the term "religion," as he has previously done, then he explores the link between the Faith and the three components of human life: the individual, society, and the state. Finally, he presents the view of the Faith on topics such as patriotism, work, and peace.

In the final pages of his work, Hippolyte draws a vibrant, life-giving portrayal of the Faith and its significance for the evolution of a society whose values seem, to him, to have completely fallen into disuse:

> In this rapid sketch we have merely wished to indicate the universal character of the Bahá'i religion and morality, and

> to point out that it is indeed a practical religion, a way of life applicable to every environment, and the best, we believe, for the development and progress of the individual and of society. The end of the reign of dogma opens up that of human reason. It is no longer in the secrecy of deserted sanctuaries that man goes to explore the Eternal Mystery: every day science throws the illuminating light of its torch farther into the domain of nature, from which even the supernatural is not excluded. [. . .]
>
> But religion always remains the most solid and most necessary basis of all social organisations, and the only possible bond between societies. In order to fulfil its aim, it cannot remain stuck in stereotypes adopted in its earliest form: it must evolve concurrently with the progress of humanity, of which it is, moreover, the efficacious mainspring. If the different religious ceremonies [rites], which are nearly all that now remain of the ancient religions, then they must be allowed to fall into disuse; if no creed can any longer be imposed [by reason of birth, culture, or nationality], it is all the more important that our actions, by their morality, come more and more up to the ideal of beauty about which we all agree. The more and more we understand that in order to really live, we must endeavour with all our might to serve the divine work of the universe![4]

With the publication of this essay, Hippolyte makes available an introductory work to the Faith that, together with *Some Answered Questions* and his three previous translations *(the Book of Certitude, the Hidden Words, Precepts of Baha'ism)* offer the French public a wide panorama of the different aspects of the Cause.

After the release of Hippolyte's essay, Clément Huart publishes an account that is a little over two pages long in the *Journal Asiatique.*[5] His first words allow us to better understand the significance of this work and to grasp the scholarly repute attained by Hippolyte in recent years in the highly specialized and exclusive world of European orientalists: "Mr. H. Dreyfus has done very well to bring together in this small volume, of an attractive reading and a convenient format, the result of his previous studies on the current state of Behaism, this transformation of the Báb's religion which has turned it into a universalist doctrine. No one was better qualified than he to deal with them wisely: through his travels, he was able to realize the current state of the Béhai communities, widespread in Indochina; through his works, he is one of the most erudite that exist, and the warmth he brings in his various pleas indicates a deep and respectable conviction."[6]

Clément Huart analyzes the teachings of the Faith as follows: although they are "not new, these doctrines, nevertheless deserve to be proclaimed loud and firm." Although he sometimes finds "naive optimism" in the ideas presented, he stresses the importance of this work because "the moral doctrines of the new teaching have never been brought together in a clearer whole."[7]

In a second report published a few weeks later in *Revue de l'histoire des religions,* Clément Huart draws a parallel between the ideas of the religiously inclined spiritualists of Europe of the late eighteenth century and the Faith, which he presents as "the converging point where the common aspirations of all religions meet, all of which tend to the knowledge of the truth [. . .]. Also, Behaism does not ask that one abandon the religion in which one was raised; it is content to purify its dogmas, to represent a teaching freed from ancient superstitions, to abandon the dead letter in order to penetrate the living and invigorating spirit."[8]

In this second piece of literary criticism, Clément Huart, even if he is now less dithyrambic in his assessments, notes that some ideas are somewhat "risky"—such as "the comparison between the different prophets" or the fact "that there is nothing for a Béhaï that is outside nature"—and concludes his article, written in a most gracious and beautiful manner, with an invitation to read the book: "The most extraordinary optimism reigns throughout the pages of this endearing little volume; Dr Pangloss[9] would be amazed to see the cultists he still counts, at the dawn of the twentieth century. But if we want to realize what Behaism is now, the nature of its teaching, its dreams and its plans for the future, we must read the new book of Mr. H. Dreyfus; we will not have wasted our time."[10]

A positive review appears at the same time in *La Revue diplomatique.*[11] In the words of Sébastien Voirol, this book, which the reader "will read with benefit," allows us to be "better informed" about the nature of a religious movement whose "liberal and progressive ideas [as] represented [in] their doctrine" are changing Persia, where "the believers are today legion," and the West, where "in all the major cities of Europe and America groupings have been formed for the propagation of ideas of liberalism and religious unification." Voirol briefly presents some principles of the Faith, such as the importance of education, the adoption of an international language, the creation of international courts, the role of the press . . . and concludes, "This essay on a wondrous religious movement, little known to the masses, is undoubtedly the best and clearest we have had in our hands so far, and its author, a distinguished orientalist, reveals himself as a subtle writer and enlightened sociologist."[12]

Essai sur le Béhá'ísme also has a significant impact outside of France. It is translated into English the same year and published in London by Cope and Fenwick under the title *The Universal Religion: Bahaism, Its Rise and Social Import.*[13] Its release is the subject of announcements and reports in the British press, such as the *Westminster Gazette, The Scotsman, The Evening Standard, The Guardian, The Daily Telegraph, and The Glasgow Herald.*[14]

Martha Root would later recount that *Essai sur le Béhá'ísme* was one of the books she took with her on her heroic journeys to spread the Faith in South America, particularly in Brazil, where she handed over copies to several libraries.[15] Laura Barney also tells us that the Guardian liked this work so much that he ordered ninety copies for the archives in the Holy Land.[16] Also, the Guardian would later encourage the friends to work on a new edition that would be released in 1934. Excerpts from *The Purpose of a New World Order* by Shoghi Effendi, as well as several chapters from *The World Economy of Bahá'u'lláh* by Horace Holley, would be added to Hippolyte's original text.[17]

A few weeks after its publication, Leo Tolstoy[18] receives a copy of the French version of the book. This dispatch follows the attempts, since the beginning of the century, of Hippolyte and other believers to present the Faith to the Russian writer. Already in 1904, Hippolyte had sent him his translation of the *Book of Certitude,* but the response from the prominent Russian writer had been far from positive.[19]

Tolstoy's reaction to reading *The Universal Religion* is of a completely different nature: Tolstoy is strongly impressed by the concepts of unity and Bahá'u'lláh's analysis of nationalism,[20] particularly when He says: "The most splendid fruit of the Tree of Knowledge is this exalted Word: Ye are all fruits of one tree and leaves of one branch. Glory is not his who loves his own country, but glory is his who loves his kind."[21] In a letter he writes a few weeks later to his writer-friend Ivan Ivanovič Gobunov-Pasadov,[22] Tolstoy advises him to read Hippolyte's work: "It is absolutely necessary to insert the admirable chapter on pages 79–80."[23]

Most interestingly, a few papers in the United States would mention, in later years, thanks to Hippolyte's efforts, Tolstoy's particular interest in the Faith. For instance, the *Tampa Tribune* would publish in 1911:

> From a letter written nearly a year ago to a friend in Paris, it has been learned that Count Tolstoy probably left the notes or completed manuscript of an important book of which nothing has since been heard. This book, if discovered, will throw a new and great light on his teachings, and it is therefore regarded as all the more important that systematic search for it be made. Interested persons here, including several Americans, intend to bring the matter to the attention of Count Tolstoy's daughter, who was so greatly loved by her father and who was among the last of his family to receive his confidences. With her consent and aid Tolstoy's notes will be gone over, in the hope of finding something on the subject of the letter.
>
> The following letter, written to M. Hippolyte Dreyfus, the well known Orientalist and traveller, of Paris, translated, reads as follows:

> "Sir—I am grateful to you for your book on the life of Abbas Effendi that I just have received, I intend to profit by it in the greatest way possible in order to write a popular book on the Bahaist doctrine." Leo Tolstoy. March 7, 1910.

> Dreyfus is one of the leaders of the Bahai sect in Paris. It is well known that Count Tolstoy was in sympathy with the movement that started in Persia and which has many points in common with his own philosophy, although of a broader scope and greater universality than the teachings of the famous Russian. It was Tolstoy's often expressed interested in the work of Abbas Effendi ['Abdu'l-Bahá], the present head of the movement, that caused Dreyfus to send him the book referred to in the letter.[24]

1909 is a year in which Hippolyte is particularly prolific; the other members of the Parisian community are likewise preoccupied and busy with service to the Faith. In response to a letter from Ahmad Sohrab asking him for information on the development of the Faith in France, Hippolyte writes:

> Until the present day, meetings have been held regularly, both in French and in English, two or three a week, at the houses of Mr. Remey, Mme Sanderson, Mr. Dreyfus, Mme Jack, Mr. Scott, Mirza Habib'ullah Chirazí, Mme d'Astre, Miss Barney etc . . . Outside of these meetings, some of them being strictly private, while others open to inquirers, the Cause was spread by the way of lectures and publications [. . .] Every one in Paris has been working according to his capacity for the spreading of His Cause, disregarding personal desires, and it is due to the constant unity of all, in the service of Baha'u'llah, that we owe the little results we have now obtained. I wish we will be able later on to be of greater service to the Cause.[25]

In the summer of 1909, May Bolles (now May Maxwell after her marriage to William Sutherland Maxwell), who has been living in

Canada since late 1902, comes to France for a few weeks to meet her "spiritual children" and support them in their teaching efforts. May and Hippolyte are in constant communication. When he learns of her impending arrival, he writes to her: "Dear May, just after writing to you yesterday, I received your telegram, and now comes your sweet letter. Yes, you need not fear, May: there is not and never will be any misunderstanding between us; and I love above everything those impetuous words in which the spontaneity of your beautiful soul reveals itself. You must never refrain from telling me all your thoughts, and just as they come to you, for unexpressed thoughts might reach me still, and in a wrong way—I am so dull at times!"[26]

Also in 1909, Hippolyte publishes a study of about ten pages on a subject that is particularly close to his heart, the Mas͟hriqu'l-Ad͟hkár. This short treatise is first published in French under the title *Une institution Béhaïe: le Machreqou'l-Azkar d'Achqabad,*[27] then translated into English in the following weeks.[28] Based on the ordinances of Bahá'u'lláh in the Kitáb-i-Aqdas and his visit to the site in 1905, Hippolyte explains how the Mas͟hriqu'l-Ad͟hkár, "the most important institution of humanity," is both a place of devotion and an institutional center around which social and civil life is organized. Here are some extracts from this treatise:

> We must know that the Mashrequ'l-Azkar [Mashriqu'l-Adhkár] is especially the centre of quite a civil organisation called by Bahā'ou'llāh [Bahá'u'lláh] in the verse we have just quoted, a "town of God," and its nature is commented upon by numerous passages of his works and of those of 'Abdu'l-Baha. We know that 'Abdu'l-Baha is today the leader of the Bahá'i movement, and that, from 'Akká where he has lived for nearly forty years, he keeps himself in contact with the faithful of different parts of the world in order to give them the commentaries and explanations they may desire. Thus it is that in an epistle of which we possess the manuscript, he says, with regard to the monument which interests us: "The Mashrequ'l-Azkar is one of the most important institutions of humanity, and its dependen-

cies are numerous." The Mashrequ'l-Azkar is indeed a place for devotion, but also it should be in connection with a hospital, a dispensary, a house for the reception of travellers, a school for orphans, and a university for the teaching of the higher sciences. Each Mashrequ'l-Azkar should be connected with these five foundations. [. . .]

Bahā'ou'llāh has then observed that the Mashrequ'l-Azkar should not only be a place reserved for prayer, solemn and splendid as it is proper, but also that it should be the centre of quite a social organisation [the central ornament of the entire spiritual complex], responding to the highest needs of all, recalling to each his responsibilities and duties, reproducing in letters of stone this idea often expressed by him in his books, namely, that true prayer is action, and that religion ought to be practised in all acts of life. [. . .]

We have merely wished to inquire into the origin and meaning of the monument of Ashqabad [Isqabat]. It has appeared to us interesting to state how the Bahá'is, by this institution, claim to conciliate [reconcile] the indefeasible aspirations of the soul, which sometimes oblige man to seek in the churches the peaceful seclusion which is necessary to him in order to be able to pray sheltered from the agitation of life, with the measures which should hinder the constitution of the clergy and the formation of rites; and also how Bahā'ou'llāh has endeavoured, so to speak, to bring religion into all social functions, and to make it the visible sign, the principal centre of the effort of humanity in its work of brotherhood and of progress.[29]

13 / Inspiring the Believers in North America

In early 1910, Hippolyte decides to travel to the United States to meet and encourage the communities that are flourishing in North America. At this time, the visits of the believers such as Hippolyte are vital for engendering the growth and uplifting the vision of the believers residing in various local communities; these visits allow the traveling visitors to share the latest news from the Holy Land when speaking at gatherings of believers who do not have the opportunity to travel, and local believers can rejoice in receiving news of the progress of the Bahá'í Cause, can deepen their knowledge and understanding of the Teachings, and thus can begin to envision the international reach of the Faith.

Before his departure, the friends of Paris receive a letter from 'Abdu'l-Bahá in response to a telegram previously sent by Hippolyte. The Master wishes them happy holidays—probably Naw-Rúz (New Year's Day)—and then addresses a few lines to Hippolyte: "I am greatly pleased with thine approach, thine upright conduct and the determination and constancy thou hast shown, my dear friend. I hope that thou wilt be confirmed and assisted in thine endeavours, at all times and under all conditions."[1]

When the friends of the United States learn of Hippolyte's imminent arrival on the American continent, many local communities reach out to invite him to their respective cities. In June, the Los Angeles Assembly writes to him:

Our dear Bahai Brother:

We have just learned that you are to give an address for the Bahai Assembly of Baltimore at the home of Mrs. Struven some time during July or August.

The Los Angeles Bahai Assembly hereby most cordially invites you to visit California at your convenience and deliver one or more public addresses and meet the members of the Los Angeles Assembly which includes the believers at Pasadena, Tropico, Hollywood and Long Beach.

The homes of the believers will be open for your entertainment. Your presence will be especially appreciated and give great joy to those whom you have known and met in Paris.

Yours in the service of El Baha,

Los Angeles Bahai Assembly[2]

The same week, Hippolyte receives a letter from the Seattle Assembly:

My dear Mr. Dreyfus and Bahai Brother,

I am so glad to hear of your presence in America and hope you will find the Bahais here are well advanced in the knowledge and practice of Faith as you expected.

The Bahai Assembly of Seattle extend you an invitation to come to us, extend your trip further west and see how wide spread the teachings really are. It is quite a journey to these parts but the trip will quite repay you for the effort, to see the wild uncultivated western country and the wonderful strides of these cities where but 50 or 60 years ago there stood almost impenetrable forests.

I sincerely hope you may consider the trip toward the Pacific Coast to your advantage. We know your coming will be of untold advantage and great spiritual uplift to all the Assemblies in this state, Spokane, and Seattle; Portland in Oregon; Oakland, Pasadena and Los Angeles in California, and many smaller towns and hamlets.

Yours in service to the Cause of God,
Ida A. Finch[3]

We wish to also mention the beautiful letter sent by Corinne True on behalf of the Chicago community:

My dear Brother in El Baha, Mr. H. Dreyfus,

Word has reached us that you are visiting America. The Bahai Assembly of Chicago, at their morning service in Corinthians Hall today instructed this maid servant to extend to you the warmest Abha greeting and to beg you to visit us at your earliest convenience. I write this on behalf of the entire Assembly.

I presume our good brother Mr. Remey will accompany you West and I wish to extend to you both the hospitality of our home during your visit to Chicago. My daughter Arna remembers your great kindness to us while in Paris and were she here, would join me in sending greetings.

Please let me know what your plans are and when we may expect you to visit the Temple City.

Greetings of Abha to you and also the other Brothers and Sisters

In His Holy Name,
Your Bahai Sister, Corinne True.[4]

Hippolyte sets out at the end of May 1910 and first makes a detour through London, where he meets the fifty Bahá'ís of the city. He gives "an inspiring talk" at one of the weekly meetings held every Friday night by believers at 10 Chemiston Gardens, Kensington.[5]

He then embarks on a journey to New York, where he arrives in early June. He gives "beautiful talks" at various gatherings organized by the Spiritual Assembly. He is also the guest of honor at a meeting held at the home of his friend, Mr. Hooper Harris.[6]

A few days later, he arrives in Baltimore. He speaks at one of the meetings organized by the Spiritual Assembly as part of a series of weekly lectures that take place every Sunday at Mrs. Rose Struven's house. These events are planned to span the three months of summer. Hippolyte is among the speakers alongside prominent believers such as Mrs. Pauline Hannen, Mirza Ahmad Sohrab, Mr. Hooper Harris, Mr. Joseph H. Hannen, Ms. Louisa Getsinger, Dr. Amínu'lláh Faríd, Mr. Howard MacNutt, and Mr. Charles Mason Remey.[7]

From Baltimore, he leaves for Washington, where he gives "most helpful" presentations on June 15 and 17. On June 16, a reception is held in honor of Hippolyte, Mason Remey, and Farajullah Khan, who were also passing through the nation's capital. Remey opens the evening with a few introductory words, then leaves the floor to Hippolyte, who speaks about the evolving fortunes of the Faith in the world and shares his experiences of travel through Asia. This very casual meeting is extremely inspiring, and the three friends respond "in a very interesting way" to the questions asked by the guests, who are curious to know more about the progress of the Faith in Europe, Asia, and America. Joseph Hannen writes, "We found the expositions of this brother most helpful, and his presence was inspiring."[8]

Hippolyte then spent three days in Chicago. On Saturday, he speaks at a specially organized meeting at Mrs. Eva Webster Russell's house. On Sunday morning, during the weekly community meeting, he gives an "excellent" presentation on the teachings of the Kitáb-i-Aqdas, the Most Holy Book. On Monday, he participates in the consultations of the members of the "Consultative Spiritual Assembly," and in the evening he resumes his arduous schedule of talks. This time, he speaks to an audience made up of people from very diverse backgrounds who are gathered at Mrs. Gertrude Buikema's house. From the testimony of the participants, Hippolyte's journey to Chicago "has acted as a stimulus to all departments of Bahai activity in this city."[9]

Hippolyte also takes advantage of his stay in Chicago to visit, in the northern suburbs of the city, the site chosen for the future Mashriqu'l-Adhkár of the American continent. Hippolyte, accompanied by his friend Zia Baghdadi, is strongly impressed by the beauty of the place where the shadows of nature and the rays of the sun are reflected on the waters of Lake Michigan. Zia Baghdadi remembers, "I brought him to this sacred place (. . .) on the grounds of the Baha'i Temple. The weather was warm and lake Michigan seemed so delightful that in a few minutes he dived in, and, oh, how he loved the water! Indeed he loved America, and the Americans . . ."[10]

Around this time, under the aegis of the American community, the first major periodical entirely dedicated to the Faith appears: *Star of the West.*[11] During his stay in the United States, Hippolyte, who received it and read with great interest every publication, wrote a letter to the publishers in response to an article published on the Mashriqu'l-Adhkár:

> To the Editors of the BAHAI NEWS.
>
> Dear Friends: I trust I will be allowed to use the publicity of the BAHAI NEWS for sending to all the Assemblies of America, which I am not able to visit in this too short a trip, the love and greetings from our friends in Paris; and also for conveying to all a little suggestion, which reading the 4th issue of your publication, giving the account of the Convention in Chicago, and only just received from Paris, has led me to deem advisable.
>
> I really think that we should make a point never to use the name "Temple" with regard to the Mashrigu'l Azkar [Mashriqu'l-Adhkár]. There are words in Persian and Arabic to say "temple," but Mashrigu'l Azkar has quite another meaning, much broader and much more beautiful. It means, as you know, "the Dawning place of the Mentions of God," and this plural in itself is quite significant, inasmuch as it reminds us that BAHA'U'LLAH has taught that we should not be satisfied by praying to God only in a place prepared for our meditations, but that we should above all pray to Him by our actions, in serving our brothers, taking care of the weak ones, giving hospitality and spreading instruction and knowledge. And the House of prayer, which is to be the centre of the Mashrigu'l Azkar, gets its true significance, in this new dispensation, from its connec-

tion to the different social institutions which 'Abdu'l Bahá[12] has often indicated to us, and which symbolize the whole activity of our future communities.

By calling it a Temple, not only, it seems to me, are we belittling one of the greatest Foundations of this Cause, but I fear that we are driving away from us many sincere souls who, in our days, have left churches, mosques, and temples, in search of a broader ideal.

Besides, don't you think that the word Mashrigu'l Azkar is harmonious enough to acquire citizenship in our occidental languages with Quran, algebra, sultan, jasmine and many other words which also come directly from the East? Let us be the pioneers of this linguistic reform, which will enable us to implant new ideas more easily into the world.

Yours truly in the Cause of Al Abha,

H. DREYFUS.[13]

This letter is published in the next issue of *Star of the West.* When one ponders his earnest words of reasoning, one begins to discover the qualities of Hippolyte as a truly devoted and humble servant of Bahá'u'lláh who is endeavoring to clarify a very important concept of worship, according to which prayer and devotional worship are directly linked with service to humanity; and we discern the clarity of his conceptual understanding of the Faith under his beloved Master's tutelage. We admire his intellectual and scholarly capacity for explicating on the unique features of the Bahá'í dawning place for the remembrance of God.

From Chicago, he goes to Montreal for a few days, the last stop of his journey.

Upon his return to France, Hippolyte receives a letter from 'Abdu'l-Bahá. The Master congratulates him on his teaching work in the United States: "[Thy missive from America] brought great spiritual joy. Praise thou God that thou hast been able to serve the Kingdom of the Lord in that region, disseminating the divine fragrances and raising the Call in His Name. The grace of God assisted thee, enabling thee to render this service."[14]

In the following days, Hippolyte works on a new project with Laura Barney—the translation into French of a play about the Faith that Laura had just published in London under the title *God's Heroes.* This piece traces different passages from the life of Ṭáhirih, the outstanding heroine of the Bábí Dispensation. These events took place between 1848 and 1852, and the play depicts the heroic actions of the first Bábí believers, as well as the courage they showed in the face of the violent persecutions of which they were the victims. Laura, an artist, actress, and sculptor by training, had long felt an ardent desire to use the arts to promote the Faith, and it seems she found inspiration in a similar piece, written by Isabella Grinevskaya, which was a great success in Russia:[15] *The Báb: a dramatic Poem from the History of Persia.*[16] In the preface to the work, Laura explains her choice to use the arts, "a mighty instrument for spreading ideas broadcast (. . .) to awaken [the] interest in this great movement, the universal religion of Baha'ism, which is today bringing peace and hope to an expectant humanity."[17]

It is also around this time that Hippolyte meets Florence George, an Englishwoman living in Paris. Accompanied by his friend Edith Sanderson, he has several intense discussions with this English lady, who is very receptive to the ideas of the Faith. She then enrolls in a Bahá'í class given by the believers in Paris, and as a result of this experience, she eventually embraces the Bahá'í Cause. In the years that followed, Florence George will be respectfully referred to as "Mother George," not least because of her exceptional efforts, along with John Esslemont, in the development of the Faith in England and the formation of the first Bahá'í group in Bournemouth in 1915.[18]

At this stage of Hippolyte's life, we discern an important role played by him in service to the Cause of Bahá'u'lláh. In France and during his travels abroad, Hippolyte is now entrusted with a very special mission by 'Abdu'l-Bahá, which is that he is, in a very real sense, the diplomatic representative of the Master. Now he is entrusted with the responsibility of meeting officials of the Persian government—most of the time when they are traveling to Paris—in order to plead the interests of the Cause and to clarify the positions of the Faith on certain important subjects. At the end of 1910, Hippolyte receives a letter from the Master in which He congratulates him on his actions and, as the Master often does in His letters, invites Hippolyte to show the greatest tenderness and kindness to the Persians he meets in Paris. The following letter is also very interesting because it shows the position of the Bahá'í community in the face of the internal revolutions that are convulsing Persia:

> Act towards Jalálu'd-Dawlih[19] and other refugees from Persia with utmost consideration and kindness. Thou hast written that Mumtázu'd-Dawlih, during his visit to the house of the Minister of the Court, Mumtázu's-Salṭanih, asked why the Bahá'ís did not come forth in support of the constitutionalists. Thou didst give an excellent response. Well done! The aim of the Bahá'ís is to raise aloft the banner of the world's Great Peace, to eradicate the foundations of war and conflict throughout all regions, to gather together all the divers nations and peoples beneath the single-hued Tabernacle of God, and to eliminate prejudice—whether racial, national, religious, sectarian, or political—from the face of the earth, so that all countries may become as one country, all races as one race, and all nations as one nation. Thus may the world of creation attain unto peace and tranquility. With such lofty goals, how can they sully themselves with these conflicts and disputes which are the playthings of the people of politics? His highness Mumtázu'd-Dawlih is well aware that such conflicts spring from the base motives of a handful of individuals on both sides. Their intentions are not at all pure. How then can the Bahá'ís be involved?[20]

The end of the year 1910 is approaching. Hippolyte's father is getting more and more feeble, and life seems to be leaving him little by little. At the beginning of 1911, on January 4, his father's spirit leaves this mortal realm and takes flight to the Abhá Kingdom at the age of seventy-one. The Dreyfus family publishes an obituary, which they sign off with the Báb's famous quote "All that is in heaven, and on earth, and in between, is God's."[21] The passing of Hippolyte's father is announced in the January 1911 volume of *Star of the West;* an obituary in the *Bahá'í News* (Chicago) states that "the family are all Bahais and this has enabled them to accept the separation with courage."[22]

Following the death of his father, Hippolyte receives several letters from friends of the community, including one from Thornton Chase, the first American believer. This testimony in these extracts shows that the bonds between the believers, even though they may not have known each other very well, were so strong that they reached across borders:

> Dear Mr. Dreyfus,
>
> Your remembrance of this stranger-friend in the time of your bereavement touches my heart. It beats with love for you and sympathy with you and your good mother in the grievance of separation which must naturally be your trial at this time. Accept my sincere regards and condolences. [. . .]
>
> Let us not grieve, but consider the joy of love and await patiently the time when we shall pass from the earth of dust and separation, into the heaven of Unity, Love and Permanence.
>
> Greetings and Joy to you in His Name, who is Love Eternal.[23]

Hippolyte, extremely touched by all these gestures on the part of the community, sends the following note, a few weeks later, to his friends through *Star of the West:* "Dear friend, the last issue of Bahai News just reached me and I want to thank you most sincerely for the kind words you have written in the Persian section on behalf of my beloved father. The sympathy of the friends has been in this great bereavement a great consolation, and it has made real even more than before the Great Unity of Al Abha."[24]

14 / Marital Union for Joint Service to the Cause

During the years from 1901 until 1911, Hippolyte has developed a strong friendship with Laura Barney, whom he has now known for about ten years. It is a friendship characterized by deep esteem, care, and respect for her.

Laura Barney (1879–1974) is an early American believer. She is the daughter of Albert Barney, a wealthy railroad car builder, and Alice Pike Barney, a famous American artist. Around 1900, while studying art in Paris, Laura met May Bolles, who introduced her to the Faith. After joining the Cause, she made numerous visits to the Holy Land and rendered important services to the Holy Family. For example, she helped to purchase and renovate a home[1] to accommodate 'Abdu'l-Bahá and His household, and she recruited a British tutor who was placed in charge of the education of Bahá'í children residing in Haifa, including Shoghi Effendi. Laura thus became an intimate friend of the Master's family. She remembers, "The first meeting with Hippolyte Dreyfus that I can recall was in 1900 in Paris on the outside of May Bolles' apartment[2] near the École des Beaux Arts. He was leaving, I was arriving to hear more of the Bábí epilogue. Although I was away from France almost constantly from 1901 to 1906, I knew that he had become an outstanding Bahá'í and that his father and mother, his sister and brother-in-law, had all joined the Cause."[3]

Between 1901 and 1906, although Laura is mostly outside France, the two friends get to know each other. They meet several times at the believers' meetings in Paris, they spend time together in Port Said when Hippolyte goes and returns from his trip to India[4] and, of course, they stay together for several weeks on their trip through Persia. However, it is especially when they work together on the translation of *Some Answered Questions,* as Laura would later recount, that they discover their mutual joy at collaborating on the work,[5] their common love for the Faith, and their attachment to each other.[6]

Laura is deeply drawn and attracted by the kindness, the gentle tender loving care, and the great patience that Hippolyte shows toward her. Above all, Hippolyte makes Laura laugh a lot and her intellectual brilliance is always tinged with the right amount of humor.[7] Marianne Girard, a relative of the family, remembers, "I think back to before your wedding and see Hippolyte so deeply in love with the beautiful Laura. What a beautiful couple you made. And you the beautiful and distant Laura you had been conquered by this man so charming, so intelligent and so worthy of your love."[8]

In 1911, Hippolyte announces in a letter to 'Abdu'l-Bahá their desire to marry and asks for His consent. The Master responds very quickly, confides to them how much this news fills Him with joy, and brings all His blessing to this marriage between "two radiant stars of the Kingdom of God, united in love, unity and friendship."[9]

Meanwhile, on April 15, 1911, Alice Pike Barney, Laura's mother, is making the headlines. Widowed since the death of her husband Albert Barney in 1902, she chooses to marry a young American artist, Christian Hemmick,[10] to whom she is thirty years his senior. The ceremony takes place at the town hall of the 8th arrondissement of Paris in the presence of a few guests, among whom we find Hippolyte, attending as one of Christian's wedding witnesses, and Laura.[11]

The wedding ceremony between Hippolyte and Laura takes place a few days later, on April 25, 1911, at the town hall of the 16th arrondissement in the presence of their respective families and certain members of the community, such as Mrs. Jackson and Miss Faith Chevalier. As witnesses, Hippolyte chooses his mother, Miss

Lea Dreyfus-Cardozo; and one of his uncles, Mr Albert Rodrigues-Pimentel; Laura chooses Hippolyte's sister, Miss Yvonne Meyer-May; and her sister, Natalie Clifford-Barney.

The couple then moves to 15 rue Greuze, still in the 16th arrondissement, and chooses to combine their surname: they become Hippolyte and Laura Dreyfus-Barney. The event is announced in the American press under the headline "Laura Barney is bride of Bahaist high priest"[12] and states that "as Mr. Dreyfus is the leader of the Bahaist Church, the ceremony will be according to the rites of the Persian religion."[13] For their honeymoon, the newlyweds travel to *Daro's-Salam,* the Dreyfus' second home, and to Montreux in Switzerland, then spend some time in Italy to visit various cities, among them Florence, Perugia, and Genoa.

Hippolyte and Laura, Mont Pèlerin, 1911

Their marriage is announced in the Persian section of *Star of the West* under the title "Marriage of Mr. Dreyfus and Miss Barney":

> On this day, the good news of the wedding of Mr. Dreyfus and 'Amatu'l-Bahá Miss Laura Clifford Barney in Paris delighted the Star of the West team and brought joy to the hearts of the

Hippolyte and Laura, Mont Pèlerin, 1911

Bahá'ís. In truth the union of these two firm friends in the Covenant is significant in every respect. Mr. Dreyfus, one of the lawyers and scholars of France, belongs to a noble family. In recent years, he has tirelessly rendered important services to the Faith, spread the religion of God to lands near and far, written articles and books on the Cause of God that have been published in various newspapers and magazines. It seems that he attained to the presence of 'Abdu'l-Bahá two or three times. To spread the divine teachings, he made a trip to India. Two or three years ago,[14] he made an important trip to Persia with Miss Barney and Mrs. Lacheney. They visited friends there. After their return, he came to the United States where he gave eloquent lectures at Bahá'í meetings and spoke about the influence and steadfastness of the followers of the Faith in the eastern countries, which was very pleasant. 'Amatu'l-Bahá Miss Barney, is a firm American Bahá'í, appreciated and loved in the Bahá'í

> world in both the East and the West. Her services and sacrifices in the Cause of God are innumerable. The Bahá'í community in Washington is where it is today, thanks to her efforts and those of a few other esteemed friends. For more than a year she was in the presence of the Master at Acre, where she learned the Persian language and the teachings of the Faith; the book Some Answered Questions is the result of this stay. 'Abdu'l-Bahá, in many of his writings, encouraged friends to study this book, which is now studied in numerous meetings in the United States. Her journey to Persia aroused enthusiasm and attraction for the Cause of God. Recently, she published a book on the heroes of God and the life of Tahirih which prompted European and American intellectuals to research the Cause. Thus, the members of the Star of the West team, present their congratulations to Mr. and Mrs. Dreyfus, hoping that they would be able to render many services to the Cause of God, which is the instrument of the unity of the human race and of universal peace. If it pleases God, this union and sincere relationship will illuminate the world and bring joy to the hearts of the Bahá'ís of the East and the West.[15]

A few days after their wedding, Hippolyte receives a new letter from 'Abdu'l-Bahá in which He reaffirms His joy and confides His hope that this union would become the source of new ardor and ever more enthusiasm in their service to the Cause so that Paris and France would awaken and become a center of spiritual light.[16] Of their marriage, the Master also says, "Mr. Dreyfus and Mme Barney are actually busy serving. I ask for them the confirmations of the Abhá Kingdom, so that with each breath they may achieve new successes in their service: by establishing assemblies of holiness in Paris, by making souls spiritual and by stimulating hearts."[17]

Hippolyte's life will from now on be totally intertwined with Laura's, and vice versa: the following years transform the couple into a team unfailingly dedicated to the service of the Cause and united in their deep love for the Master.

Hippolyte and Laura, London

Their union will be one of the finest examples of the Bahá'í concept of marriage as taught by 'Abdu'l-Bahá: a partnership, based on mutual support, both intellectual and spiritual, in the service of the Cause:

> Among the people of Bahá, [. . .] marriage must be a union of the body and of the spirit as well, for here both husband and wife are aglow with the same wine, both are enamoured of the same matchless Face, both live and move through the same spirit, both are illuminated by the same glory. This connection between them is a spiritual one, hence it is a bond that will abide forever. [. . .]

When, therefore, the people of Bahá undertake to marry, the union must be a true relationship, a spiritual coming together as well as a physical one, so that throughout every phase of life, and in all the worlds of God, their union will endure; for this real oneness is a gleaming out of the love of God.[18]

Hippolyte and Laura, France, 1912

15 / Welcoming 'Abdu'l-Bahá to Europe

From 1908, following the uprising of the Young Turks[1] movement against the autocratic rule of the Ottoman monarch, Sultan 'Abdu'l-Ḥamíd II,[2] 'Abdu'l-Bahá, like many other political prisoners, gradually regains His freedom. In 1910, the Master finally obtains permission to travel, and He expresses a desire to travel to the West. The believers around the world look forward to the coming of the Master in their respective countries, particularly those of Europe and the United States.

In September 1910, after having been severely weakened by a life of severe deprivation, arduous exile, and prolonged imprisonment, 'Abdu'l-Bahá first departs for Egypt, where He hopes to be able to recover physically. However, He spends most of his time deepening and enriching the faith of the believers in the local community, welcoming Western pilgrims on their way to 'Akká, and meeting local personalities. As a result of this rigorous schedule, the Master's moments of rest are both rare and sporadic.

During the winter of 1910, Hippolyte receives a letter from 'Abdu'l-Bahá in which He reassures him of His state of health and calls him to continue his teaching activities in Paris so that when the Master comes to France, He can "travel in joy and gladness."[3] The news of the coming of the Master to Europe intensifies, and the communications between Hippolyte and the entourage[4] of 'Abdu'l-Bahá begin to multiply.

In a letter addressed to his friend Albert Windust at the end of 1910, Hippolyte confides all the excitement surrounding the eventual and long-awaited arrival of 'Abdu'l-Bahá in Paris: "My dear brother, Alas! no, 'Abdu'l Bahá is not in Paris! He is in Alexandria until he leaves for Cairo. The truth is that on the 22 September, I received a telegram from Port Said telling me that he had left for Marseilles. I was in Munich and left at once to go and receive him, but on my way received another cable from him saying that (. . .) he had postponed his trip, and stopped in Alexandria. Let us hope that after the winter is over, if his health is stronger, we may see him here! But God knows better!"[5]

A few weeks later, a letter from the Master explains to Hippolyte the reasons for His inability to make the journey. The Master relates that He intended to leave Port Said, but that when He boarded the boat, He felt so unwell that He was forced to disembark. Then the Master reassures him by telling him that He would come, God willing, after spring.[6]

In July 1911, one of the first large-scale anti-racism events in the world is held in London as the First Universal Races Congress. Between July 26 and 29, speakers from around the world are invited to discuss the issue of race relations and ways of improving them, and over fifty countries and twenty governments respond positively to this initiative by sending representatives. 'Abdu'l-Bahá is invited to speak, but unfortunately, He is still recuperating in Egypt. He therefore decided to appoint a small number of believers, including Hippolyte, to represent the Faith and read a letter on His behalf.[7]

This congress is also an opportunity for the Bahá'í community in London to organize a large number of activities both at the venue of the congress and at other locations. A large public meeting is arranged at Caxton Hall in Westminster, during which Hippolyte, Wellesley Tudor-Pole, Louise Waite, Jeanne Stannard, and other believers give talks to present the Cause, its links with other religions, and its principles of unity. This event is reported in the press, which describes the contributions of the speakers as "fascinating."[8]

The long-awaited coming of the Master to France is approaching. On August 11, 1911, 'Abdu'l-Bahá boards the French liner *Orénoque* at Alexandria and reaches Marseille five days later. Hippolyte is on the dock to receive Him. From this date, Hippolyte will have the immense joy and the immeasurable privilege of being able to accompany and serve the Master daily for several weeks. Among his many responsibilities, he will organise the Master's daily schedule, plan His trips, receive an unceasing flow of His visitors, and serve as the main interpreter at His public speeches.

In Marseille, where the Master and His friends decide to rest for a few days, Hippolyte accompanies 'Abdu'l-Bahá on His daily walks through the city, which gives them the opportunity to consult on the Master's stay in Europe. 'Abdu'l-Bahá and His Persian companions, as well as Hippolyte, eventually take the train on August 20 to Geneva, where they arrive at around midnight. The next day, they take a boat, cross Lake Geneva, land in Thonon-les-Bains, and reach the *Grand Hôtel du Parc,* where Laura is waiting for them.

During this stay of a little over a week on the shores of Lake Geneva, Hippolyte is in constant communication with the friends in order to best arrange their meetings with the Master. Thus, many believers—such as Juliet Thompson, Horace Holley, Annie Boylan, Percy Woodcock, Tamaddunu'l-Mulk, Edith Sanderson, Lillian Frances Kappes, Elizabeth Stewart, the Ahmadov brothers—will have the sacred opportunity of entering the presence of 'Abdu'l-Bahá. Horace Holley, Hippolyte's close friend, left us the following testimony of his meeting with the Master at Thonon-les-Bains:

> ABDUL BAHA ['Abdu'l-Bahá] at Thonon, on Lake Leman! This unexpected news, telegraphed through the courtesy of Mr. Dreyfus, brought my wife and me to the determination we had long agreed upon of making a pilgrimage to the Master at our earliest opportunity. With only a few days intervening before his journey to London, we set out immediately from our home in Siena, and arrived at Thonon in the afternoon of 29 August.

> The Hotel du Parc lies in the midst of sweeping lawns. Groups of people were walking quietly about under the trees or seated at small tables in the open air. An orchestra played from a near-by pavilion. My wife caught sight of Mr. Dreyfus conversing with others, and pressed my arm. I looked up quickly. Mr. Dreyfus had recognized us at the same time, and as the party rose I saw among them a stately old man, robed in a cream-coloured gown, his white hair and beard shining in the sun. He displayed a beauty of stature, an inevitable harmony of attitude and dress I had never seen nor thought of in men. Without having ever visualized the Master, I knew that this was he. My whole body went into shock. My heart leaped, my knees weakened, the thrill of an acute, receptive feeling flowed from head to foot.[9]

Despite the very many interviews and the long hours given to His colossal correspondence, 'Abdu'l-Bahá takes the time to engage in verbal exchange with Hippolyte and Laura; He loves both of them so much, and He affectionately regards them as His confidants. They engage in pleasant discussions, and Laura notes that "The Master liked talking with this refined Frenchman skilled in conversation. (. . .) There was no restraint between them. Hippolyte Dreyfus never put himself forward, but he was always ready to carry out the most difficult tasks that might be asked of him."[10]

An anecdote is also reported to us by Juliet Thompson about the unique relationship of trust and devotion, and the sense of loving complicity that existed between Hippolyte and his adored Master. One afternoon, when Hippolyte is laughing in delight while listening to a story of a dream Juliet is recounting, the Master, amused, tells Hippolyte that the funniest thing about this story is that he (Hippolyte) does not believe in dreams. Then, more seriously, he explains to them that there are three kinds of dreams: "There are three kinds of dreams: dreams that come from some bodily disorder, symbolic dreams, and those in which future events are clearly foretold. When the soul is in a state of perfect purity it is able, He said, to receive a direct revelation from God. Otherwise, it sees in symbols."[11]

When time permits, which, as it turns out, is rarely, Hippolyte takes 'Abdu'l-Bahá on a ride in his car through the lush landscapes of the Haute-Savoie and the pristine beauty of the Alps, and they explore the surrounding nature that the Master loves so much.[12] One afternoon, Hippolyte leads the Master, Laura, and Juliet to the site of the g*orges du Pont-du-Diable* (Devil's Bridge gorges). Let Juliet Thompson recount for us the details of their excursion:

> "Did you ever think, Juliet," said the Master, laughing, as we got into the car with Him, "that you and Laura would be riding in a car with Me in Europe?"
>
> We drove to a country inn where a little later, after a walk, we were to have our tea. As the Master stepped down from the car, about fifteen peasant children with bunches of violets to sell closed in on Him, formed a half circle around Him, holding up the little purple bunches, raising their eyes to His Face with grave astonishment. They pressed so close that they hid Him below the waist, and the blessing in the look He bent on them I shall never forget. Of course He bought all the violets, drawing from His pocket handfuls of francs. But when He had given to each child bountifully, they held out their hands for more!
>
> "Don't let them impose!" cried Laura.
>
> "Tell them," said the Master very gently, "that they have taken." [they have already received their portion]
>
> He turned and walked into the forest, followed by Laura, Hippolyte, and myself. Hippolyte had told Him of "the Devil's Bridge" deeper down in the forest, a place celebrated for its beauty, and the Master wanted to see it. His excitement over beauty is wonderful to see and perfectly heart-rending when you think of His long, long life in prison. He—our Lord—led us to the Devil's Bridge! I can see Him now, just ahead of us, the white robe, the black 'abá, the white turban, the beautiful sway of His walk among the trees.
>
> "What is it," I said to Laura, "that makes that stride of the Master's so unique? Its absolute freedom?" Laura found she

> couldn't walk as far as the Devil's Bridge, so I waited in the woods with her, both of us sat on a rock, while Hippolyte followed our Lord.[13]

The afternoon draws on; 'Abdu'l-Bahá remains captivated and continues to marvel at the natural beauty of the surrounding scenery. By a remarkable chance, they discover a waterfall which is as beautiful as it is spectacular. The Master sits on a rock, fascinated by the torrent of light, and enters into deep contemplation. On the way back, they pass a huge drawing painted on a stone wall. The Master points to what turns out to be an advertisement of a chocolate brand and asks Hippolyte what it says. Responding to Hippolyte's explanation, He bursts into laughter and asks, "Is chocolate so important in Thonon?"[14]

On August 23, an unexpected and historic meeting takes place at the hotel where the friends stay. The infamous Prince Ẓillu's-Sulṭán, responsible for the horrible persecutions against the Bahá'ís in Persia and who is now in exile with some members of his family in Geneva, happens to be on the terrace of the *Grand Hôtel du Parc!* Juliet Thompson writes:

> The day before I arrived, Zillu's-Sultán came over to Thonon for a few hours, and straight to the Hotel du Parc. Hippolyte Dreyfus, when he was in Persia, had met this Prince, had visited him in his tent while he—the prince—was on a hunting trip. And now he met him again on the terrace of the hotel. The Master too was on the terrace, pacing up and down at a little distance. Hippolyte was standing in the doorway when he saw Zillu's-Sultán coming up the steps. The prince approached and greeted him, then turned and gave a startled look toward the Master.
>
> "Who is that Persian nobleman?" he asked.
>
> "That," answered Hippolyte, "is 'Abdu'l-Bahá."
>
> And now Zillu's-Sultán spoke very humbly.
>
> "Take me to Him," he begged.

> Hippolyte told me all about it: "If you could have seen the brute, Juliet, mumbling out his miserable excuses! But the Master took him in His arms and said: 'All those things are in the past. Never think of them again.' Then He invited Zillu's-Sultán's two sons to spend a day with Him." And so it was that Prince Bahrám came to lunch.[15]

'Abdu'l-Bahá's and Hippolyte's stay in Thonon-les-Bains ends on August 30. They travel onward to Geneva where they stay for five days to prepare for 'Abdu'l-Bahá's journey to London. On September 4, Hippolyte "entrusts" the Master to the good care of Lady Blomfield, now in charge of organizing the Master's schedule.

In London, even if Hippolyte is not constantly in the presence of 'Abdu'l-Bahá, Whose days are punctuated by numerous meetings and public talks, he has occasion to visit with his beloved Master. Lady Blomfield's book makes a warm reference to Laura and Hippolyte Dreyfus-Barney, and she leaves us with an unforgettable impression of a brilliant and lovely man and his brilliant American wife: "Foremost amongst our visitors were Mr. and Mrs. Dreyfus-Barney, the brilliant French scholar and his no less brilliant American wife, who spoke Persian with 'Abdu'l-Bahá, translated for Him, and were altogether helpful, courteous, and charming."[16]

16 / 'Abdu'l-Bahá's First Visit to Paris

On October 3, 1911, 'Abdu'l-Bahá and His companions leave London for Paris, at which they arrive in the late afternoon. The Master goes directly to the home of Hippolyte and Laura, at 15 rue Greuze, to get a few days of rest.

He then moves into an apartment prepared by the couple, located in the Trocadéro district, near the Eiffel Tower. Lady Blomfield remembers, "When the days of 'Abdu'l-Bahá's first visit to London (in the autumn of 1911) were drawing to a close, His friends, Mr. and Mrs. Dreyfus-Barney, found an apartment for His residence whilst in the French capital. It was charmingly furnished, sunny and spacious, situated in the Avenue de Camoëns (no. 4), whence a flight of steps led into the Trocadéro Gardens; here the Master often took solitary, restful walks. Sheltered in this modern, comfortable, Paris flat, He Whom we revered, with a secretary, servitors, and a few close friends, sojourned for an unforgettable nine weeks."[1] It is also in this apartment that 'Abdu'l-Bahá will speak on the phone for the first time.[2]

During 'Abdu'l-Bahá's stay in Paris, Hippolyte is constantly by His side. Hippolyte organizes the Master's daily schedules and plans His travels, serves as a point of contact with the many friends who desire to meet the Master, uses his network of acquaintances to arrange private meetings and public speeches, welcomes the guests in an unceasing flow of visitors, acts as an interpreter-translator and, most of the time, introduces 'Abdu'l-Bahá to those who come to listen to the Master. Every morning, 'Abdu'l-Bahá gives an address to a wide range of participants. Lady Blomfield has written, "Every morning, according to His custom, the Master exposed the principles of the Teaching of Bahá'u'lláh to those who gathered round Him, the learned and the unlearned, eager and respectful. They were of all nationalities and creeds, from the East and from the West, including Theosophists, agnostics, materialists, spiritualists, Christian Scientists, social reformers, Hindus, Sufis, Muslims, Buddhists, Zoroastrians, and many others. Often came workers in various humanitarian societies, who were striving to reduce the miseries of the poor. These received special sympathy and blessing."[3]

Each public talk or informal discourse given by the Master is a life lesson for the participants. Lady Blomfield and her daughters take

'Abdu'l-Bahá in Paris—1911. Standing, from left to right: Hippolyte, Ághá Mírzá Báqir Shírází, unknown, Mountfort Mills, Laura Dreyfus-Barney, the Häfner family. 'Abdul-Bahá is sitting in the center.

notes that will result in the publication of the famous compilation known as *Paris Talks*.[4] Though not considered authentic Bahá'í text, *Paris Talks* is a very readable and charming compilation of the Master's discourses during His sojourn in Paris.

Hippolyte translates daily the public talks delivered by 'Abdu'l-Bahá in Paris. Hippolyte fascinates the audience with his instant rendering of Persian, French, and English, and many are impressed by his linguistic talents. In the newspaper *Liberté*, Myrtil Airel testifies, "Abdou'l-Baha smiles at the audience. He clasps his hands outstretched and then sits down and, in a nuanced voice, speaks in Persian. Barely uttered, each sentence is translated to us by Mr. Hippolyte Dreyfus, the most zealous Parisian follower of Baha'ism . . ."[5]

Similar sentiments are expressed by Remy de Gourmont[6] in the *La France* newspaper: "[The] philosophy at once candid and gentle, against which one seeks in vain [to raise] objections [. . .] was taught to me yesterday by the Master, in discourse rich with flowery language which M. D. [Monsieur Dreyfus] translated into the French language with an ease that amazed me almost as much as the [principles or tenets of] Baha'ism itself."[7]

Also worthy of note are the words of Mr. Louis Le Leu[8] who, in his speech before the talk given by 'Abdu'l-Bahá at the Spiritualist Assembly, declared, "I do not want to infringe upon the ground over which you are going to lead us, assisted by your devoted interpreter, Mons. Dreyfus, who has already[9] given us a volume of great clearness on the principles and history of Bahaism."[10]

The effect of 'Abdu'l-Bahá on Hippolyte and the other believers goes far beyond the vastness and profundity of the Master's wisdom and knowledge. With Him, they can see how the Bahá'í Faith is to be lived and how its principles are to be put into practice. The following anecdote, told by Alice Breed[11] in *Star of the West*, deeply affects Hippolyte:

> After a morning talk given by Abdul-Baha at his apartment No. 4 Ave. de Camoëns on 15 October 1911, all those present were invited that Sunday afternoon to meet him at 4 pm at

22 rue Seeden Rollin [Ledru Rollin] Pré-Saint-Gervais (Seine) outside the walls of Paris, where a real Bahai settlement work is carried out by Mons. V. Ponsonaille and his good wife. They are poor people. He is employed as a collector for one of the large department stores in Paris. Having received the Message, he felt his work for the Cause of God was among the very poor children, waifs and those who had no parents; so with his wife, some years ago settled his home here and by going without their noon day meal (which to the French means a lot) they could give it to these little ones. They started in an old car where they met together to read the Tablets and hear the Word of BAHA'O'LLAH [Bahá'u'lláh]. It was not long before many came and it grew so that the clergy of many sects desired to have it consolidated under them. Mr. Ponsonaille did not consider this the way to serve best and he declined all these offers. At last, they grew so very jealous that they, with the help of the priests, took the car from him. The Bahai friends in Paris offered to build a place for his work and Mons. Ponsonaille told them that if they would furnish him with the boards and nails, he would build it himself, which he did, and it was here that we went, and after three months spent going around Paris every day, I assure you, I had never seen such a dirty, miserable quarter.

After leaving the train on the main street, we walked down to the end of a narrow lane or street without sidewalks, on which doors opened to places where soldiers and women were drinking and screaming, while from the small windows bedclothes were hanging out, and women and children could be seen. It was with joy we at last saw a familiar face and Mons. De Scott [Mr Scott], the artist, pointed to the small gate through which we passed and by the discarded car into a small board cabin about 20x25 feet. At one end was a raised platform and desk of rough boards. I can only say as my eyes fell first upon The Greatest Name hanging in a frame from this desk and I saw the crowd of miserably poor, dear little ones gathered there, and as my ears caught the music of their voices (for they were singing), tears filled my eyes and a great lump choked me. Then I looked and saw we were but a half dozen who had come as guests, and all, like myself, were deeply affected. It was Madam Ponsonaille, a woman with a strong, kind and most intelligent face, who obviously had taught the children to sing and who with her whole heart was leading and keeping time for them, as they had no instruments. After the song Mr. Ponsonaille read a Tablet sent by the Master, for he called Abdul-Baha "The Master," and it is quite evident that they all know him as the Master. Mr. Ponsonaille, who has a delicate, most refined face—that of a gentleman in its fullest sense—talked for a time; they sang again, and then all their little heads were turned toward the entrance and it was evident that their hearts were full of expectation and they longed to see the One who had promised to come to visit them. The oldest of these children were not over fifteen—from that down to babies in arms—all ages and kinds, clothed cleanly in clothes that were not fitted, or were misfits rather.

At last there was a silence. Then all rose to their feet as Abdul-Baha quickly entered and walked up the narrow centre passage to the front and stood. Mr. Dreyfus-Barney and Tammadon-ul-Molk took their places on the side. Mr. Dreyfus-Barney acted as interpreter. Abdul-Baha said: "I am very glad to be here with you. I am very glad to see you all here. I love you very much. I have been in many beautiful houses, but this is more beautiful to me than any of the others, for the spirit of the love of BAHA'O'LLAH is here. You are all receiving the teachings of God and learning how to act and live and some day you will be great and wise for having learned the truth. I have seen many beautiful rich children, but to me you are more beautiful, and I love you all (as Christ loved little children) here. Mr. and Mrs. Ponsonaille are your spiritual teachers. They give you food and understanding of eternal God, while your parents are giving you your material food and care for your bodies. You must love these good friends." Turning to Mr. and Mrs. Ponsonaille, he [said:] "This is a great work you are doing for the love of God in this great day, through the power of BAHA'O'LLAH. Your station is great. Your names will go down through all the ages. Kings and Queens have never been talked of and remembered as you will be. You are workers in the Kingdom of ABHA and I am very happy and love you very much." Then with his head upturned and the palms of his hands upturned together, as if to receive in them the pouring down of the Holy Spirit, he sang a prayer and blessing, and coming down from the small elevation, on which he was standing, to where the children were, all crowded close around him, and laying his hands caressingly upon some of their heads and taking the hands of others with a loving smile to all, with difficulty he passed down the aisle to the door. Near me were some rough boys whom I was often obliged to quiet before Abdul-Baha entered the hall. But after he came they never moved nor spoke and when he passed out they fell over each other in their great desire to have him take their hands.

Outside the door stood Mr. Ponsonaille, and Abdul-Baha, putting his hand inside his gown, took out many gold pieces and gave to him as he bade him good-bye. He walked down the street toward the carriage so quickly that our little party was at least twenty feet behind. Oh! what a sight. In every doorway and window were people—and such people! A very poor man held the carriage door open as Abdul-Baha entered with his little party, Mr. and Madam Dreyfus-Barney and Tammadon-ul-Molk. The crowd were fighting and calling names but a gendarme and Mr. De Scott protected us as we passed on safely.

So ended a never-to-be-forgotten day, having seen Abdul-Baha among the children of the poor of the streets of Paris and I thought again of the light I saw twice on Fridays in Acca and wondered if they were missing him and longing for his return and loving help. The thought comes to me now of what the world's poverty will be after his departure and to us who have been fed from his hand on the Bread of Life.[12]

During his stay, 'Abdu'l-Bahá also visits Hippolyte several times to have lunch or dinner and participate in the "spiritual meeting" held every Friday at his home. These gatherings, in which believers, friends of the Faith, and seekers participate, usually take place as follows: Hippolyte chooses an excerpt from the Writings of Bahá'u'lláh that he reads in the original language, in Persian or Arabic, before translating it into French. Then he shares his understanding of the text until the participants can grasp its meaning and fully enjoy it. Finally, the evening ends with the singing of prayers, in the melodious voices of the believers, most often in Persian.[13]

During His nine weeks in Paris, 'Abdu'l-Bahá attends most of these weekly meetings. The program is, of course, adapted to take into account the presence of the Master. Hippolyte usually takes the floor first to introduce 'Abdu'l-Bahá (when necessary) and present the theme of the evening. Then, he leaves room for the Master, Who develops the chosen subject. 'Abdu'l-Bahá then begins to expound on many subjects, such as divine knowledge, the role of the Manifestations of God, religious prejudice, the progress of the soul, the relationship between body and soul and spirit, to name a few. Finally, after a question-and-answer session, participants have the privilege of being able to listen to the Master chanting a prayer.[14]

Hippolyte's desire to be constantly at the service of the Master and to relieve Him as much as possible from the fatigue that overwhelms Him also translates into simpler everyday actions. When 'Abdu'l-Bahá comes to his house for dinner, Hippolyte and Laura prepare Persian dishes; when the Master has appointments outside the apartment, Hippolyte drives Him there in his car. For example, on October 26, the two men travel in Hippolyte's car to the headquarters of the Theosophical Society, where 'Abdu'l-Bahá gives a speech on the founding principles of the Bahá'í Faith, which Hippolyte translates from beginning to end. After the Master receives resounding applause, Hippolyte drives the Master back to His apartment.[15]

The bond of loving communion between the Master and His devoted aide is strong. 'Abdu'l-Bahá, for His part, often invites

Hippolyte to accompany Him on His daily walk through the streets of Paris. This time together offers intimate and privileged moments during which they can discuss matters of the Faith in complete freedom. The Master also takes advantage of His stay in Paris to meet several members of Hippolyte's family, including his sister and brother-in-law, Yvonne and Paul Meyer-May, who eventually also accept the Faith. The Master even goes to their home at 21 boulevard Beauséjour, on the evening of October 29, to give a short speech, and this event is attended by several other friends.[16]

Significantly, it is at the Dreyfus residence that 'Abdu'l-Bahá delivers the last talk of His Paris trip, known as "The Last Meeting." Here is an extract:

> Tonight I come to say farewell to you—but bear this in your minds, that although our bodies may be far apart, in spirit we shall always be together.
>
> I bear you one and all in my heart, and will forget none of you—and I hope that none of you will forget me.
>
> I in the East, and you in the West, let us try with heart and soul that unity may dwell in the world, that all the peoples may become one people, and that the whole surface of the earth may be like one country—for the Sun of Truth shines on all alike. . . .
>
> Now I say "Good-bye."
>
> This I say only to your outer selves; I do not say it to your souls, for our souls are always together.
>
> Be comforted, and rest assured that day and night I shall turn to the Kingdom of the Most Glorious in supplication for you, that day by day you may grow better and holier, nearer to God, and more and more illuminated by the radiance of His Love.[17]

On December 2, Hippolyte accompanies 'Abdu'l-Bahá and His entourage to the Gare de Lyon where they take the train to Marseille; they arrive at 10:45 in the evening. On December 6, Hippolyte and the Master go to the headquarters of the Theosophical Society in

Marseille; the Master gives a speech, which Hippolyte translates into French, "on materialism, in its clear, simple and just style."[18] Hippolyte notes, "All the theosophists applauded these words so full of life and spirituality."[19] The next day, 'Abdu'l-Bahá and His companions leave Hippolyte, Marseille, and France to travel to Alexandria, Egypt.

17 / Traversing the United States

In the spring of 1912, the Bahá'í community receive news from the Holy Land that 'Abdu'l-Bahá is preparing for a long trip to North America. Hippolyte and Laura decide, instantly, to go there to meet their friends and believers and, if the opportunity arises, to enter the presence of the Master once again.

Hippolyte—Passport, 1911

Before His departure, Hippolyte receives a letter from 'Abdu'l-Bahá to reassure him about the arrangement of His trip to the United States, and as it turns out, the very devoted Mr. MacNutt will be responsible for organizing it. 'Abdu'l-Bahá also expresses His gratitude for Hippolyte's efforts during His stay in Europe, and He notes that all the arrangements for Him in Paris and London had been very well organized. He shares His hope that positive outcomes will become evident as a result of the efforts of the friends from Paris.[1]

When 'Abdu'l-Bahá arrives in the United States on April 11, the couple is not yet in Washington. Hippolyte and Laura embark on the SS *Kaiserin Auguste Victoria,* stationed at Cherbourg, on April 17. The tragedy of the *Titanic*[2] is on everyone's mind. The giant liner had hit an iceberg a few days earlier, and the list of the number of victims continues to grow. The atmosphere in the port is heavy, and Hippolyte confides, "conversations are rare [. . .] each bearing in themselves the burden of the horrible disaster that had just engulfed the largest ship in the world."[3]

After several days of ocean crossing, the couple arrives in New York. It is the second time Hippolyte lands on American soil, and he admits that he does not "feel the impression of audacity, grandeur, or vertigo" that it had given him the first time.[4] The couple hurries to their Washington home where they find Laura's mother, Alice, and her new husband, Christian Hemmick.

For His part, the Master, after spending nine days in New York, takes the train to Washington on April 20. The time of His arrival had not been correctly communicated to the believers eagerly awaiting Him, and Marzieh Gail remembers:

> It was noon, 20 April, 1912. Florence and Khan were at luncheon, and like the other Washington Bahá'ís, they were wondering when 'Abdu'l-Bahá would arrive in the capital. Suddenly there came a phone call from Mason Remey: "Hurry! The Master is arriving at the station in half an hour!" They dropped forks and knives, collected Rahim and Marzieh, and ran out into the street, breathless, trying to catch a public Victoria[5]—their

Bar Harbour, Maine, United States, 1912

chance of reaching the station on time. With fervent prayers, and urging shortcuts on the driver, they made it five minutes before the train pulled in. Florence rushed to the florist's in the station and bought two bouquets for the children to present, violets for Rahim and red roses for Marzieh. Mason Remey and Joseph Hannen were there, and one Persian friend. There had been no time to inform the others, except for Mrs. Agnes Parsons. (The Master was to spend His first week at her beautiful home, newly built, and furnished to be ready for His visit. Then He would leave for Chicago to lay the Temple cornerstone.) Three cars drew up outside the station to receive the party, one bringing Hippolyte Dreyfus-Barney.[6]

The reunion is obviously extremely joyful. During the short week that 'Abdu'l-Bahá spends in Washington, He gives nearly fifteen talks, including two at Studio House, an art studio owned by Laura's mother.

After the departure of the Master from Washington, Hippolyte and Laura remain with their family. Hippolyte especially loves the city of Washington: "how pretty the capital is under the thick coat of foliage in the first days of May! [. . .] the greenery, the houses paved with wisteria, the bright rhododendrons under the porches."[7] In the absence of the Master, the days are also busy but more mundane: bridge, polo, walks in Rock Creek Park and night receptions follow one another. About Hippolyte's moments of rest, Laura shares, "Hippolyte Dreyfus was a well-balanced and independent person. He liked both thought and action. He could sit at his desk and translate and read all day and late into the night. Or he could go for a swim or horseback ride with friends or alone."[8]

Swimming and horse riding seem to be the two favourite hobbies of this tireless worker. Natalie, her sister-in-law, confirms this observation and writes, "He loved horse riding through the woods of Saint-Cloud or of Saint-Cucufa. He made the worst rental horse docile, amiable even, by his attention. [. . .] He was a wonderful swimmer, and gave me confidence because he never lied; when he said we had a foot, we had it; and when we no longer had it, he was there, offering solid security without haste."[9]

On May 8, the Master and His entourage return to Washington after being in Chicago, Cleveland, and Pittsburgh. They are once again greeted at the station by friends—Hippolyte and Laura; Agnes Parsons; Ali-Kuli Khan and his wife; Ahmad Sohrab; and Joseph and Pauline Hannen are present. All these wonderful souls then drive to Mrs. Parsons' house for tea, but Hippolyte and Laura cannot stay.[10]

At the end of May, Hippolyte travels to Cincinnati for a few days to meet the believers and deal with some family business issues. Cincinnati is the birthplace of Laura and her mother, and in early June, the couple leaves for a long journey through the United States. Their first stop is Minneapolis, in which Hippolyte notes the charm and rhythm of life of the local Bahá'í friends and writes, "Nothing equals the charm of these houses, where you find yourself in the evening in the simplicity of friends' meetings, after days spent at the factory or at the bank."[11] From Minneapolis, he writes the following to his sister, whom he has just learned is bedridden and about to be hospitalized:

> My dear, I can't tell you how sorry I am to be away from Paris right now! Paul's letter came to me last night, at midnight, and you know what a night I had; I thought about going back to Washington immediately to return to France. But I also thought that now all your worries have probably passed and that I will arrive when I am no longer needed. I am waiting every moment for a dispatch that Laura has asked Paul to send me to Chicago and that I must be followed here. If I do not receive it today, I will telegraph him to wire me your news to my next address. Did you suffer a lot before the operation? I know how brave you are and how easily you will have decided: but what emotions for Paul and the children! And what a torment for me to be so far away! And poor mother how did she know about it? In her last letter, she torments herself knowing that you suffer from the intestines, but that is all: she puts this on the account of your overwork as always. Finally, here is a summer that we will remember in the family!
>
> My journey is very interesting from the point of view of the Cause which has taken on a considerable importance in America: but to find myself in this way alone, with the sad news and the lack of news, it is sometimes very hard. (. . .) I leave tomorrow for Vancouver and Seattle; then I must stop in Portland, San Francisco, Los Angeles, Denver without counting some smaller assemblies where I am also expected. What a beautiful trip it would be if I had peace of mind!
>
> Finally, my dear, I can do nothing but pray that you will recover quickly, and that this operation will return all your strength and all your drive. My thoughts are with you continually and I can think only of when we will all be reunited again.[12]

Back in New York, 'Abdu'l-Bahá writes to Hippolyte to share His experience in Philadelphia. With extreme humility, He also shares His hopes regarding the couple's journey through the United States:

> I visited Philadelphia, for a few days, at the invitation of two ministers and at the request of the friends of God. Two large congregations gathered in the two churches, and I spoke within the measure of my incapacity. But the confirmations of the Abhá Kingdom, as evident as the sun, descended and enfolded us. Although we are powerless, He is Mighty. Although we are poor, He is All-Sufficient. The import of this blessed verse became truly manifest: "We shall aid whosoever will arise for the triumph of Our Cause with the Concourse on high and the company of Our favoured angels." [. . .] It is our hope that you and the handmaiden of Bahá[13] will be able to render important services during this trip, and you will become the cause of the proclamation of the word of God.[14]

From Minneapolis, Hippolyte and Laura take the *Canadian Pacific* train to the Rocky Mountains. They thus cross the American continent from east to west; Hippolyte is dazzled by the beauty of the landscapes, "the fields of wheat and the grasslands where the herds of horses and oxen graze [. . .] in the middle of the bread basket of the world!" They then arrive in the Canadian province of Alberta and spend several days in the midst of its dizzying mountains and snow-capped peaks; Lake Louise and its turquoise waters amaze Hippolyte.

At the end of June, Hippolyte and Laura travel along the west coast, pass through the cities of Seattle and San Francisco, then visit the Grand Canyon in Arizona. Of course, Hippolyte takes advantage of this trip to visit the communities that had so warmly invited him in 1910 but which he had unfortunately not been able to meet earlier for lack of time. In Los Angeles, Hippolyte finally receives reassuring news about Yvonne from his brother-in-law, Paul, to whom he gives, in a letter entitled "Don't show Mother!!", also some news of his trip:

My dear Paul,

Your letter of June 7th came to me here: you can imagine the emotion with which I read it. It is terrible to be so far away at such times, and I have relived all the anxieties you must have had to go through. As for your dear Yvonne, we can only admire her courage. I hope that she will now be completely rid of all her miseries, and that she will return to perfect health. She will need this summer, as you say, care and comfort, and I think she can have the summer that suits her. As for mom, I have a letter from her where she writes that she does not want at any cost that I come back for her, because she is getting better and better. What is exaggerated in what she says? I cannot know. So, I am determined to come back anyway if you telegraphed me that you find it necessary. (. . .)

As for me, I intend to be back in Chicago by the beginning of the second week of July: I will have completed my tour of visits and conferences. But then I will have to go with Laura to W. Virginia where there are properties that her mother has overlooked, without them having been occupied for 10 years. (. . .)

Kiss Yvonne and the kids for me,
Very affectionately,
Hippolyte[15]

Back in Washington, they go to New York to benefit one last time from the presence of 'Abdu'l-Bahá. On July 21, they attend His daily talk titled "services beneficial to the world of humanity."[16] A few days later, Hippolyte and Laura are invited to the wedding of two friends from the American community, Grace Robarts and Harlan Foster Ober, in Jersey City. The ceremony takes place in the presence of 'Abdu'l-Bahá, Who recites a short prayer. Annie Boylan writes:

The friends gathered at 'Abdu'l-Bahá's house at 309 West 78th St for the usual meeting. Instead of a meeting, however,

> Edward Getsinger announced that there would be a surprise. A few minutes later, Harlan and Grace came down, Grace dressed in a white dress and carrying a large bouquet of white roses. Juliet Thompson was present as well and recorded her impressions: "Grace and Harlan stood together, transfigured; they seemed to be bathed in white light. Mr. Ives, standing opposite, married them. Back in the shadow sat the Master . . . At the end of the wedding He blessed the marriage." Howard Colby Ives remembered: "'Abdu'l-Bahá rose . . . He swept the room with a glance at once enfolding and abstracted. He raised his hands, palms upward, level with his waist. His eyes closed and He chanted a prayer . . . in tones to me unequalled in all experience, mellifluous (honey-like), is the nearest descriptive word, but how inadequate . . . my heart certainly moved far more by the chanting Voice and the flowing musical periods, than by the interpreter's version of the wedding prayer, beautiful as it is."[17]

Beyond the beauty and magic of the ceremony, it is a historic moment attended by friends, as it is the first marriage between two Western believers celebrated by the Master Himself outside of the Holy Land.[18]

With summer coming to an end, it is time for Hippolyte and Laura to return to France to continue their teaching work, and, above all, to prepare for the second journey of 'Abdu'l-Bahá to Europe.

18 / 'Abdu'l-Bahá Returns to Europe

On December 5, 1912, after 239 days on the American continent and having visited more than forty cities, 'Abdu'l-Bahá and His companions embark in New York on the White Star liner *Celtic,* bound for England. After a week of ocean crossing, they dock in Liverpool, in the darkness of the night, on December 13. Hippolyte is at hand to welcome them in the company of a group of a dozen believers from Manchester, Liverpool, and Leeds, among whom are Elizabeth Herrick and Isabel Fraser. Still aboard the ship, 'Abdu'l-Bahá waves toward the friends and, with a gesture, invites Hippolyte to join Him on the deck. The Master takes him in His arms and kisses him on both cheeks. Once disembarked, they go to the Adelphi Hotel[1] with Mírzá Mahmúd.[2]

The next morning, Hippolyte goes to the Master's room to bring Him the important correspondence from the East that has been awaiting His arrival. 'Abdu'l-Bahá devotes the whole morning to answering letters. At noon, Hippolyte joins 'Abdu'l-Bahá for lunch and listens to the Master recount different events that occurred during His trip to California.

In the evening, 'Abdu'l-Bahá and Hippolyte go to the headquarters of the Theosophical Society in Liverpool, where 'Abdu'l-Bahá speaks about the three natures of the human being: animal, human, and spiritual. He encourages the audience to focus on the latter, rather than devoting the entirety of their time to material and human problems, and to try to become a reflection of the image of God.

Hippolyte is responsible for translating His words into English.[3] In the evening, they dine together in the Master's room; the supper, consisting of a polow,[4] is prepared by Siyyid Assadu'lláh.[5]

On the morning of December 15, 'Abdu'l-Bahá and Hippolyte, accompanied by Ahmad Yazdí,[6] take a long walk through the center of Liverpool. After lunch, back at the hotel, Hippolyte converses with the Persian friends; Siyyid Assadu'lláh recounts to them some events that happened during their stay in the United States, and these anecdotes cause all the friends to laugh a lot. In the evening, at Pembroke Chapel,[7] in a talk attended by over 1,500 of its congregation, 'Abdu'l-Bahá delivers an address on the unity of religions and the need to abandon prejudices. He then returns to the hotel, where He dines with Hippolyte and His entourage in the hotel dining room.[8]

The next morning, the friends prepare to leave Liverpool for London. Hippolyte travels before everyone else to the station to buy train tickets for all the friends. 'Abdu'l-Bahá and His companions join Him soon afterward, and everyone boards the train. Hippolyte shares the same compartment as the Master, along with Ahmad Yazdí, Mrs. Fraser, and Mrs. Herrick.[9]

As with the previous visit of 'Abdu'l-Bahá to London, Hippolyte "entrusts" the Master to the good care of Lady Blomfield, assisted this time in her task by Mrs. Thornburgh-Cropper. Present by their side during most of the Master's stay in England, Hippolyte makes himself available as soon as the need arises. He serves as a translator, presents different individuals to the Master, and sometimes drives 'Abdu'l-Bahá to His appointments. Hippolyte also has the opportunity to engage in several intimate conversations with the Master and to accompany Him on His walks in the city parks.[10]

In London, Hippolyte tries to arrange a private meeting between Professor Browne[11] and 'Abdu'l-Bahá, but unfortunately, despite several invitations, Professor Browne is unavoidably detained by his work. The letters exchanged between the two men allow us to better perceive the magnitude of the impact of the Master's visit to London and the respect that binds the three men. Here is an extract of a letter from Hippolyte to Edward Granville Browne:

> Abdu'l-Bahá's stay in London is likely to last until the end of the month; unfortunately, if you cannot come before the 20th it is my wife and I who will be deprived of the pleasure of seeing you: I hope you can arrange to come before our departure, because I would be sorry, as well as Mrs. Dreyfus, to miss you. It goes without saying that 'Abdu'l-Bahá will be delighted to meet Mrs. Browne.[12] Notify me by telegram of the day of your visit and the time that suits you so that I can arrange things, because there are always a lot of people and you need to have a special interview. [. . .] The interest caused by his ['Abdu'l-Bahá's] visit to London is considerable. There are about sixty visits every day and he has had articles in all the newspapers. He spoke last Sunday at the City Temple, and next Sunday Archdeacon Wilberforce[13] asked him to come to Westminster. I admire the religious liberalism of your country, which contrasts singularly with French indifference or sectarianism.[14]

On December 18, Laura travels from Paris and joins Hippolyte. The same day, a long consultation with the Master is undertaken in order to better prepare for His next visit to Paris. Then 'Abdu'l-Bahá addresses the crowd of visitors who have come to meet Him about the aspirations of the spirit and the need to rise beyond worldly desires. Hippolyte translates this exciting talk, a discourse that is a source of great inspiration for the audience, into English. On the same day, at Hippolyte's insistent invitation, Professor Browne finally meets 'Abdu'l-Bahá. There is a record of what the Master reportedly said: "'The last time I met you,' He told the distinguished Orientalist, 'was twenty-two years ago in Acca under a different environment, but now I have the pleasure of seeing you in London.'"[15]

The three men exchanged views for over an hour on different topics, such as Persia, the history of the Faith, and the education of women, but their conversation is eventually interrupted by the arrival of new visitors who have appointments with 'Abdu'l-Bahá. Professor Browne is invited to come back the next day, and the prospect that they will all see each other again makes everyone very happy.

On December 20, the Master goes to the Westminster Palace Hotel, where He addresses a large crowd of people who have come to listen to Him. He chooses to speak out on the theme of love and hate. At the end of 'Abdu'l-Bahá's speech, at His invitation, Hippolyte steps onto the stage and, addressing the audience, says the following words:

> Ladies and Gentlemen,
>
> After the beautiful and interesting speech you have heard, I have to make you a promise, it is, not to take up too much of your time, but I wish to say what a joy it is to me to see the wonderful interest that the movement has now awakened in London.
>
> Is it a religion, this movement? Some say no, looking only at the philosophical aspect of the teachings, looking only to its code of ethics; but I say yes, and you certainly will say so, too, after having heard what you have from this platform. It is a religion because it is founded upon the knowledge of God. The knowledge of God is the first thing we should try to acquire. It has, in former times, I think, been very difficult for, in the past, the esoteric part of religion was hidden from the people and the truth was only given in symbols. But in this day BAHA'o'LLAH [Bahá'u'lláh] appeals to our reason.
>
> Reason is the greatest gift of God to man, and it is through reason we can know God. How? BAHA'o'LLAH teaches us that we can know Him [God] best through His Manifestations. What does that mean? I think we should say, in order to make ourselves understood, through the greatest manifestation of God, because everything in the world manifests God to a greater or lesser degree. We can find the divine in the beautiful melodies that are sung by the birds in the forests, the divine in nature, but we find it specially in man, who is at the summit of creation, and especially in those supreme beings who are called the prophets. It is in understanding their teaching that we can reach the knowledge of God. But I said in the beginning that I

did not want to take up too much of your time. I think we can move in a high spirit in thanking the Chair for this wonderful gathering, which I hope will be the beginning of many similar gatherings in this city."[16]

On December 29, Hippolyte and Laura leave London for Paris to complete the final preparations for the next visit of the Master, scheduled for the middle of January. A few days after his departure, Hippolyte successively receives two letters from 'Abdu'l-Bahá. In the first letter, the Master relates that He has been in the home of Mr. Whyte in Edinburgh, that He is in good health, and that He is scheduled to appear at a large gathering in the afternoon and meet with several dignitaries.[17] He further says that He will, on the following day, speak to a group of women who are advocating for their rights, and He ends the letter by conveying His greetings to Laura.[18] In the second letter, the Master relates that His health has taken a turn for the worse, that He has developed a fever and has not slept very well, and He asks Hippolyte to prepare a modest apartment for His arrival in Paris on the 20th or 21st of the month.[19]

Two weeks after their departure, on January 13, Hippolyte returns to London, certainly at the request of 'Abdu'l-Bahá. On that same day, he translates several private conversations between the Master and His visitors. In the evening, he accompanies the Master to Caxton Hall[20] where the Peace Society[21] has organized a meeting between its members and 'Abdu'l-Bahá.

19 / 'Abdu'l-Bahá's Second Stay in Paris

The arrival in Paris of 'Abdu'l-Bahá and His fellow travelers is imminent. Hippolyte's first task is to find an apartment that is functional, pleasant, and, most importantly, spacious enough to accommodate all the believers, their friends, and the simply curious who, every day, will want to enter into the presence of the Master. Hippolyte and Laura are delighted to find suitable premises at 30 rue Saint-Didier, in the 16th arrondissement. This apartment is located in an elegant Haussmann-style building, close to the place the Master had stayed in during His first visit to Paris. It has a large bright living room and is very convenient for welcoming visitors.[1]

On January 21, 1913, on a cold and gloomy day, Hippolyte, Laura and some friends are waiting for 'Abdu'l-Bahá at Saint-Lazare station, where the Master is to arrive shortly. Once He gets off the train, Hippolyte leads 'Abdu'l-Bahá directly to His own apartment, where a traditional Persian dinner, specially prepared for the occasion, is waiting for them.[2]

During the following months, Hippolyte is once again constantly in the presence of 'Abdu'l-Bahá. Well-supported by Laura, he again has the privilege of organising the Master's daily schedule, serving as a translator, introducing Him to different personalities, and sometimes driving the beloved Master to meetings in his own car.[3]

The Dreyfus-Barneys inform others of the Master's new place of residence sparingly, in the hope that He could rest for a few days before resuming the intense rhythm of daily visits and talks. However, from the first days, friends and believers flock in large numbers to the apartment on rue Saint-Didier.[4]

The Master's daily routine during this second visit to Paris is more or less similar to that of his first stay in 1911. Isabel Fraser remembers:

> Each morning a group assembled at his apartment, at 30 rue St. Didier, where he spoke informally; sometimes answering questions, or, on request, explaining points touched on in public addresses. In this way, although there are seeming repetitions, many abstruse subjects are elucidated in these informal lectures. [. . .]
>
> On these occasions Abdul Bahá would sometimes sit by the window over-looking Paris and anon [occasionally] the majestic white-robed figure would pace the room as he discoursed. Every Friday evening, he addressed an assemblage at Mr. and Mrs. Dreyfus-Barney's, 15 rue Greuze and every Monday afternoon he visited a group at Mr. Scott's studio (an American artist), in the Latin quarter, 17 rue Boissonade.
>
> His time in Paris was completely occupied. In the afternoons and evenings one found him surrounded by French scholars and lovers of truth who sought an audience with this master of wisdom. All of a sudden he would sweep majestically forth, and should an attendant make as though to follow, he would wave him aside—"I walk alone!" Many an hour did this man of mystery wander the streets of Paris dispelling the fogs of ignorance.[5]

Between requests for a private interview or the arrival of unexpected visitors, the organization of the Master's schedule is not easy. In general, Hippolyte or Laura receives the guests and leads them one by one, or two by two, to the Master's room; whenever He asks, Hippolyte or Laura stay to help with the translation.[6] The morning talks of 'Abdu'l-Bahá are mostly translated by Hippolyte; when the number of participants is too large, the audience is separated into two groups. Hippolyte then translates into French for the Francophone group, and Laura into English for the Anglophone group.

Between the morning talk and lunch, the Master regularly leaves the apartment for a walk through the streets of the French capital. He sometimes walks alone, and sometimes He is accompanied, although rarely by the same people. Often He is with Hippolyte, who takes Him to discover unknown places.[7] Thus, one afternoon, Hippolyte accompanies 'Abdu'l-Bahá to the Department Stores of the Louvre to buy umbrellas, which the Master wants to give as gifts when He returns to the Holy Land.[8] Another time, they travel in Hippolyte's car to Versailles, and the Master is impressed by the visit to the palace and their stroll through the sumptuous gardens.[9] When 'Abdu'l-Bahá asks him to do so, Hippolyte takes the Master's Persian traveling companions, such as Maḥmúd Zarqání and Ahmad Sohrab, for walks in the streets of Paris; the latter noted in his memoirs that he particularly enjoyed car rides in the Bois de Boulogne, along the banks of the Seine and as far as Saint-Cloud.[10]

During this stay, several daily anecdotes reveal to us all the very special spirit of loving collaboration between Hippolyte and 'Abdu'l-Bahá who, despite the many responsibilities that fall on them, do not forget to share laughter and smiles. One afternoon, when Hippolyte has just arrived at the apartment on rue Saint-Didier, he realizes that he has forgotten the bag of tea he had just received for 'Abdu'l-Bahá. The Master teases him:

> "Whatever! Give us this tea that gives the heart eternal joy, because the pleasure of this tea lasts only a few minutes."
>
> Hippolyte replies: "But we need a special samovar for this kind of tea!"
>
> 'Abdu'l-Bahá: "I expect this samovar to be in Paris!"[11]

On another occasion, Hippolyte offers to take 'Abdu'l-Bahá to see the Eiffel Tower. Ahmad Sohrab tells us about their conversation:

> "Would you like to climb to the top of the Eiffel Tower to see Paris?"
>
> "I can see Paris without climbing the Eiffel Tower."

> "From up there you could breathe new life into all of Paris."
> "That's what I do from here."[12]

Their conversations are, for the most part, an opportunity for the Master to deepen the knowledge and understanding of the earnest learner Hippolyte. One afternoon, while discussing the visit of King Alfonso XIII of Spain to France, 'Abdu'l-Bahá confides to him, "I am always thinking how to carry the loads of others and not to put my own loads onto their shoulders. The Blessed Perfection [Bahá'u'lláh] has taught me this. We must prove this through deed and not by mere words."[13] On another day, the Master tells him at great length about the sacrifices made by Christ's first disciples in their endeavors to promote His teachings.[14]

In 1913, the weekly meetings[15] at Hippolyte's and Laura's home are still very popular, and in general, the three living rooms of their apartment are crowded.[16] The meetings are usually bilingual, in English and French,[17] and follow a very specific agenda: after the reception of the participants—believers, visitors, seekers, and supporters[18]—Hippolyte presents the agenda for the evening, reads one or more Holy Writings of Bahá'u'lláh in the original Persian or Arabic, then in French. Most often, the selected excerpts come from Hippolyte's personal translation work.[19] Then 'Abdu'l-Bahá takes the floor to give a short address; in His usual style, the Master encourages other believers to speak on topics of their choice, or to share news from the Bahá'í world.[20] When 'Abdu'l-Bahá is absent, it is Hippolyte who applies himself to answering questions, asked by the guests, about the Faith.[21] The meetings end with prayers chanted in Arabic or Persian by the Master, or by one of His Persian companions. A very special moment then brings the evening to a close: 'Abdu'l-Bahá always takes the time to shake hands with each of the participants and offer His blessings before retiring.

Many meetings are also organized outside the apartment on rue Saint-Didier by Hippolyte and the friends of the community to provide the Master with more and more opportunities to spread the Cause. Thus, 'Abdu'l-Bahá has conversations with eminent personalities and diplomats, both Persians and Europeans, in large hotels. For example, He presents the principles of the Faith at the annual banquet of Esperantists;[22] He expounds by way of revelatory utterance His unique perspective on the divine spirit in the historical center of the Theosophical Society;[23] and He protests against the stupidity of war and calls for the promulgation of universal peace with a high sense of urgency at the headquarters of the Spiritualist Alliance.[24] Most of the time, Hippolyte—always with the greatest devotion—drives the Master from His apartment to His meeting place, presents 'Abdu'l-Bahá to the audience who have come to listen to Him, translates His words, then transports the Master back to His place of residence.

The continuous flow of visitors keenly eager to meet 'Abdu'l-Bahá, and the press coverage that flourished during the Master's stay in Paris, testify to the success of this second visit to France. Unfortunately, however, the joy of all this good news is frequently tarnished by the activities of the Covenant-breakers.

During His stay in Paris, 'Abdu'l-Bahá has several lengthy conversations with Hippolyte on the subject.[25] Although the subjects of these conversations are not known, one issue on which 'Abdu'l-Bahá requests (in an undated letter) Hippolyte's assistance concerns the deposit of certain untrue yet inflammatory and divisive manuscripts written by Mírzá Yaḥyá in major national libraries, in Paris and London in particular.[26] In an undated letter from 'Abdu'l-Bahá to Hippolyte, the Master had already warned him, before he came to Paris, of this situation and of the confusion regarding the Faith that reigned in Europe due to the scheming falsehoods perpetrated by Mírzá Yaḥyá and his followers:

> Regarding the books thou didst mention: Áqá Aḥmad will be tasked with sending them, so that thou mayest present them to the Paris Library. Those by Yaḥyá are, in truth, a source of embarrassment, for his words are empty and without meaning. Make it clear to them that Yaḥyá's writings have no connection with the Cause of the Abhá Beauty. A Bahá'í is different from a Bábí.[27] The Bahá'ís follow the Kitáb-i-Aqdas and abide by

> its laws, and are not connected to the Bábís. The Bábís have a different path, different conduct, different motives. [. . .]
>
> The Bahá'ís are at peace with all the communities of the world, treating all with sincerity, honesty and goodwill. The Bábís seek to promote conflict between peoples. The Bahá'ís treat enemies as friends, dealing fairly even with a despot. The Bábís' highest aspiration is bloodshed and war. The Bahá'ís act with nothing but kindness and compassion towards followers of other religions; nay, rather, they deem it their duty to nurture, to cherish, to praise, to seek the well-being of all. The Bábís aim to undermine the foundation of religion and destabilize nations. Behold how great is the difference in their ways! These two groups are distinctive in all respects and cannot be compared. [. . .]
>
> In Europe, some seditious individuals have misled others by calling the Bahá'ís Bábís, and stating that both have the same foundation and principles, the same attitude and beliefs, the same commandments and precepts. This is a great mistake. Thou shouldst explain this. We do not hate the people of the Bayán, but our path and approach are incompatible with theirs. We therefore wish to avoid misconceptions.[28]

The second area of concern for 'Abdu'l-Bahá is Dr. Faríd's actions in the United States and England. Dr. Amínu'lláh Faríd (Ameen U. Fareed) was a nephew of 'Abdu'l-Bahá's wife, Munírih Khánum. In 1901 he moved to the United States where he studied, and in 1912 he served as the Master's interpreter during His trip to the United States. He then dishonored himself by using his relationship with the Holy Family to insistently request money from the believers of the American community. His greed led him to spread deceitful and self-serving rumors that the Master needed money but that He would never openly accept help from friends. Dr. Faríd therefore proposed to be the intermediary and to offer the opportunity to believers to be able to "relieve" the Master. His actions caused great pain and suffering to 'Abdu'l-Bahá Who, after a long period of silence, ordered him in 1913 to return to live in Haifa. Soon, however, Dr. Faríd, unhappy with living far away from the United States, disobeyed the Master's instructions and returned to the United States, where he resumed his fraudulent schemes. Hippolyte's role in serving the Master to deepen the believers and protect them from Dr. Faríd's machinations will be discussed later in the book.[29]

We return now to the mainstream of the narrative on the Master's second visit to Paris. Another milestone appointment arranged by Hippolyte is the new interview between 'Abdu'l-Bahá and Professor Browne. The latter shows up at the apartment on rue Saint-Didier with his wife, Alice Caroline, who, after the usual pleasantries, goes out for a walk in the company of Laura Dreyfus-Barney. This renewed conversation between the two men, to which Hippolyte is also invited, lasts almost three hours. Among the topics of discussion, some of the professor's unfortunate remarks about the Faith that appeared in the English press need to be clarified.[30] In a letter he had earlier addressed to Hippolyte, Professor Browne confided in him:

> I feel some diffidence about this, as I fear he ['Abdu'l-Bahá], with the other Bahá'is, must be disappointed in me, as I have regarded the movement rather as a historian and a critic than as a believer. It interests me very deeply, but I am puzzled about several matters, both doctrinal and political. I have often wished to talk over these matters with you, for you and your wife are the only European and American Bahá'ís I have met with who possess the knowledge and grasp of the subject which makes utterance authoritative. [. . .]
>
> I recognise the high Ethics presented by Baha'ism but I do not see that they are higher than those presented by Christ, nor do I see what motive force is to give them greater effect. The difficulty is not to know wherein virtue consists but to make ourselves follow the path of virtue. [. . .] Nor do I think that the Bahá'is are free from the intolerance that they denounce. I was very much distressed by the evidences of such intolerance which I met with, especially in Egypt in 1902. [. . .].[31]

Toward the end of their interview, Professor Browne seems satisfied and reassured by the explanations given by the Master, and he receives a printed pamphlet of a talk by 'Abdu'l-Bahá on the life of the soul after death. Delighted, Professor Browne also thanks 'Abdu'l-Bahá and Hippolyte for sending him new Tablets of Bahá'u'lláh in their original language, and a new discussion of the Writings begins between the two Orientalists and the Master.[32]

Hippolyte also arranges meetings between the Master and certain members of his family. During His stay in Paris, 'Abdu'l-Bahá is invited to lunch on several occasions, and also to have tea or to dine at Hippolyte's and Laura's, where He meets Hippolyte's sister Yvonne; her husband and their children; as well as Hippolyte's cousin, Carle Dreyfus, curator at the Louvre Museum; and his uncle Gustave Dreyfus and his wife Henriette Obermayer Dreyfus. Yvonne, for her part, often invites other family members to dinner with friends of the community, and despite the absence of accessible written testimonies, it may be assumed that a large number of Dreyfus family members may well have met the Master during this period.[33] On several occasions, 'Abdu'l-Bahá visits Hippolyte's mother, who is very ill.[34] Ahmad Sohrab remembers one of these encounters and writes, "The Master entered her room and was very loving and kind to her. She is in bed and very weak physically. She loves the Master. Whenever his name is mentioned her eyes are filled with tears. He read her a short, beautiful, prayer and most touchingly kissed her forehead."[35]

From the end of February, 'Abdu'l-Bahá appears to the friends to be more and more marked by fatigue.[36] Hippolyte and Laura, extremely concerned about the health of the Master, redouble their efforts and attention in order to try to offer Him as much relief as possible.[37] Laura regularly brings Him beautiful bouquets of flowers to decorate His room, as the Master loves nature.[38] Hippolyte also takes Him on car tours[39] or accompanies Him so that He can take walks on the streets of Paris more and more often.[40] Hippolyte also attempts several times to invite Him to go out for a dinner at a restaurant with the Persian friends, but he succeeds only once: they spend a short evening with a dozen Persian friends at the restaurant Le Petit Durand located at 27 Avenue Victor Hugo.[41] The most important thing is that he manages to convince 'Abdu'l-Bahá to take the time to consult a doctor so that He would receive a prescription of some restorative medicine.[42]

In the afternoon of March 19, Hippolyte, Laura, and some Persian friends meet at the apartment on rue Saint-Didier in order to help the Master and His companions pack their bags, as the apartment needs to be vacated.[43] As 'Abdu'l-Bahá and His entourage have to leave in less than two weeks for Germany and Eastern Europe, they decide to stay in a small hotel, the Martha-Pension, located at 97 Lauriston Street.[44] From this date, the Master's meals are most often cooked at the home of the Dreyfus-Barneys[45]—despite the reluctance of 'Abdu'l-Bahá, Who did not want to impose on Hippolyte and Laura—then brought to the hotel. Or, if the Master's schedule permits, the friends all have lunch together at Hippolyte's and Laura's home.[46]

On March 21, it is the feast of Naw-Rúz. A young Persian student in Paris named Achraf Achraf, someone who is close to Hippolyte, tells us about this very special day:

> In the afternoon we went to the Iranian Embassy. The Iranian Bahá'ís, whether passing through or residing in Paris, were obliged, according to the instructions of 'Abdu'l-Bahá, to come to the embassy. All arrived, gradually. The students stayed longer than the others in order to present their problems to the Minister Plenipotentiary Momtázu's-Saltanih. It was then that 'Abdu'l-Bahá, accompanied by Mr. Dreyfus, entered the great hall of the embassy. The Minister invited all the students to greet 'Abdu'l-Bahá. We took places around the large room—we were about thirty people. 'Abdu'l-Bahá extended his care and kindness to all [. . .] and spoke in detail about the historical antecedents of the Arab and European cultures. [. . .] The entire audience listened in silence with the greatest concentration and respect. [. . .]

> Before leaving, Mr. Dreyfus told the Bahá'í students that a meeting would be held at his home that evening. Thus, after having dinner in a restaurant, we went to Mr. Dreyfus' apartment. The audience was made up of numerous Iranian and Western Bahá'ís. 'Abdu'l-Bahá was giving explanations about Naw-Rúz. He went through the history of the creation of this holiday, from ancient times to the era of Bahá'u'lláh, and described the traditions and customs of the Iranians—dressing in new clothes, eating and drinking treats, rejoicing. Finally, he compared the feast of Naw-Rúz with the divine revelation and the inauguration of a new era. He recalled the custom of the ancient kings, which was to plan and found, on such a blessed day, charitable institutions, to lay the foundations of assemblies for peace, so that there would remain a memory of the feast, and that it could be said, in the future, that such work represented the result of the feast of Naw-Rúz of such a year. 'Abdu'l-Bahá spoke in Persian, and Mr. Dreyfus translated. When the Master finished his speech, he shook the hand of each person present and then left the room.[47]

On April 1, Hippolyte, accompanied by Laura, goes to the hotel early to meet 'Abdu'l-Bahá. The Master and His entourage are preparing to leave Paris for Stuttgart, Vienna, and Budapest where they plan to stay for a month. Hippolyte drives the Master in his car to the *Gare de l'Est,* where many people come to greet Him.[48]

'Abdu'l-Bahá and His companions return to Paris on May 1 and stay at the Baltimore Hotel, located at 88 bis of Avenue Kléber.[49] The next day, Hippolyte brings the Master a large package of letters from the United States. Then 'Abdu'l-Bahá tells Hippolyte about His journey to Hungary and Germany, and He praises the qualities of the Germans, whom He found to be "very civilized. They are serious and earnest. They are industrious and energetic."[50]

The agenda for the next six weeks is as busy as ever. Tirelessly, Hippolyte organizes the Master's days, brings Him His mail and helps with translation. He takes 'Abdu'l-Bahá to His meetings outside the hotel, to visit other believers such as Mrs. Jackson and Edith Sanderson, who are residing in Paris. He also takes Him to the hospital where His daughter, Rúhá, had come from the Holy Land for treatment. The Master is often invited to lunch, or to have tea, at the Dreyfus' home, as Hippolyate and Laura are constantly concerned about his health. Maḥmúd Zarqání notes that 'Abdu'l-Bahá is truly "happy with all the efforts made by the friends."[51]

The weekly meetings at the Dreyfus's continue at the same pace. The Master participates when His health permits Him; if He cannot go, He encourages His fellow Persian travelers to stand in for Him.[52] There is a growing number of participants and different speakers from week to week. During this period, Consul Albert Schwarz, Miss Hart,[53] Horace Holley, and other believers share the news coming in from various parts of the Bahá'í world and facilitate the talks. When the Master is present, His speeches are mostly focused on the importance of spreading the Faith, and He invites the friends to strive to teach, "perchance the sleeping ones may be awakened by the celestial strains of the city of melody and hear the soft, delicate music which is streaming down from the kingdom of El-Abha."[54] The date for the Master's scheduled departure from Paris draws nearer.

On May 23, all friends are invited to Hippolyte's and Laura's home to celebrate the Declaration of the Báb.[55] While the guests are slowly arriving, 'Abdu'l-Bahá rests in a nearby room. The evening begins with the singing of prayers in Persian by Mírzá Mohamet, and Hippolyte explains the meanings of each prayer. He also talks about the deep mystery of these two events falling on the same day[56] and the great good fortune they enjoy by virtue of having the Master in their midst. Then, Mrs. Claire Bernard takes the floor and praises the qualities of the Master. 'Abdu'l-Bahá then enters the room, and everyone stands up. He talks about the life of the Báb and ends with these reported words: "I congratulate you on this sacred day, the anniversary of the declaration of the Bab—the day when for the first time on this earth BAHA'O'LLAH'S name was mentioned and in the world the dawn appeared on the horizon. May all of you become the cause of joy and of renewing the fire of the love of God in all hearts."[57]

Finally, the Master asks Beatrice Irwin to read a few passages from The Hidden Words. The friends then move on to the social part of the celebration, and exchange ideas freely over a cup of tea and some sweets. The Master seems particularly happy to be able to share this special moment with such sincere, loving friends from all over the globe.[58]

In their constant efforts to relieve the Master of the strain imposed by the grueling programme of engagements, Hippolyte and Laura try to show imagination and creativity. At the end of May, cognizant of the Master's love for nature, Hippolyte takes him to the *Spring Exhibition of the National Horticultural Society of France,* where thousands of fruit trees, plants, and flowers are exhibited in the open air.[59] By the greatest stroke of luck, they come across a group of Bahá'ís. Fanny A. Knobloch[60] recounts:

> While in Paris, we made a trip to Versailles. One afternoon, [as we] sat on the upper deck of the trolley car, we passed some black tents. Small open spaces gave us a glimpse of beautiful flowers, and when we heard "This is the Parisian flower show," we descended immediately. While strolling about, admiring the beauty displayed, we were greatly surprised and pleased when Abdul Baha suddenly appeared at the end of the walk. He was advancing slowly, in his usual way, looking to the right and left, admiring, whilst we stood silently watching. We then saw Mr. Hippolyte Dreyfus following in the rear. When finally, Abdul Baha came nearer, he greeted our little group with a brilliant smile and walked up to a young German lad who was with us and kissed him on both cheeks. Needless to say, we returned to our hotel very happy indeed.[61]

On another occasion, when 'Abdu'l-Bahá speaks of how much He loves and honors Mary Magdalene[62] and praises the firmness of her faith, Hippolyte offers the Master a suggestion that they should go out for the evening and watch a play on her life then being performed in Paris. The Master gladly accepts Hippolyte's idea, and on the same evening, they attend the performance given at the *Théâtre du Châtelet.*[63] These two short breaks in the Master's hectic schedule afforded Him a brief respite, a much-needed rest from His daily travails.

On June 12, it is time for the departure. Hippolyte and Laura pick up 'Abdu'l-Bahá at His hotel and have one last cup of tea with the Persian friends.[64] Hippolyte then drives the Master to the *Gare de Lyon,* where He is to board the train to Marseille. At the station, about fifty people are waiting for the Master; He takes time to shake hands and say a few words to every person. He arrives in Marseille in the late evening, and on June 13, He embarks on the SS *Himalaya,* bound for Port Said, Egypt.

Just after the Master leaves, Hippolyte and Laura send him a telegram: "A thousand regrets to see you parting, and not being able to accompany you. We hope that your voyage will be pleasant and we trust that we will see you again soon. Rúhá[65] is well. In thought, she joins us in sending you affectionate greetings."[66]

20 / The Epistle to the Son of the Wolf

Despite the sense of emptiness left by the departure of the Master, 'Abdu'l-Bahá's last words of farewell spoken to the friends who came to see Him in Paris on the day of His departure still resonate in the hearts of those who love the Master:

> I have been in your midst for a few months. Only God knows how much I have grown to love you. Your love beats in my heart like the artery of life. During my stay, I have explained to you the divine ideals. I have ignited in the chamber of your hearts the light of the love of God. Strive day and night that its lustre and brightness may increase, so that the light of God may illuminate all the regions, that the Kingdom of God may be established and the Glory of Abha be revealed. Do not rest for one moment. Make ye a noble effort so that you may guide the souls, confer life upon these dead ones, make mindful those who are heedless, awaken those who are asleep, enkindle the extinct men and women with the consuming fire of the love of God, and exhilarate the souls with the Tablets of the wine of knowledge.
>
> I leave you here and I go to Egypt, but I expect to receive good news from you, that your meetings are glowing with the light of faith and assurance.[1]

Thus, Hippolyte, taking to heart the parting words of the Master, resumes his work of spreading the Faith. First, he completes his translation of the Epistle to the Son of the Wolf[2] and publishes it in 1913 at the Honoré Champion Bookshop. This Tablet, dated 1891, is considered to be the last major work revealed by Bahá'u'lláh before His death in 1892. It is addressed to the terrible Shaykh Muḥammad-Taqí (1846–1914), a Muslim religious leader and son of the cruel man whom Bahá'u'lláh gives the nickname "Wolf" Shaykh Muḥammad-Báqir (1819–1893), who conspired with Ẓillu's-Sulṭán to foment the bloody persecutions against the Bahá'ís in the Isfahan region. In this Tablet, Bahá'u'lláh describes certain historical events, such as the martyrdom of the two brothers known as the "King of Martyrs" and the "Beloved of Martyrs," His own arrest, and the political machinations to which He was subjected in Constantinople. This work is of particular interest to the general public because Bahá'u'lláh quotes many of His own previous Writings, thus offering a captivating presentation of the fundamental teachings of the Faith.

After summarizing in the introduction of the book the history of the two martyrs and setting the historical context surrounding the revelation of this Tablet, Hippolyte explains why he chose to translate this work:

> The *Epistle to the Son of the Wolf* (it is indeed by this name that it is known among the disciples) derives its value to us, not only because it is one of the last writings of the Prophet, but also because it constitutes a true summary of his work done in the hope of softening one of the most violent opponents of the Cause. [. . .] From another point of view, the book is interesting. It is known that from the beginning of His mission, Bahá'u'lláh found pitted against Him a number of Bábís who could not accept the impulse towards universalism, which He had given to the doctrine of the Báb. They gathered around His half-brother Sobhi Azal [Subh-i-Azal] who, until recently, directed against the Cause the most bitter, as well as the most barren, of struggles. [. . .] It is thus that Bahá'u'lláh and the

> Baha'is are accused of diminishing, despising even, the personality of the Báb, in order to exalt that of His successor, and thus preventing all the faithful Bábís from joining the movement. [. . .] In reading the *Epistle to the Son of the Wolf*, an impartial critic will, on the contrary, see that Bahá'u'lláh draws, so to speak, from the writings of the Báb, eschatological evidence of the authenticity of His own mission. The impartial observer will not be able to conceive how such an accusation could be spread: for to weaken the authority of the person of the Báb, would be, for Bahá'u'lláh, to weaken His own authority.[3]

In a report published in the *Journal Asiatique,* Clément Huart congratulates Hippolyte for his work: "Thanks to the zeal of Mr. H. Dreyfus, the literature of the Béhâîs is successively made available to the general public by means of the elegant translations he gives us."[4]

Another review of the work, published by *Studies of the Society of Jesus,* also praises Hippolyte's work: "The publications of Mr. H. Dreyfus, composed with the fervour and seriousness of a neophyte, have undoubtedly helped to give (the movement) its—so little deserved—notoriety. He gives us today the translation of the Epistle to the son of the Wolf. It is an open letter, addressed by the founder of the Bahoullah sect around 1892, to his main opponent, gallantly described, among the followers, as the son of the Wolf."[5]

In *Revue critique d'histoire et de littérature,* the author, although he acknowledges that Hippolyte has "left all its splendour to the original Tablet, and its translation must be excellent," questions the scope of this work, which he considers extremely difficult for the uninitiated reader to grasp.[6] It should also be noted that the famous French newspaper *Le Figaro*[7] announced the publication of the work in its edition of 7 February 1913.[8]

In July of the same year, Hippolyte is invited to speak at the Sixth Congress for Religious Progress, as a representative of 'Abdu'l-Bahá Who, having gone back to the Holy Land, cannot be present. Credit for taking the initiative of organizing this congress belongs to the American Unitarians who founded in 1900 an International Committee to "bring together in all countries those who strive to unite pure religion and perfect freedom, and to increase among them confraternity and solidarity, those who have the same hunger and thirst for justice and love, human brotherhood and mutual respect."[9]

Researchers, theologians and representatives of different faiths and religions, including some twenty members of the clergy whom 'Abdu'l-Bahá had met in England, Canada, the United States, or France, are invited to engage in discussion for several days on topics such as universalism, theological uniqueness, the spiritual unity of religions, the reconciliation of science and religion, subjects very much in tune with the fundamental principles of the Bahá'í Faith.

In his address, unlike his colleagues, Hippolyte does not seek to justify the benefit of universal solidarity or the need for unity among religions, but he demonstrates, boldly and persuasively, how the Bahá'í Faith is already putting these ideals into practice throughout the world and unifying, in a universal movement, people of various cultures and beliefs. Hippolyte first addresses the topic of the oneness of God and religion: "I want to point out right away that Bahaism, unlike other religions that seek universalism in the conversion of unbelievers, does not claim to suppress old beliefs, nor does it ask its followers to abjure their errors. Bahá'u'lláh achieves unity because he sees all religions as different systems explaining the same Truth, and he says to men: 'You are all the flowers of the same garden, the drops of water of the same ocean.' He shows, how, [. . .] their founders are the messengers of the same God, bringing to men the same teaching, adapted only to the requirements of the time."

In a second part, he explains how communities in the west and the east that have received the message of Bahá'u'lláh are undergoing a process of transformation all around the world:

> Baha'ism has achieved it [universal unity], [. . .] its followers have been recruited in all parts of the world, and today form singularly active communities whose efforts are increasingly successful every day. That these ideas find a favourable reception in the liberal circles in Europe and America may seem to

> some extent natural: but their success in the fanatical East, and in India itself, so deeply divided by castes, is quite characteristic. It is necessary, in fact, for a religion to be truly universal, for it to become Religion, that it adapts not only to our mentalities as Westerners, but also to those of the peoples [. . .] in which the superstitions of the past are more deeply rooted.

On the other hand, he reminds us that true religion must reconcile science and religion: ". . . we just have to leave to each [science and religion] their own domain, and to not pretend to explain the unknown with the help of formulas imposed on the faith. Bahá'u'lláh said: 'Religion cannot contradict science, for the opposite of science is error. Religion must evolve with the science it must inspire, just as it must inspire all spheres of human activity.'"

Finally, he advances the idea that religion is not a set of dogmas but a lifestyle that aims at advancing the social progress of all humanity:

> . . . and it does not make the exercise of religion consist in the accomplishment, at certain determined times, of various rituals, but in a life lived in harmony with the moral and social principles which govern humanity. Bahá'u'lláh intended that his religious reform should also be a social reform, and [taught] that by freeing themselves from dogmas, men become aware of their duties of solidarity: from this arises the importance that he places upon the instruction and education that must make possible the equality of sexes and races, a better social organization, including [international] arbitration courts that must succeed in suppressing wars.

His speech is well-received and met with resounding applause. The text is published at the end of the year by the Fischbacher Bookshop in the volume titled *Proceedings of the 6th International Congress of Religious Progress.*[10]

In his report of the lectures published at the *Maison de la Bonne Presse,* the editor writes about the Faith:

> The Behaïs of the East, in turn, are animated by the highest liberalism. They call for the cycle where hatreds will disappear, where animosity between beliefs will change into brotherhood, where the instruments of war will turn into tools of agriculture and commerce. God has always raised up guides and teachers among men. Each of them, in different ways and in different languages, preached the same principles. Whether they were called Moses, Buddha, Jesus, Muhammad or BéhaOullah (founder of Behaism, who died in 1892), they were all the emanation of the same spirit. Behaism has no special rites or ecclesiastical hierarchy.[11]

During the winter of 1913, the health of Hippolyte's mother, Mrs. Inès Dreyfus Cardozo, unfortunately continues to deteriorate. At the age of sixty-five, her soul eventually took flight on 2 October.[12] The burial takes place a few days later in the same chapel of the Montmartre cemetery where her deceased husband had been laid to rest two years earlier.[13]

Madame Inès Dreyfus-Cordozo, by Alice Pike Barney, 1911

"Laura attentive," by Alice Pike Barney, 1912

Hippolyte Dreyfus by Alice Pike Barney, 1907

21 / Covering the Southern United States

A few weeks after the funeral of Hippolyte's mother, the Dreyfus-Barneys travel to the United States to spend the winter with Alice, Laura's mother. In a letter sent to his sister Yvonne, Hippolyte confides, "I found Little One[1] as young and as kind as ever, always lively and delighted to have us with her: Christian's sister who lives almost opposite is also charming. I ride horses with her husband. Apart from dinners, visits, lectures, there is not much to do."[2]

The three months in Washington are punctuated by the settlement of some personal affairs in Cincinnati, Dayton, and Newark, along with the visits of Bahá'í friends and the participation in receptions given by Alice and her husband, Christian, at which consuls, ambassadors, and artists meet. These social activities are important for Hippolyte and Laura because they enable them to meet diplomats and refine their preparations for their next great spiritual undertaking, a journey to the East. The couple has indeed decided to go to Asia for a journey to experience the diverse cultures there and, above all, to share the Cause with as many people as possible. Hippolyte, who corresponds regularly with his sister Yvonne, writes to her in December, "So, as I said, we booked our places for Honolulu and Yokohama. We will embark on the *Mongolia* on 5 March [1914] in San Francisco. [. . .] We will leave Honolulu around 26 March on the *Shinyo Maru* which arrives in Yokohama around 5 April. [. . .] Our immediate projects are not yet finalised."[3]

At the same time, the couple continues their efforts to spread the Cause. Two major events mark this period: Hippolyte and Laura give a lecture on the Faith together at the Washington Conservatory of Music on December 10,[4] and Hippolyte travels to Baltimore to present the Cause.

Before their departure for the Far East, Hippolyte travels on January 14 to Key West in Florida, where he takes a boat the same day to Havana; he stays in Cuba for a week. In a letter, he confides in Yvonne that "throughout the journey, he meets charming people."[5] At the present time, we know very little about his stay on the island of Cuba; what we do know is that just a few days later, Hippolyte is back in the United States.

Back in Washington, Hippolyte and Laura fine-tune the organization of their journey. They plan to travel to the southern United States first with Alice. While waiting for the departure date, they spend a few days in New York; it is an opportunity for them to participate in several meetings and, to their utmost delight, to see once again some of their faithful friends: Edith Sanderson, May Bolles Maxwell, Mountfort and Adele Mills, Manuel Enrique, and Ellen Goin Rionda.[6] The connection between Hippolyte and the New York Bahá'í community is very strong, and the New York Spiritual Assembly will write later: "He [Hippolyte] is and will be especially dear to the members of our Baha'i community in New York City from the fact that through his constant association with the beloved Master and his knowledge of the Persian tongue he was greatly beloved, trusted and listened to during those years when we so badly needed reliable information and advice."[7]

February 30, 1914 is the day of the grand departure on which they have spent so much time preparing to embark. The first city they visit is New Orleans. They stay three days, but Hippolyte is very disappointed, as he had heard so much about this bubbling artistic center. Few things pleasantly surprise him except the Creole cuisine[8] and the meetings with a large number of people who speak "a kind of French."[9]

They leave Louisiana for Texas and stop in San Antonio, and Hippolyte writes to Yvonne, "The city is interesting, you almost think it's Mexico, except for the cold."[10] They then take the train to El Paso, just one step from the Mexican border: "The railroad follows the border, first through the desert where thousands of prairie dogs are seen, then along the Rio Grande where the first Mexican dwellings made of dried mud meet."[11]

It should be noted that since 1913, Mexico has been in the middle of a revolution: President Francisco Madero[12] has just been assassinated following a military coup, organized by General Victoriano Huerta.[13] The latter, meanwhile, must face uprisings in the north of the country led by the famous revolutionaries Emiliano Zapata[14] and Pancho Villa, himself at the head of the fighting in the Juarez region, on the border of Texas.

Hippolyte, so close to the zone of conflict, decides to go there for a visit. He says in a letter to Yvonne:

> Immediately after dinner, while these ladies were resting, I took the tram that crosses the bridge going to Juarez. The city is the capital that General Bandit Villa chose for himself with the tacit protection of the United States; the contrast is strange when leaving El Paso, to be in this city of low houses, streets only lit by the lights of the casinos and saloons. Because since November when the rebels seized it by surprise, massacring the 300 feds who garrisoned it, nothing is going on, except roulette, Kino, a sort of lotto, and poker. [. . .]
>
> It was an unforgettable impression to see this city of Juarez for the first time at night with patrols of comic opera bandits with their huge pointed hats, mounted on their little horses and wrapped up with their blankets up to their noses.[15]

After a few days in Texas, Hippolyte, Laura, and Alice get back on the road, and their destination is Los Angeles. They stay there for one night, then go to San Diego for three days. Hippolyte, always very attentive to his family, takes the opportunity to write to his niece, Valentine, and tell her, in a most affectionate tone, about the vagaries of their journey: "My dear Valentine, we only stayed one night in Los Angeles, and came here to San Diego to the most beautiful place one could dream of. The hotel is surrounded by date trees, giant bamboos, and flowers of all colours. There is a Japanese garden, monkeys, seals, a swimming pool, everything one can dream of. [. . .] I hope that you have become a successful skater, and that you and Jacques[16] have as much fun as work. Aunt Laura and I send you our love."[17]

The main objective of their visit to San Diego is to meet Katherine Augusta Tingley (1847–1929), head of the American branch of the Theosophical Society, to better understand this school of thought that, at this time, is flourishing in Europe and becoming increasingly popular in the United States. Mrs. Tingley takes them first on a tour of the community, then presents to them the fundamental principles of the movement. When Hippolyte and Laura hear about the concepts of universal brotherhood and love of humanity so dear to the Theosophist movement, they are very enthusiastic; however, when Mrs. Tingley explains the occult beliefs of the Theosophical Society, the couple is quite disappointed, and the discussion ends rather abruptly.[18]

Hippolyte, Laura, and Alice then return to Los Angeles for three days. On February 18, Hippolyte gives a lecture "in a large auditorium that the believers rented for him."[19] The next day, he plans to spend the day with Laura and Alice in Santa Barbara, but heavy rains flood the outskirts of Los Angeles, so they choose to go straight to San Francisco, where friends eagerly await them.[20]

The meetings with California believers are very important. Hippolyte and Laura are instructed by 'Abdu'l-Bahá to warn and protect the community against Dr. Faríd's deceptive schemes. At the end of 1913, Dr. Faríd traveled to London to create new dissensions and rally the local community to his side; in response, the Master asked Annie Gamble to watch over the British community and suggested to George Latimer and Mason Remey, who were both on a teaching journey to Europe, to go to London. Now back in the United States,

Dr. Faríd makes a long journey across the country with the same goals; he is particularly active in California where he has made his home. 'Abdu'l-Bahá has no alternative but to exclude Dr. Faríd from the community. At the same time, the Master instructs Hippolyte and Laura to explain to the believers, on His behalf, the reasons that led to Faríd's expulsion. The Cause is only minimally affected by Faríd's actions and expulsion; only Dr. Faríd's immediate family, his father and sister, and a few British believers choose to leave the Faith and continue to associate with him.[21]

During this time, 'Abdu'l-Bahá writes a letter to Hippolyte describing how deeply saddened He is by Dr. Faríd's actions. The Master recounts how, from Dr. Faríd's childhood, He treated both Dr. Faríd and his parents with extreme kindness and benevolence so that he would distinguish himself in his service to the Cause. He regrets how Dr. Faríd has now turned against the Cause and reminds Hippolyte that no one can resist the power of the Covenant and that those who choose to break the Covenant will suffer the same spiritual extinction as Covenant-breakers of the past.[22]

On February 28, Hippolyte gives another address, this time to the believers of the San Francisco community, gathered especially for the occasion. This public talk by Hippolyte is significant as it shows us how Hippolyte takes advantage of these meetings with believers to encourage them to serve and teach the Cause as the Master exhorts us all to do. After a brief historical reminder outlining the spiritual connection between the Báb, Bahá'u'lláh, and 'Abdu'l-Bahá, he speaks about one of the difficulties that believers seem to encounter when they wish to share the teachings:

> Now, one of the greatest difficulties that some of us encounter when we wish to give the Message, as we say, to spread this Cause, at least one of the things that has always seemed to me the most serious, difficult, is that we meet in the world many people, many societies, many organizations, who are very broad, who are striving to do a lot of good, and who are accomplishing a lot.

And often we feel that it is very difficult to point out to them something that they are lacking, to explain to them what we have that they do not [yet] possess. Well, in order to confront that difficulty, we must first acknowledge the beauties that we see outside. We must acknowledge the truth wherever it is, and we must take example from Abdul Baha's broad-mindedness. Then we must remember that this Cause is not a cause of antagonism, that the purpose of this Cause is to unite the different organizations of the world, and that it is important for us to show to those people who are doing so much good that we are with them, that we only desire to help them, until they realize that in our abnegation itself, is the proof of what we possess. There is no doubt to me that if someone is sincere, he is bound to acknowledge that there is no greater instrument for the universal good than the Cause of Baha'o'llah [Bahá'u'lláh]. All of these different organizations that exist in the world are accomplishing their work, but they need acknowledge to themselves how limited they are.

The Cause of Baha'o'llah is the one universal instrument, and when we meet such organizations, such people doing the work we are trying to do, we must remember that all these organizations, all these new branches of human activity, all started at this same time, that they are really other forms of the same vibrations, or other vibrations of the same movement instituted by God.

It is important, before all, to renounce absolutely the spirit of sectarianism. You see how Baha'o'llah and Abdul Baha speak in different words, according to the people whom they are addressing. What does it mean but that there are different languages to express the truth? And we must always remember that if we are right it does not mean that the one who is not thinking exactly like us is wrong. And we can only make unity in a religion by realizing, as Baha'o'llah said, that we are all flowers of one garden, all different flowers in one garden—and that all those flowers have the same right to exist.[23]

He then expounds on several concepts: unity—unity among men, unity of religions—the fundamental agreement between science and religion, the importance of prayer and the spiritual practices of the Faith, and the need for the application in our daily lives of the principles revealed by Bahá'u'lláh. He is about to conclude his speech when Laura asks him to share a few thoughts about the institutions of the Faith. Hippolyte resumes his presentation, explaining how the Faith aims at a renewal of political, social, and judicial institutions. He concludes, "It is this work that we should all have in mind, in order not to be satisfied to see only the group of our friends [enrollment of our fellow believers] increasing, little by little as it has, but in order to see the superb ideals of Baha'o'llah reaching all centres until they are universally adopted."[24]

On March 5, it is time for the separation between the couple and Alice. The latter decides not to continue on the proposed journey to the Far East with her daughter and son-in-law. Hippolyte and Laura then embark in San Francisco on the *Mongolia,* bound for Honolulu, the capital of Hawaii.

22 / Exploring the Far East

On March 7, 1914, the Dreyfuses land in Honolulu. Their arrival is announced in the *Honolulu Star Bulletin,* a daily newspaper that reports the arrival of notable persons and people of high society.[1] The Dreyfuses stay about three weeks, and their time is divided between discovering the different islands of the archipelago, making contacts during lunches and dinners or random excursions, and having several meetings and conferences with the believers, who are very active on the main island. Hippolyte, in a letter dated March 15, 1914, shares his first impressions with Yvonne:

> We are in a state of rapture with this country, where the vegetation is admirable, and the temperature is delicious. [. . .] Heavy black clouds float in the air, cling to the mountains and die, giving the vegetation an incomparable wealth. The country is fantastic, with volcanoes everywhere, most extinct but some still active, and on the 21st, we plan to go to the biggest island to spend 2 days on the Kilauea volcano, the largest in the world it seems. [. . .]
>
> Here an old Colonel Parker,[2] parent of the fallen queen, who was her Prime Minister at the time of the annexation, and to whom the Spreckels[3] recommended to us, takes us everywhere in his car. Today he gives a lunch to 25 people in our honour, with indigenous food and music. There are many believers, and

> last night we gave a much-appreciated talk. We'll do it again the day after tomorrow.[4]

At the end of March—most probably on the 27th—they embark on the *Shinyō Maru*. After ten long days at sea, they reach Japan and the port of Yokohama, late at night. Laura describes her first sensations: "It was night when our ship docked. Japanese shadows swinging paper lanterns, were running hither and thither, strange shapes carrying on their backs children, bedding or bundles. The toc-toc, of their hundreds of wooden sandals sounded like the croaking of frogs at the fall of day."[5]

They spend a day in Yokohama and take the opportunity to discover the city by rickshaw. The next day, they travel to Kamakura to visit the beautiful Buddhist and Shinto temples, as well as the famous Daibutsu, the giant statue of Buddha. Then they head back to Tokyo, where they spend a week. They are welcomed into the capital city of Japan by the Dodge[6] family, who organize several meetings for them with Japanese friends, thus giving them the opportunity to present the Faith to many well-wishers and seekers.[7] Also, the Dreyfuses have several appointments with ambassadors and visit the parks and temples of the capital. Unfortunately, their movements are more or less limited, as the city is in a state of mourning following the death of Empress Shoken.[8] Hippolyte describes a city "huge and awful but which has admirable temples, exquisite parks even more beautiful as it is the season of blossoming cherry trees."[9]

They then go to Nikko where they visit temples as well as a public school; after that, they return to Yokohama to meet with an American friend who guides them for several days around Myanoshita and Hakone; this is the opportunity for the couple to admire the snowy peaks of Mount Fuji. They resume their journey to Kyoto and make two stops in the cities of Nagoya and Ise. Hippolyte is under the spell of the former imperial capital [Kyoto]; he tells Yvonne in a letter dated 25 April 1914: "This is the real Japanese city, and we can't decide to leave. There is such a profusion of things to see, interesting excursions, and so many silk shops and bric-a-brac, that the days pass without anyone noticing. Even the Buddhist temples, whose extravagant ornamentation and richness of lacquers end up giving us indigestion, are here in such beautiful places that we always want to see a new one. You do not imagine this countryside with cherry trees, azaleas and wisteria, or shrubs [. . .] all this in a site of high mountains like in Bavaria!"[10]

Japan, 1914

As Hippolyte writes in this letter, the couple spends a lot of time rummaging in small shops in search of valuable art objects and furniture, which they can then resell on their return to Europe to collectors or antique dealers. This activity is one way for them to finance their many journeys for the Cause, as they had decided to devote their abundant family resources to the service of the Faith.[11]

In the same letter, Hippolyte reminds us of how different the travel conditions at that time were from what we can imagine today: "As Laura saw that there was smallpox in China, she wanted to have us vaccinated by a local doctor. You should have seen that this morning. Jacques' young colleague knew about as much mixed English and

German as I did of Japanese: and I did not really understand what virus he inoculated us with. It is true that apart from the smallpox in China, here there is the plague and typhus, chances are that it is something good."[12]

They spend a day on the beautiful site of Nara, then return to Kyoto to immerse themselves once again in Japanese life. They meet and talk with geishas, have bentos for lunch, take jiu-jitsu classes, and perform the walking-on-fire ceremony . . . Over the course of meetings and discussions, Hippolyte and Laura observe the rise of increasingly strong patriotism in the Japanese empire which, after annexing Taiwan, also occupies Korea.[13]

A few days later, they reach Kobe, where they board a boat to visit the small islands of the inland sea. They spend several days on the sacred island of Miyajima,[14] where "neither birth nor death must happen" and where "at the top of the mountain, in a Buddhist temple burns a fire lit 1300 years ago by the great saint Kobo Daishi."[15] Finally, they go to Shimonoseki to board a steamboat, the *Chosen,* for Korea.

Rumors of the imminent outbreak of a world war are increasingly worrying, so much so that Hippolyte and Laura do not know how to plan the rest of their journey. Already in Kyoto, Hippolyte wrote to Paul, the husband of his sister Yvonne: "We do not know what we will do when we arrive in Peking[16] [. . .] we hear so many conflicting opinions about [. . .] the trouble, that it is impossible to decide anything now."[17] Despite all these uncertainties, they continue their journey to Korea and China.

They disembark in Busan and travel the same day to Seoul. The atmosphere in Korea, occupied by Japan since 1910, is described by Laura as "heavy with torpor, poverty and discouragement seem the lot of the people,"[18] Japanese soldiers are omnipresent in the streets. They do not linger and hastily journey on to Mukden[19] in Manchuria, a territory controlled by the *Fengtian* clique, a Manchu armed faction, supported by Japanese forces, in northeastern China. From there, they go to Tianjin, and after a few hours by train, they eventually arrive in Beijing.

Hippolyte in Japan, 1914

Laura in Japan, 1914

The Republic of China, proclaimed two years earlier following the abdication of the last emperor, is going through a period of total confusion, fueled by the revolutionary insurrections of the warlords. Beijing is still reeling from the Boxer Rebellion, and several districts of the city are under foreign administration. In these neighborhoods where foreigners are exempt from Chinese law, a large number of diplomats, soldiers, sinophiles, academics, and travelers meet. Laura describes how much the Chinese capital disconcerts them; it is so vastly different from anything they have been able to see so far:

> Look down on the city from the tower of the ancient Observatory, and you will see the long grey rooves [roofs] of the houses lying in the dust, like scaled horned dragons. Further off are vast patches of green, and you get the impression that Peking has many trees and gardens. As the sun's rays glisten through

> the veil of dust, you see a magic vision: a city of burnt amber and of green jade. In the street, the impression of space and verdure has vanished, you move in crowded thoroughfares, where everything is surprising to conventional eyes: an orgy of form and of colour, reeling in rags and brocades. You begin to distinguish the passer-by, a woman with hoof-like feet striking the earth as she stumps forward, a Chinese gentleman taking his stroll with a birdcage in either hand, a blind man bangs a gong as he feels his way in the crowd, familiar sounds must aid his lack of vision. Now it is the flute or cymbal of the venders as they push along their wares; again, it is the wail and beat of musical instruments in a procession of marriage or of death. But the traveller is bewildered, he feels under the influence of some narcotic when sounds dwindle and crash forth afresh. The misery and the dirt make him dread the outburst of ulcerated life; more than the stench of the narrow streets, emotions drive him back to the refuge of the hotel.[20]

These picturesque and gruesome conditions do not deter them from exploring the city: the Forbidden City, the Summer Palace, the Temple of Heaven, the Great Wall, and the Ming Tombs are all on their itinerary. Contact with the local population is almost impossible due to the significant social stratification and language barriers that complicate interactions between the Chinese general population and Westerners, so Hippolyte and Laura concentrate their efforts to share the message with the strangers they meet during their visits, at lunches, dinners, or simply when they rest in the lobby of the hotel. In a letter addressed to Yvonne, Hippolyte concisely summarizes their days in the Chinese capital and writes that their daily schedule consists of meetings and social dinners with the authorities, which evidently are forming part of his most important mission for the Faith during this trip; visits; excursions; and fortuitous meetings emerging from his persistent desire to meet with people in Chinese society. He writes, "We like it a lot here, and now that we have done the temples and palaces, we are studying a little bit of Beijing life which is even more interesting. We gave dinner on Saturday to Conty,[21] Mr. de Laas[22] and Mrs. Slater, a former family friend. Saturday is the chic day at *Les Wagons-lits:* dinner with music, followed by a ball until 1 a.m., and it is an extraordinary spectacle to see the toilets of Paris and the costumes of the pretty Chinese neighbours at the small tables."[23]

China, 1914

In Beijing, Hippolyte and Laura also participate in the burial ceremony of a Japanese Minister, along with Chinese and foreign personalities from Beijing society.

> I come home from the funeral of the Japanese Minister and find your letter of May 20. (. . .) The Shinto ceremony was most interesting. We built a huge, all-white hall decorated with all the wreaths we had sent. In the background [there was] an altar with the urn containing the ashes of the deceased, surrounded by paper flowers, offerings of fruits and cakes, and images of grimacing devils. All the diplomatic corps in full dress. Then arrived our friend Sze,[24] representing the President, escorted by

> the Chinese officers in white silk uniforms adorned with gilding. Finally, the widow in a white kimono, with her hair down. Then the priests in purple and yellow robes. The incense, the bells and gongs, the liturgical songs, all this was very impressive. And outside, the sounds of the bugles of the Japanese regiment that made the funeral honours gave an even stranger note to this ceremony from another age. Too bad you only see all this through my descriptions![25]

After a few weeks in the Chinese capital, they travel to Kalgan,[26] a city northwest of Beijing known as the last gate before Mongolia, or the Northern Gate of Beijing. Hippolyte confides in a letter he sends to Paul on May 28 about their trip:

> Our trip to Kalgan was one of the most interesting. We were the hosts for the British American Tobacco because there are no hotels there and no more than 9 Europeans including 4 missionaries. It is a city of 100,000 souls on the border of Mongolia, in a superb site, at the entrance of a pass in the mountain from which the caravans of camels leave for Urga[27] and Russia: the country is not yet very safe, and the Chinese have an army of 15,000 men because the Mongols have been in insurrection since the government had their living Buddha treacherously murdered. Nevertheless, I was able to make, without the slightest danger, despite the presence of all these soldiers, a very interesting cart ride along the border. The day before our departure the notable merchants of the area gave in our honour a Chinese dinner whose menu I send you for Jacques as we brought the dishes. On the way back we stopped one day and one night in Nankou to see the Great Wall and the Ming Tombs, two of the [famous] wonders of China. We had in Kalgan our first real sandstorm; and we were able to see, as we were an hour from our house, the suffering that such storms can cause to caravans.[28]

Back in Beijing, they decide to visit the region of Jehol, a province north of Beijing that is wedged between Manchuria and Mongolia. They embark on this new adventure despite the dissuasive advice, which does not worry them, from the people with whom they speak: "too dangerous, you must be armed," "too hard for a woman," "too hot in this season," and "if you can stand that journey, you can go anywhere in China."[29] The state of the roads to northern China is excruciating, and the five-day journey turns into an experience of prolonged agony for Hippolyte, who has nothing to hang on to when their cart, pulled by two mules, bounces off large stones or sinks into the potholes that punctuate the road. Nevertheless, as usual, he does not complain and keeps smiling.[30]

During their afternoon and evening stops, they have an opportunity to meet the inhabitants of the villages along the way and, thanks to the help of the interpreter who accompanies them, to engage them in conversation. The discussions invariably turn into a medical consultation, during which Laura offers the medicines she brought with her. She had originally brought the medicines to safeguard her and Hippolyte's health during their journey, but now, faced with the villagers who clearly needed them more than she did, she shares them with the villagers without hesitation. The rest of the journey is, as expected, extremely difficult, and after having to face the dust and heat, they must endure torrential rains that force them to take refuge in an abandoned temple and spend the night on the floor.[31]

Eventually, they reach Jehol,[32] the former summer capital of the Manchu emperors during the Qing dynasty. The head of the district, who has been informed of their arrival, offers them a room belonging to the great Buddhist temple of the city. They travel through Jehol for a few days and meet the only foreigners in the city, a family of missionaries from Scotland who opened a dispensary in a poor neighborhood:

> Yesterday morning at 7:30 I went to see the general for whom Conty had given me a letter. But the brave warrior who

Manchuria, 1914

had made the wedding until 4 am apologized "for not being able to receive me in pyjamas" and put one of his men at my disposal to show us around the Palace (that was all I wanted). So, we left at 9 am with our boy carrying lunch, and we spent a delicious day in this beautiful park of several hundred hectares with its lakes, its pagodas, and its palaces with tiles of a thousand colours. (. . .) The country is superb: a real oasis in the middle of the bare mountains where the rocks affect the most extravagant forms: and it is a real change after the heat of the last days of Peking, and of the road. This is where the emperors came in the 18th and 19th century, to spend the summer months, and real treasures were accumulated in this palace that are now to be found in the museum that is built in Peking, a place sheltered from the theft and purchases of the merchants. On returning, I went to see the general, around 5 o'clock in the evening: he was charming, and made himself entirely available. From there, we visited a Scottish missionary who is with his wife the only European living in the country! He has been in Mongolia and China

> for 27 years. They are lovely people, having learned that we had no bread since Peking, they have just sent us 3 loaves just out the oven for our trip; and there goes our diet intentions.[33]

They choose to leave Jehol via the Luanhe River. On their arrival in Luanzhou, touched by the strenuous efforts expended by the two rowers, who under the harassing heat did everything to facilitate their crossing, Hippolyte offers them the rest of their provisions and a little more money than had been agreed. From Luanzhou, Hippolyte and Laura take a train back to Beijing. On their return to Beijing, Hippolyte tells us about a slight incident that demonstrates the sense of justice that animated him, even in the smallest details of his life: "We returned last night without incident to Peking, except that after our arrival at the hotel I learned that my cook had been arrested at the station for taking the left instead of the right at the exit, and when I got to the table, I had to take a rickshaw to go to the station to yell at the officer and have him release him [the cook] immediately!"[34]

Upon their arrival at the hotel, very bad news awaits them. They learn that Archduke Franz Ferdinand, heir to the Austro-Hungarian Empire, has been murdered in Sarajevo. The start of a large-scale war is imminent! The couple, still unfazed, nevertheless decides to go to Shandong Province to visit the homeland of Confucius. They travel to his hometown, Qufu, and then climb the sacred Taoist mountain, Taishan. They also visit the capital of the province, Jinan, and eventually go to the city of Qingdao, then a German concession.

A few days later, war is declared, and all kinds of news begins to spread. The wildest rumors even announce that German soldiers are bombing Edinburgh, are landing on the English coasts, and invading the British Kingdom.[35] On the first of August, Qingdao city falls under martial law. The city is in total chaos; German military planes are flying in the sky, warships are appearing in the port, German officers confiscate travel papers and luggage from travelers. Word is out that the Russians will bomb the city soon! On August 3, Hippolyte takes his pen to share with his sister their anxieties of the moment:

> My dear Yvonne, when and how will this letter reach you? Since my last, events have rushed with maddening speed and we have gone through days of which you can imagine the anguish, because here we are absolutely deprived of news and we know only what the German government wants to tell us. The state of siege has been declared, and we feel as if we're trapped on a German battleship. On July 29, the news of Russia entering the line caused panic here, and the next day we were told that the Russians, the English, and the French were going to have to go. At the same time, all boat services were stopped, all banks were closed and handed over their funds to the German bank, and the arrangements were made as if Tsing-Tau was going to be attacked by the combined forces of the Triple Entente.
>
> As for us, we are not in a hurry to go to Shanghai (. . .) as long as France is not at war we remain here for a while. Although the military and patriotic marches are not very pleasant, the Germans are very kind, and commit us to stay.[36]

After a few days, Hippolyte contacts the French diplomatic authorities to find an exit. Laura recalls, "He never 'borrowed trouble'; he faced situations with ease and when the occasion demanded with unflinching courage. He was rapid in decision but deliberate in manner. While he and I were in Qingdao, China, ready to journey up the Yangzi River and overland by trail to Kunming (Yunnan), the war broke out in 1914. Through his adroitness we got away from the German colony and returned to France in time for him to assume his military obligations."[37]

Arrangements are negotiated by the consulates so that foreigners can leave Qingdao city by train and reach the south of the country as soon as possible. Hippolyte manages to get two places for Shanghai.[38]

Upon their arrival in Shanghai, Hippolyte presents himself to the French consulate. He, too, has been called up by the French army and must return to France quickly to fulfill his military duty. But first, he must find a way out of China and the city of Shanghai, which is also beginning to disintegrate. The few boats returning to Europe are crowded, and it is impossible to get a place on board.

Eventually, Hippolyte manages to secure two tickets on a steamship bound for the United States via Japan. Their stress eases, and as Laura confides, "Now that I know that there is a way back to France, the nervous tension of this isolation is less terrifying."[39]

The next day, they leave Shanghai by sea for Japan. They remain stranded at sea for a few days, as the Japanese coast is plagued by a terrible typhoon. Finally, the boat reaches Nagasaki. The streets are crowded with men in uniform, and a multitude of red and white flags for the empire's glory flutter in the sky. Hippolyte and Laura pass through Kobe, Tokyo, and Yokohama before their boat heads finally to the United States of America. They arrive in Hawaii during the second week of September and return to Washington at the end of the same month. Hippolyte reports to the French embassy, where he is received by the vice consul, who gives him an official statement of presentation to the consulate,[40] as well as an authorization to take up his military assignment in France.[41]

One last critical point to settle before Hippolyte returns to France is whether Laura should stay in the United States with her family or return to France with him. Hippolyte writes to Yvonne, "We stopped here [Washington] where it was essential that we make arrangements to return to France and where I hoped to leave Laura with her mother, not wanting her to return to Paris at this time. But I believe that she will eventually overcome my objections, and that we will go back together, and that if she cannot render services to the Red Cross or to the hospitals, which she cares most about, she may come to see you at the Pèlerin [Daro's-Salam]."[42]

In the end, Laura manages to convince Hippolyte of the importance of returning together to France, and the Dreyfus-Barney couple return to New York a few days later to embark on the *France,* bound for the port of Le Havre.

23 / First World War

On October 19, 1914, about two months after their harrowing departure from China, Hippolyte and Laura land in Le Havre. The atmosphere is terribly heavy. People are polite and kind, but they are also consumed by anxiety and are terrified by the approach of wartime suffering and deprivation. The French, Belgian, and English soldiers who roam the city have scarred faces, and they have clearly already witnessed bloody battles.[1]

From Le Havre, the couple go to Paris. After eleven hours by train, they find the same fear and trepidation in the capital, a far cry from the effervescence that animated the city before their departure. Several buildings have been transformed into reception centers for refugees who have managed to flee the fighting at the battlefronts, and the large gardens, such as the Bois de Boulogne, are used as parks for livestock. The friends they meet briefly all have a terrible story to tell, such as the death in battle of a child or the disappearance of a loved one. Death is omnipresent.[2]

In Paris, Hippolyte learns that the military administration, having considered his linguistic abilities, his high level of education, and his military rank, has chosen to assign him to the postal services of Marseille, where he will be in charge, among other duties, of controlling communications.[3] Laura volunteers with the American Ambulance Corps in Paris then serves with the Red Cross, where she works to comfort soldiers who are wounded, have had limbs amputated, or have been mentally broken by the horrors experienced on the battlefields. Laura will eventually participate in the creation of the first children's hospital in Avignon.

During the four years of the war, Hippolyte and Laura are mostly separated, but they meet up in Marseille when conditions allow. Along with her Red Cross companions, Laura is sent as close as possible to the conflict, and she travels to the Oise department, at the edge

Hippolyte's military passport

Hippolyte and Laura in Marseille, 1914

Hippolyte and Laura in Marseille, 1914

of the trenches. Hippolyte is assigned to various checkpoints around the country—most of which are kept secret—and he must travel to several villages to deliver important letters to families or soldiers. Laura recalls one of these many distressing memories, in which she saw an old woman and men of a village as Hippolyte approached to deliver mail: "Covered with dust, [Hippolyte] joined us where we stood, and the old woman went about her work, while we watched the men gather round the 'regimental postman.' To some came joy and courage, to others grief and anxiety, to many disappointments, as they turned away empty handed."[4]

For a certain period, Hippolyte is assigned to the Montagne Noire area, at the southwestern end of the Massif Central, north of the Haut Languedoc region. Laura visits Hippolyte and recalls, "Wherever I went, I saw France mustering her forces to expel the abhorrent intruders; wherever I went, I saw women and children in mourning, and cripples from the front. All over the country I encountered the courage that can live through pain, ruin and bereavement; all over the country I came face to face with the spirit of the French."[5]

Hippolyte and his infantry regiment

The first World War eventually ends on November 11, 1918. At the end of this conflict—the most murderous that humanity has known so far—Hippolyte and Laura, who have seen so much suffering and sorrow, realize that their firmness in the Faith has grown even stronger, along with their appreciation of the urgency with which the ideas of the Cause must be propagated.

Deeply scarred by the trauma they have witnessed, Hippolyte and Laura have an intense desire to return to the Master to receive new instructions. The couple tries every method of resuming their communications with the Holy Land. At the end of 1918, Hippolyte writes to his friend George Latimer who is then in France: "The news of Palestine has indeed been comforting news, [. . .] as soon as it has been possible, I have sent a cable to 'Abdu'l-Bahá and I hope to receive an answer soon through the British authorities who have been most kind in helping me to get my cable through."[6]

In January 1919, Hippolyte says to Latimer in another letter, "I am glad to hear that you have permission to go East [Palestine]: we may meet you there as we are intending to go some time in spring."[7]

'Abdu'l-Bahá walking outside 7 Haparsim Street in Haifa, c. 1919

At the same time, the ministry of war, through a general who is chief of staff of the French army, gives Hippolyte a report expressing his profound appreciation of "the conscientiousness, the zeal and the competence that Secretary Dreyfus Hippolyte showed in the exercise of his duties as Reader—Interpreter at the Postal Control."[8]

In 1919, the Treaty of Versailles, which concludes a peace agreement between Germany and the Allies, introduces a new organization in charge of preserving peace in Europe: The League of Nations. Based in Geneva, it aims at disarmament, the prevention of wars through the principle of collective security, the resolution of conflict through negotiation, and the overall improvement of the quality of life. The League's approach is revolutionary in that it recommends collective negotiation and the abandonment of secret diplomacy. Hippolyte welcomes this experience with great enthusiasm and sees it as a pragmatic step toward the eventual union of all nations. He travels to Geneva several times to follow the debates over whether and how the League should be established and to speak with statesmen and experts who, like him, sees the League as an indisputable step toward peace.[9]

At the beginning of 1919, travel conditions are still extremely complicated, but Hippolyte and Laura have been separated from the

Master for far too long; for them, the wait is unbearable. In March 1919, they decide to go to the Holy Land despite the instability that still prevails in the Middle East. In Marseille, they board a British ship bound for Egypt and manage to dock at Port Said after being stranded for several days at sea due to the violent revolts that are shaking the country.[10] Laura recalls, "As there was violent rioting in Egypt, it was [well] nigh impossible to get permission to land. But 'Where there is a will, there is a way' was interpreted by [Hippolyte] to read 'Where there is a way, have the wits to find it,' so we landed in Port Said, and that day we were the only civilians that took the train for Cairo, passing through the stations which the insurgents had freshly burnt."[11]

In Cairo, thanks to the help of their friend, Major Tudor-Pole, they obtain a residence permit for Palestine.[12] From Cairo, they go to Haifa, not by sea as in the past, but by train, thanks to the new railway line built by the British during the war. After overcoming all these obstacles, they finally arrive in Haifa, and it is Shoghi Effendi who personally welcomes them at the railway station and takes them straight away to the House of 'Abdu'l-Bahá, where they will be staying.[13] In a letter dated April 5, 1919, Shoghi Effendi recounts to Ahmad Sohrab this very particular day:

> Dear [Ahmad],
>
> From the city of Cairo on March 31st the following telegram was dispatched.
>
> "Expect arrive Saturday love all ~ Dreyfus Barney"
>
> Startling and unexpected as the news broke upon us, it nevertheless filled our hearts with joy and rapture for today at noon we were to welcome two well-known friends of the Cause who are really the first to arrive from Europe, from belligerent countries, from a region that has been devoured by war and pillage, and has undergone the severest trials.
>
> (. . .) We had hardly bid them farewell [Shoghi Effendi was saying good-bye to other visitors], when the train arrived and we

instantly recognized the old, intimate friends who were looking out eagerly to meet a familiar face. The landau of the Master took them directly to the House of the Beloved where they put up and [a] few minutes later the Beloved arrived. Oh! How glad and grateful they were to meet Him, to speak to Him, to hear His voice, to sit beside Him and to feel the touch of His hand. What a terrible time they had both experienced, how uncertain were the conditions they had lived in, how strenuous was the Red Cross Relief work for the Refugees that had been undertaken by Mrs. Dreyfus throughout the war, how delicate and even perilous had been the situation in which Mr. Dreyfus had often found himself, once taken to China and there falling into trouble with the Germans and the story of his return safely to Europe, once "garde-de-voie"[14] of the railway service and once the censor in one of the south French departments at which latter post he had been of service to the Cause. But all was forgotten, every hardship vanished at meeting the face of the Beloved and casting a glance on His radiant countenance.

In the evening, the Beloved sent all the friends to greet and welcome guests at Mirza Jalal's house and there they all gathered, including a group of the Bahai [Bahá'í] students of the American University who had recently arrived for the Easter vacation from Beirut. Their names are as follow: Messrs Ruhi Afnan, Soheil Afnan, Mohamed Ali Afnan, Tofic Yazdi, Seyed Kazim, Mirza Ali Moh. Bakir. The rest due to pressure of work and preparations for final examinations were detained from enjoying these joyous festal days. The friends all extended to the newly arrived guests their heartiest welcome, after which Mr. Dreyfus spoke on some of his bitter and sweet experiences during the war in France and elsewhere.

The news these welcomed friends impart to us reveal the safety, the activity, the loyalty and the longing of the friends of God and the maid-servants of the merciful on the continent of Europe and elsewhere.[15]

As Shoghi Effendi eloquently intimates in his letter, at long last Hippolyte and Laura are reunited with 'Abdu'l-Bahá: they are the first Western Bahá'ís to arrive in the Holy Land since the outbreak of the First World War.[16] The Dreyfus-Barneys spend several days around Mount Carmel, where they have the opportunity to recharge their spiritual "batteries," receive new instructions and advice from the Master, and interact with the Persian friends living in Haifa and 'Akká.

Pilgrimage, 1919. Front and center: 'Abdu'l-Bahá. In the first row: Shoghi Effendi is seated sixth from the left. Hippolyte is seated fifth from the left, and Laura is seated fourth from the left.

One morning, Hippolyte and Laura have a meeting with the students who had greeted and welcomed them upon their arrival, and they engaged in conversation with them on different topics, all related to their mutual experiences during the war. Later in the day, Hippolyte and Laura and a few of the friends have the bounty of entering the central chamber of the Shrine of the Báb, where 'Abdu'l-Bahá joins them.[17] In the words of Shoghi Effendi:

> In the afternoon, we had a most spiritual and delightful meeting. When the Beloved entered the middle room of Makam, all rose to greet him, and the seat the Beloved occupied was in the central position with Mr. and Mrs. Dreyfus on his left, and Haji Mirza Haidar Ali and Mulla Abu Taleb on his right. He spoke as follows in a direct, impressive dignified tone. [. . .] The Beloved then ordered tea to be served and led the friends to the interior of the Tomb where a most ardent and inspiring prayer of praise and thanksgiving was offered; on the whole, as Mrs Dreyfus intimated it was a very lovely and spiritual meeting.[18]

A few days later, the Dreyfus-Barneys, accompanied by Shoghi Effendi and some of the friends from Haifa, have the immense privilege of visiting 'Akká and later praying at the Holy Shrine, the resting place of Bahá'u'lláh at Bahjí.[19] Shoghi Effendi shares the details of this unforgettable day in a letter written to one of his friends:

> Wondrous and remarkable has been the day which we have passed in Acca [Akká]. In view of the lack of time and in order to fulfill previous engagements, a party consisting of Mr. and Mrs. Dreyfus, Ruhi Effendi, two other members of the household and myself, started under a pelting rain and a dark and gloomy sky on our lovely drive along the beach to Acca. The wind changing every now and then in different directions was blowing fiercely and together with the heavy rain and the boisterous waves of a stormy sea added a great deal to the adventurous and unique experiences which we have had today. When we reached the city's gates all alighted from the carriage and with Agha Hassein Ashcha as our guide we went directly to the Barrack in order to visit the old and sacred sites where Baha'o'llah [Bahá'u'lláh] and His seventy followers and co-sharers in exile spent the first weeks and months in their confinement in this fortress of Acca. One after another, imbued with a profound sense of affliction, sympathy and respect visited the long and dark corridors where the friends of the Blessed Beauty were

confined and where they had their meals and rest. We passed then to the well-known sleeping room of the Beloved which was nothing but a dark, small, damp and low-roofed cabin where corpses were washed and wrapped in their shrouds and from the roof of which rain water leaked constantly, so much so that it necessitated the Master's removing his bed and mattress from one spot to another. From there on the same storey we found the remnants of a poorly built and imperfect bath, the remains of a kitchen in which Aga Reza prepared a hot soup at night and a light pilou [polow] at noon for the seventy patients accompanying Baha'o'llah to Acca and whose shares were given and distributed from the hands of the Beloved. Close to it we stood before a room which at present is almost in ruins where Baha'o'llah spent His first days in Acca until a proper and permanent place would be prepared for Him in a higher story of this spacious yet most unhealthy barrack. Going up to the next floor, the different rooms designed to the special attendants and relatives of Baha'o'llah were pointed out to us until we reached the place where the Blessed Beauty and His family lived for nearly a couple of years. We stood silent, deeply touched and prayerful at the Threshold of the room were Baha'o'llah used to stand by its window which faced the walls of the rampart beyond which stood the anxious longing and hopeful pilgrim who had covered long distances in order to catch a glimpse from afar of the Countenance of the Blessed Perfection and to gaze once more in the distance at His Brilliant Beauty.

What was most touching and sad was when we were pointed out a spot on the roof which at that time was not fully constructed and from which, Aghaye Ghosueh Abhar,[20] the younger brother of the Beloved fell to the ground while meditating and absorbed in his evening supplications. The incident related to us was indeed tragic and heartrending and this constituted the end of our survey of that memorable significant moment—the barracks where Baha'o'llah spent His first years of exile in Acca.

> In the afternoon, after having had our lunch to Acca, we drove to Bahjeh [Bahjí] where our friends after years of separation and longing met at the Holy Threshold, visited the Holy Shrine and spent some time in that hallowed spot in deep reverence and profound gratitude.
>
> We returned before sunset and were just in time to be present at the evening meeting and thus to complete a whole series of inestimable and dear experiences which have been ours on this glorious day.[21]

In mid-April, Hippolyte and Laura, revitalized by their stay with the Master, leave Haifa. As Shoghi Effendi testified, "Mr. and Mrs. Dreyfus, due to unavoidable arrangements could not remain long this time with the Beloved but left with a determination to visit again the Master toward the end of this year about November and December. Guided and enlightened by the instructions and the exhortations of the Master they started to Egypt via Jerusalem and thence to France where after remaining for awhile will start for the United States of America and from there will return to the Holy Land."[22]

Hippolyte and Laura decide to take advantage of their presence in Palestine to travel to Jerusalem together for the first time. With the end of the war, amidst the call for the return of Jews to Palestine and the rise of Zionism, the atmosphere in the holy city of Jews, Christians, and Muslims is very tense. By chance, their arrival coincides with the celebration of Easter, which in 1919 falls on the same day for Catholics, Greek Orthodox Christians, and Copts. Intrigued, the couple attends the processions in the holy sepulchre with keen interest. They then return to Egypt via Port Said and board a ship back to France at the end of April.[23]

24 / The Tablets of the Divine Plan

Back in France, Hippolyte and Laura hurry to share the good news from the Holy Land with the community of believers. Then, very quickly, they plan their next journey: it is time for the couple to go to the United States to visit Laura's family, whom they have not seen for more than four years now. Alice needs—even more than ever before—Laura's support, care, and wisdom, as her marriage to Christian is coming to an end.[1]

There is also a second reason that prompts Hippolyte and Laura to go to America as soon as possible: during their stay in Palestine with the Master, the Tablets of the Divine Plan were unveiled in New York.[2] These fourteen Tablets, written by 'Abdu'l-Bahá between 1916 and 1917, during the darkest hours of the first world war, were addressed to Bahá'í communities of the United States and Canada. Considered as the "mandate" and "the supreme charter for teaching," they contain the guidelines for spreading the Message of Bahá'u'lláh throughout the world.[3] The first eight Tablets were written between March 26 and April 22, 1916, and the last six were revealed between February 2 and March 8, 1917, only a month before the United States entered the war. Of the first Tablets, five were published in the *Star of the West* of September 1916. As all communications with the Holy Land were interrupted during the war, the other Tablets were kept for the duration of the war under the Shrine of the Báb on Mount Carmel. At the end of the war, they were sent to the United

States and unveiled to believers at the end of April 1919 during a historic ceremony.[4]

In these Tablets, the Master calls believers to travel throughout the American continent and beyond to spread the Faith. His advice is extremely pragmatic: He names the regions and countries where the Cause needs dedicated servants, and He invites believers to go there to establish new Bahá'í communities and Local Spiritual Assemblies. The arrival of Hippolyte and Laura is therefore eagerly awaited by the different communities of believers. Finally, they will be able to receive the latest information from the Holy Land and listen to the instructions the couple has just received from 'Abdu'l-Bahá. There is also no doubt that this call to action on the part of the Master has affected Hippolyte in a profound manner, for as we know by now, he has always been, and is always ready, to respond immediately and fervently to the instructions and directives of 'Abdu'l-Bahá.

On August 9, they set sail to Le Havre on *Le France,* the same ship that had brought them back from New York to Le Havre five years earlier. A few weeks after they arrive in the United States, Hippolyte receives a letter from 'Abdu'l-Bahá, Who rejoices at his presence in the United States and entrusts him with His hopes:

> Praise be to God that thou hast arrived in thy homeland under His divine protection, and wert able to rest and once again meet with the friends. I beseech God that thou mayest help them to remain firm and steadfast in the Covenant [. . .]
>
> My hope is that when thou dost sojourn in America, thou shalt infuse the spirit of the Covenant into those souls as well, attaining unto a new joy every day. Upon thee rest the Glory of the Most Glorious.[5]

In Washington, they spend time with Laura's family and visit as many friends and believers as they can among those residing in nearby communities. In a letter written in September to a believer in California, Hippolyte confides that he and Laura are busy meeting the friends of Washington, New York, Boston, and Green Acre, with whom they share the latest instructions given by 'Abdu'l-Bahá.[6] In addition, their activities of spreading the Faith continue: every Friday evening, starting from 5pm, they receive the people who come to listen to their talks in the residence they share with Alice.[7] Hippolyte seems to be fairly busy, but, as he intimates to his sister in a letter dated December 3, 1919, the placid and mundane conditions are monotonous and unsatisfying for this indefatigable servant of the Cause: "We cannot leave Washington yet: before six weeks, there is no need to move, and Laura feels that her duty is with her mother who needs her company.[8] Life is monotonous: dinners at home two or three times a week, everyone is very friendly and 'Little One'[9] is always popular. I do bridge at the circle every day from 4 to 7 with retired old admirals and generals, and the rest of the time is devoted to the Cause. Did you announce the wedding to 'Abdu'l-Bahá?[10] It could be that in February we will find ourselves in Haifa. But nothing is decided yet."[11]

In the winter of 1919, Hippolyte, undoubtedly because he was determined to respond promptly to the Master's call, prepares a journey to the countries of the Caribbean and South America, to locations specifically mentioned by 'Abdu'l-Bahá in the Tablets of the Divine Plan. Between December and January, he visits various embassies and consulates and receives visas for Costa Rica, Peru, Chile, the British West Indies[12] (a travel pass to Jamaica and the Bahamas), Cuba, and Panama.

On January 15, 1920, Hippolyte is in Havana; he writes to Yvonne, "There is a dockers' strike here as elsewhere but a very special climate. The journey so far has been remarkably pleasant, and it augurs well for the rest. I will return here in 15 days and will leave the ship to spend a few days with the Riondas[13] in the interior."[14]

One week later, on January 21, 1920, Hippolyte is in Panama! From his hotel in the Ancón district of Panama City, the Tivoli Hotel, he writes to Yvonne, "My dear, the most interesting trip. Unfortunately, the flu in Havana prevented us from disembarking in Jamaica on the way. We will do this on the return. I hope that I can still be in Havana on the 29th where I have to give a lecture. You have no idea what the Americans have done here: it is fantastic. We leave tonight for Costa Rica and if the sea continues to be so beautiful, it will be really delicious: like a hundred travelers only on a large steamer of 1500 tons."[15]

Which countries did he visit after Cuba and Panama? The rest of his journey remains shrouded in mystery at the time of this writing; it is not known if he was able to travel to all the countries he wanted to visit. We only know that, in March 1920, two months after his departure from America, Hippolyte returns from Panama to Washington, DC, where he receives a new passport that will allow him to return to France. In the days following his return, Hippolyte, relentless in his eagerness to promote the Cause, gives a speech on "The Unity of Mankind" at the Pouch Gallery in New York on March 14.[16]

From New York, the Dreyfus-Barneys, accompanied by Alice, take a ship, the *Canada,* to Sicily. After a stopover in Oran so that the *Canada* can refuel with coal, they arrive on March 31 in Palermo after an excellent crossing. They first disembark from the ship and head to the *Hotel des Palmes,* then travel to Taormina—a picturesque, slow-paced town on the east coast of Sicily—where they can properly rest. Alice, by contrast, decides to stay at the famous luxury hotel *Villa Igiea,* which was the most prestigious hotel in the region. A few days later, they all leave for Tunis, in Tunisia.

Very interestingly, when they are in North Africa, Shoghi Effendi, who is a student in the United Kingdom at this time, is traveling to France. Hippolyte, always very much aware of the latest news concerning the Cause, writes to Yvonne, who was still living in Paris at the time, "I learned at the time that Shoghi Rabbani, the grandson of Abdul-Baha, a very nice boy of about 22 years old speaking good French and English, has arrived in Paris to rest. He is at Borghese, 29 boulevard Victor Hugo in Neuilly, where Rouha [Rúhá] has been for some time. He is her nephew. Do you want to call and see if we can do something for him, and tell him that we plan to go home around June 10th? If he needs anything, do it for me and we will settle it when I get back. I'm sure you'll be glad to get to know him."[17]

In Tunisia, Hippolyte is asked by the Master to carry out a very special mission: he is to visit the small community of local believers and, as always, to encourage them. Above all, he is to meet the French colonial authorities to discuss the situation of the Bahá'ís in the protectorate. Indeed, a decade earlier, during his journey to Persia, Hippolyte had met several consuls and ambassadors, including French diplomats stationed in Tehran. During one of their conversations, one of these diplomats told Hippolyte how impressed he was by the effect of the Faith on the Persians and suggested that the presence of the Bahá'ís in the protectorate of Tunisia might be a good idea. After consultation with 'Abdu'l-Bahá, Hippolyte was given the task of facilitating the arrival of Persian teachers into the French-speaking countries of North Africa. Hippolyte then relied on his professional network to establish a transparent and continual communication with the diplomat and orientalist Eustache de Lorey.[18]

As Hippolyte tells Mrs. Mary Rabb[19] in a letter, the first teacher to visit Tunisia was Shaykh Muḥyí'd-Dín Ṣabri, who stayed for several weeks and won many victories in his work of spreading the Faith.[20] It is important to know that since Bahá'í teachers generally are not paid to reside abroad, they must find work to support themselves. Mr. de Lorey then proposed bringing in Persians with professional skills in sectors where the Tunisian government had identified a need, such as carpentry, weaving, or tapestry. He also suggested placing them in local companies where foreigners (Syrians or Egyptians) were already recruited, so that their integration would be more natural.[21]

Then, with the beginning of the first world war, all these teaching projects were suspended. The arrival of Hippolyte in 1920 therefore does the greatest good for the nascent community and allows them, as Laura mentions, "[to obtain] from the French authorities' permission to have the Bahá'í teachings promulgated in Tunisia."[22] After Hippolyte's death, the Guardian would also make it a point to acknowledge Hippolyte's role in "the stimulating encouragement to the Bahá'í community of Tunis on the northern shores of Africa."[23] In two letters written to Yvonne during his stay in Tunisia, Hippolyte shares his thoughts about two important events. He writes, "I was delighted with my tour in the South where I met interesting religious leaders. I continue my research here with Puaux[24] who is extremely intelligent, and who sees my activity very favourably. He will introduce me to the Bey[25] next week. As all this may still take me some time, Laura and her mother who has enough of Tunis leave tomorrow for Hammam Keskhoutine, Constantine, Timgad, and Biskra. I'll join them as soon as I can."[26]

A few days later, he writes:

> It is I who opened your letter to Laura, because Little One having had enough of Tunis, they left yesterday morning at 6am for Algeria. I will join them in a few days, but do not want to leave again because I am meeting the most interesting personalities of the Muslim world. Yesterday I was received by the Bey surrounded by his ministers at the Palace of la Marsa.[27] The Director of protocol introduced me, and I told him of the interest in spreading Baha'i ideas in these regions. In short, by leaving here I will leave the ground well prepared for those whom Abdul-Baha will want to send. It is certain that the importance of the movement will not be realized in France until England, the United States and Germany, which are increasingly inspired by it, have fully joined it. The work accomplished here by France is indeed the most interesting, and in many ways far superior to that of the English in Egypt. You have no idea of the superb roads that sink in the south to the middle of the Sahara; and in general, the indigenous recognizes the benefits of the protectorate. But spiritual culture should not be neglected for too long, or civilization will one day bring the disorders of Europe here.[28]

All these efforts, associated with a constant correspondence with the authorities, will lead to great victories in the following year. In a letter dated May 1921, Hippolyte shares some exciting news with his sister: "I received a very good letter from the Tunisian government, eager to see the Cause spread in the country. My missionary,[29] an Arab from Cairo University must be on his way now and I hope there will be good results although the difficulties are many. The Mills[30] are in Haifa: I guess you will see them in Paris on the return: make them our friends and tell them to wait for us or come to meet us. Laura and I each send you much love."[31]

After Hippolyte communicates to Haifa this stirring news, 'Abdu'l-Bahá invites Shaykh Muḥyí'd-Dín, in a missive dated 1921 and written in both Arabic and Persian, to return to Tunis to teach the Faith. Once there, the activities of the shaykh do not remain unnoticed. On October 4, 1923, Mr. de Castillon Saint-Victor,[32] delegate to the General Residence of France in Tunis, writes to the French Minister for Foreign Affairs:

> I have the honour to inform you that Sheikh Mohieddine Sabri,[33] a 55-year-old Persian teacher in Cairo, and Mohamed Sesbi Kesroui, a 20-year-old merchant from Medina in Damascus, are currently on a journey to Tunisia. The second descends from a Kairouan family. [. . .] Mohieddine Sabri makes Behaiste propaganda and distributes a small pamphlet on this doctrine. He made contact in Kairouan with the destourians[34] of the locality. [. . .] The Tunisian "old turbans," especially the members of the Chara naturally welcomed without pleasure the news of the passage of Sheikh Behaiste within the Regency. [. . .] A local newspaper even asked for his expulsion.[35]

Thus, despite the difficulties and the danger, the Faith can, little by little, emerge from obscurity and spread in Tunisian territory. In 1923, Hippolyte writes, for a daily newspaper published in Tunis, *La Vie Tunisienne,* a multi-page article titled "Le Bahaïsme."[36]

25 / Adventures at the Borders of Indochina

Back in Paris, Hippolyte and Laura are already planning their next journey, and this time, it will be to the Far East! Eager to respond to the best of their ability to the instructions revealed in the Tablets of the Divine Plan, the couple, in regular and frequent consultation with ʻAbdu'l-Bahá, decide to go to Asia to visit as many of the territories specified by the Master as possible in reference to this part of the globe.[1]

During the preparation for their journey, Hippolyte and Laura welcome Shoghi Effendi while passing through France. Shoghi Rabbani, age twenty-three, is resting for a few weeks in Neuilly-sur-Seine before continuing on his way to Oxford, where he is enrolled as an undergraduate student. One afternoon in July, the believers in Paris, then gathered at Loulie Mathews' house, are surprised and delighted to see Shoghi Effendi appear and join their gathering. Marzieh Gail writes:

> A knock at the tall double-doors during the afternoon [. . .] and a young Zoroastrian Bahá'í stepped into the room and in some excitement announced the arrival of Shoghi Effendi who then immediately and joyfully entered the room.
>
> What unspeakable delight ensued, amongst one and all, as we were individually greeted by him. He appeared so fresh and radiant, so powerful, and joy-inspiring!

> The Guardian (as he [Shoghi Effendi] was to become) was invited to address us, and he did so, in his perfect and cultivated English. He read the Tablet, written by 'Abdu'l-Bahá, that introduced him to the friends in Europe and other foreign lands.
>
> In this Tablet, the first names mentioned were Ali-Kuli Khan and Mrs. Khan, with loving words of praise; Mr. and Mrs. Dreyfus, with praise; the two American painters (in whose studio Bahá'í meetings were often held) Mr. and Mrs. Scott, with praise, and in the end, the names of Mrs. Mathews and her daughter (Wanden) of whom 'Abdu'l-Bahá had written this line—"They are faithful."[2]

Around the same time, Hippolyte receives a new letter from 'Abdu'l-Bahá. In a very moving way, the Master confides in him how sorrowful He is to learn of the death of Hippolyte's paternal aunt because everything that brings grief to Hippolyte "makes him sad." Then 'Abdu'l-Bahá tells Hippolyte how delighted He is to have regular correspondence with him and that He is looking forward to his visit to Haifa this winter. Finally, as usual, He reiterates His hope that the flame of the love of God will be ignited in Paris.[3]

Before their departure, Hippolyte obtains two letters of recommendation from his diplomatic friends, which will be very useful, as formal written introductions, to enable him to meet expatriate officials in Asia. They will also be necessary for the smooth progression of a difficult and risky journey. The first, signed by the minister of foreign affairs to the diplomatic and consular agents of France in the Far East, states, "This letter will be presented to you by Mr. H. Dreyfus-Barney, who is accompanied by Mrs. H. Dreyfus-Barney, on a pleasure and art journey around the world and especially in the Far East. Although our compatriots are always assured of receiving the best welcome from you, I would nevertheless like to make a special recommendation to you, Mr. and Mrs. H. Dreyfus-Barney, and I would be obliged if you would be willing to lend them the support of your good offices if necessary."[4]

The second is written by Philippe Berthelot,[5] Plenipotentiary Minister, Head of the Ministry of Foreign Affairs office: "Dear friend, please give your best welcome to my friends Mr. and Mrs. Dreyfus-Barney, who are making an art journey to Asia. Please also recommend them to your friends in Indochina and give them a letter for the governor? I would be very grateful. Yours sincerely, ..."[6]

On their journey to the Far East, they first stop in the Holy Land. On November 6, 1920, Hippolyte and Laura board the liner SS *Narkunda* for Egypt, dock at Port Said, journey onward to Kantara,[7] and eventually arrive in Haifa on November 15.[8]

Upon their arrival in Haifa, they find that several American believers are also present. Helen Goodall, Ella Cooper, Kathryn Frankland, and Georgia Ralston—all from California—are completing their pilgrimage, and it is an opportunity to form new friendships and strengthen old ones. This time, Hippolyte and Laura stay ten days with the Master, the Holy Family and the believers serving in Haifa, receiving valuable advice in order to best prepare them for their journey to the far reaches of Asia. As Hippolyte writes in a letter to Yvonne, "We have just spent a wonderful week here, in the house of Rouha [Rúhá] who is always so affectionate: her children are charming. The Master is in excellent health and at the moment has about forty visitors, some of whom have been there for several months."[9]

On November 25, Hippolyte and Laura return to Port Said. From there, they embark on the *Princess Juliana,* bound for the Dutch East Indies.[10] The crossing lasts sixteen days, and the liner makes only one stop, in Colombo, on the island of Ceylon.[11] Hippolyte, true to himself, does not lose any opportunity to share the message, and he takes advantage of his meetings onboard the ship to talk about the Faith. On December 12, as the ship approaches the Indonesian coast, he gives a lecture in which he sets out the principles of the Faith. When we now look back at this sea voyage, we can see clearly that Hippolyte is making every effort to meet a lot of people on the ship. The enthusiasm animating his many conversations results in his being invited to give a public talk on the ship, in which he presents the tenets of the Faith. Concerning Hippolyte's gift of friendship, and his talent for befriending strangers, Laura recalls, "[He made] friends easily wherever he went. Sometimes on a train or a steamer, at the bridge table, at the Sorbonne, and again in long walks which he liked to take through the city and in the country."[12]

A few days after their departure, 'Abdu'l-Bahá shares the following words with His family and friends:

> The friends who have departed recently, that is, the friends from America—Mrs. Goodall, Mrs. Cooper, Mrs. Ralston, Mrs. Frankland, and from France, Mr. and Mrs. Dreyfus, have determined to strive to promote and spread the Word of God with all their energy. They have confined all their thoughts to this excellent intention . . .
>
> They departed from here with utmost sincerity of purpose and devotion to Bahá'u'lláh. The truth of this statement was not so well known while they were here, but after they return home, this will become manifest, and you will hear what they will achieve. Now you should pray for them and supplicate confirmation and assistance for them that they may be able to promote the Word of God and be favoured with the privilege of serving the world of humanity, that they may help to establish universal peace and lay the foundation of the oneness of the world of humanity. They should be kind to all people and prefer the welfare of others to their own. When they attain to these characteristics, the Hosts of the Supreme Concourse will assist them, and the confirmations of the Kingdom of Abha will surround them. Every one of them will become a brilliant candle and a victorious banner, not only they themselves, but others will become astonished; but they are in need of your prayers. Whenever you are begging [supplicating for divine assistance] ask confirmations for them.
>
> Today every soul who gives up his own thoughts and desires and mingles with the people with utmost sincerity, such a one is surrounded by the Hosts of the Supreme Concourse: as a mag-

> net attracts iron these benevolent intentions similarly attract the divine confirmations. You shall see before long that every one of the friends will be confirmed to achieve distinguished services. Do not think that he or she is weak or without fame; consider his characteristics, his sincerity, truthfulness, willingness to serve, trustworthiness, and so on . . . , not his position in society. Such a person is confirmed, otherwise all doors of confirmation will be closed.
>
> Therefore, you should supplicate and pray for such friends as these and implore confirmations and assistance.[13]

On December 13, late in the day, Hippolyte and Laura land in Sabang, on the northwestern end of Sumatra Island. The vegetation is lush, the weather is heavy, and the air is extremely humid. They spend the night in the port and leave the next morning; they sail along the coast of Sumatra Island, cross the strait of Malacca, make a short stop in Singapore, a British colony, and arrive on December 18 at Batavia,[14] capital of the Dutch colony, located on the island of Java. A few days earlier, Hippolyte summarized for his sister his first impressions:

> The boat emptied yesterday of half the passengers in [Belawan], and since then we have been sailing lazily on a lead-colored sea with floating palm debris. There must have been a cyclone lately, but today it is calm and flat: we avoided another one off Jokarta and our trip was most happy.
>
> Our stopover in Sabang, the first port of Sumatra was most interesting: a small mountainous island covered with lakes and forests that come to the sea. We all went for a swim in a freshwater pool in the shade of the rubber trees while the monkeys called us from the tops of the branches. How beautiful—and the sunsets!
>
> Tomorrow we arrive in Singapore where I will have our passports prepared for Java and Saturday in Batavia.

> I gave a lecture on Baha'ism which was very successful and brought me interesting relations for Java—among others, Helfrick [Helfferich],[15] the brother of the Minister whose cabin we occupied from Port Said and who was burning with desire to get to know us.
>
> Our plan of travel to Java, and the people we will meet there is now specified, and I can only indicate it to you briefly because we must not, unfortunately, think of hearing from you there.[16] After 8 days in Batavia, we will go to Buitenzorg where I have a friend from the control.[17] Then in Bandoeng [Bandung], Djokjakarta [Yogyakarta], Surabaya, Tegen, Gebirg, Garoet and the island of Bali where we will be received by the resident. We will probably be in Saigon at the end of January.[18]

They stay about three weeks on the island of Java. They cross jungle, lakes, rivers, and make stops in the cities of Buitenzorg [Bogor], Garoet [Garut], Djokjakarta [Yogyakarta], Borobodur [Borobudur], Surakarta, Tosari, and Surabaya. They divide their time between discovering religious sites where Buddhist, Hindu, and Muslim civilizations coexist in an exceptional way,[19] and they meet with many of the local authorities,[20] indigenous princes, expatriate Europeans,[21] and Arab merchants. They also try, when they go to the markets, to establish contacts with the local population.

Hippolyte and Laura then go to the island of Bali, where they stay for about ten days. They pass through the towns and villages of Denpasar, Bangli, Kintamani, Karangasem, and Singaraja. On their first day on the island, the city of Denpasar is abuzz; it is the festival of cockfighting. The Dreyfus-Barneys attend with heightened attention to this spectacular blood sport, which is as unusual as it is disturbing.[22]

On the island, boarding houses called "rest houses"[23] are made available to travelers by the colonial authorities, if they are not then occupied by colonial officials during the course of their travel duties. In one of these rest houses, they meet the regional opium controller[24] with whom they become acquainted.[25] He takes them around in his car and introduces them to his friends, the local governor, and also to one of the princes of the island with whom they spend an evening. This chance meeting with the regional controller of opium enables them to establish more and more contacts.

On January 18, 1921, they leave Bali, cross the island of Java from east to west, and reach the Strait Settlements,[26] a territory including Penang, Malacca, Singapore, and administered by the East India Company for the British Colonial Empire. They stay one short week in Singapore, where they observe Englishmen, Indians, Chinese, and Malays living in harmony. Life there is "comfortable and easy," and the friends they meet are "settled pleasantly."[27]

On January 30, they leave Singapore by ship for Indochina. French Indochina is one of the major objectives of the Tablets of the Divine Plan, and Hippolyte and Laura's visit has a unique historical character, as they are most probably the first Bahá'ís to visit this part of the world. They arrive in Saigon[28] on February 2 and are greeted by Hippolyte's friends,[29] who house them in their large colonial mansion. Laura recalls, "After four months traveling, we [were][at last] in a real home, a home such as one could have in our countries a score of years ago—spacious, comfortable, and peaceful."[30]

In 1920, French Indochina is a vast territory consisting of the colony of Cochinchina (southern Vietnam), the protectorates of Annam and Tonkin (central and northern Vietnam), the protectorate of Cambodia, the protectorate of Laos, and the Chinese leasehold territory of Kouang-Cheou-Wan (peninsula to the west of Guangdong province).

The couple spend a week in the company of their friends visiting Saigon and the nearby region. On February 9, they travel to Phnom Penh by car, in their friends' small Renault, and they reach the capital of the Cambodian protectorate after 280 kilometers of road and three river-crossings by ferry boats. One evening, they participate in a reception organized by the King of Cambodia for diplomats, foreign personalities, and the Prince of Siam[31] and his royal family. Hippolyte takes this opportunity to form new friendships with those who are gathered there.[32]

On February 14, after a four-hour drive to the Great Lakes region, a seven-hour rowboat crossing, an hour by sampan up the Siem Reap River, and an hour by car, Hippolyte and Laura reach Angkor. They are amazed and enchanted by the archaeological site of the ancient capital of the Khmer Empire and its temples dedicated to Hindu deities. Some sites are totally buried in the forest, while others are only accessible via a ride in a howdah on an elephant's back. After three days of excursion, Hippolyte and Laura return to Phnom Penh, then to Saigon, where they arrive on February 20 after two days of stormy navigation on the Mekong River.[33]

They stay about six weeks in Cochinchina, three in Saigon, and three in Cape Saint Jacques,[34] a resort destination for privileged colonials that is known for its pleasant seaside. During these six weeks, Hippolyte makes contacts in two ways: first, he uses his address book to meet personalities who invite him to lunches, dinners, or to participate in other activities; secondly, he takes advantage of their stay in hotels to engage in conversation with people who sit to rest in the reception halls, or at meals when they share the same table with other travelers. His new contacts are therefore mainly Europeans or Annamites who have received a European education and speak French or English. In his personal travel diary, he notes the names of the director of the Continental Hotel in Saigon, the governor of the province of Cochinchina, mayors and general residents, hunters, and farmers.[35]

The complexity of the social and ethnic divisions that exist between Europeans and Vietnamese, and also between Vietnamese and ethnic minorities, make their objective of meeting with the local population particularly difficult to achieve. During their stay in Indochina, Hippolyte and Laura take lunch breaks in the villages, meet groups of natives in the middle of the forest, stop along the Mekong River in the fishing villages, and engage in pleasant exchanges with their Annamite servants. However, due to the language barrier, it is often difficult for them to have in-depth conversations with those they meet.

At the beginning of April, Hippolyte and Laura return to the north of Indochina. They cross the Annam and pass through Tourane,[36] where they meet American missionaries who, alas, "are of the narrow variety not feeling the need of spreading their gospel by works of social value. They denounce Buddhism, Confucianism and Catholicism. They have been unable to see the bond of brotherhood linking together the great teachers."[37] Then they climb the Col des Nuages,[38] and stop for six days in Hue, the ancient capital of the Annam empire that is crossed by the famous Perfume River (Sông Hương).

On April 14, Hippolyte and Laura reach Hanoi, capital of the protectorate of Tonkin and French Indochina. As in Saigon, they establish new contacts through meetings organized by their friends. In particular, they spend several days in the company of the very progressive indigenous governor of the city and his family, all of whom speak French. During their two weeks in Hanoi, Hippolyte and Laura take two days to visit Hạ Long Bay and admire the limestone karsts and caves that dot the emerald waters of the Gulf of Tonkin.[39]

On May 1, they decide to explore the north of Tonkin. They roam the mountains, jungles, and rice fields on the plateau for ten days. On their return to Hanoi, Laura falls seriously ill, and her fever rises to over 104 degrees. Her strength seems to leave her, and the doctors are unfortunately unable to make a consistent or definite diagnosis. In a letter dated May 24, Hippolyte shares with Yvonne the events of the last weeks:

> Please excuse me for letting yesterday pass without writing to you for your feast, although I often think of you, but I am still looking after my patient. Laura has been in the same condition for 16 days. Still do not tell her mother or Natalie who would torment each other unnecessarily. Dr. Degarce who sees her every day seems satisfied that she has no functional disorder, not even the mildest migraine, and confines himself to prescribing bed rest, baths when her temperature exceeds 38.5 and a liquid diet every two hours. You see how my time goes; in the evening from 6 to 8, I do bridge at the circle, or a car ride with the Lochards. In a few days we will make a new serodiagnosis,

> and maybe we can then give a name to this fever before which we are only helpless spectators.[40]

A week later, Hippolyte sends the latest updates to his family:

> By this same mail, I write to Natalie to tell her that Laura has had a fever for a few days (I do not tell her 20 days) and that today the doctors wondered if it was malaria, they said that it was a slight pleural condition. (. . .) Finally! I believe that all this will change our plans and that the trip to Yunnan is compromised. When the sweetheart has recovered, I will think about returning. But at this time and until November, we must not think of returning via the Indian Ocean due to the monsoons which make travel very difficult so it will no doubt be through America that we will return. You have no idea how good the Lochards are to us: they give us their clothes, every night they come to take me for a ride in the car and make me get some air. They really treat us like brother and sister![41]

Laura remains bedridden for five weeks and finds great comfort in Hippolyte's delicate and dedicated attention: "The incomplete part was to force myself to take my nourishment or to stand on my feet when I went to take one of my too numerous baths. All of this difficulty was made easier for me by [Hippolyte], who was always there to care for me with solicitude and skill."[42]

On June 27, Laura finally recovers. They leave together for southern China, to Yunnan Fu:[43] from Hanoi, they go to Laokai where they take a truck to cross the Sino-Vietnamese border. Seven years after leaving the country in the utmost panic and confusion, they are back in China, this time in the south, in Amicheou.[44] Then, they take a train to the region's nerve centre, Yunnan Fu, 1,800m above sea level, the perfect place to escape the enervating heat of summer.

They spend the three summer months in a house made available to them by one of their friends in Tonkin. During their stay, most often during dinners, they meet several official figures, as well as a few Chinese people, often businessmen. The instability in the region, where lurking rebel troops and brigands specialize in the kidnapping of foreigners, forced them not to leave the city. They observe in the streets the daily life of the many ethnic minorities who populate the city, but an "invisible wall" separates local Chinese life from the "world" of foreigners, and Laura would later say that, alas, the Chinese "have remained hidden from my observation."[45] In a new letter written to his sister, Hippolyte writes:

> Fortunately, we are very well here, and the country is very interesting. I am now in contact with the Muslim leaders who receive me at the mosque and who have allowed me to take pictures there. Within a few days we will start excursions in the surrounding area. Only the Chinese authorities dissuade us from spending the night outside because of the pirates, which for a while at least will prevent us from going too far. I send you on the reverse of an invitation to lunch the summary menu of the meal offered to us yesterday by the Director of the Chinese telegraph, in a delightful pavilion on the edge of a lake covered with pink lotus. In the evening we had dinner at the Consulate, big hoopla, 16 seats and as many French dishes this time—if that were to continue our next stop would be at Royal.[46]

On September 25, they leave Yunnan Fu and return to Hanoi. On October 1, they travel to Hong Kong by sea. They spend a day with Persian friends who take them around the island and invite them to dinner at their home. Once again, their days are punctuated by meals: they meet Sir Catchick Paul Chater, a member of the executive council of the British territory of Hong Kong, and spend time with a clergyman named "Father Robert."[47] Hippolyte and Laura spend a day strolling in the alleys of the island of Macau to discover and explore the Portuguese colony.[48]

From Hong Kong, they go to Shamian, a Franco-British concession located on the Pearl River, west of central Canton in mainland China, and then to Canton (now Guangzhou). They spend an afternoon with Dr. Wu Ting Fang,[49] whom they had already met in Shanghai in 1914. They have "a long heart to heart talk" with him, and their conversation focuses first on the political situation in China during which, with tears in his eyes, Wu Ting Fang confides his difficulties in moving his country forward. Then, they address the topic of religions and faith. Laura writes, "We found him as always a fervent Theosophist and interested in Baha'ism, and it was with hope in our hearts for the welfare of China that we bade goodbye to the wise living old man."[50]

After a few days in Canton, Hippolyte and Laura decide to travel to Wuchow, despite the dissuasive advice of their friends: indeed, this port city is known for being one of the largest hideouts for pirates and brigands in the region. Regardless, they spend a day there and meet the missionaries of the city who, despite the dangers and difficulties that surround them, try to spread the gospel to the local people. From there, they return to Hong Kong on October 26, then to Saigon, which they reach on November 8.[51]

After two weeks in Saigon, they visit, once again, the majestic site of Angkor in Cambodia. This time, they stay five days, and they feel the same awe and wonder as before. They spend the following week in southern Cambodia, where they visit a leper home in the middle of the jungle, and then return to Saigon. With the end of their stay in Indochina approaching, they decide to go to Dalat and Nha Trang, cities they have not yet visited, located to the north of Saigon.[52]

On December 18, 1921, they embark on the *Kishu Maru,* bound for Burma. They make a twenty-four-hour stop in Singapore, another in Penang on Christmas Day, and reach Rangoon in the last week of December. Hippolyte is now back in the Burmese capital, more than sixteen years after his first visit to Rangoon (now Yangon).[53]

Upon their arrival, the couple go to Spark Street, where the Persian friend who had hosted Hippolyte lived in 1905. They tell themselves that this friend will be able to direct them to the other Bahá'ís in the city; however, when they reach Spark Street, they are dismayed. Everything there has been demolished, and the land on which the house once stood has been converted into a public garden! They then head to one of the Persian restaurants in the city, but no one knows how to contact the Bahá'ís. They decide to return to their hotel, the Strand Hotel, and, at the height of their disappointment, they discover to their delight that the director is an Armenian Persian. The latter, thanks to his contacts with the Persian community, manages to find two Bahá'ís from the city.[54]

In the early days of their stay in Rangoon, Hippolyte accompanies Laura to visit the main tourist attractions of the city, including the Shwedagon Pagoda, a stupa of great beauty that, according to legend, contains relics of four ancient Buddhas, including the hair of Buddha Gautama. On the afternoon of December 27, they eventually have their first contact with Bahá'ís in over a year since their departure from Port Said. Laura describes this meeting with the two believers:

> One was a blind, elderly Persian; the other, a young professor Cashmere. To be more at ease to talk, we had refreshments served in a small private dining room of the hotel. The old gentleman spoke of the time when [Hippolyte] had been here years and years ago; the young man asked twice if we had received news from Haifa. I wondered at his insistence, as I had already answered that we had received our last mail [during] the first part of November in Saigon. "But you must have newer news?" He began to cry and said, "The news is not good." Silence. I hardly spoke out the words: "The Master is dead?" And he nodded, adding, "on the 28 November; it is only yesterday that we received the cable from Bombay."[55]

Hippolyte is stunned by the announcement of this news, so painful, so sudden, so totally unexpected. The departure of the beloved Master for the Kingdom of Abhá seems completely unimaginable and leaves him speechless. Laura is devastated and disconsolate.[56]

After gradually regaining their composure, they send a telegram to the Holy Family to offer their condolences and ask them whether they should hasten immediately to Haifa or continue their teaching journey to India and visit the communities of believers, as the Master had asked them. As Hippolyte has not been in contact with his own family for several weeks now, he sends to Yvonne the following message, a letter that poignantly reveals to us his profound spiritual maturity, as expressed in the last three sentences in the passage quoted below:

> We learned of Abdul-Baha's death when we arrived in Rangoon where the friends announced it to us: we were far from expecting it, because we had another letter from him a few weeks ago, not even two months ago: we have no details yet, but in response to a dispatch, the Jalals[57] have begged us to come as soon as possible. Our stay in the Indies will therefore be considerably shortened, and we will probably be in Haifa toward the end of February. It is a great loss for all of us, a light that goes out in the world . . . and the responsibility of each will be greatly increased. I hope he left some instructions that we can carry out. For him, he reached the goal he desired, and he had truly accomplished his work![58]

Over the next four days, they participate in two meetings organized by the local community. The first takes place at the home of one of the believers in central Rangoon. Laura writes, "One month after the departure of the Master, we went to a meeting of Bahá'is in a home in Rangoon. Everyone had the firm composure of those who know where their duty lies and how their love and loyalty can be expressed."[59]

The second meeting takes place in the outskirts of Rangoon, in Kamayut. The atmosphere is the same, and the friends know that despite the sadness of the news of the Master's departure, their task now is to help the world by teaching the Faith, by living a dignified life, and by reflecting the teachings that the Master had devoted Himself to disseminating, with patience and love, throughout His entire life of selfless service.[60]

On December 31, they leave Rangoon for Calcutta, which they reach on January 3. Upon their arrival, they receive several telegrams from the Holy Land, which inform them that their presence in Haifa is expected as soon as possible.[61]

Hippolyte and Laura do not hesitate. To get to the Holy Land, they must travel to Bombay, where ships depart for destinations in the Middle East. On January 9, 1922, Hippolyte and Laura embark on a crossing of India, which takes them from the far east of the country, Calcutta, to its western tip. They travel more than two thousand kilometers in less than a month and pass through Benares, Lucknow, Agra, New Delhi, Jaipur, and Ahmedabad.[62]

In Ahmedabad, the manager of the hotel where they reside writes them a letter of recommendation so that they can meet his friend, Mahatma Gandhi.[63] When they arrive at Gandhi's house, a young Indian greets them and warns them that his master will receive them shortly but that he cannot speak, as it is his day of silence. This interview therefore takes place in the following way: Hippolyte asks his questions aloud, and Gandhi answers them in writing. Their conversation, short and respectful, is mainly about the country's independence movement, although, presumably, Hippolyte would have spoken about the Bahá'í Faith when he met the Mahatma. The only record we have been able to find of this meeting so far are Laura's recollection of questions asked by Hippolyte regarding the political situation in India:

> Gandhi: "I am very sorry; today is my day of silence. You may speak but I must only write my answers, I am glad to meet you, but you must excuse me for not being able to speak to you today."
>
> Question: "What difference is there between civil disobedience and non-cooperation?"
>
> Gandhi: "Non-cooperation is a wider term, and includes civil disobedience. When I don't keep a title, I do not offer civil disobedience, but when I don't pay a tax, I do. Both acts are non-cooperation."

Question: "Isn't the movement turning to Anglophobia? French seems to me more in favour than British."

Gandhi: "The movement is neither against the British nor against the other foreigners. It is against the system of practical slavery that the British have established. We refuse to participate in the symbols of our own slavery. That is human nature as it is. Those who do good turn to one are liked. Those who do harm are disliked. The movement is going beyond the lower part of our nature and teaching us to convert even the evil doer."

Question: "What is the minimum you expect to get through this campaign?

Gandhi: "At the present I do not think we have sufficiently purified ourselves to gain what we want. But I do expect, if all goes well, in a short while, to be able to again redress of the Khalifat[64] [Khilafat] and the Punjab wrongs and the Swaraj[65] in accordance with a scheme drawn up by popular representatives."

Question: "How do you hope to settle the Khalifat question?

Gandhi: "Turkey should have all the territories which are predominantly Turkish in nationality, and foreign influence should be entirely removed from Arabian territories. If the British people accept the Mussalman [Muslim] position and sincerely work with us, it will meet the case. The Shias are with the Sunnis in thought at any rate on the question of the Khalifat."

Question: "And the Punjab wrongs?"

Gandhi: "There are certain things that do need to be done about the Punjab. The officials who have grievously wronged the Punjabis should no longer be in our services or our pay.

The men who have been wrongly fined must have their fines refunded, and the men who are still wrongly in prison should be discharged."

Question: "How do you account for the retirement of the President of the Congress?"

Gandhi: "The President's retiral is still an enigma to me. He has been always noted for his patriotism. This is one of the things which it is so difficult to explain. I have called it cussedness in private conversation. He was nettled and he was thrown off his balance. He is new to the renovated life in the country."

Question: "Will civil disobedience start next month?"

Gandhi: "If nothing comes out of the talk of round table conference, and if nothing unforeseen appears in our ranks, civil disobedience in specified areas will commence next month."

Hippolyte: "I must apologize for taking so much of your time."

Gandhi: "Do please ask all the questions you wish."

Hippolyte: "Please sign."

Hippolyte: "May I take your picture?"

Gandhi: "I never give a sitting. You may take the picture without asking me to take up any position. You will have a walk around the Ashram and see the spinning and weaving we are doing. It means to me perhaps the greatest part of my outward activity. My secretary will take you around."

Hippolyte: "Thanks for having so kindly received strangers."

Gandhi: “You are not foreigners to me.”[66]

This meeting is one of Gandhi’s first with the Bahá’ís and therefore has an important historical significance. The Mahatma would later meet with Mr. Mani Mehta, chairman of the Mumbai Spiritual Assembly; and Mrs. Shirin Fozdar, the first woman elected to the National Spiritual Assembly of India, who would introduce him more widely to the Faith. Around 1937–38, Martha Root would send Mahatma Gandhi a copy of *Gleanings from the Writings of Bahá’u’lláh*. All these efforts of the friends led Gandhi to declare in the *Bombay Chronicle* newspaper in 1944[67] that the Faith was for him “a solace to humankind.”[68] After exchanging sincere thanks, Hippolyte and Laura visit the Ashram,[69] then head back to Bombay.

They arrive in Bombay on January 24. They then spend a week in the city and wait for the departure of the next ship to Egypt. They also meet Persian friends and attend several gatherings with the believers residing in the city. Then they embark on the SS *Cracovia* on February 1, reach Port Said on February 13, and finally arrive in Haifa on February 15, where Shoghi Effendi and the Holy Family warmly welcome them.[70]

Thus ends this historic journey of nearly fifteen months to the Far East, during which a multitude of seeds were sown in the hearts of those Hippolyte and Laura met during their historic journey.

26 / The Days of the Guardian

When Shoghi Effendi, then a student in England at Balliol College, Oxford, learns of the passing of 'Abdu'l-Bahá, to Whom he has always been devoted and for Whom he felt immense unconditional love, he is utterly devastated. In his own words, "'the pain, nay the anguish of His bereavement is overwhelming.'"[1] A few days later, he returns to the Holy Land with his sister Rúhangíz and Lady Blomfield. Upon his arrival, the Will and Testament of 'Abdu'l-Bahá[2] is read before the members of the Holy Family and the believers gathered specially for the occasion. Here, he receives another thunderbolt of shock! Shoghi Effendi, then twenty-four years old, learns that the Master has appointed him Guardian of the Cause, and in accordance with the Will of the Master, Shoghi Effendi is now the new leader of the worldwide Bahá'í community and the authorized interpreter of the Holy Writings of the Faith.[3]

Shoghi Effendi, still deeply affected by the Master's ascension and overwhelmed by the enormity of his responsibilities, suffers even more when he learns that members of his own family have decided to turn against him and not recognize him as the Guardian of the Faith. Despite this, he finds the strength to convene an international group of believers in March 1922 to reflect on the immediate developments of the Faith. Among them are Hippolyte and Laura, Lady Blomfield (UK), Emogene Hoagg (USA), Ethel Rosenberg (UK), Roy Wilhelm (USA), Mountfort Mills (USA), Charles Mason Remey (USA), Alice and Albert Schwarz (Germany), and Wellesley Tudor-Pole (UK).

Two Persian Bahá'í teachers, 'Abdu'l-Husayn Ávárih and Jináb-i-Fáḍil, are also expected in Haifa, but the journey from Persia to Palestine is extremely complicated, and their arrival is therefore delayed. In addition, during the long weeks that follow, Siyyid Muṣṭafa Rúmí from Burma and Corinne True from the United States also join the consultations.[4]

Hippolyte has known Shoghi Effendi since the latter's childhood and, as Rúḥíyyih Khánum writes in *The Priceless Pearl*, Shoghi Effendi regards Hippolyte as a friend and collaborator "whom he evidently felt he could be open with as an intimate friend."[5] In the correspondences of this period, Shoghi Effendi often confides to Hippolyte how physically and mentally exhausted he is by "'the atrocious vexations which have afflicted me for so long.'"[6]

Shoghi Effendi was still a child when he first met Hippolyte, who was then on a pilgrimage to the Holy Land. As mentioned in the previous chapter, when Shoghi Effendi was resting in Neuilly-sur-Seine, Hippolyte and Laura had come to visit him and take him for a walk in Paris. When he had to travel to Oxford for his studies, Shoghi Effendi often made stops in Paris to meet friends and spend some time with the Dreyfus-Barneys. As Hippolyte and Laura's two families are steeped in culture and art, Shoghi Effendi enjoyed discussing music and painting with them. When Shoghi Effendi became Guardian of the Faith and began to construct the terraces on Mount Carmel, it was to Hippolyte that he turned for assistance when he wanted to buy certain specific species of grass and flowering plants that were found in France.[7] The Guardian writes about Hippolyte, "None, I can confidentially assert, among the Baha'is of the East & the West, combined to the extent that he did the qualities of genial & enlivening fellowship, of intimate acquaintance with the manifold aspects of the Cause, of sound judgment & distinctive ability, of close familiarity with the problems & condition of the world—all of which made him such a lovable, esteemed & useful collaborator & friend."[8]

Beyond the sincere and deep affection that exists between the two men, if Hippolyte is invited to take part in these consultations of such enduring historical significance after the passing of the Master, it is, above all, because of his deep understanding of the Faith, his profound knowledge of the Holy Writings, and his valuable contributions to the Cause.

Hippolyte and Laura stay almost six weeks in Haifa with Shoghi Effendi and the other assembled friends. The main subject of consultation is whether the time has come to establish the Universal House of Justice. As Lady Blomfield says, "Oh! What a unique and thrilling part of the world's history is being enacted here and now!"[9] At first Hippolyte seems to be leaning toward an election of the first Universal House of Justice;[10] however, after weeks of consultation and study of 'Abdu'l-Bahá's Will and Testament, it becomes clear to the friends gathered there that this option would be premature.[11] For the Universal House of Justice to be elected and to function fully, local and national Assemblies must be firmly established in all the countries where Bahá'ís reside; however, in 1922, this administrative foundation is almost nonexistent. At the time of the passing of 'Abdu'l-Bahá, there were only a handful of local Assemblies, mostly scattered throughout the United States and Persia, in the Bahá'í world.

Therefore, from that very moment, a historical evolution occurs in the Faith, as the formation of institutions in Bahá'í communities will become, alongside the propagation and protection of the Faith, the primary mission of the Guardian and the most important endeavor of the Bahá'í world.

This period was a momentous and historically significant time in the growth and evolution of the Faith (and, by definition, in the history of the maturation of humanity as a whole). It marked a watershed, a time of change in the culture of the fledgling Bahá'í community. The early believers had to adjust to a culture of change, and some of them could not understand or embrace the need for such a change in the Bahá'í community. However, this was not the case for Hippolyte Dreyfus. He participated in the deliberations, and he fully abided by the decisions arrived at after consultation among the believers summoned to the Holy Land. He was firm in the Covenant.

Several events also mark the Dreyfus-Barneys' stay in the Holy Land. A prayer meeting is held in memory of Helen Goodall, one of the first American believers. A table is set up with utmost simplicity, on which are placed a few dishes of cookies, refreshments, and beautiful red and pink roses. For the occasion, Shoghi Effendi chants a Tablet of 'Abdu'l-Bahá, revealed in honor of Helen Goodall's daughter, Ella Cooper.[12]

It is also an opportunity for all the believers present to accompany Shoghi Effendi to the Shrine of Bahá'u'lláh to meditate and to pray. Lady Blomfield depicts these unique moments for us: "The friends stood together in the little alcove, and so we could see Shoghi Effendi as he approached the Threshold. One could never forget his face. The expression of adoration and humbleness, combined with a great majesty, cannot be put into words. Then he sang and of course, his voice is heavenly, but there, it was surely the voice of an angel singing."[13]

It seems, however, that the Dreyfus-Barney couple could not join each of these sessions because, as an American believer reports, Laura "had contracted a terrible disease last summer, so she had to be careful. Moreover, they were most often busy translating important documents for Shoghi Effendi."[14] In a letter written on March 18, Hippolyte describes to his sister Yvonne the latest events happening in the Holy Land:

> We still have a lot to do here, but things inevitably drag on. I am afraid we will leave before the Persians we have called in arrive, and we may have to come back here later. In addition, there are issues where the government must intervene, and it is waiting for the mandate to be confirmed in England, which can last a few more years.
>
> There are always crowds here: fortunately, most people are very active and interesting: the Schwarz of Stuttgart tell us about the progress of the Cause in Germany, and the development that Bad Mergentheim[15] has taken, of which they are the main shareholders since Abdul-Baha's visit there. [. . .] [Mountfort] Mills and [Roy] Wilhelm will leave at the end of the month and will be in Paris around April 10. I hope you can see them: they will give you interesting news.[16]

On March 21, the day of Naw-Rúz, all the pilgrims gather in the Master's House for a unique event: in front of them are unveiled the portraits of the Báb and Bahá'u'lláh, to which was added, for the first time, a photo of 'Abdu'l-Bahá. After gathering in the Master's room, the pilgrims reconvene in the afternoon at the pilgrim house to have tea with the Guardian. He then leads them to the Shrine of the Báb to pray, and at the entrance to the Shrine, he pours rose water on each of their hands. In front of the Shrine of the Báb, the pilgrims stand while Shoghi Effendi chants the Tablet of Visitation; they then enter the adjacent rooms which form the repository of 'Abdu'l-Bahá earthly remains, where, seated, they listen to two of the friends chant several of the Holy Writings.[17]

On March 24, Hippolyte, Laura, Lady Blomfield, Albert and Alice Schwarz, Mason Remey, and Mountfort Mills decide to organize a small celebration for the fifty Persian friends, who had been recently joined by twelve pilgrims from the province of Khorasan, remembered in the history of the Faith for the unfortunate and brutal murders of believers in 1852. Lady Blomfield also describes for us this memorable evening: "We pushed the tables up to the wall, opened the double doors into the three bedrooms, put rugs into the doorways, the rest of the rugs we spread on the floor, about 3 dozen chairs, the others sat on the floor on their heeds [heels]—the dears, they all wrote their names in my book. They enjoyed their delicious tea and cakes and candies. Laura is worthy to be Earl Marshal so amazingly well did she manage it all . . ."[18]

The friends are deeply touched by the stories told by the Persian Bahá'ís of the first heroes of the Faith who sacrificed everything, including their lives, for the advancement of the Cause.[19]

As this is the first visit of their friend Lady Blomfield to the Holy Land, Hippolyte and Laura decide to take her for a tour over a few days to explore Palestine and Lebanon, which was then occupied by France. Toward the end of their stay, Hippolyte rents a Buick and leads the friends through desert roads and orange orchards that stretch as far as the eye can see. The three of them make a stop in Beirut, where they meet some young Bahá'ís who are studying at the

American College or at the Jesuit school in the city. Lady Blomfield exclaims, "They all know Laura and Hippolyte and positively adore them, small wonder! I know of none to equal them!"[20]

From Beirut, Lady Blomfield, Laura, and Hippolyte travel to Damascus, cross into completely different terrain, and enjoy the unusual landscapes as they traverse rivers, valleys, and mountains. Here, too, they are greeted by Bahá'í friends who invite them to dinner several nights in a row. After a few days, they return to Haifa. This trip will remain engraved forever in Lady Blomfield's memory. Delighted by her journey, she confides in her daughter, Mary,[21] all the good she thinks of her dear friends: "They are darlings—and the best Baha'is in the world I think from the mental as well as the spiritual plane. . . . I could tell you reams of their adventures in Indochina—always working for the Divine Cause of Peace and Unity without the narrow sectarianism which is likely to be a danger in the future—a real pitfall to be avoided . . . The Dreyfus' adventures also broadened out to jungles and tigers and things."[22]

It is soon time for Hippolyte and Laura to return to France. As the Guardian majestically pointed out to them, the Cause is entering a new age,[23] and the Bahá'í Faith must now be recognized as an independent religion alongside other religions. Additionally, the worldwide Bahá'í community must continue to labor unceasingly for the establishment of the administrative institutions of the Bahá'í world order as revealed by Bahá'u'lláh and gradually set up by 'Abdu'l-Bahá, and the Heroic Age of the development of the Faith must now give way to the Formative Age. It is with this clear and penetrating vision that the couple, despite the sadness and emptiness left by the departure of the Master, prepare on April 10, 1922, to return, confident and determined, to Paris. In a letter to his sister, Hippolyte informs his family of his return to France and gives them the latest news concerning the Guardian:

> I just spent three extremely busy and interesting days here. Laura stayed in Haifa where she still had a lot to do, and she must join me tomorrow evening in Port Said to embark us on

the 12th on the *Cracovia* for Venice. This is the same boat that returned from Bombay two months ago.

Do you know that Shoghi left a few days ago to rest, at an unknown destination? The poor boy really needed solitude and tranquillity after all the emotions of the last few months. It may be that he meets us this summer and we will spend a few weeks together in the mountains.[24]

27 / The Writings of Bahá'u'lláh

Back in France, Hippolyte resumes his writing and translation work. His new goal is to publish a compilation of Bahá'u'lláh's most important Writings.

In 1923, he publishes, in the Ernest Leroux Editions, the first volume of *l'Œuvre de Bahá'u'lláh* [The Writings of Bahá'u'lláh]. It includes (1) The Most Holy Tablet,[1] (2) The Hidden Words, (3) The Seven Valleys, and (4) The Letter on the Bayán.

In this book Hippolyte presents a revision of his translations of The Most Holy Tablet and the Seven Valleys; the very first French translation of the Arabic section of the Hidden Words, to which he adds the Persian section; and, above all, he introduces to the general public a document he referred to as the Letter on the Bayán, which is said to be a Tablet in which Bahá'u'lláh explains the relationship between His station and that of the Báb as a Manifestation of God, but which has yet to be identified.

In the foreword, Hippolyte evaluates the influence of the Cause and explains why it attracts more and more followers:

> The influence of the modern Prophet of Persia today has crossed the boundaries of Islam. The teachings of Bahá'u'lláh have indeed spread in the West in recent years, where the breadth of its praised tolerance, the generosity and wisdom of its social conceptions, the nobility of its ethics, could not fail to attract those who still believe in the possibility of a new and better

> order, and whose ambition is to collaborate in its establishment. [. . .] Whether they regard him as the modern "Christ," or they see him as one of the Great Inspired Beings who will lead a reconciled humanity to universal Peace, his followers recognize in his writings an inspiration that they seek in vain in the many outdated churches, and many are, in Europe, in America, as well as in the East, the assemblies of the believers, who regard the work of Bahá'u'lláh as a new Gospel.[2]

Lucien Bouvat,[3] in his report published in the *Journal Asiatique,* presents the relevance, for the reader, of the works selected in this compilation: "it includes quite different works of form and inspiration, but all interesting in various ways: *Les Paroles cachées* (the Hidden Words), of which mysticism is the essential character; *Les Sept Vallées du Voyage vers Dieu* (the Seven Valleys of the Journey to God), in which the principles of Sufism are recognized; the Most Holy Tablet, which is an appeal to Christians, and the Letter on the Bayan, where the analogies of the manifestations of the Báb and Bahá'u'lláh are exposed."[4]

In *Revue critique d'histoire et de littérature,* Félix Lacôte[5] writes an appreciative review of Hippolyte's translations of texts whose very particular style can challenge readers who are unfamiliar with the themes of Middle Eastern culture, Islamic references, and mysticism. He writes, "Mr. H. Dreyfus, for many years, has for us made himself the spokesperson of Baha'ism. [. . .] The mystical outpourings of Bahâou'llâh come from a soul so clearly genuine and tender, they are poured out with a lyricism so ardent and colourful, though sometimes monotonous, that one cannot deny them a minute of sympathy, nor deprive oneself of the pleasure of having the fleeting illusion of surrendering to it. The translation by Mr. H. Dreyfus is excellent; in a French of the best quality, it brings to life the mystical ardour of the original."[6]

In parallel with his translation work, Hippolyte delivers several lectures, which he regards as new opportunities to introduce the principles of the Faith to the general public. He delivers one of his most striking discourses in Geneva, on February 28, 1924, during a series of lectures organized by the Swiss magazine, *Towards Unity,* which promotes liberal spiritual research. This French-language journal invites different authors and specialists in the humanities such as philosophy, sociology, and religion to present their research around the theme of unity.

The title Hippolyte chooses for his address is eloquent: "Baha'ism—Unity through religion."[7] As usual, his foray into the subject is marked by an audacity that reflects his firm conviction: "Few movements are as worthy as Baha'ism to attract the attention of those who rightly care about the future of humanity, and who nurture the ambition to contribute to making it better than the present. It is that indeed [which] Baha'ism draws from the spirit of its founder, the Prophet Bahaou'llah [Bahá'u'lláh], a universal force that only a religious movement can have, and [. . .] by its very nature, it is addressed without discrimination to all the peoples of the world."[8]

Hippolyte first demonstrates how universalism and unity are at the center of religions but how, unfortunately, because of man's limited vision and misconceived notions, these ideal conditions cannot be realized. Next, he explains how the Bahá'í Faith, unlike other religions, considers all religions as representative of the same essential truth, with each religion uniquely and successively revealed in a progressive unfolding of religious truth:

> Baha'ism, unlike other religions that seek universalism through the conversion of unbelievers, does not claim to suppress ancient beliefs and does not demand any abjuration from its followers. Bahaou'llah achieves unity because He sees all religions as different systems that explain the same Truth. He shows them how, through the diversity of dogmas and symbols, religions are only the result of the effort of different humanities to solve, with the teaching of an inspired Prophet, the great problem of the unknown; and that their founders are the messengers of the same God, bringing to men the same doctrine adapted to the requirements of their mentality.[9]

In a second step, he explains how new followers, coming from different cultures and religions, have decided to join the Faith to build a new type of community that is centered on service to others. Finally, after demonstrating how the Faith must be the source of unity between religions, between men, and between cultures, he recalls that it must also be in accord with unfettered thought and with scientific reasoning: "And also, it is important that it works for reconciliation [. . .] deemed impossible of religions with Free thought, and that the alleged opposition between science and religion be once and for all eliminated. For this it is enough to leave to each of the two their own domain, and not pretend to explain the Unknown with the help of formulas imposed on [grounds of blind unquestioning] faith. Bahaou'llah said: 'Religion cannot be at odds with science, for the opposite of science is error. Religion must evolve with the science it must inspire, just as it must inspire all forms of human activity.'"[10]

He ends his presentation by recalling that true religion is not obedience to rites or cults in a predetermined way, but is instead the action of leading a life in harmony with the moral and social principles that govern humanity.

The text of his speech is published the following month in the journal *Vers l'unité.* The introduction written by the editor is admirable:

> The exposition of this religion, this philosophy or this morality, which we have the pleasure to make known here to the readers of the journal, served as a kind of preamble to the very beautiful lecture that Mr. Dreyfus-Barney, Doctor of Law, Lawyer at the Court of Appeal of Paris, gave in Geneva on 28 February 1924, under the auspices of *Vers L'unité.* This is a movement to which the principles of this Unity which we all have at heart to seek and to live are related in a singular manner. The doctrine of the Prophet or the Messenger Bahaou'llah, Baha'ism, dates, as we know, from 1844. Starting from this East from which the Light comes, it went around the world; in every country, it encountered a warm welcome that attested to its inspired origin and a deep concern for social and religious reorganization. Baha'ism

> is certainly a harbinger of New Times; it strengthens our hope in the coming of this New Spirit who will make of all flesh the living Temple of the One God and who consecrates Mankind to his Name.[11]

Also in 1924, Hippolyte published the second volume of *l'Œuvre de Bahá'u'lláh* [The Writings of Bahá'u'lláh—Volume II]. This new compilation includes translations of: (1) The Tablet of the Temple and (2) Letters to the Kings.[12]

Hippolyte introduces the book in the following words:

> Written during the last years of [Bahá'u'lláh's sojourn in] Adrianople and the first months of his imprisonment at 'Akká (1868–1869), it constitutes Baháou'lláh's appeal to the peoples of the world, the first effort towards the universalization of His doctrine, which was to be pursued with the zeal and success that His son Abdou'l-Bahá is known to have. [. . .] Until then, Baháou'lláh had only addressed the Bábís of Persia. [. . .] If Suratou'l Haykal, the Chapter of the Temple of God, is still written especially for the Bábís, it is nevertheless also an appeal to Christians, since Baháou'lláh proclaims the coming of the Father announced in the Gospel, the Supreme Manifestation of God. The Letters to the sovereigns, to the Pope, to Napoleon III, to the Tsar of Russia, to the Queen of England, which form the second part of Suratou'l Haykal, constitute direct appeals to Christian Europe, so that it may join the great movement of religious unification, which alone can ensure the felicity of humanity [. . .] Nowhere more vividly than in these writings are we able to penetrate the unique character of Baháou'lláh's thoughts, His prophetic inspiration, combined with a startling awareness of social necessities.[13]

In *Revue de l'histoire des religions,* Clément Huart welcomes this second volume, as usual, by focusing on the quality of Hippolyte's translation work: "The second volume of the translation of the

Works of Baháou’lláh, disciple of the Báb and founder of Behaism, which has become familiar to the readers of the Journal, has just been published, as well as the formal promise given earlier. The translator wanted to continue his courageous work: it takes, in fact, a certain courage to try to convey into French, a language that likes clarity, the sometimes-cloudy exhortations of an author writing in Persian. Mr. H. Dreyfus certainly succeeded in the task he had set himself, and his translation is read with pleasure.”[14]

28 / Traveling on Behalf of the Guardian

Besides his endeavors to translate the Holy Writings, Hippolyte, accompanied by Laura, also travels at the request of the Guardian to many European countries, as well as to the United States. The purpose of these journeys is twofold: on the one hand, they will clarify the importance of setting up administrative institutions, and on the other hand, they will encourage the friends in their teaching activities.[1]

A very particular feature of the personality of Hippolyte deserves to be noted here: throughout his life, and despite the various crises that rocked the foundations of the Faith, his perspicacity and dedication always empower him to understand the needs of the Cause, at any juncture in the history of its development, and to serve its exigencies and protect its vital interest under the direction of the Master and, subsequently, of the Guardian.

In the early years following Hippolyte's conversion, the emphasis had to be on the translation and propagation of the Writings of Bahá'u'lláh. This difficult work he carried out with great ardor after committing himself to master two new and complex languages and giving up his practice of law. When communities of believers outside France needed travel teachers to deepen their understanding of the Faith, Hippolyte traveled to the far corners of the world to teach, to explain, to inspire, and to support his fellow Bahá'ís in strengthening their understanding of the infant Faith. In the early 1920s, when the Bahá'í world is shaken by a difficult period of transition—passing from what the Guardian has called the "Heroic Age" to the "Formative Age" of the Faith, a time of change that demanded from the believers, orphaned by the passing of 'Abdu'l-Bahá, a significant cultural shift—Hippolyte immediately grasps its exigencies and requirements and, at the instruction of Shoghi Effendi, arises instantly and travels to different continents to explain the importance of building the administrative systems that are indispensable for the development of the Cause.

In 1925, Hippolyte and Laura travel to Mexico, then the United States, and spend several months in California among various communities of believers in the region. Hippolyte and Laura's arrival in the United States is announced in the January edition of *Bahá'í News:* "The friends will be delighted to learn of the arrival in this country of Mr. and Mrs. Dreyfus-Barney from Paris, their plans including a visit of several months in California with Mrs. Dreyfus-Barney's mother. The world-wide Baha'i experience of Mr. and Mrs. Dreyfus-Barney, their intimate knowledge of the history and teachings of the Cause, and their unique proficiency in the Persian language bring to the American believers a mental and spiritual reinforcement that will assist us greatly."[2]

Now a well-known orientalist and scholar of the Faith who is recognized internationally, Hippolyte's stay in California is announced in the press. In an article in the Pasadena Post dated February 28, 1925, we read:

> The Baha'i Assembly Meets on Sunday afternoon from 3:30 to 4:30 in the blue room of the Vista del Arroyo hotel. A cordial welcome extended to all meetings. Information and literature may be had by calling Mrs Madsen, Colorado 4380, or the secretary, Mrs Stuart W. French, Fair Oaks.
>
> Next Sunday the speaker will be the noted scholar and author who has long been identified with the Baha'i cause, Monsieur Hippolyte Dreyfus-Barney of Paris, France. M. Dreyfus will speak upon the subject of the "Significance of the Revelation of Baha'u'lllah [Bahá'u'lláh].[3]

On April 9, 1925, the Assemblies of Los Angeles, Glendale, and Pasadena hold a grand dinner colloquium in Hollywood on the theme of "Unity." The gathering, composed of more than 250 people, is particularly diverse. Alongside the guest of honor, the well-known Bahá'í teacher Mírzá Asadu'lláh Fáḍil-i-Mázandarání,[4] the guests include artists, musicians, consuls, reverends, rabbis, university professors, and representatives of various philanthropic associations. Hippolyte, who is asked to be the master of ceremonies, introduces the theme by speaking "in a most gracious and eloquent" manner of the "constructive ideals for world unity." Then he calls on the various speakers and invites them each to expound their ideas. The evening is successful and provides an opportunity for all participants to deepen their understanding of the concept of unity and to reflect on its practical implementation.[5]

In July, Hippolyte makes a journey at the Guardian's request to visit Green Acre, in Maine, to attend North America's "Seventeenth Annual Convention and Bahá'í Congress."[6] During the Convention, the seventy delegates at the Convention elect Mountfort Mills as chairman and Horace Holley as secretary of the National Assembly. Hippolyte, representing France, is elected honorary delegate. When invited to speak, he outlines the progress of the Cause in France, reiterates the importance of building the Administrative Order, and voices the hope that the activities of the Green Acre Bahá'í school—similar to any other Faith-related activity—will be placed under the supervision of the National Spiritual Assembly. Finally, he announces that the Bahá'í world has now nine National Spiritual Assemblies: The United States and Canada; Persia; Germany; Great Britain; India and Burma; Egypt; the Caucasus; Turkey; and Iraq.[7]

Between 1923 and 1927, Hippolyte, sometimes accompanied by Laura, will visit many European countries and territories, such as Germany, England, Corsica, Denmark, Scotland, Spain, Ireland, Italy, Norway, the Netherlands, Portugal, and Switzerland.[8] Their journeys are coordinated by the Guardian. Needless to say, Hippolyte and Laura chose these destinations in response to the Master's call for the believers to pioneer to the numerous localities specified in

Hippolyte in the late 1920s

the teaching plan revealed by 'Abdu'l-Bahá in the Tablets of the Divine Plan: "Therefore, O ye believers of God! Show ye an effort and after this war spread ye the synopsis of the divine teachings in the British Isles, France, Germany, Austria-Hungary, Russia, Italy, Spain, Belgium, Switzerland, Norway, Sweden, Denmark, Holland, Portugal, Rumania, Serbia, Montenegro, Bulgaria, Greece, Andorra, Liechtenstein, Luxemburg, Monaco, San Marino, Balearic Isles, Corsica, Sardinia, Sicily, Crete, Malta, Iceland, Faroe Islands, Shetland Islands, Hebrides and Orkney Islands."[9]

In early 1923, Hippolyte is invited by London believers to attend the first gathering of the first National Spiritual Assembly of the British Isles. During this historic meeting, six members of the London community—two from Manchester and one from Bournemouth—

are elected. Invited as an observer, Hippolyte participates in the consultations around the drafting of legal statutes specific to the Assembly (such as trust, bequests, donations) and draws upon the knowledge he has acquired on the subject during his deliberations with the National Spiritual Assembly of the United States and Canada.[10]

Hippolyte makes many journeys back and forth to the United Kingdom to accompany the formation of Local Spiritual Assemblies and to participate with other friends, such as Martha Root and Mountfort Mills, in various teaching activities. For instance, they visit the eminent orientalist Reynold A. Nicholson (1868–1945), Professor Browne's successor as the chair of Oriental Studies at the University of Cambridge. Laura, for her part, addresses the National Council of Women and the Religious and Ethics Committees of the League of Nations.[11]

The believers work together continually in their efforts to spread the Faith. Martha Root, for example, mentions several times how she multiplied contacts during her various travels in Europe and Asia and relied on the Dreyfus-Barneys to follow up with these contacts. Martha sometimes asks Hippolyte and Laura to maintain correspondence with the seekers she has met, or she invites them to visit the most receptive souls, or—most often—she requests that they send these seekers Bahá'í literature—usually works published by Hippolyte, which are often available in English and German.

During this time, the Guardian is in constant communication with Hippolyte. The Guardian closely follows his work, and above all, due to repeated requests from Hippolyte, gives news about his state of health. Shoghi Effendi writes to him:

> On my way to the Bernese Oberland which has become my second home. In the fastnesses and recesses of its alluring mountains, I shall try to forget the atrocious vexations which have afflicted me for so long . . . It is a matter which I greatly deplore, that in my present state of health, I feel the least inclined to, and even incapable of, any serious discussion on these vital problems with which I am confronted and with which you are

> already familiar. The atmosphere in Haifa is intolerable and a radical change is impracticable. The transference of my work to any other centre is unthinkable, undesirable and in the opinion of many just scandalous . . . I cannot express myself more adequately than I have for my memory has greatly suffered.[12]

Hippolyte also focuses on community development in France. In the minutes signed by the Bahá'í Spiritual Assembly in Paris dated November, 1925, we read:

> We are coming together again, and we hope that this winter will be a time of good and fruitful work. We had a meeting at the home of our good and devoted friends Mr. and Mrs. Scott. There, we decided in principle to meet twice a month, once at Mr. and Mrs. Scott's house, another time at Mr. and Mrs. Dreyfus's house. These two meetings will be considered as working sessions and, so to speak, will constitute the Spiritual Assembly. Apart from these two centres, the members who attend them will have special meetings at their own home to instruct newcomers to our good Cause. In this way the work will be shared, and these newcomers will soon be able to call themselves Bahá'ís and attend the bimonthly meetings.[13]

29 / Legal and Diplomatic Protection of the Faith

During his early years as the Guardian of the Cause, Shoghi Effendi is able to repeatedly utilize Hippolyte's legal skills and keen sense of diplomacy, and he entrusts him with special missions.

In 1926, the Guardian invites Hippolyte to Haifa to examine the legal status of the Bahá'ís in Egypt. In the first days of January, Hippolyte and his friend Mountfort Mills embark in Marseille for Port Said, where they take the train to Haifa via Kantara. In Haifa, the Guardian warmly welcomes them and, with the utmost care and kindness, does everything to ensure their stay is pleasant.[1]

During the consultations, Hippolyte, who has been working on the subject for several years, recalls that in Egypt, as in most surrounding Muslim countries, laws concerning personal status (marriage, divorce, civil law . . .) are administered by religious courts. In this judicial system, only members of state-recognized religions[2] can argue their case. Therefore, if Bahá'ís want to appeal to these bodies, they can only do so by identifying themselves as Muslims, Christians, or Jews—which means they must deny their religious identity and recognize the authority of Islamic law over their Bahá'í principles. As it is unthinkable for Bahá'ís residing in Egypt, or anywhere else, to deny their Bahá'í identity, they are effectively deprived of the means for advocating legally for their rights.[3]

Hippolyte, on his part, has met several times with the friends of Egypt and for several years has provided them with advice and support with their legal procedures, in the hope that the authorities would recognize the independent character of the Bahá'í Faith and, in fact, their right to call on independent courts to handle their civil cases.[4]

In 1925, a tragic event turned the situation upside down. In the small Egyptian town of Beni Suef,[5] the leader of the town incited the inhabitants to rise up against three married men who had become Bahá'ís. A divorce petition was sought by the families who could not accept that their female relatives were "married to heretics."[6] On May 10, the appellate religious court of Beba,[7] after an exhaustive study of the teachings of Bahá'u'lláh, declared that the Bahá'í Faith was distinct and irreconcilable with Islam, condemned the husbands for violating the laws and ordinances of Islam, and annulled their marriages.[8] This conviction was described as historic by the Guardian, because for the first time in the history of the Faith an official court had recognized the independence of the Bahá'í Faith from Islam. In summarizing the outcome, Shoghi Effendi quoted the following words from the verdict: "'The Bahá'í Faith is a new religion, entirely independent, with beliefs, principles and laws of its own, which differ from, and are wholly in conflict with, the beliefs, principles and laws of Islam. No Bahá'í, therefore, can be regarded a Muslim or vice-versa, even as no Buddhist, Brahmin, or Christian can be regarded a Muslim or vice-versa.'"[9]

In light of these new events, Shoghi Effendi asks Hippolyte and Mountfort Mills to travel once again to Egypt to plead with the Egyptian authorities for the national legitimization of this local verdict and for the recognition of independent civil status for members of the Bahá'í community.[10]

The two friends travel to Cairo at the end of January and manage to secure appointments with the prime minister, the minister of the interior, and the British high commissioner and his adviser. At each of these meetings, Hippolyte and Mountfort Mills are received with great courtesy, and their interlocutors show a benevolent understanding of their petition for recourse to justice. Despite the complexity of the problem, the various authorities seem to be sincere in their willingness to act. Mountfort Mills explains the outcome of the discussions and the role played by Hippolyte in the negotiations: "The Orient moves slowly. We did, though, I believe, persuade those particular men to recognize the independence of the Faith. To obtain official Government recognition was another matter. A full report of our interviews was given the Guardian [. . .] Needless to say, much of whatever success resulted from our journey was due to Hippolyte's rare gifts of analysis and diplomacy."[11]

The second mission entrusted to Hippolyte by the Guardian concerns the home of Bahá'u'lláh in Baghdad. Known as "The Most Great House," this site, located near the banks of the Tigris River, was the residence of Bahá'u'lláh in Baghdad for most of His exile in Iraq; this is where the Kitáb-i-Íqán was revealed.[12]

In the early 1920s, the keys to the house are illicitly confiscated by the enemies of the Faith in Baghdad. Shoghi Effendi instructs Hippolyte and Mountfort Mills to deploy their legal skills to advocate for the Bahá'ís' rights over this house. A long and difficult legal battle ensues. Between 1921 and 1926, the case is presented successively before several bodies, including the Court of Justices of the Peace and the Baghdad Court of Appeal, and several times the appeals lead to the annulment of a decision made by a lower court. During this period, Hippolyte and Mountfort Mills advise the friends of Iraq during the preparation and the presenting of their case. Mountfort Mills travels twice[13] to Iraq[14] to meet King Faisal[15] and plead the cause of the Bahá'ís, and he is severely assaulted during one of his journeys.

In 1926, the two friends, after consultation with the Guardian, decide to bring the case to the League of Nations. By now, even though Hippolyte understands well how the League functions, the proceedings are long and tedious. The two friends provide their full support and their legal expertise in drafting a petition signed by the Bahá'ís of Iraq.[16] The petition is submitted to the members of the Mandates Commission at the League of Nations on September 11, 1928. The case is being considered before the fourteenth session of the Mandates Commission, who ultimately issue a statement that recognizes the right of Bahá'ís to property and strongly urges the government of Iraq to find a solution to the conflict. This victory brings much joy and comfort to the Guardian, as well as to the Bahá'í community, even though, as a matter of historical fact, this particular legal battle is far from over and will last many years.[17]

Finally, the Guardian also draws on Hippolyte's legal acumen and negotiating skills in the management and safeguarding of the Bahá'í heritage in the Holy Land.[18] From 1922 onward, beginning a few weeks after the reading of the Will and Testament of 'Abdu'l-Bahá, relatives of Shoghi Effendi, frustrated by the Master's last wishes, vehemently demanded inheritance rights over certain properties and rebelled against the authority entrusted to Shoghi Effendi. Harassed and heartbroken as a result of his relatives' prolonged and unceasing rebellion against 'Abdu'l-Bahá's sacred will, Shoghi Effendi would eventually have no choice but to declare them Covenant-breakers.

During this dark period of the Guardian's life, which he would consider the most distressing and exhausting of his tenure,[19] Shoghi Effendi finds comfort in the advice and unwavering dedication evinced by Hippolyte who, with his training in inheritance law, works to find viable legal solutions with the local authorities and prevent Bahá'í Holy Places from falling into the hands of the Covenant-breakers, who for a time unlawfully occupied the Mansion of Bahjí[20] and certain adjacent buildings.[21]

30 / Until the End of his Days

In 1925, Shoghi Effendi loses one of his closest collaborators residing in the Holy Land, Dr. John Esslemont, who passed away after contracting tuberculosis. Deeply saddened by the loss of this steadfast worker of the Cause, Shoghi Effendi is looking for a new assistant capable of effectively relieving him from the "oppressive burden of responsibility and care which it is my lot and privilege to shoulder."[1] He first contacts Horace Holley, whose qualities and dedication he highly appreciates. Hippolyte, who is in constant correspondence with the Guardian and the believers around the world, writes to his friend Horace in support of the choice made by Shoghi Effendi and urges his friend to give due deference to the Guardian's request. He writes, "Shoghi Effendi is now enjoying a much-needed rest in Switzerland and preparing for next years' work. He feels greatly the need of having the proper kind of assistant when he returns to Haifa, as he misses Esslemont tremendously. I hope the time will come when, having put the Cause on a firm basis in America, you and your dear wife will be able to give him your valuable help. But I know for the present, the friends would not spare you."[2]

After consultation, it is decided that the presence of Horace Holley in the United States is of the utmost importance to the establishment and consolidation of the administrative order on the American continent. Shoghi Effendi thereafter turns to Hippolyte and writes to him in 1926:

> I stand in need of a capable, trustworthy, hard-working, methodological, experienced secretary who will combine the gift of literary expression with a recognized standing in the Bahá'í world. Dr Esslemont was a most suitable companion, unhampered, painstaking, devoted, lowly and capable. I mourn his loss . . . A capable, painstaking secretary, wholeheartedly devoted to his work, and two chief advisers who would represent the Movement on specific occasions, with dignity and devotion, together with two Eastern associates, mentally awake and expert in knowledge, would, I feel, set me on my feet and release the forces that will carry the Cause to its destined liberation and triumph . . . I cannot express myself more adequately than I have for my memory has greatly suffered.[3]

There is no doubt that on reading these exchanges, Hippolyte, always ready to alleviate the heavy pains and workload that overwhelm the Guardian whom he loves and respects so unreservedly, must have felt the full weight of the grief and burden of a heavy heart . . . all the heavier that he himself could not respond positively to Shoghi Effendi's request for, as it turns out, from 1927, Hippolyte's health abruptly deteriorates and forces him to limit his movements to the barest requisite minimum.

Hippolyte toward the end of his life

Hippolyte spends more and more time in *Daro's-Salam* in Switzerland and several small towns in France, where he tries to rest and devote himself fully to writing.[4] In 1928, he publishes the third volume of his compilation of the Writings of Bahá'u'lláh, *L'Œuvre de Bahá'u'lláh—volume III.*[5] The main content is an improved and annotated reissue of his first translation of the Kitáb-i-Íqán, published in 1904. The introduction, which is the same as the preface to the 1904 edition, tells us that the first edition is completely out of print in 1928.

Many of his French translations, which he has been working on for some twenty years, will unfortunately not be published; among the most important are The Will and Testament of 'Abdu'l-Bahá;[6] the Tablet revealed by Bahá'u'lláh after the Martyrdom of Badí';[7] the "Treatise on Politics,"[8] written by the Master; as well as several prayers revealed by Bahá'u'lláh and 'Abdu'l-Bahá.[9] The most valuable is certainly his translation of the Most Holy Book, the Kitáb-i-Aqdas,[10] that he translated very early in his life and that was gradually revised and annotated following discussions with 'Abdu'l-Bahá during their meetings in the Holy Land.[11]

In addition to his writing and translation work, his many lectures, his uninterrupted correspondence with souls in search of spirituality, his innumerable journeys, and the weekly meetings he organized at home, Hippolyte—always unwavering in his desire to serve the development of the Faith—established throughout his life relations with the great libraries of France,[12] the United Kingdom, the United States, and especially Germany, to which he systematically sends his translations and historical works, as well as some original manuscripts of inestimable value.[13]

In some of His letters to Hippolyte, 'Abdu'l-Bahá repeatedly reaffirmed the importance of this work and assures Hippolyte of the assistance of the friends of the Tehran community in sending one or more Tablets each month so that he can make regular deposits with the libraries.[14] To the National Library of France, he donated three major documents: The Alwáh (made up of the Lawḥ-i-Salmán, the Lawḥ-i Khalíl, and the Lawḥ-i Yúsuf), recorded as "Persian supplement 1754" (dated 1295 AH / 1878 CE) and transcribed by the hand of Alí Taqí ibn Abú Tálib al-Husayní; the *Alwáh-i muqaddasa,* recorded as "Persian supplement 1753" (dated 1326 AH / 1908 CE), transcribed by the hand of Alí Akbar Mílání; and a version of the Kitáb-i-Aqdas, recorded under the words "Arab funds 6397" (dated 1314 AH / 1896 CE).[15]

In March 1928, Hippolyte is in recovery in Cannes; the meeting minutes of the Bahá'í Spiritual Assembly in Paris provide news of his state of health: "Our meetings have resumed but unfortunately our dear friend Mr. Dreyfus has been seriously ill, he has had to leave Paris and is recovering in Cannes from where we receive better news from him."[16]

A few months later, it would seem that Hippolyte must be feeling better, as he applies for and receives a new passport in June 1928, and in August he is back in Switzerland.[17] Unfortunately, his physical condition does not improve, and a few months later, he is hospitalized again, this time at the American Hospital in Neuilly-sur-Seine.

Friends visit him in large numbers, and no one, at the sight of his sincere enthusiasm and natural *joie de vivre,* seems to notice that his strength is increasingly declining. When Natalie, Laura's sister, comes to see him during the month of December, he jokes about this situation that forces him to stay bedridden and that deprives him of good food: "and to say that I had such a good fork!"[18] True to himself, he does not complain, and Natalie tells us, "The last time I saw him, in his hospital room, which he suffered with displeasure but never complained about, he was dressed in beautiful Japanese silk wrapped around his wrists. I saw, without noticing them, some white threads mixed with his colourless beard, and a tender regret in his sick eyelids. That day I stopped all my attention on the faint colours of the pink "Glory of Dijon"[19] of his ears, which seemed auspicious to me. I told him, he smiled enigmatically, and always without the slightest emphasis."[20]

At the end of the year, he leaves the hospital and returns to his Parisian home. However, a few weeks later, his health deteriorates again, severely, and as suddenly as it is unexpected, Hippolyte's soul takes flight to the Abhá Kingdom on December 20, 1928. He was only fifty-five.[21]

One of the nurses of the American Hospital writes to Laura, "You must know that I feel very keenly the sad news conveyed in your letter this morning. Little did I dream that such remarkable progress would be cut short so soon after leaving the hospital."[22]

No one had expected this sudden and tragic news, not even the Guardian who writes to Laura in the days that follow: "I will forever regret that, not realizing the gravity & the hopelessness of the illness which afflicted him, I failed to demonstrate in a fuller manner, the feelings of profound & abiding affection that I have always cherished for him in my heart."[23]

The funeral is announced in the press, most prominently in the newspapers *Le Temps*[24] and *Le Matin*[25] by the following press release: "We learn with regret the passing of Mr. Hippolyte Dreyfus-Barney, a literary man, which occurred on December 20, 1928 in Paris. The funeral will be held strictly with family. On behalf of Mrs. Dreyfus-Barney, Mr. and Mrs. Paul Meyer-May and their children, Mrs. Alice Barney, Miss Natalie Barney and the entire family."[26]

The funeral takes place on December 21 at the Montmartre cemetery in Paris. Hippolyte is buried in the same chapel as his mother and father.[27] On the same day, the family receives two cables of condolences from the Holy Land:

> HAIFA > FAMILY, FRIENDS, GRIEF STRICKEN DEEPLY FEEL HIS LOSS OFFERING HEARTFELT CONDOLENCES PRAYING FOR HIS BELOVED SOUL —SHOGHI.[28]

> HAIFA > MOTHER MYSELF OVERWHELMED WITH UNSPEAKABLE SORROW MEMORY OF HIS INESTIMABLE LOVING SUPPORT IN DAYS OF DARK AFFLICTION FOLLOWING MASTER'S PASSING EVER ENSHRINED IN OUR HEARTS ASSURES YOU TENDEREST SYMPATHY —SHOGHI.[29]

On the same day, Shoghi Effendi writes to Laura:

My dear Laura Khánum:

We were all profoundly moved when we received the news of the passing of our dear Hippolyte, and I assure you that since the ascension of our Beloved [‘Abdu’l-Bahá], the family, and myself included, never felt the sense of loss & the pain of overwhelming sorrow as acutely as we did the night we received your wire, announcing the passing of one who was close & dear to us all.

Needless to say, how overpowering is the sense of his loss to me, in particular, who received from him such comfort and support in perhaps the darkest days of my life & cherished the fondest hopes for his future contribution to the advancement of the international work of the Cause.

None, I can confidentially assert, among the Baha’is of the East & the West, combined to the extent that he did the qualities of genial & enlivening fellowship, of intimate acquaintance with the manifold aspects of the Cause, of sound judgment & distinctive ability, of close familiarity with the problems & condition of the world—all of which made him such a lovable, esteemed & useful collaborator & friend.

I have, impelled by my love & admiration for him, addressed the enclosed message to my co-workers throughout the West, that those who knew him not may recognize his standing & appreciate his achievements. I am certain that the National Spiritual Assemblies of America & Persia, responding to my cabled request, will take the necessary measures for the holding of memorial gatherings as a tribute to one who advanced so effectively the international interest of the Cause. [. . .]

My mother wishes me to express to you her deep sense of affectionate sympathy in the loss of one who proved such a sustaining & sympathetic friend in her gloomiest hours of anxiety & sorrow.

Rest assured, dear Laura Khánum, that in my hours of prayer & meditation at the holy Shrines, I will frequently & tenderly remember my dearly beloved friend & fellow-worker who has served so well our beloved Cause & is now receiving from the hands of our Master the reward of his notable achievements.

With kind regards & deepest sympathy, Yours affectionately, Shoghi.[30]

A statement is also published in the press, in the newspapers *Le Figaro*[31] and *Le Temps*,[32] to thank all the people who have offered their condolences: "Mrs. Dreyfus-Barney, Mr. and Mrs. Paul Meyer-May, Miss Natalie Barney and the family, for whom it is impossible to individually thank all of those who expressed their sympathy at the death of Mr. Hippolyte Dreyfus-Barney, ask them to find here the expression of their heartfelt thanks."

Countless letters of condolence pour in from all over the world, from the Holy Land, the United States, France, England, Switzerland. Messages of condolence also arrive from believers, Spiritual Assemblies, orientalists, friends, diplomats, and family members. In the space of a few weeks, Laura and Hippolyte's relatives receive more than three hundred letters and telegrams.[33]

The news of Hippolyte's departure is met with dismay and great suffering. His friend Ahmad Yazdí tells in a very moving letter that Shoghi Effendi is extremely affected and that the women of the Holy Family shed many tears upon hearing the sad and sorry news of the passing of Hippolyte, whom they considered a full member of their family.[34]

Munavar, fourth daughter of 'Abdu'l-Bahá, confirms in a letter to Laura, "I cannot find words to express to you my sympathy and deep sorrow for the passing away of our dearly loved Hippolyte. Indeed, I feel his loss as a loss of a most precious and beloved brother and friend."[35]

It is also clear from reading these many testimonies and letters of condolence that Hippolyte's last days were long and painful . . . but that his departure was sudden.

Lady Blomfield writes, "I had hoped and thought that he was recovering! It seemed so when I last saw him in July! When he said 'younger ones must henceforth carry on the work, I have done what

I could!' he looked so vital and so young, that he could continue to render to the Cause greater service than ever, that only he could achieve!"[36]

George Townshend confides, "When we left Paris the news of his condition was better and I thought he was turning the corner and would soon be out of danger."[37]

A friend of the family wrote, "although knowing your husband very afflicted and demanding great care, we could not think of a misfortune so close."[38]

Edith Sanderson consoles herself by writing, "at least, our Hippolyte is out of his struggles."[39]

Laura Dreyfus-Barney poignantly reflects on how Hippolyte remained noble and worthy until his very last days: "He never grumbled. He took life as it came. In suffering he showed the simple fortitude which manifested a mature soul. He was ready to die."[40]

Hippolyte leaves us with the memory of a man of extreme kindness, admired for his serenity and dignity and respected for his intelligence and culture. He was a source of inspiration because of his dedication and his generous heart, and he was an unshakable servant in his love for the Master, in his unwavering support for the Guardian, and in his determination to spread the Cause.[41]

From his relatives, we learn a little more about the kind of person that Hippolyte was in private. Natalie Barney testifies:

> Hippolyte, my brother-in-law, a gentle man with a beard, smooth skin on little Asian cheekbones, eyes slightly narrowed and predisposed to the East, seemed a passive force placed between two American sisters like an insulator between two batteries. [. . .]
>
> He accepted us as we were, but his presence prevented the short circuit of our overstretched nerves and, when he could not prevent anything, he remained, with a small whirlwind of folds in his forehead, on the sidewalk where some combination or abrupt decision had just torn us. He did not try to understand,

> or to follow us, he would walk away with the good step of a man who knows that walking rests. [. . .]
>
> He did not ever subject others to any tyranny and he did not submit to any oppression himself. A precious thing in a family, the drama did not get to him. He was orderly and independent—it would have been as impossible for him to change his tastes as to impose them.[42]

Let us leave the last word to the one person through whom the glorious Hippolyte Dreyfus story all began, May Bolles Maxwell, his spiritual mother. Below is her personal tribute to him. Her heartfelt words serve as a summation of the essence of all these many messages of condolence and bereavement:

> As a profound scholar, a loved and trusted friend among his associates, as a man of deep sympathies, intellectual attainment and sound judgment, he was well prepared to grasp and accept the sublime teachings of Baha'u'llah and become their greatest advocate and exponent in France. [. . .]
>
> His activities and services in the spread of the Baha'i faith were by no means confined to France, for Mr. Dreyfus-Barney visited most of the European countries, the United States and Canada, China, Japan, Egypt, Algiers, Persia, the cradle of the Baha'i faith, and other countries, everywhere leaving the impress of his lofty character, his breadth of vision, his mature knowledge of the religion of Baha'u'llah. His presentation of the Cause among all peoples enhanced its honour and prestige, and among the friends he was invariably a unifying influence, welding them in those deeper bonds of brotherly love which is the essence of the Baha'i faith. [. . .]
>
> Like many Baha'is he combined a rare sweetness of nature with great firmness and strength, and his criterion for estimating the true worth and status of his fellow Baha'is is a standard for all. He said that he considered every soul in their relation

to God and to the Cause, never in their relation to him. Thus, he said if anyone hurt or wronged him he did not allow this to influence his judgment, this being merely a transient personal matter, but always considered each person in their relation to God and their service to the Cause. [. . .]

In these brief and fragmentary memories of early associations with one who has become an internationally known figure in the Baha'i Cause, I pay my humble tribute to a great soul and a lifelong friend.[43]

Epilogue

Laura Dreyfus-Barney overcomes the inexpressible sadness and loneliness she experiences after the loss of her husband and closest companion by intensifying her efforts for the development of the Faith, which she knows is the Cause for oneness and unity, for universal peace, and for global prosperity. At the same time, she also finds solace and refuge by actively serving the Guardian with whom she thereafter engages in regular communication. The memory of Hippolyte is never far away. In 1929, Shoghi Effendi writes to Laura to ask if she could send him a picture of Hippolyte because he wants to place it in his office, where the two men had "spent delightful hours conversing & collaborating with regard to the affairs of the Cause."[1]

In the same year, Shoghi Effendi himself writes in his inimitable style a final tribute, which is certainly one of the most moving and lengthy he has been given reason to write. Published in *Bahá'í World*,[2] his words consecrate Hippolyte's life of total dedication with precision and clarity:

> Dearly beloved brothers and sisters in 'Abdu'l-Bahá:
>
> With feelings of profound sorrow, I am moved to send you these few lines, mourning the loss which the Cause has undoubtedly sustained by the passing of one who, for many years and in circumstances of exceptional significance, rendered the sacred Threshold distinctive and inestimable services.

The hand of Divine Decree has removed, by the death of our talented and dearly beloved friend, Mr. Hippolyte Dreyfus-Barney, yet another outstanding figure in the Cause of Bahá'u'lláh, who, by his brilliant gifts of mind and heart as well as by the diverse achievements of his life, has truly enriched the annals of God's immortal Faith.

A pioneer of the Cause of Bahá'u'lláh ever since its celestial light first warmed and illuminated the West, he has, by his close association with the person of 'Abdu'l-Bahá, by his numerous and extensive travels in Eastern and Western lands, by his contact with all sections of society, by his scholarly presentation of the history and fundamentals of the Faith, and lastly by his unforgettable share in the settlement of the complex and pressing issues that called for expert assistance in the days following 'Abdu'l-Bahá's passing, achieved a standing which few have as yet attained.

The days of his spiritual communion with 'Abdu'l-Bahá and His household within the walls of the prison-city 'Akká, wherein he imbibed the principles which he later so ably expounded to the peoples of the West; his pre-eminent role on his return to Paris in kindling the torch which is destined to shed eternal illumination upon his native land and its people; the links of abiding fellowship which he forged with our Persian brethren in the course of the historic mission entrusted to his charge by our Beloved; the seeds which he scattered far and wide during his subsequent travels to the heart of Asia, throughout India, beyond the remotest villages of Burma and as far as the eastern borders of Indo-China; the able support he showed in its initial and intermediary courses to the case of Bahá'u'lláh's house in Baghdad; his unhesitating intervention with State officials in paving the way for the ultimate emancipation of our Egyptian brethren from the yoke of orthodox Islam; the stimulating encouragement his visit caused to the Bahá'í community of Tunis on the northern shores of Africa; and last but not least

> the ability and diligence with which he applied himself to the solution of the difficult and vexing problems of the Holy Land in the critical years following 'Abdu'l-Bahá's ascension—all stand out as memorable landmarks in a life that was as varied in its international aspects, as it was rich in its spiritual experience.
>
> His gifts of unfailing sympathy and penetrating insight, his wide knowledge and mature experience, all of which he utilized for the glory and propagation of the Message of Bahá'u'lláh, will be gratefully remembered by future generations who, as the days go by, will better estimate the abiding value of the responsibilities he shouldered for the introduction and consolidation of the Bahá'í Faith in the Western world.
>
> Suffering as he did in his last days from the effects of a slow and painful illness, he bore heroically his share of the afflictions of the world and is now in the realms of blissful deliverance partaking his full share of the goodly reward which he certainly deserved. To me, and particularly amid the storm and stress that have agitated my life after 'Abdu'l-Bahá's passing, he was a sustaining and comforting companion, a most valued counsellor, an intimate and trusted friend.
>
> With much emotion and the deepest sense of gratitude and supplication at the holy Threshold I request that you join with me in my prayers for the spiritual advancement in the realms above of a soul who by the sheer merit of the signal services he rendered already deserves to rank highly among the departed faithful.
>
> May he forever rest in peace.[3]

With his characteristic humility, the Guardian confides a few weeks later to Hippolyte's sister, Yvonne, also very much saddened by the loss of her brother: "What I have written and attempted to express is indeed only an inadequate tribute to the many and unforgettable services he has rendered to the Cause and humanity in the course of his rich & fruitful life."[4]

A few years later, Shoghi Effendi bestows the title of "Disciple of 'Abdu'l-Bahá" upon Hippolyte Dreyfus and eighteen other Western believers and thereby sanctifies their service to the Cause during the ministry of 'Abdu'l-Bahá. The list is published in *the Bahá'í World* of 1930 and 1933, and alongside Hippolyte, we find other prominent believers such as John Esslemont, Thornton Chase, Lua Getsinger, and others.[5]

In the 1940s, when Shoghi Effendi unveils the project to build the magnificent superstructure to cover the mausoleum of the Báb, Laura makes a large donation in the name of Hippolyte and receives the deep gratitude of the Guardian.[6] Widowed and childless, she will survive Hippolyte for more than forty-five years, during which time she will be appointed a "Knight" in France, then an "Officer of the French Légion d'Honneur." She receives these awards for her tireless commitment to the many humanitarian and social causes she has advanced and defended throughout her service on the International Council of Women and on the Subcommittee of Experts on Education of the League of Nations, and later of the United Nations.[7]

Vault of the Meyer-Dreyfus family

Disciples of 'Abdu'l-Bahá
"Heralds of the Covenant."

The Bahá'í World, vol. 4 (1933): 118–19

1. Dr. J. E. Esslemont: Distinguished Bahá'í author.
2. Mr. Thornton Chase: First American Bahá'í.
3. Mr. Howard MacNutt: Notable Bahá'í teacher.
4. Miss Sarah Farmer: Founder of Green Acre.
5. Monsieur Hippolyte Dreyfus-Barney: Author, translator, and international promoter of the Faith.
6. Miss Lillian Kappes: Notable teacher of the Tarbíyat School in Tehran.
7. Mr. Robert Turner: First African-American Bahá'í in America.
8. Consul A. Schwarz: Pioneer for the Faith in Germany.
9. Mr. W. H. Randall: Eloquent upholder of the Bahá'í Cause in America.
10. Mrs. Lua M. Getsinger: Renowned and devoted international Bahá'í teacher.
11. Mr. Joseph Hannan: Indefatigable servant of the Cause.
12. Mr. C. I. Thacher: Zealous Bahá'í worker.
13. Mr. Ch. Greenleaf: Firm supporter of the Faith.
14. Mrs. J. D. Brittingham: Trusted and energetic sower of the seed of the Faith.
15. Miss E. Rosenberg: Pioneer of the Faith in England.
16. Mrs. Helen S. Goodall: Ardent establisher of the Cause in America.
17. Mr. Arthur P. Dodge: Staunch advocate of the Cause.
18. Mr. William H. Hoar: Prominent Bahá'í teacher.
19. Dr. J. G. Augur: Pioneer of the Faith in the Pacific Islands.

Glossary

Age: Refers to one of the three phases of development in the history of the Bahá'í Faith—namely, the Heroic Age, the Formative Age, and the Golden Age. The Heroic Age, or Apostolic Age, is the period from the Declaration of the mission of the Báb in 1844 until the passing of 'Abdu'l-Bahá in 1921. The Formative Age, or Transitional Age, began with the Guardianship and will last until the establishment of the Golden Age. Shoghi Effendi stated that during the Formative Age, the Administrative Order would be completed with the establishment of the Universal House of Justice, the Kitáb-i-Aqdas would be codified and its laws promulgated, the Lesser Peace would be established, and mankind would unite and reach maturity. The Golden Age is the final age of the Bahá'í Era and will ultimately lead to the establishment of the "Most Great Peace," to the World Bahá'í Commonwealth, and to the "birth and efflorescence of a world civilization."

Apostle of Bahá'u'lláh: A title Shoghi Effendi bestowed upon nineteen prominent believers who, through their sacrifice, courage, and steadfastness played a critical role in the development of the Faith, notably through their teaching activities, during the lifetime of Bahá'u'lláh.

Bahá'í Temple Unity: The first body formed by the American Bahá'ís to represent their national community. It was elected for the first time during the National Convention in 1909 by thirty-nine delegates representing thirty-six different cities. Its initial purpose was to coordinate the endeavors to build the first House of Worship in the United States. Its duties and fields of action progressively grew, and it was superseded in 1925, on the instructions of the Guardian, by the National Spiritual Assembly of the United States and Canada.

Covenant-breaker: A term referring to a member of the Faith who attempts to create internal division or disunity among the community by challenging the succession of one of the heads of the Faith (Bahá'u'lláh, 'Abdu'l-Bahá, Shoghi Effendi, and now the Universal House of Justice). For more information, see "The Covenant and Covenant-breaker" by Moojan Momen (unpublished), available online at https://bahai-library.org/momen_encyclopedia_covenant.

Disciple of 'Abdu'l-Bahá: "Herald of the Covenant," a title Shoghi Effendi bestowed upon nineteen Western Bahá'ís to acknowledge the inestimable services they rendered during the ministry of 'Abdu'l-Bahá. The list of the Disciples was published twice in *The Bahá'í World* (Vol. III, pp. 84–85; Vol. IV, pp. 118–119).

Hand of the Cause: A group of fifty prominent Bahá'ís appointed first by Bahá'u'lláh, then by 'Abdu'l-Bahá, and later by Shoghi Effendi to stimulate the propagation of the Faith and ensure its protection. 'Abdu'l-Bahá described their responsibilities as follows: "The obligations of the Hands of the Cause of God are to diffuse the Divine Fragrances, to edify the souls of men, to promote learning, to improve the character of all men and to be, at all times and under all conditions, sanctified and detached from earthly things. They must manifest the fear of God by their conduct, their manners, their deeds and their words" ('Abdu'l-Bahá, *Will and Testament of 'Abdu'l-Bahá,*

p. 13). Four were designated by Bahá'u'lláh, four were named posthumously by 'Abdu'l-Bahá, and forty-two were appointed by Shoghi Effendi, among which ten were named posthumously.

Mashriqu'l-Adhkár: Meaning *The Dawning-place of the remembrance of God* in Arabic. It is a Bahá'í House of Worship, a place open to all for worship and prayer and serves as a comprehensive center for community life, education, and service. Its various dependencies enhance its function, fostering an environment that promotes spiritual growth, social action and dialogue for all. The first House of Worship was built in Turkmenistan, between 1902 and 1908, but was damaged by an earthquake in 1948 and was eventually razed in 1963. There are currently eight continental Mashriqu'l-Adhkárs, in Australia, Chile, Germany, India, Panama, Samoa, Uganda, and the United States; two national Mashriqu'l-Adhkár in the Democratic Republic of Congo and Papua New Guinea; and four local Mashriqu'l-Adhkárs in Cambodia, Colombia, Kenya and Vanuatu. Several new Houses of Worship are currently under construction, notably in Brazil, Canada, Malawi, and India.

Spiritual Assembly: The name of an elected Bahá'í administrative institution composed of nine members forming a governing body that coordinates, guides, and manages the affairs of the Bahá'í community. The area of jurisdiction of a Spiritual Assembly can be local (Local Spiritual Assembly) or national (National Spiritual Assembly). The establishment of these assemblies is prescribed in the Will and Testament of 'Abdu'l-Bahá, and these institutions are central to the administrative order of the Bahá'í Faith, as it has no clergy.

Ten Year Crusade: A collective endeavor launched by the Guardian in 1953 to strengthen the foundations of the structure of the Administrative Order and expand the presence of the Bahá'í Faith worldwide. Twenty-seven objectives were formulated, encompassed in four primary goals: (1) the development of institutions at the World

Center, (2) the consolidation of the twelve countries where the Faith was well established, (3) the consolidation of all other territories already open, and (4) the opening of the remaining "chief virgin territories on the planet" (Shoghi Effendi, *Messages to the Bahá'í World 1950–1957,* p. 42).

Universal House of Justice: The supreme international governing and legislative body of the Bahá'í Faith. Its nine members are elected every five years by the members of each National Spiritual Assembly. The Universal House of Justice today guides the growth and development of the global Bahá'í community. Its Constitution entrusts it with the duty to exert a positive influence on the general welfare of humankind and to promote a permanent peace among the nations of the world. It was elected for the first time in 1963.

Glossary of Names

'Abdu'l-Bahá (1844–1921): The "Servant of Bahá," a title given to Abbas Effendi, first son of Bahá'u'lláh. After Bahá'u'lláh's passing in 1892, 'Abdu'l-Bahá became the Head of the Faith and leader of the Bahá'í community, as prescribed by Bahá'u'lláh in the Kitáb-i-'Ahd (Book of the Covenant). He is appointed in this Tablet as the Center of the Covenant and the authorized Interpreter of Bahá'u'lláh's Writings. He is regarded as the perfect Exemplar of Bahá'u'lláh's teachings.

Afrúkhtih Yúnis (?–1948): A physician by training, born in Persia, who served as secretary and interpreter for 'Abdu'l-Bahá from 1900 to 1909 in the Holy Land. After returning home to Tehran, this indefatigable promoter of the Faith was elected to the Local Spiritual Assembly of Tehran and the National Spiritual Assembly of Iran. He traveled to America and Europe several times. He is the author of *Memories of Nine Years in 'Akká,* his memoirs of the nine years he spent in the service of 'Abdu'l-Bahá.

d'Ange d'Astre, Georgina, Baronne (1874–1946): A Bahá'í who was a member of the Paris community in its early years. A nurse at the Red Cross, she worked in French military hospitals in Turkey, Greece, and Serbia. She also traveled to the Holy Land with Mr. & Mrs. Howard McNutt to meet the Master and published several articles regarding the Faith in French newspapers and *Star of the West.*

Ávárih, 'Abdu'l-Ḥusayn (1873–1953): A Persian Bahá'í who traveled extensively to deepen the new believers in their knowledge of the Faith. Unfortunately for him, he withdrew from the Faith in 1927 and publicly attacked the Institution of the Guardianship and Shoghi Effendi's efforts to build the Administrative Order.

Azízí, Azíz'u'lláh (1873–1949): Known as Jináb-i-Azízí, he was a Persian Bahá'í from a Jewish background. He was very close to and had a strong friendship with 'Abdu'l-Bahá, journeyed to the Holy Land eight times, and met the Master during His travels in both Paris and London. His memoirs are available at http://bahai-library.org under the title *Crown of Glory*.

Ahmadov, Áqá Ḥusayn 'Alí (years of birth and passing unknown): A businessman who was, with his brother, one of the leading members of the Bahá'í community in Ashgabat. He was instrumental in resisting the attacks of the Covenant-breakers in the region, particularly in Georgia. His father was Ḥájí Aḥmad, a Persian Bahá'í who met the Báb in Tabriz and helped in the highly risky task of concealing from the enemies of the Faith the remains of the Báb after His martyrdom.

Ali-Kuli Khan (1879–1966): A prominent Persian Bahá'í who served for many years as amanuensis for 'Abdu'l-Bahá and as His interpreter. He moved to the United States, where he made his career as a diplomat. In 1904, he married Florence Breed (1875–1950); their union was praised by the Master as one of the earliest intercultural marriages and "the fruit of the prophecy of Bahá'u'lláh that the East and the West shall be united like unto two beloved ones." (National Spiritual Assembly of the Bahá'ís of the United States and Canada, "In Memoriam: Francis William Breed," *Bahá'í News* (1931), no. 49, p. 3, col. 2.)

Báb, the (1819–1850): The title, meaning "the Gate" in Arabic, is one of the titles of Siyyid 'Alí-Muḥammad, the Prophet-Founder of the Bábí Faith in 1844. As the Forerunner and Herald of the Bahá'í Faith, He foretold during His ministry the coming of "Him Whom God shall make manifest" and was martyred in Tabriz in 1850.

Badí' (1852–1869): Also known as Áqá Buzurg-i-Níshápúrí, most famous for being the bearer of a Tablet written by Bahá'u'lláh for personal delivery to Náṣiri'd-Dín Sh̲áh. For doing so, he was arrested, tortured for three days and killed at the age of seventeen. He was posthumously named an Apostle of Bahá'u'lláh by Shoghi Effendi.

Bag̲h̲dádí, Zia Mabsut (1884–1937): Born in Beirut, he was the son of the Apostle of Bahá'u'lláh Muḥammad Mustafá al-Bag̲h̲dádí (1838–1910). In 1909, he went to the United States, where he established himself as a physician. He accompanied the Master during His stay in the United States, was elected a member of the Bahá'í Temple Unity, and served as the editor of the Persian pages of *Star of the West.*

Bahá'u'lláh (1817–1892): The "Glory of God" is the title of Mírzá Ḥusayn-'Alí, Prophet-Founder of the Bahá'í Faith. He proclaimed world unity and universal peace and taught that all people were created and nurtured by the same loving and merciful God. He advocated principles such as equality between men and women, the abolition of prejudices, harmony between science and religion, and the need for universal education. Clerical leaders and authorities of Persia and the Ottoman Empire rose up against Him, banished Him from Tehran to Baghdad, to Constantinople, to Adrianople, and eventually to the prison-city of Akká. In the evening years of His life, He resided at the Mansion at Bahjí, where He passed away in 1892.

Bahíyyih K̲h̲ánum (1846–1932): The daughter of Bahá'u'lláh and a sister of 'Abdu'l-Bahá. She is known by the title "The Greatest Holy Leaf." She accompanied Bahá'u'lláh throughout His exiles and dedicated her whole life to the service of the Faith. She was an unfailing and faithful companion to the Master after the passing of Bahá'u'lláh and an indefatigable support and solace to Shoghi Effendi after the passing of 'Abdu'l-Bahá.

Baraghani, Fátimih (1817/18–1852): Known as Ṭáhirih (The Pure One) or Qurratu'l-'Ayn (Solace of the Eyes), she was an eloquent poetess, an ardent protector of the Báb, and the only woman among the Letters of the Living (the first eighteen persons to have recognized the Báb as the Return of the Qáim, in addition to Siyyid 'Alí-Muḥammad, the Báb Himself). Thanks to her legendary courage, she will forever stand in the annals of the Faith as a prominent symbol of the emancipation, education, and equality of women.

Barney, Alice Pike (1857–1931): An American Bahá'í and famous painter who was the mother of Laura Clifford Barney and Natalie Barney.

Barney, Laura: See Dreyfus-Barney, Laura Alice Clifford.

Barney, Natalie (1876–1972): Laura Barney's sister. American playwright, poet, and novelist, she spent most of her life in Paris. For more than sixty years, she hosted a salon every Friday at her home, where prominent artists and writers from all around the world would gather and converse about poetry, literature, and social issues. Some of them would later write about the Faith or even about 'Abdu'l-Bahá during His stay in Paris.

Blomfield, Lady Sara Louisa (1859–1939): A Bahá'í from Ireland who lived most of her life in London. She became a Bahá'í in 1907 and took extensive notes of 'Abdu'l-Bahá's discourses during public meetings in Paris; these materials were used in preparing the volume called *Paris Talks*. A very active humanitarian, she took part in the founding of Save the Children, an NGO dedicated to improving the lives of children.

Boylan, Annie (1869–1933): An American Bahá'í who lived in New York. She met 'Abdu'l-Bahá in Thonon-les-Bains in 1911 and subsequently served on numerous Bahá'í administrative bodies in the United States.

Breakwell, Thomas (1872–1902): The first Englishman to become a Bahá'í and one of the "three luminaries of the Irish, English and Scottish Bahá'í communities."(Shoghi Effendi, *Messages to the Bahá'í World, 1950–1957,* p. 174). He was taught the Faith by May Bolles Maxwell during the summer of 1901 and traveled to the Holy Land to meet 'Abdu'l-Bahá a few weeks thereafter. At the Master's request, he returned to Paris, where he served and taught the Cause with great enthusiasm and intense devotion. By reason of his exceptional spiritual maturity and purity of heart, he became the first Western Bahá'í to pay Ḥuqúqu'lláh. In 1902, he contracted tuberculosis, and after long months of sufferings, he passed away at the age of thirty.

Buikema, Gertrude (1874–1942): An American Bahá'í who, along with Albert Windust (1874–1956), was responsible for the editing and distribution of *Star of the West,* a Bahá'í periodical published in the United States.

Carra de Vaux, Bernard (1867–1953): A French orientalist who mentioned the Bábís in several of his publications.

Chamberlain, Isabel Fraser (1871–1939): An American Bahá'í from California who compiled some of the talks of the Master during His travels in the West and published them under the title *'Abdu'l-Bahá on Divine Philosophy.*

Chase, Thornton (1847–1912): An American Bahá'í who was designated by 'Abdu'l-Bahá as the first American believer. He played a major role in developing Bahá'í communities in Chicago and Los Angeles, and in the diffusion of the first publications about the Faith in English. He was posthumously named a Disciple of 'Abdu'l-Bahá by the Guardian.

Chevalier, Faith (1851–1935): An American Bahá'í who lived in Los Angeles and who was a very good friend of Hippolyte and Laura Dreyfus-Barney.

Chirazí, Habíbu'lláh (years of birth and passing unknown): A Persian Bahá'í who was born in Shiraz and who was the son of Áqá Riḍá Qannád. Named "Aynu'l-Mulk" ("the Eye of the Nation"), he collaborated with Hippolyte on his first translation of the Holy Writings in French. Habíbulláh was very active during the early years of the twentieth century and played an essential role in the propagation of the Faith in Paris. However, as the years passed, he became very ambitious and drifted away from the Faith.

Cooper, Ella (1870–1951): An American Bahá'í who was Helen Goodall's daughter. Upon returning from her second pilgrimage in 1908, she published with her mother their personal impressions in a book called *Daily Lessons Received at Akká.*

Cropper, Mary Virginia Thornburgh (1857–1938): An American Bahá'í living in London who is considered the first believer to have accepted the Faith in the United Kingdom in 1898. She joined the group of the first Western pilgrims who met the Master in the Holy Land in 1899. She went several times to the Holy Land and was instrumental in organizing the visits of the Master to the United Kingdom in 1911 and 1912. She was also elected to the first Spiritual Assembly of the Bahá'ís of the British Isles in 1922.

De Bons, Theodora Edith: Born MacKaye (1879–1959), she was a French-American Bahá'í who was taught the Faith by May Bolles Maxwell and who became the second believer in Paris. She was one of the first believers to reside in Switzerland when she left Paris in 1903.

Dreyfus, Carle (1875–1952): Hippolyte's cousin and son of Gustave Dreyfus (see Dreyfus, Gustave Louis). He was a curator at the artifacts department of the Louvre. 'Abdu'l-Bahá visited the museum in 1913 during His second sojourn in Paris.

Dreyfus, Gustave Louis (1837–1914): Hippolyte's uncle. Between 1861 and 1864, he worked in Egypt for the construction of the Suez Canal. He acted as a jury member to several prominent international art expositions. He was a renowned art collector; he amassed an important collection of which one item, "La Madone Dreyfus," is currently exhibited in the National Gallery of Art in Washington, DC. He was honored by being named *Chevalier de la légion d'honneur* (Knights of the Legion of Honor) in 1878.

Dreyfus, Georges Arthur Lucien (1840–1911): Hippolyte's father. A stockbroker, in 1872 he married Léa Cardozo, with whom he had two children, Hippolyte and Yvonne. He became a Bahá'í in the early years of the twentieth century. His death was announced in *Star of the West.*

Dreyfus-Cardozo, Léa Marie Sophie Inès (1848–1913): Hippolyte's mother. A descendant of a Jewish family who left Portugal to live in France, she married Georges Dreyfus in 1872. She became a Bahá'í in the early years of the twentieth century and met with 'Abdu'l-Bahá several times in Paris in 1911 and 1913.

Dreyfus-Barney, Laura Alice Clifford (1879–1974): Hippolyte's wife. Born in the United States, she attended boarding school in France and later studied art in Paris. Artist, painter, and sculptor, she visited Haifa and 'Akká several times and stayed with the Holy Family for long periods of time. During her visits, she took down her conversations with 'Abdu'l-Bahá, which she compiled into a book titled *Some Answered Questions.* During the First World War, she served in the American Ambulance Corps and the American Red Cross in France, and she helped to establish the first children's hospital in Avignon. She was very active in the International Council of Women and an ardent advocate who represented different NGOs accredited to the League of Nations and to the United Nations. She was named *Chevalier* (Knight) in 1925 and *Officier of the French Légion d'Honneur* (Officer of the Legion of Honor) in 1937 for all the many services she performed in France.

Esslemont, John (1874–1925): A British Bahá'í born in Scotland. A physician by training, he became a Bahá'í in 1915. He was the author of the introductory book on the Bahá'í Faith, *Bahá'u'lláh and the New Era,* first published in 1923 and eventually translated into dozens of languages. In 1951, he was posthumously named a Disciple of 'Abdu'l-Bahá, and a Hand of the Cause by the Guardian.

Faraju'lláh-Khán, Mírzá (years of birth and passing unknown): A Persian Bahá'í who served as a French teacher at the Tarbiyat School for Boys in Tehran. He was sent by 'Abdu'l-Bahá several times to the United States to deepen the American communities.

Frankland, Kathryn (1872–1963): An American Bahá'í who lived in California. An outstanding teacher of the Faith, she taught many people, such as the very devoted Saichiro Fujita (1886–1976). At the request of the Master, she traveled to South America and eventually homefront pioneered to Texas for many years.

Gail, Marzieh (1908–1993): An American Bahá'í who was the daughter of Ali-Kuli Khan and Florence Breed Khan (1875–1950). She was a very prolific author and translator. In the early 1930s, responding to the instruction of the Guardian, she moved with her husband to Tehran to teach the Persian Bahá'ís about the Administrative Order. In 1954, in response to the Ten Year Crusade, Marzieh and her husband moved to France, Austria, and the Netherlands to support the formation of the first Local Spiritual Assemblies in Nice, Salzburg, and Arnhem.

Gamble, Annie (1848–1947): One of the first British Bahá'ís. In 1912, 'Abdu'l-Bahá gave a talk at her home. She was asked by the Master to protect the community in London against the doubts spread by Dr. Faríd.

Getsinger, Louisa Aurora Moore (1871–1916): Better known as Lua Getsinger, she was one of the first American Bahá'ís. An outstanding teacher of the Faith, she traveled around the world, taught many believers, notably May Bolles Maxwell, and joined the group of first Western pilgrims who met the Master in the Holy Land in 1899. Referred to as the "mother teacher of the American Bahá'í Community" and "herald of the dawn of the Day of the Covenant," she was posthumously named a Disciple of 'Abdu'l-Bahá by the Guardian (Shoghi Effendi, *This Decisive Hour,* p. 101).

Goin, Ellen (1877–1966): An American Bahá'í, she was Laura Barney's cousin. She married a wealthy Cuban businessman, Manuel Rionda, with whom she lived in New Jersey.

Goodall, Helen S. (1847–1922): An American Bahá'í who lived in California. She heard about the Faith for the first time in 1898 from Lua Getsinger and eventually traveled to New York with her daughter, Ella Cooper, to learn about the Faith from Anton Haddad. A tireless teacher of the Faith, she helped establish the Bahá'í Faith on the west coast of the United States and in Hawaii. She was posthumously named a Disciple of 'Abdu'l-Bahá by the Guardian.

Gulpáygání, Mírzá Abu'l-Faḍl (1844–1914): One of the foremost Bahá'í scholars who helped spread the Faith in Egypt, Turkmenistan, and the United States. Although he never actually met Bahá'u'lláh, he was posthumously named an Apostle of Bahá'u'lláh by the Guardian.

Haddad, Anton (1862–1924): Born in Lebanon, he was the first Bahá'í to move to the United States in 1892. A skilled translator, he was an ardent supporter of 'Abdu'l-Bahá against the Covenant-breakers' activities in the United States.

Ḥájí Ákhúnd (1842–1910): Also known by his full name, Ḥají Mullá 'Alí-Akbar Shahmírzádí, he was one of the four Hands of the Cause appointed by Bahá'u'lláh. Praised for his forbearance and fortitude under severe persecution and for his zeal in the propagation of the Cause, he was arrested and imprisoned many times, notably during seven months in 1872, two years in 1882, and two years again in 1891.

Haney, Mariam (1874–1939): An American Bahá'í who was elected to the first National Spiritual Assembly of the United States and Canada in 1925. She was the mother of Hand of the Cause of God Paul Haney (1909–1982).

Hannen, Joseph (1872–1920): Born in the United States, he became a Bahá'í in 1902 in Washington, DC. During 'Abdu'l-Bahá's visit to America in 1912, he was one of the believers who took notes of many of His talks, which were later published in *The Promulgation of Universal Peace*. He was elected and served many years on the Bahá'í Temple Unity, and he was posthumously named a Disciple of 'Abdu'l-Bahá by the Guardian.

Hannen, Pauline, née Knobloch (1874–1939): A German American Bahá'í who married Joseph Hannen. During His visit to America, 'Abdu'l-Bahá gave several talks at their home. In 1925, she and her sister became the first Bahá'ís to visit Southern Rhodesia (now Zimbabwe).

Harris, (William) Hooper (1866–1934): An American Bahá'í who, together with his wife Sarah, encountered the Faith for the first time in 1899. He went to the Holy Land in 1906 to meet 'Abdu'l-Bahá, Who suggested he travel to India to teach the Cause, which he immediately did. He visited many cities in India and Burma and eventually returned to New York in 1907, where he was a very active member of the community. He was posthumously named a Disciple of 'Abdu'l-Bahá by the Guardian.

Ḥasan-i-Adíb, Mírzá (1848–1919): Also known by his full name Hájí Mírzá Ḥasan-i-Adíb, he was one of the four Hands of the Cause appointed by Bahá'u'lláh. Instrumental in dealing with the activities of the Covenant-breakers, he participated in the formation of the first Spiritual Assembly in Tehran.

Herrick, Elizabeth (1864–1929): A British Bahá'í from Liverpool, she spent most of her life in London. She is the author of *Unity Triumphant: The Call of the Kingdom,* an introductory book to the Faith published in 1925.

Hoagg, Emogene (1869–1945): An American Bahá'í, considered the first Bahá'í to reside in California. Among her countless services, she went pioneering in Alaska in response to the call of the Master in the Tablets of the Divine Plan. She also pioneered to both Italy and Cuba.

Holley, Bertha D. Herbert (1879–1969): A Bahá'í who taught the Faith to many prominent believers, such as Lady Blomfield and Horace Holley, whom she would marry in 1909. During a trip to Paris, while she was living in Italy, she met 'Abdu'l-Bahá in Thonon-les-Bains in 1911.

Holley, Horace (1887–1960): An American poet, he became a Bahá'í in 1909. He served on several Local Spiritual Assemblies before being elected to the National Spiritual Assembly of the United States and Canada in 1925 for which he served as secretary for thirty-four years. The Guardian named him a Hand of the Cause in 1951. After the passing of Shoghi Effendi, he was chosen in 1959 to serve as a Custodian—one of those who served as stewards of the Faith until the election of the first Universal House of Justice in 1963—to replace a member who could no longer serve. He passed away in 1960.

Jack, Marion (1866–1954): A Canadian Bahá'í, she encountered the Faith in Paris. In 1908, she visited the Holy Land and stayed in 'Akká for a short time to teach English to members of the Holy Family. A prominent teacher of the Faith who was also known as the "Immortal Heroine" and "General Jack," she passed away in 1954 at her pioneering post in Sofia, Bulgaria, where she had been serving since 1931, disregarding all manner of danger and privation.

Jackson, Mary Edith (1849–1914): An American Bahá'í living in Paris, she was a Bostonian who married James Jackson, a wealthy Frenchman. Her first Bahá'í teacher was May Bolles Maxwell, who taught her in Paris. She went to the Holy Land in 1901, where she met 'Abdu'l-Bahá. Her encounter with the Master left her "full of faith."

Jamál Effendi (?–1898) or Sulaymán Khán, a Persian Bahá'í from Tunukábun. He was sent by Bahá'u'lláh to India in the 1870s to teach the Cause. He traveled extensively to India, Sri Lanka, Burma, Southeast Asia, and Central Asia until the end of his life, and he won countless victories for the Faith.

Kappes, Lillian Frances (1878–1920): An American Bahá'í from New Jersey. In 1911, she moved to Tehran to serve at the Bahá'í school for girls, first as a teacher, then as a professor, then as director. With Elizabeth Stewart, she met 'Abdu'l-Bahá in Thonon-les-Bains in 1911. She died of typhus fever in Persia and was buried in Tehran next to the tomb of Varqá. She was the first Western Bahá'í to die in the Cradle of the Faith, and she was posthumously named a Disciple of 'Abdu'l-Bahá by the Guardian.

Lacheny, Emmanuella (years of birth and passing unknown): We have very little information about Mme Lacheny, other than she was a friend of Laura Dreyfus-Barney with whom she, together with Hippolyte, visited Persia in 1906. Her name is sometimes spelled Lachnay, Lacheny, or Lacheney.

Latimer, George Orr (1889–1949): An American Bahá'í who met 'Abdu'l-Bahá in November 1919 and published, in 1920, his impressions in a book called *The Light of the World.* He worked closely with Leroy Ioas and John Bosch in helping to open the first Bahá'í school in the West, in Geyserville, California. He was a member of the National Spiritual Assembly of the United States from 1933 to 1939, and from 1941 to 1949.

MacNutt, Howard (1858–1926): One of the first Bahá'ís in the United States. He served as a member of the Bahá'í Publishing Society, the principal publisher of Bahá'í literature in the English-speaking world. He prepared *The Promulgation of Universal Peace,* a compilation of 139 talks given by the Master when He was in America in 1912. He was posthumously named a Disciple of 'Abdu'l-Bahá by the Guardian.

Mathews, Loulie (1869–1966): An American Bahá'í who, in response to the Guardian's call, traveled to South America with her husband, notably in Guatemala and Mexico, where they proclaimed the Faith to many.

Maxwell, May Bolles (1870–1940): Born in the United States, she was among the first contingent of pilgrims to visit the Master in the Holy Land in 1899. She was the spiritual mother of the Bahá'í community in Paris, and she was elected to the first National Spiritual Assembly of the United States and Canada in 1925. She married William Sutherland Maxwell (1874–1952), who was eventually named a Hand of the Cause. She was the mother of Mary Maxwell, who would marry Shoghi Effendi in 1937.

Meyer May, Jacques (1896–1975): Hippolyte's nephew, son of Yvonne Dreyfus and Paul Meyer May. He had several careers, including physician and surgeon, medical geographer, and nutritionist. He traveled to Vietnam, Thailand, and the United States for research projects. He died on July 3, 1975 in an automobile accident in Tunisia.

Meyer May, Paul (1868–1944): Husband of Hippolyte's sister, Yvonne Dreyfus Meyer May. He met 'Abdu'l-Bahá on several occasions in Paris in 1911.

Meyer May, Valentine (1898–1979): Hippolyte's niece, daughter of Yvonne Dreyfus and Paul Meyer May. During World War II, she managed to flee from France to the United States with her husband, Robert Maroni, and their daughter Claudine. She would live in the United States until the end of her life.

Meyer-May, Yvonne (1874–1941): Hippolyte's sister. She met 'Abdu'l-Bahá several times in Paris in 1911. In 1913, she participated with Hippolyte, as a representative of the Bahá'í movement to the International Congress of Religious Progress.

Mills, Mountfort (1874–1949): An American Bahá'í who spent his life between Paris and New York. A lawyer by training, he represented the Faith in some important legal cases, notably in Egypt and in Iraq, and together with Horace Holley, he drew up a draft of a Declaration of Trust and the by-laws for the National Spiritual Assembly of the United States and Canada.

Mihdí, Mírzá (1848–1870): The youngest son of Bahá'u'lláh; he was given the title "The Purest Branch." He died at the age of twenty-two in the prison-city of 'Akká. While walking back and forth in enraptured prayer on the rooftop of Bahá'u'lláh's cell, he fell through a skylight, landing on top of a crate below him, whose splinters mortally pierced his lungs. He died of his injuries twenty-two hours later.

Muḥammad-'Alí, Mírzá (1853–1937): Eldest son of Bahá'u'lláh by His second wife; he was the main leader of the Covenant-breakers during the ministry of 'Abdu'l-Bahá.

Munírih Khánum (1847–1938): Known as the Holy Mother, she married 'Abdu'l-Bahá in 1873 and was His unwavering support and beloved confidante all her life. They had nine children together, but only four—all daughters—survived to adulthood: Ḍíyá'íyyih Khánum (Shoghi Effendi's mother), Rúḥá Khánum, Ṭúbá Khánum, and Munavar Khánum.

Ober, Grace née Robarts (1869–1938): A Canadian Bahá'í. She became a Bahá'í in 1906 after being taught by Lua Getsinger. Her wedding with Harlan Ober was celebrated by 'Abdu'l-Bahá when the Master was in New York in 1912.

Ober, Harlan Foster (1881–1962), American Bahá'í. He became a Bahá'í in 1905 after attending conferences held in Green Acre. He traveled extensively for the Faith to India, Burma, the Middle East, and South Africa. He passed away at his last pioneering post in Pretoria in 1962.

Parsons, Agnes (1861–1934): American Bahá'í from Washington. She visited 'Abdu'l-Bahá in the Holy Land in 1910 and 1920 and organized His stay in Washington in 1912. 'Abdu'l-Bahá told her, "I want you to arrange in Washington a convention for unity between the white and coloured people." She carried out His instructions by organizing, with the support of several American believers, the first Race Amity Conference, which was held in Washington, DC in 1921.

Ponsonaille, Désiré Jacques Victor (1851–1937): A French Bahá'í who moved in 1911 with his wife into a very poor quarter outside Paris in order to help children there. Through great sacrifices, they were able to feed and give free education to a large number of children.

Rabb, Mary (1872–1940): An American Bahá'í who, in 1926, published a compilation of the Writings of 'Abdu'l-Bahá titled *The Divine Art of Living.*

Ralston, Georgia (1869–1950): An American Bahá'í who heard about the Faith in 1910 from her childhood friend, Ella Cooper. She met 'Abdu'l-Bahá many times, notably in New York in 1912 and in the Holy Land in 1920.

Remey, Charles Mason (1874–1974): An American Bahá'í who was introduced to the Bahá'í Faith by May Bolles in Paris in 1899 while he was a student at *l'École des beaux arts* in Paris. He traveled extensively to teach the Faith, visited Bahá'í communities across the world, proposed architectural designs for the Houses of Worship in Uganda and Australia, and was eventually named a Hand of the Cause in 1951 by Shoghi Effendi. After the Guardian passed away, he was elected as one of nine Custodians to oversee the administration of the international Bahá'í community. However, a few years later, he claimed to be the second Guardian of the Bahá'í Faith. After several months of consultation, the Hands of the Cause made the decision to declare him a Covenant-breaker in 1961.

Root, Martha Louise (1872–1939): An American Bahá'í whom Shoghi Effendi called "the foremost travel teacher in the first Bahá'í Century." A journalist by training, she became a Bahá'í in 1909 after meeting Roy C. Wilhelm and several other members of the Bahá'í community. From 1919, she started her travels all around the world to proclaim and teach the Faith. She is famously known for meeting Queen Marie of Romania, who is considered the first royalty to have accepted the Bahá'í Faith. Martha Root was posthumously named a Hand of the Cause by the Guardian.

Rosenberg, Ethel (1858–1930): one of the first Bahá'ís to accept the Faith in the United Kingdom, in 1899. An outstanding promoter of the teachings of Bahá'u'lláh, she visited the Holy Land three times, helped organize the visit of 'Abdu'l-Bahá to London, and served as secretary of the Guardian.

Rúḥá Khánum (circa 1880–?): Third daughter of 'Abdu'l-Bahá. Born in the prison-city of 'Akká, she married Mírzá Jalál Shahíd, with whom she had four children. He was a son of Mírzá Muḥammad-Ḥasan (the "King of the Martyrs").

Rúmí, Siyyid Muṣṭafáy-i- (1846–1945): One of the Hands of the Cause appointed by Shoghi Effendi in 1945. Born in Baghdad, he grew up in Madras, India. He served the Cause in India and in Burma, where he helped establish communities in Rangoon, Mandalay, and Daidanaw, a village in the south of Burma where more than eight hundred residents converted to the Faith.

Russell, Eva Webster (1856–1914): An American Bahá'í who was very active in the Chicago community. She was a very much appreciated painter and miniaturist.

Ṣabri, Shaykh Muḥyíd-dín (circa 1860–circa 1940): A Persian Bahá'í who was a teacher in Cairo. He was sent by the Master to Tunisia to teach the Faith, then to Iraq by the Guardian.

Samandar, Shaykh Muḥammad Káẓim-i- (1844–1918): A prominent Persian Bahá'í from Qazvín who was named an Apostle of Bahá'u'lláh by the Guardian, he traveled extensively in Persia to teach the Bahá'í Faith and to protect the Covenant in the time of both Bahá'u'lláh and 'Abdu'l-Bahá. He is the father of Tarázu'lláh Samandarí, who would be named a Hand of the Cause in 1951.

Sanderson, Edith (1870–1955): An American Bahá'í. She became a Bahá'í in 1901 after meeting May Bolles Maxwell. A close friend of Hippolyte and Laura, she dedicated her life to the promotion of the Faith in France.

Sanderson, Margaret (1839–1913): Spouse of the seventh chief justice of the Supreme Court of California, Silas Sanderson, and mother of Edith Sanderson and Sibyl Sanderson. After her husband's passing, she took her daughters to Paris to pursue their studies.

Sanderson, Sibyl (1864–1903): A famous operatic soprano, widely considered as the muse who inspired some of the works of the renowned pianist, Jules Massenet.

Schwarz, Albert (1871–1931): A German diplomat who became a Bahá'í at the same time as his wife after hearing about the Faith in 1912 from Edwin Fisher, an American Bahá'í who pioneered to Germany. Albert Schwarz met 'Abdu'l-Bahá when the Master visited Stuttgart in 1913. He was elected chairman of the inaugural National Spiritual Assembly of Germany and Austria in 1922, where he served until his passing. He was posthumously named a Disciple of 'Abdu'l-Bahá by the Guardian.

Scott, Frank Edwin (1862–1929): An American painter who lived in Paris. With his wife Josephine (1863–1955), he was an active teacher of the Faith. Their studio, where the Master gave talks in 1911 and 1913, was one of the most dynamic centers of activities in Paris at the beginning of the twentieth century and was used as the first Bahá'í library in France.

Shoghi Effendi (1897–1957): Great-grandson of Bahá'u'lláh and eldest grandson of 'Abdu'l-Bahá. He was appointed Guardian of the Bahá'í Faith by 'Abdu'l-Bahá in His Will and Testament. During his ministry, he developed the administrative structure of the Bahá'í community, launched the Ten Year Crusade, translated into English many of the Holy Writings of Bahá'u'lláh, the Báb, and 'Abdu'l-Bahá, and wrote many letters and several historical books. Additionally, he oversaw the restoration of Bahá'í Holy Places, the completion of the superstructure of the Shrine of the Báb, and the landscaping of the gardens at the heart of the World Center. Between his appointment as Guardian and his passing, the number of believers increased significantly, and the number of countries opened to the Faith increased from 35 to 250.

Sohrab, Mírzá Ahmad (1893–1958): A Persian-American author who served as 'Abdu'l-Bahá's interpreter, translator, and secretary between 1912 and 1919. He wrote several historical books on Bahá'u'lláh and 'Abdu'l-Bahá. After rejecting the Guardian and opposing the Spiritual Assembly of New York and the National Spiritual Assembly of the United States, he was eventually declared a Covenant-breaker in 1939. His wife and daughter eventually changed their names and remained faithful to the Cause.

Sprague, Sydney (1875–1943): An American Bahá'í who was an art and music teacher. He was Hippolyte's traveling companion during their journey to India and Burma in 1905. He visited many places, particularly in Persia and Russia, to promote the Cause. He moved to Persia and married one of the nieces of 'Abdu'l-Bahá. After a few years, her family broke the Covenant, and he left the Faith. Toward the end of his life, in 1941, he applied to be reinstated and was finally accepted in 1941.

Stewart, Elizabeth Harnill (1867–1926): An American Bahá'í who, in 1911, moved to Tehran to serve at the Bahá'í school for girls as a nurse—a position at which she served until 1924. With Lillian Kappes, she met 'Abdu'l-Bahá in Thonon-les-Bains in 1911.

Struven, Howard (1882–1977): An American Bahá'í whose mother, Rose Struven, was the host of many Bahá'í meetings at their home in Baltimore. He accepted the Faith in the late 1890s after meeting with Lua Getsinger. At the end of 1927, responding to 'Abdu'l-Bahá's suggestion, he traveled with Charles Mason Remey for a teaching trip to circle the globe. They traveled to Hawaii, Japan, Shanghai, Singapore, Burma, India, and Palestine.

Tamaddunu'l-Mulk (years of birth and passing unknown): A Persian Bahá'í from Shiraz. He met 'Abdu'l-Bahá in Thonon-les-Bains in 1911 and accompanied Him during His long visit to Europe. In 1913, he attempted to divide the Bahá'ís of Tehran and was eventually expelled from the Faith.

Thompson, Juliet (1873–1956): An American Bahá'í who lived in Paris in the early 1900s. She was a close friend of Lua Getsinger and May Bolles, and in 1909, she met 'Abdu'l-Bahá in the Holy Land and accompanied and attended to the Master during His stay in Thonon-les-Bains in 1911. In 1912, she painted a portrait of the Master in New York; it was on this occasion that New York City was designated by the Master as the "City of the Covenant" ('Abdu'l-Bahá, quoted at "City of the Covenant," https://www.bahai.us/city-of-the-covenant/).

True, Corinne (1861–1961): An American Bahá'í who was named a Hand of the Cause by the Guardian in 1952. She played an instrumental role in the establishment of the Mother Temple of the West, the first Bahá'í House of Worship on the American continent, in Wilmette, near Chicago.

Tudor-Pole, Wellesley (1884–1968): A spiritualist, a British Bahá'í, and a fervent admirer of 'Abdu'l-Bahá who wrote a book about the Master and the Bahá'í Faith titled *Writing on the Ground* (1968). In 1917, as a major in the British army, he played a decisive role in protecting the Master in Haifa while the British troops, led by General Allenby, were invading Palestine. It was in his office in London that Shoghi Effendi first learned of the passing of 'Abdu'l-Bahá.

Waite, Louise (1866–1939): One of the early believers in America, she joined the Faith shortly after Thornton Chase in 1894. She served many years as a member of the Spiritual Assembly of Los Angeles and composed several well-known songs, such as "The Temple Song" and "The Benediction."

Wilhelm, Roy C. (1875–1951): A very successful American businessman who became a Bahá'í in 1907 while accompanying his mother on pilgrimage. She had been a believer since 1898. A member of the Executive Board of the Bahá'í Temple Unity in 1909, he remained a member until he was elected to serve as a member of the first National Spiritual Assembly of the United States and Canada. He was posthumously named a Hand of the Cause by the Guardian.

Windust, Albert (1874–1956): An American Bahá'í who was elected to the first Spiritual Assembly of Chicago. In 1910, he became editor of *Star of the West* and was responsible for the distribution of Bahá'í literature in the United States.

Winterburn, Rose and George (years of birth and passing unknown): American Bahá'ís who accepted the Faith in Paris in the early 1900s. Their pilgrim notes from 1904 were published in 1908 under the title *Table Talks with 'Abdu'l-Bahá.*

Woodcock, Percy (1855–1936): A Canadian Bahá'í and well-known artist, he studied the arts at *l'École des beaux arts* in Paris and, later, in the Netherlands. He met 'Abdu'l-Bahá in Naples in 1912 and traveled with Him on the SS *Cedric* on their way to the United States.

Yaḥya, Mírzá (1832–1912): The half-brother of Bahá'u'lláh and primary leader of the Covenant-breakers during his time, who attempted to poison Bahá'u'lláh.

Zarqání, Maḥmúd (1875–1924): A Persian Bahá'í who, during his youth, traveled around and taught the Faith in Persia. Beginning in 1903, he began traveling outside of Persia, particularly in India. He was one of 'Abdu'l-Bahá's main secretaries during His trip to the West, and "he was a careful and faithful chronicler and engaged in assembling and publishing his work with the permission of the beloved Master" (Letter dated April 30, 1984 from the Universal House of Justice to the National Spiritual Assembly of the Bahá'ís of the United States). His impressions were compiled and published in a book titled *Mahmúd's Diary*.

Notes

Foreword

1. See Glossary under "Age."
2. "The Disciples of 'Abdu'l-Bahá," *The Bahá'í World* (New York), vol. 3, 1928–1930 (1930): 84–85.
3. Now spelled "Qingdao."

Foreword to the English Edition

1. The Universal House of Justice, "Message to the Friends Gathered in Battambang, Cambodia, for the Dedication of the House of Worship," 1 September 2017.
2. Bahá'u'lláh, in *The Compilation of Compilations, volume 2,* p. 332.
3. The Universal House of Justice, Message to the Conference of the Continental Boards of Counsellors, 30 December 2021.
4. The Universal House of Justice, *Message to the Bahá'ís of the World,* 25 November 2020.

Author's Note

1. *Hippolyte Dreyfus: Apôtre d'Abdu'l-Bahá.* Written by the Committee for the History of the Bahá'í Faith in France. (Paris: Librairie bahá'íe, 1996).

2. Unfortunately, a large portion of Laura's personal archives was lost during the Second World War when Paris was bombarded and, later, when it fell under German occupation.
3. See http://bahai-library.com and https://bahai.works.
4. Shoghi Effendi, *The World Order of Bahá'u'lláh,* p. 5.

1 / Early Years

1. According to his birth certificate delivered by the Prefecture of the Department of the Seine. Rue Rovigo (Rovigo Street) is now named the rue de la Bienfaisance.
2. Natalie Barney, *Hippolyte mon beau-frère . . .* , National Bahá'í Archives of France, Laura Dreyfus-Barney Folder, File: "Documents postérieurs à Hippolyte Dreyfus-Barney" (1AP-I-F).
3. The Dreyfus affair (l'Affaire Dreyfus) was a social and political scandal centering around the accusation of Captain Alfred Dreyfus of national treason. He was accused of passing French military secrets to the German Empire. This scandal disturbed the French society for more than twelve years, from 1894 until 1906, and deeply divided it between Captain Dreyfus' supporters and his accusers. Dreyfus was convicted but eventually exonerated, released, and reinstated in the French Army.
4. Laura Dreyfus-Barney, "Hippolyte Dreyfus-Barney," article for *Bahai World.* National Bahá'í Archives of France, Laura Dreyfus-Barney Folder, File: "Documents postérieurs à Hippolyte Dreyfus-Barney" (1AP-I-F).
5. Founded in 1803, The Lycée Condorcet is one of the four oldest high schools in Paris. During the nineteenth century, it was known for its liberality and was the first choice of the French bourgeoisie for the education of their children. Prominent individuals such as Paul Verlaine, Marcel Proust and Henri Bergson attended the Lycée Condorcet.
6. Hippolyte Dreyfus, *Des droits de succession du conjoint survivant dans le droit français et dans les principales législations étrangères* (Paris: Arthur Rousseau, 1898).

7. François Thévenet (1845–1910) was a French lawyer and politician. He was a member of the parliament, a senator, and was eventually appointed Minister of Justice and Religious Affairs between 1889 and 1890.
8. Laura Dreyfus-Barney, "Hippolyte Dreyfus-Barney," article for *Bahai World,* (1AP-I-F).
9. The Visitors' Society (la Société des Visiteurs) is a charitable association founded in 1896 with the aim of helping the unemployed, sick, or injured workers.
10. Yvonne Meyer-May (Dreyfus), "Curriculum vitae et activités d'Hippolyte Dreyfus," National Bahá'í Archives of France, Laura Dreyfus-Barney Folder, File: "Documents postérieurs à Hippolyte Dreyfus-Barney" (1AP-I-F).
11. Cécile Brunschvicg to Laura Dreyfus-Barney, Jan. 26th, 1929. Laura Dreyfus-Barney (1AP) Folder, File: "Documents postérieurs à Hippolyte Dreyfus-Barney" (1AP-I-F). Cécile Brunschvicg (Kahn) (1877–1946), one of Hippolyte's distant relatives, a prominent feminist, was appointed as Minister in Léon Blum's government during the Third Republic.

2 / First Encounter with the Bahá'í Faith

1. May Maxwell, "Hippolyte Dreyfus-Barney: The Passing of a Bahá'i Scholar and Lecturer." *The Bahá'í Magazine: Star of the West,* vol. 20, no. 1 (April 1929): 26–27.
2. Jean Lefranc, "Le bahaïsme et son prophète." *Le Temps,* no. 18386 (3 Nov. 1911): 4, col. 2–3.
3. Ibid.
4. Jules Massenet (1842–1912) was a French composer of the Romantic area. Extremely prolific, he composed more than thirteen operas, including the famous *Manon* and *Werther.*
5. 'Akká, Akko, or Acre, is a city located on the Northern part of Haifa Bay, in Israel. In the 19th century, 'Akká (known by its Christian name of Saint-Jean-d'Acre) was a penal colony, well known for being extremely desolate, isolated and dirty, and

the most execrable prison city of the Ottoman Empire. It was to that city that Bahá'u'lláh and His family were banished in 1868, and in the vicinity of which, at Bahjí, Bahá'u'lláh, the Prophet founder of the Bahá'í Faith, passed away.

6. École des beaux-arts (The Beaux-Arts school of Paris) is a French *Grande École* founded in 1671. The school was renowned for being one of the best in the world, and offered instruction in drawing, painting, sculpture, architecture, and engraving to students selected by competitive examination. The Beaux-Arts is the classical and historical School of Fine Arts in France.
7. Hogenson, Kathryn Jewett, *Lighting the Western Sky: The Hearst Pilgrimage and the Establishment of the Bahá'í Faith in the West,* pp. ix–x.
8. Ibid., p. 181.
9. One of the honorific names by which ardent believers refer to Bahá'u'lláh.
10. Violette Nakhjavani, *The Maxwells of Montreal: Early Years 1870–1922,* pp. 145–46.
11. Hippolyte Dreyfus-Barney, "Bibliography." National Bahá'í Archives of France, Laura Dreyfus-Barney Folder, (1AP). File: Hippolyte "Manuscrit-œuvre" (1AP-I-B).
12. Clément Huart (1854–1926), was a French orientalist. After graduating with a focus in Arabic, Persian, Turkish, and modern Greek, he joined the Ministry of Foreign Affairs and was sent to Damascus and eventually to Istanbul. Back in France, he held the Chair of Persian at the School for Oriental Languages *(École des langues orientales)* and was finally appointed Director of Studies for Islam and the religions of Arabia at the *École pratique des hautes études.*
13. Joseph Arthur de Gobineau (1816–1882), known as the "Comte de Gobineau," was a French writer and diplomat. Known for his work on race theory, he wrote several historical books on Persia, particularly *Religions and Philosophies in Central Asia (Les Religions et les philosophies de l'Asie Centrale)* in

1865, which was considered during many years the foremost work of reference about the Bábí Faith.

14. Louis Alphonse Daniel Nicolas (1864–1939), was a French orientalist and diplomat, better known under his pseudonym "A.L.M. Nicolas." Born in Persia, he spoke Persian and Russian fluently. Attracted by the Bábí Faith, he translated several Holy Writings of the Báb into French and wrote his own books on the Bábí Faith. For more information, see Edith Sanderson, "An Interview with A. L. M. Nicolas of Paris," in *The Bahá'í World*, vol. 8 (1942): 885–87.
15. Joseph Ernest Renan (1823–1892), was a French author, philosopher, and historian. Known for his research on the concept of nations, most of his works were dedicated to religion.

3 / Recognition of the Divine Message

1. A copy of this letter is held at the Department of the Archives at the Bahá'í World Center in Haifa. In general, letters written to the Head of the Faith are considered to be confidential communications and are not made public. Therefore, only a short summary is provided here. (Memo dated February 1, 2019 from the Research Department to the Universal House of Justice)
2. 'Abdu'l-Bahá to Hippolyte Dreyfus [undated], National Bahá'í Archives of France (Letter-1). Provisional translation from the Arabic prepared by the authors, reviewed and improved by Ms. Hoda Seioshansian and Ms. Mary Victoria, to whom we are grateful.
3. Yvonne Meyer-May (born Dreyfus), "Curriculum vitae et activités d'Hippolyte Dreyfus," (1AP-I-F).
4. Several of Hippolyte's study notebooks can be found in his personal belongings. Among these, a twelve-page notebook is dedicated to prophecies in the Bible that announced the coming of Bahá'u'lláh. These prophecies are cross-referenced with passages from the Kitáb-i-Íqán. In another notebook, Hippolyte studies the historic context surrounding the Rev-

elation; in a third one, he gathers all his notes regarding the colonization of Palestine. See National Bahá'í Archives of France, Laura Dreyfus-Barney Folder (1AP), File: Hippolyte "Manuscrit-œuvre" (1AP-I-B).

5. Laura Dreyfus-Barney, "Hippolyte Dreyfus-Barney," article for *Bahai World,* (1AP-I-F).
6. The word *Tablets* refers to letters or documents revealed or written by Bahá'u'lláh, the Báb, or 'Abdu'l-Bahá.
7. Mavaddat-Baghdadi Roxana, "Un oiseau parmi les oiseaux du paradis" in *Baha'i France,* no. 167, pp. 19–21.
8. 'Abdu'l-Bahá, in Ariane Schaller Haenni, *Edith Mackaye de Bons,* p. 170, National Bahá'í Archives of France.
9. Shoghi Effendi, "Hippolyte Dreyfus-Barney: An Appreciation," *The Bahá'í World,* vol. 3, 1928–1930 (1930): 210–14.
10. Youness Afroukhteh, *Memories of Nine Years in 'Akká,* p. 148.
11. See chapter 1, note no. 3.
12. Youness Afroukhteh, *Memories of Nine Years in 'Akká,* p. 148.
13. Ibid., p. 149.
14. Hippolyte Dreyfus to Yvonne Meyer-May 1 Feb. 1903. Dreyfus, Hippolyte (great-uncle of Claudine Harris): letters, 1903–1914, Box: 3. Iowa Women's Archives.
15. Jean Lefranc, "Le bahaïsme et son prophète." *Le Temps* (Paris), no. 18386 (3 Nov. 1911), p. 4, col. 3.
16. Yvonne Meyer-May (Dreyfus), "Curriculum vitae et activités d'Hippolyte Dreyfus," (1AP-I-F).
17. Established in 1868, the school had six sections when Hippolyte enrolled: Mathematics, Physics and Chemistry, Natural Sciences and Physiology, Philological and Historical Sciences, Economics, and Religious Sciences.
18. Hartwig Derenbourg (1844–1908) was a French orientalist. A specialist in Islam, Arabic, and Semitic languages, he was notably a professor of Arabic at the École pratique des hautes études.
19. See ch. 2, note no. 10.

20. Jean Lefranc, "Le bahaïsme et son prophète." *Le Temps* (Paris), no. 18386 (3 Nov. 1911), p. 4, col. 2–3.
21. Roxana Mavaddat-Baghdadi, "Un oiseau parmi les oiseaux du paradis" in *Bahá'í France* (Paris) no. 167, p. 19.
22. 'Abdu'l-Bahá to Hippolyte Dreyfus [undated], National Bahá'í Archives of France (Letter-2). Provisional translation from the Persian by the authors.
23. 'Abdu'l-Bahá to Hippolyte Dreyfus [undated], National Bahá'í Archives of France (Letter-8). Provisional translation from the Persian by the authors.
24. 'Abdu'l-Bahá to Hippolyte Dreyfus [undated], National Bahá'í Archives of France (Letter-2). Provisional translation from the Persian by the authors.

4 / Arising to Serve the Cause

1. Muzzafar al-Dín (1853–1907), or Mozzafar-al-Dín Sháh, was the shah of Persia between 1896 and 1907. At the end of his reign, the constitutional revolution forced him to create a constitution and a National Consultative Assembly in 1906. He died of a heart attack forty days after granting these reforms.
2. Velda Piff Metelmann, *Lua Getsinger: Herald of the Covenant,* pp. 59–67.
3. Laura Dreyfus-Barney, "Hippolyte Dreyfus-Barney," article for *Bahai World,* (1AP-I-F).
4. Azíz'u'lláh Azízí, *Crown of Glory: Memoirs of Jináb-i-Azíz'u'lláh Azízí,* translated from the original Persian by Christopher and Nahzy Buck, p. 90.
5. Janet Ruhe-Schoen, *A Love Which Does Not Wait: the Stories of Lua Getsinger, May Maxwell, Martha Root, Keith Ransom-Kehler, Hyde Dunn, Susan Moody, Dorothy Baker, Ella Bailey, and Marion Jack,* pp. 18–19.
6. Azíz'u'lláh Azízí, *Crown of Glory: Memoirs of Jináb-i-Azíz'u'lláh Azízí,* p. 91.

7. Lua Getsinger, quoted in Violette Nakhjavani, *The Maxwells of Montreal: Early Years 1870–1922,* p. 145.
8. Hippolyte's father and mother.
9. Hippolyte's sister.
10. Velda Piff Metelmann, *Lua Getsinger: Herald of the Covenant,* pp. 59–67.
11. Janet Ruhe-Schoen, *A Love Which Does Not Wait,* pp. 18–19.
12. See Glossary.
13. Hasan M. Balyuzi, *'Abdu'l-Bahá: The Centre of the Covenant of Bahá'u'lláh,* pp. 90–99.
14. Youness Afroukhteh, *Memories of Nine Years in 'Akká,* pp. 173–74.
15. Violette Nakhjavani, *The Maxwells of Montreal: Early Years 1870–1922,* p. 202.
16. Turkish word, derived from the Arabic word wali, which refers here to the governor of a province during the Ottoman Empire.
17. Hasan M. Balyuzi, *'Abdu'l-Bahá: The Centre of the Covenant of Bahá'u'lláh,* pp. 95–96.

5 / Early Stirrings of the Cause in Paris

1. The letters of declaration written by Yvonne and her husband, Paul Meyer-May, are in the archives of the Bahá'í World Center.
2. Youness Afroukhteh, *Memories of Nine Years in 'Akká,* pp. 326–27.
3. Born in 'Akká, Mírzá Ḥabíbu'lláh Chirazí was the son of Áqá Reza Qannad Shírází, an early follower of the Bahá'í Faith. In his early twenties, he relocated to Paris to study French and help grow the Bahá'í community. Shortly after his arrival, he and Hippolyte became central to the teaching activities in the city and contributed significantly to the proclamation of the Bahá'í Faith in the emerging community.
4. Ibid., p. 327.

5. Ibid., p. 142.
6. Hippolyte Dreyfus, "Le Babisme et le Béhaïsme" [Bábism and Behaism]" quoted in Théodore Reinach, et al. *Religions et sociétés: Leçons professées à l'École des hautes études sociales,* pp. 247–86. At the beginning of the nineteenth century, the transcription of the Persian words into the Latin alphabet was not standardized yet; therefore, different spellings were used to designate the Bahá'í Faith in French (Béhaïsme, Bahaïsme . . .), the Bahá'ís (béhaïs) or Bahá'u'lláh (BéhaUllah) and 'Abdu'l-Bahá (Abdoul Beha).
7. Ibid.
8. Ibid.
9. Théodore Reinach, et al. *Religions et sociétés: Leçons professées à l'École des hautes études sociales,* pp. 247–86.
10. Henri Mazel (1864–1947), was a French journalist, poet and playwright. He was in in charge of the column regarding social issues in the magazine *Mercure de France.*
11. French gazette founded in 1672, first published under the title *Mercure galant.* It was intended to inform its readers about life in the court, the latest intellectual debates and artistic life by featuring poems, art reviews, songs. It was acclaimed for its tone of liberality and its capacity to be unconstrained by traditional journalistic rules.
12. Henri Mazel, "Revue de la quinzaine: Science sociale," *Mercure de France* (Paris) t. 60, no. 191 (1 June 1905): 429.
13. Jean Réville (1854–1908) was a French theologian and Protestant pastor born in the Netherlands. He was appointed professor of theology at *l'École pratique des hautes études,* and at the *Sorbonne.* He was editor of the *Revue de l'Histoire des Religions* for more than twenty years.
14. French quarterly journal founded and launched by Emile Guimet in 1879. Its editorial committee was established at the *Collège de France.* Its main goal was to publish, free from bias or partisanship, historical and analytical articles regarding

all aspects of religion; it encompassed Judaism, Catholicism, Islam as well as new creeds and traditional beliefs found in Egypt, Greece, China, etc. . . .

15. Jean Réville, "Revue des livres: Analyse et compte-rendu: *Religions et Sociétés.* Leçons professées à l'École des Hautes études sociales." Paris: F. Alcan, 1905. *Revue de l'histoire des religions* (Paris) t. 53; no. 1 (1906): 363.
16. French magazine launched in 1865. It mainly focused on publishing critiques and reviews on new publications in the fields of history, literature, and philology.
17. M. D. "Dans le volume *Religion et société, Leçons professées à l'École des Hautes études sociales."* Revue critique d'histoire et de littérature (Paris) t. 61, no. 17 (30 April 1906): 291.
18. A magazine founded in 1854 by intellectuals from various backgrounds, such as scientists, clergymen, and writers to resist those schools of thought and doctrines opposed to the truths of Christianity or that distorted the teachings of Christ.
19. "Les livres: Religions et Sociétés. Leçons professées à l'École des hautes études sociales . . ." *Revue chrétienne.* (Paris) t. 1 (1 Jan, 1905): 412–13.
20. French Catholic magazine, issued every two months. It was published from 1895 to 1920 and aimed at popularizing works in the field of religious sciences among clergymen.
21. Joseph Bricout, "Religion et églises," *Revue du clergé français* (Paris), t. 43, (1905): 129.
22. "Hippolyte Dreyfus, *Babism and Bahaism.* Address delivered March 1, 1904 at the School of Higher Social Studies, University of Paris, translated by Rosa V. Winterburn, Extract from the work Religions et Sociétés." Unpublished typewritten manuscript. National Bahá'í Archives of France.
23. Hippolyte Dreyfus, *Babismus und Behaismus: [und] Der Islam in seinen Derhältnis zur modernen Zivilisation* von Baron Carra de Vaux. Übers. v. Margarete Platte (Frankfurt am Main: Neuer Frankfurter Verlag, 1909).

24. May Maxwell, "Hippolyte Dreyfus-Barney: The Passing of a Bahá'í Scholar and Lecturer," pp. 26–27.
25. Lua Getsinger to Hippolyte Dreyfus, [1903], National Bahá'í Archives of France, Laura Dreyfus-Barney Folder (1AP), File: Hippolyte "correspondance passive" (1AP-I-D4).
26. Bahá'u'lláh, *Le Livre de la certitude,* traduit du persan par Hippolyte Dreyfus et Mirza Habib-ullah Shírází, (Paris: Ernest Leroux, 1904).
27. Shoghi Effendi, *God Passes By,* pp. 218–19.
28. Hippolyte Dreyfus, in Bahá'u'lláh, *Le Livre de la certitude,* traduit du persan par Hippolyte Dreyfus et Mirza Habib-ullah Chirazí, (Paris: Ernest Leroux, 1904).
29. Ibid.
30. Ibid.
31. Jacques Brieu (1866–1921), was a French writer, acting as editor at the *Mercure de France.* He specialized in esotericism, mysticism, and psychic sciences.
32. Jacques Brieu, "Revue du mois: Le livre de la certitude," *Mercure de France* (Paris) no. 179, t. 52 (Nov. 1904), pp. 481–82.
33. Swiss literary magazine founded in 1862. It published chronicles on a wide variety of subjects, from scientific and political articles to critical reviews on literary works published in, among other countries, France, Switzerland, Italy, Germany, and the United States.
34. R. F. "Le Livre de la certitude, traduit du persan par H. Dreyfus . . ." *Bibliothèque universelle et Revue suisse* (Lausanne) t. 45 (1907), pp. 660–61.
35. Clément Huart. "Analyses et comptes rendus: Beha-ullah—Livre de la certitude (Kitab-el-Ikan). Trad. H. Dreyfus et Mirza Habib-ullah. Paris: E. Leroux, 1904," *Revue de l'histoire des religions* (Paris) t. 50, (1904), pp. 116–21.
36. Bahá'u'lláh's.
37. See Glossary.
38. Ishqábát, now Ashgabat (also spelled 'Ishqábád, Ashkhabad),

is one of the largest cities of Turkmenistan and is located near the Iran-Turkmenistan border. The first Bahá'í House of Worship was built in the city in 1908 but was expropriated by the Soviet government in 1928, was badly damaged in 1948 by an earthquake, and was eventually demolished in 1963.

39. Letter from Clément Huart to Hippolyte Dreyfus, 6 Oct. 1905, National Bahá'í Archives of France, Laura Dreyfus-Barney Folder (1AP), File: Hippolyte "correspondance passive" (1AP-I-D4).

6 / In the Heart of Asia

1. One of the titles of Bahá'u'lláh.
2. 'Abdu'l-Bahá to Hippolyte Dreyfus [undated], National Bahá'í Archives of France (Letter-2).
3. Now Myanmar.
4. Sydney Sprague, *A Year with the Bahais in India and Burma,* p. 6.
5. Ibid., pp. 6–7.
6. The most holy place for the Bahá'ís. It is the site of the Shrine of Bahá'u'lláh, the Prophet-Founder of the Bahá'í Faith, and it is the location of the point of adoration *(Qiblih)* to which Bahá'ís face when saying their daily obligatory prayers.
7. See Glossary.
8. Percy Woodcock (1855–1936) and his wife, a Bahá'í couple from Canada. He was a painter, a member of the Royal Canadian Academy of Arts and Ontario Society of Arts, and served on the Bahá'í Temple Unity from 1911.
9. Jean Joseph Benjamin Constant (1845–1902) was a French painter, etcher, and art teacher at l'École des beaux arts in Paris. He was especially renowned for his Oriental subjects.
10. Hippolyte Dreyfus to Yvonne Meyer-May, 1905. Iowa Women's Archives.
11. Now Mumbai.
12. William Garlington, "The Baha'i Faith in India: A Developmental Stage Approach," *Occasional Papers in Shaykhi, Bábi*

and Bahá'í Studies, no. 2 (1997). Online: https://www.h-net.org/~bahai/bhpapers/india1.htm.

13. Now Yangon.
14. Abbasali Butt, "In Memoriam: An Account of the Services of Siyyid Muṣṭafa Rúmí." *The Bahá'í World* vol. 10, 1944–1946 (1949): 517–20. Daidanaw is also known as "'Abdu'l-Bahá Village."
15. Behramji Malabari (1853–1912), was an Indian poet, writer and social reformer, known for his ardent advocacy for the protection of the rights of women and for his endeavors against child marriage.
16. A very active theosophist in Bombay and very close friend of Behramji Malabari.
17. International religious movement established in New York in 1875. At its center, it claims the existence of "one universal religion," one "essential truth" underlying religion, philosophy, and science, and thus advocates syncretism of all world religions and ancient wisdom.
18. Sydney Sprague, *A Year with the Bahais in India and Burma,* p. 15.
19. Ibid., p. 16.
20. Ibid., p. 17.
21. The most holy of Bahá'í festivals, referred to by Bahá'u'lláh as the "King of Festivals." It is a twelve-day festival commemorating the twelve days Bahá'u'lláh spent at the Garden of Riḍván, near Baghdad, where He declared that He was "Him Who Will Be Made Manifest," the Manifestation of God announced by the Báb.
22. Bahá'u'lláh.
23. Hippolyte Dreyfus to the Bahá'ís of Chicago, Bombay, April 22, 1905. National Bahá'í Archives of France, Laura Dreyfus-Barney Folder, File: Hippolyte "correspondance active."
24. Now Kolkata.
25. Also known as the Golden Pagoda, it is the most sacred pagoda of the country, as it is believed to contain relics of the four

previous Buddhas, including eight strands of hair of Buddha Gautama.

26. Sydney Sprague, *A Year with the Bahais in India and Burma,* p. 23.
27. Hippolyte must have intended to say Mandalay, not Rangoon.
28. Hippolyte to Yvonne Meyer-May, 5 May 1905. Iowa Women's Archives.
29. Sydney Sprague, *A Year with the Bahais in India and Burma,* p. 31.
30. Ibid., p. 37.
31. Ibid., p. 33.
32. Sydney Sprague, *A Year with the Bahais in India and Burma,* pp. 39–41.
33. Burma's largest river and most important commercial waterway that flows from north to south through the country.
34. Sydney Sprague, *A Year with the Bahais in India and Burma,* p. 42.
35. Ibid., p. 43.
36. Ibid., p. 44.
37. At that time, there was no Pakistan, thus India and Persia shared a common border.
38. Now Varanasi.
39. Agenda de voyages de Hippolyte Dreyfus en Inde et Birmanie [Hippolyte's travelogue of his voyages to India and Burma] (1905). National Bahá'í Archives of France, Laura Dreyfus-Barney Folder (1AP), File: Hippolyte "papiers et objets personnels" (1AP-I-B3).
40. May Maxwell, "Hippolyte Dreyfus-Barney: The Passing of a Bahá'í Scholar and Lecturer," pp. 26–27.

7 / A Man of Letters

1. 'Abdu'l-Bahá to Hippolyte Dreyfus [undated], National Bahá'í Archives of France. Provisional translation from the Persian by the authors.

2. Notification from *Ordre des Avocats à la Cour d'Appel de Paris* to Hippolyte Dreyfus, 26 Oct. 1905. National Bahá'í Archives of France, Laura Dreyfus-Barney Folder (1AP), File: Hippolyte "Papiers et objets personnels" (1AP-I-A).
3. See his passports. National Bahá'í Archives of France, Laura Dreyfus-Barney Folder (1AP), File: Hippolyte "Papiers et objets personnels" (1AP- I-A).
4. Largest city in northwestern Iran, located in the East Azerbaijan Province.
5. Arthur de Gobineau, *Les Religions et les Philosophies dans l'Asie centrale.*
6. Edith Sanderson, "An Interview with A. L. M. Nicolas of Paris" (1942), in *The Bahá'í World,* vol. 8, New York: Bahá'í Publishing Committee.
7. Mírzá Yaḥyá (1832–1912). Known as Ṣubḥ-i-Azal, he was the half-brother of Bahá'u'lláh and the main leader of the Covenant-breakers during that time.
8. 'Abdu'l-Bahá to Hippolyte Dreyfus [undated], National Bahá'í Archives of France (Letter-6).
9. Now Tabriz.
10. Most probably an herbalist selling tea and spices, or an apothecary, or a perfumer trading in attar of rose.
11. A grocer owning a small shop.
12. A. L. M. Nicolas to Hippolyte Dreyfus, 22 May 1905, National Bahá'í Archives of France, Laura Dreyfus-Barney Folder, (1AP-I-D4).
13. Professor Browne recorded his impressions of this unique encounter. See John Esslemont, *Bahá'u'lláh and the New Era,* chapter 3.
14. 'Abdu'l-Bahá to Hippolyte Dreyfus [undated], National Bahá'í Archives of France (Letter-13).
15. Reference to Laura Clifford-Barney.
16. 'Abdu'l-Bahá to Hippolyte Dreyfus [undated], National Bahá'í Archives of France (Letter-20). Provisional translation from the Persian by the authors.

17. Salomon Reinach (1858–1932) was a French archaeologist and a museum curator, as well as a professor of art history at the École du Louvre. He is best known for "secularizing" the study of religions by using a scientific method.
18. Salomon Reinach to Laura Dreyfus-Barney, 21 Dec. 1928, National Bahá'í Archives of France, Laura Dreyfus-Barney Folder, File: "Condoléances" (1AP-II-D).
19. Edgar Blochet (1870–1937) was a French orientalist, specialized in the history of religions. He spent most of his career at the *Bibliothèque nationale de France* (National Library of France) working in the department of manuscripts.
20. Introduced by the Guardian of the Bahá'í Faith as the "Charter of the future world civilization," the Kitáb-i-Aqdas was written in Arabic by Bahá'u'lláh around 1873. It is the "Most Holy Book" of the Bahá'í revelation and the "Mother-Book" of the Dispensation of Bahá'u'lláh. The Kitáb-i-Aqdas is the scriptural text in which Bahá'u'lláh introduces the laws and ordinances for His Dispensation.
21. Clément Huart to Hippolyte Dreyfus, 6 Oct. 1905, (1AP-I-D4).

8 / The Hidden Words

1. Bahá'u'lláh, *Les Paroles cachées,* traduit du persan par Hippolyte Dreyfus et Mirza Habib'ullah Chirazí (Paris, Ernest Leroux, 1905).
2. Hippolyte and Mírzá Habíbu'lláh Chirazí, quoted in Bahá'u'lláh, *Les Paroles cachées,* traduit du persan par Hippolyte Dreyfus et Mirza Habib'ullah Chirazí, p. 7.
3. French newspaper published between 1789 and 1944. It was first created to reproduce the exact records of the sessions of the National Assembly, a newly established institution in France where deputies engage in political debates. Later it became a more liberal space in which eminent figures in French society, such as Honoré de Balzac, Hector Berlioz, Joseph Kessel, Victor Hugo, and Jules Verne would express their opinions on

various subjects. At the end of the nineteenth century, it was considered, together with *Le Figaro* and *Le Temps,* one of the most important daily papers in France.

4. F. D., "Revue des livres: Mélange historique et littéraire: Béha-Ullah: Les Paroles cachés, en persan," traduction française par Hippolyte Dreyfus et . . . . *Journal des débats politiques et littéraires* (Paris) no. 121 (2 May 1905): p. 2.
5. Sébastien Voirol (1870–1930), whose real name is Gustaf Henrik Lundqvist, was a French writer and translator. Around 1902–3, intrigued—like many Europeans—by the stories of the Báb and Bahá'u'lláh, he went to the Holy Land, where he met 'Abdu'l-Bahá several times. The story of his travels was published in 1905 (see next footnote).
6. Sébastien Voirol, "Chez les bâbis." *Mercure de France* (Paris) t. 58 (1 Nov. 1905): 22.
7. Clément Huart, "Analyse et compte-rendu: Béha-ullah. Les paroles cachées, en persan . . ." *Revue de l'histoire des religions* (Paris) t. 52 (1905): 140–44.
8. B. M., "Les paroles cachées, en persan; traduction française par Dreyfus et . . . ." *Revue critique d'histoire et de littérature* (Paris), t. 61, no. 8 (26 Feb. 1906): 124–25.

9 / In the Cradle of the Faith

1. A. L. M. Nicolas to Hippolyte Dreyfus, 6 Aug. 1905, National Bahá'í Archives of France (1AP-I-D4).
2. The *Orient Express* was a fabulously luxurious long-distance passenger train service created in 1883 by *Compagnie Internationale des Wagons-Lits.* It first operated between Paris and Vienna; later, its route was extended to Venice and eventually up to Constantinople.
3. Capital of the Ottoman Empire until 1923. It is known today as Istanbul.
4. Odessa was, at the beginning of the twentieth century, one of the most important harbors of the Russian Empire. Today Odessa is located in the Ukraine.

5. Baku was at that time an important commercial center of the Russian Empire thanks to its oil fields. Today Baku is the capital of Azerbaijan.
6. Now Türkmenbaşy.
7. Moojan Momen, "Turkmenistan," *The Bahá'í Encyclopedia* online at https://bahai-library.com/momen_encyclopedia_turkmenistan.
8. See Glossary.
9. Anthony A. Lee, "The Rise of the Bahá'í Community of 'Ishqábád." *Études Bahá'í Studies* (Thornhill, Ont.) vol. 5 (Jan. 1979): 1–13.
10. Laura Dreyfus-Barney, transcript of talks. 16 May 1909. National Bahá'í Archives, United States: MS. Frank Osborne Papers, M-453, Box 1, Folder "Talks: Laura Dreyfus-Barney."
11. Moojan Momen, "Turkmenistan," *The Bahá'í Encyclopedia* online, at https://bahai-library.com/momen_encyclopedia_turkmenistan.
12. Laura Dreyfus-Barney, transcript of talks. 16 May 1909.
13. Most probably Shaykh Muḥammad 'Alí Qa'ini, one of the prominent Bahá'í intellectuals living in the region at that time and Mashhadí Yusif Milani, a prosperous merchant in Ashgabat. Both were elected to the first Bahá'í council of the city in 1895–96.
14. Tamerlane, or Timur (1336–1405), was a Turco-Mongol military commander who founded the Timurid Empire, which today would cover parts of Afghanistan, Iran, and Central Asia.
15. Today Kokand, in Eastern Uzbekistan.
16. Today Tashkent, the capital of Uzbekistan.
17. Hippolyte to Valentine Mayer-May, 18 June 1906. Iowa Women's Archives.
18. Robert H. Stockman, *The Bahá'í Faith in America, Volume 2, Early Expansion 1900–1912,* p. 262.
19. Arabic word meaning "chief." It usually referred to the dignitary or person in charge of a municipality.

20. Heider Ali, *Bahäi Martyrdoms in Persia in the Year 1903,* A. D., 2nd ed. (Chicago Bahai Publishing Society, 1917).
21. Laura Dreyfus-Barney, transcript of talks. 16 May 1909.
22. Azíz'u'lláh Azízí, *Crown of Glory: Memoirs of Jináb-i-Azíz'u'lláh Azízí,* p. 93.
23. Laura Dreyfus-Barney, transcript of talks. 16 May 1909.
24. Rastgár, Nasrulláh. *Kitáb-i táríkh-i Hadrat-i Sadrus-Sudúr (The book on Sadrus-Sudúr).* Tehran: National Bahá'í Publishing Committee, 104 E.B. / 1947–48. More about Sadrus-Sudúr in *Masábíh-i hidáyat,* vol. 5.
25. Mona Khademi, *Some Questions Answered: The Life of Laura Barney,* p. 103.
26. Mona Khademi, "A Glimpse into the Life of Laura Dreyfus Barney," *Lights of Irfan,* Papers Presented at the 'Irfán Colloquia and Seminars (Darmstadt) Book 10 (2009): 80.
27. Ibid.
28. Also known as Chemiran or Shemiranat, it is now the northernmost district of the city of Tehran.
29. During his travel in Persia, Hippolyte received (at least) one Tablet from the Master, encouraging him in his endeavors.
30. Hippolyte to his mother, 4 July 1906. Iowa Women's Archives.
31. Ẓillu's-Sulṭán.
32. Hippolyte to his mother, 7 July 1906. Iowa Women's Archives.
33. Ẓillu's Sulṭán (1850–1918), or Soltan Massoud Mirza Zell-e Soltan, is the eldest son of Náṣiri'd-Dín Sháh. He was the governor of the city of Isfahan between 1874 and 1907, and the main person responsible for the violent persecutions against the Bábís and the Bahá'ís in the region; he notably ratified the death sentence of the *King of Martyrs,* Ḥájí Siyyid Muḥammad-Ḥasan, and the *Beloved of Martyrs,* Ḥájí Siyyid Muḥammad-Ḥusayn. He met 'Abdu'l-Bahá at Thonon-les-Bains in 1911, at which meeting the Master forgave him for his past actions.

34. Located in the district of Kahrizak, it is now part of the province of Tehran.
35. Azíz'u'lláh Azízí, *Crown of Glory: Memoirs of Jináb-i-Azíz'u'lláh Azízí,* p. 93.
36. Yvonne Meyer-May (Dreyfus), "Curriculum vitae et activités d'Hippolyte Dreyfus," (1AP-I-F).
37. Azíz'u'lláh Azízí, *Crown of Glory: Memoirs of Jináb-i-Azíz'u'lláh Azízí,* p. 95.
38. Laura Dreyfus-Barney, transcript of talks. 16 May 1909.
39. Fadil-Mazandirani, Asadu'lláh. *Táríkh-i-Zuhúru'l-Haqq, (Compilation on the History of the Bahá'í Faith in Persia)* vol. 8. Tehran: Muassisih matbúát-i-Amrí. [Bahá'í Publishing Trust], 1968–1973. See *https://bahai-library.com/mazandarani_tarikh_zuhur_haqq.*
40. Alláh-u-Abhá is a greeting used by Bahá'ís when they meet; it means "God is the Most Glorious" in Arabic.
41. Julfa is the Armenian quarter of Isfahan, located in the old part of the city, along the Zayande River.
42. The Jāmeh Mosque of Isfahan was the largest congregational mosque. It has been a Unesco World Heritage Site since 2012.
43. Andarúní, the private room(s) of the women of a household.
44. Persian word to refer to Westerners or Europeans.
45. Kashan.
46. Qom.
47. Hippolyte to his mother, 20 July 1906. Iowa Women's Archives.
48. Agenda de voyages de Hippolyte Dreyfus en Perse [Hippolyte's travelogue of his voyages to Persia] (1906). National Bahá'í Archives of France, Laura Dreyfus-Barney Folder (1AP), File: Hippolyte "papiers et objets personnels" (1AP-I-A1).
49. Laura Dreyfus-Barney *The Way Reopens,* typescript, (1922), National Bahá'í Archives of France, Laura Dreyfus-Barney Folder, File "manuscrits: récit de voyage" (1AP-II-B1), p. 190.
50. A. L. M. Nicolas to Hippolyte Dreyfus, 19 Jan. 1907, National Bahá'í Archives of France (1AP-I-D4).

51. A. L. M. Nicolas to Hippolyte Dreyfus, 4 Apr. 1907, National Bahá'í Archives of France (1AP-I-D4).
52. Atabeg (spelt "Atabek" by Hippolyte), is a title referring to the governor of a nation or a province.
53. Hippolyte to Paul Meyer-May, 31 July 1906. Iowa Women's Archives.
54. Hippolyte to Yvonne, 4 August 1906. Iowa Women's Archives.
55. A prophetic figure foretold in the traditions of Shia Islam.
56. Laura Dreyfus-Barney, transcript of talks. 16 May 1909.
57. The term "Kargozar" refers to an agent of the Ministry of Foreign Affairs, who was charged with regulating relations between Iranian subjects and foreigners.
58. Vali'ahd, the crown prince.
59. Hippolyte Dreyfus to A. L. M. Nicolas, August 22, 1906, *Bibliothèque universitaire des langues et civilisations,* Paris, Fonds Alphonse Nicolas, Cote C_Religion-31.
60. Fadil-Mazandirani, Asadu'lláh. *Táríkh-i-Zuhúru'l-Haqq,* [Compilation on the History of the Bahá'í Faith in Iran] vol. 8.
61. Laura Dreyfus-Barney, transcript of talks. 16 May 1909.
62. Ibid.

10 / Intensification of Teaching Efforts

1. 'Abdu'l-Bahá to Hippolyte Dreyfus [undated], National Bahá'í Archives of France (Letter-5). Provisional translation from the Persian prepared by the authors, reviewed and improved by Ms. Hoda Seioshansian and Ms. Mary Victoria, to whom we are grateful.
2. 'Abdu'l-Bahá to Hippolyte Dreyfus [undated], National Bahá'í Archives of France (Letter-5).
3. Bahá'u'lláh, *Préceptes du Béhaïsme, comprenant Les Ornements, les Paroles du paradis, les Splendeurs, les Révélations, précédés d'une Lettre au Sultan de Constantinople, traduit du persan par Hippolyte Dreyfus et Mirza Habib'ullah Chirazí* (Paris, Ernest Leroux, 1906).

4. Ṭarázát (Ornaments)is a Tablet in which Bahá'u'lláh reveals six qualities or attributes (ornaments) that each believer should strive to obtain. (Taherzadeh, *The Revelation of Bahá'u'lláh, Volume Four: Mazra'ih and Bahjí, 1877–92).*
5. Kalimát-i-Firdawsíyyih (Words of Paradise) is a Tablet revealed in 1890 by Bahá'u'lláh in honor of one of his disciples, Ḥájí Mírzá Ḥaydar-'Alí. (Taherzadeh, *The Revelation of Bahá'u'lláh, Volume Four: Mazra'ih and Bahjí, 1877–92).*
6. Ishráqát (Splendors) is a Tablet revealed in 1885 by Bahá'u'lláh in response to questions asked by a believer from Azerbaijan called Jalíl-i-Khú'í. In this Tablet, Bahá'u'lláh, refers to nine "splendours," which are nine unique characteristics of His Revelation. (Taherzadeh, *The Revelation of Bahá'u'lláh, Volume Four: Mazra'ih and Bahjí, 1877–92).*
7. Tajallíyát (Effulgences) is a Tablet revealed around 1885 by Bahá'u'lláh in honor of Ustád 'Alí-Akbar, who designed the first House of Worship in Ashgabat. (Taherzadeh, *The Revelation of Bahá'u'lláh, Volume Four: Mazra'ih and Bahjí, 1877–92).*
8. Lawḥ-i-Ra'is, or Tablet of the Chief, was titled by Hippolyte Dreyfus in his compilation *Letter to Sultan Abdul Aziz.* Bahá'u'lláh revealed the Lawḥ-i-Ra'is in 1868, soon after the death of three of His followers. In this Tablet, addressed to 'Alí Páshá, the Ottoman Prime Minister, He denounces with vehemence Alí Páshá's violence and cruelty. This Tablet should not be confused with Lawḥ-i-Sultan, a Tablet revealed by Bahá'u'lláh after His departure from Constantinople to Adrianople and addressed to Násiri'd-Dín Sháh. (Taherzadeh, *The Revelation of Bahá'u'lláh, Volume Four: Mazra'ih and Bahjí, 1877–92).*
9. Bahá'u'lláh, *Préceptes du Béhaïsme, comprenant Les Ornements, les Paroles du paradis, les Splendeurs, les Révélations, précédés d'une Lettre au Sultan de Constantinople,* traduit du persan par Hippolyte Dreyfus et Mirza Habib'ullah Chirazí, pp. I–II.

10. Hurufism is a Sufi doctrine founded by Fażlu l-Lāh Astar- Abādī (Nāimī) at the end of the fourteenth century. Its theories are explained in the *Great Book of Eternity*. Hurufism is based on the mysticism of letters and claims that its mastery can lead men to the understanding of the principles of the universe.
11. Bahá'u'lláh, *Préceptes du Béhaïsme, comprenant Les Ornements, les Paroles du paradis, les Splendeurs, les Révélations, précédés d'une Lettre au Sultan de Constantinople, traduit du persan par Hippolyte Dreyfus et Mirza Habib'ullah Chirazí*, pp. VIII–IX.
12. The Báb, *Selections from the Writings of the Báb*, p. 3.
13. 'Abdu'l-Bahá, *Selections from the Writings of 'Abdu'l-Bahá*, no. 17.3.
14. Clément Huart, "Beha-ullah. Les préceptes du Béhaïsme." Revue de l'histoire des religions (Paris) t. 53, (1906): 392–95.
15. The Bábí Faith was already in the Larousse. Its first mention seems to have been in 1867. See Larousse, Pierre (1817–1875) *Grand dictionnaire universel du XIXe siècle* (Paris: Larousse, 1866–1890), "Bab," t. 2 (1867): 5; "Babysme," t. 2 (1867): 14–17; ibid., "Perse moderne," t. 2 (1874): 662–67.
16. "Béhaisme," *Nouveau Larousse illustré: Dictionnaire universel encyclopédique*. Supplément / publié sous la dir. de Claude Augé (Paris: Larousse, 1906): 66.
17. *Tablets of Abdul-Baha Abbas*. (Chicago, Bahai Publishing Society, 1909), vol. 1, pp. vi–viii.
18. Hippolyte Dreyfus, "Les Béhaïs et le mouvement actuel en Perse." *Revue du monde musulman* (Paris) t. 1, n° 1 (dec. 1906): 198–206.
19. A French magazine founded in 1907 that published articles and review on various subjects linked to Islam. Its publication stopped in 1926 and eventually gave birth to a new magazine called *Revue des études islamiques*.
20. Hippolyte Dreyfus, "Les Béhaïs et le mouvement actuel en Perse," p. 200.
21. 'Akká, where 'Abdu'l-Bahá, the Head of the Faith, was residing at that time.

22. Hippolyte Dreyfus, "Les Béhaïs et le mouvement actuel en Perse," p. 200.
23. Ibid., p. 201.
24. Ibid., p. 203.
25. Ibid., p. 209.
26. "La mort du chah de Perse," *Le Temps* (Paris), no. 16638 (11 January 1907): 1, col. 6.
27. Laura Dreyfus-Barney, "Hippolyte Dreyfus-Barney," *Article for Bahai World,* (1AP-I-F).
28. Bertha Herbert Holley (1879–1969), first wife of Mr. Horace H. Holley (1887–1960).
29. Robert Weinberg, *Ethel Jenner Rosenberg: The Life and Times of England's Outstanding Bahá'í Pioneer Worker,* (Oxford: George Ronald, 1995).
30. *'Abbas* is 'Abdu'l-Bahá's surname.
31. Lady Sara Louisa Blomfield, *The Chosen Highway,* introduction.
32. Robert Weinberg, *Lady Blomfield: Her Life and Times,* p. 43.
33. Hippolyte Dreyfus, "Le Béhaïsme, Conférence faite au siège de la Société Théosophique" *Les Annales théosophiques* (Paris) (1er trimestre 1908), pp. 25–46.
34. Hippolyte Dreyfus, "Le Béhaïsme, Conférence faite au siège de la Société Théosophique," p. 36.
35. Hippolyte must have wanted to say that the acquisition of wealth is praiseworthy only insofar as it is attained through just means, like honest work. As the Universal House of Justice states in a message dated 2 April 2010: "The acquisition of wealth should be governed by the requirements of justice (. . .) An employer and employee, for example, are both bound by the laws and conventions that regulate their work, and each is expected to carry out his or her responsibilities with honesty and integrity."
36. Hippolyte Dreyfus, "Le Béhaïsme, Conférence faite au siège de la Société Théosophique," pp. 36–37. Bahá'u'lláh states in a Tablet called *Tarázát,* "the first effulgence which hath dawned

from the horizon of the Mother Book is that man should know his own self and recognize that which leadeth unto loftiness or lowliness, glory or abasement, wealth or poverty. Having attained the stage of fulfillment and reached his maturity, man standeth in need of wealth, and such wealth as he acquireth through crafts or professions is commendable and praiseworthy in the estimation of men of wisdom, and especially in the eyes of servants who dedicate themselves to the education of the world and to the edification of its peoples" (Bahá'u'lláh, *Tablets of Bahá'u'lláh Revealed after the Kitáb-i-Aqdas,* pp. 34–35).

37. Hippolyte Dreyfus, "Le Béhaïsme, Conférence faite au siège de la Société Théosophique," p. 41.

11 / Spreading the Faith Across his Native Land

1. Mission laïque française (tr. "French Secular Mission") is a non-profit organization founded in 1902 by Pierre Deschamps to spread the French language and culture by establishing schools outside of France based on a secular education curriculum.
2. *Le Béhaïsme,* conférence faite le 23 mai 1908 par Hippolyte Dreyfus, docteur en droit. Publications de la Mission Laïque Française, Comité Lyonnais, 1908.
3. There were earlier public announcements of conferences mentioning the Faith of the Báb outside of Paris. See Auguste Carrière, "Les origines d'une religion nouvelle (Le Babysme): Conférence de M. Schillinger," *Le Progrès Religieux* (Strasbourg) no. 6 (5 févr. 1870): 45–48. See also Jules Balteau, (1858–1943) "Le Babysme: lecture faite par M. J. Balteau, à la Séance du 22 mai 1896," *Travaux de l'Académie nationale de Reims* (Reims) année 1895–1896, v. 99, t. 1 (1897): 195–222.
4. *Le Lyon Universitaire* was an academic newspaper published in Lyon between 1902 and 1914. It was mainly engaged in publishing the latest news related to science, arts, and literature.

5. Alfred Moulet, "Mission Laïque Française: Une religion nouvelle: Le Behaïsme." *Lyon universitaire* (Lyon) no. 286 (15 May 1908): 3.
6. Édouard Herriot (1872–1957) was a French politician. He served as mayor of Lyon from 1905 to 1940, three times as prime minister, and for many years as president of the Chamber of Deputies.
7. *Le Béhaïsme,* conférence faite le 23 mai 1908 par Hippolyte Dreyfus, docteur en droit, p. 3.
8. Ibid., p. 4.
9. Ibid., p. 4.
10. Ibid., p. 29.
11. Ibid., p. 30.
12. Ibid., p. 31.
13. "Mission Laïque Française," *Echos Lyonnais* (Lyon), 24 May 1908, vol. 7.
14. Daily newspaper founded in 1878 in Lyon. It had a circulation of more than 100,000 before the First World War.
15. "Mission Laïque Française," *Lyon Républicain* (Lyon) no. 10926, (24 May 1908): 3, col. 4.
16. Hippolyte Dreyfus, "Le Béhaïsme, Conférence faite le 23 May 1908." ([Lyon], *Publications de la Mission laïque française, comité lyonnais,* [1908]).
17. 'Abdu'l-Bahá, *Some Answered Questions,* collected and translated from the Persian of 'Abdu'l-Baha, by Laura Clifford Barney. (London: K. Paul, Trench, Trübner & Co., 1908).
18. Laura Clifford Barney, "Introduction de la première édition," dans 'Abdu'l-Bahá, *Les Leçons de Saint-Jean-d'Acre,* p. 2.
19. Laura Clifford Barney, *Les Leçons de Saint-Jean-d'Acre,* p. 2.
20. Hartwig Derenbourg, "Livres offerts" and *Comptes-rendus des séances de l'année. – Académie des inscriptions et belles-lettres* (Paris), 52e année, n°4, 1908, pp. 217–20.
21. Alma S. Knobloch, "The Call to Germany," *The Bahá'í World* (New York), vol. 7, 1936–1938 (1939): 736.

12 / Crafting a Masterpiece

1. Hippolyte Dreyfus, *Essai sur le Béhá'ísme, son histoire, sa portée.*
2. Ibid., pp. 1–2. In this connection, one of the prayers revealed by Bahá'u'lláh is very apposite and instructive as to the profundity and spiritual import of the Bahá'í Revelation: "Praise be to Thee, O Lord my God! I implore Thee, by Thy Name which none hath befittingly recognized, and whose import no soul hath fathomed; I beseech Thee, by Him Who is the Fountainhead of Thy Revelation and the Dayspring of Thy signs, to make my heart to be a receptacle of Thy love and of remembrance of Thee. Knit it, then, to Thy most great Ocean, that from it may flow out the living waters of Thy wisdom and the crystal streams of Thy glorification and praise." (Bahá'u'lláh, *Prayers and Meditations,* p. 56).
3. "This is the changeless Faith of God, eternal in the past, eternal in the future." See Bahá'u'lláh, The Kitáb-i-Aqdas, ¶182.
4. Hippolyte Dreyfus, *Essai sur le Béhá'ísme, son histoire, sa portée sociale,* pp. 102–3.
5. *Journal Asiatique* is a French bi-annual academic journal established in 1822 by the Société Asiatique to cover Asian studies.
6. Clément Huart, "Comptes rendus: Hippolyte Dreyfus. Essai sur le Béhaïsme, son histoire, sa portée sociale." *Journal Asiatique* . . . (Paris) t. 13 (March–April 1909): 309.
7. Ibid., 310.
8. Clément Huart, "H. Dreyfus. Essai sur le Béhaïsme, son histoire, sa portée sociale. . ." *Revue de l'histoire des religions* (Paris) t. 59 (1909): 361–64.
9. Pangloss, a fictional character in the 1759 novel *Candide* by Voltaire. He is a philosopher, Candide's mentor, and eternal optimist. He is always repeating "all is for the best."
10. Clément Huart, "H. Dreyfus. Essai sur le Béhaïsme, son histoire, sa portée sociale. . . ." *Revue de l'histoire des religions,* p. 364.
11. Magazine founded by Auguste Meulemans in 1891, published until 1939.

12. Sébastien Voirol, "Livres et Idées." *La Revue diplomatique* (Paris) no. 17 (25 April 1909): 12, c. 1.
13. Hippolyte Dreyfus, *The Universal Religion: Bahaism: Its Rise and Social Import.*
14. National Bahá'í Archives of France, Laura Dreyfus-Barney Folder. File Hippolyte "Documents rassemblés: coupure de presse" (1AP-I-E). For more information, see *Westminster Gazette* (12 June 1909), *The Scotsman* (14 June 1909), *The Evening Standard* (21 June 1909), *The Guardian* (4 August 1909), *The Daily Telegraph* (2 September 1909), and *The Glasgow Herald* (15 September 1909).
15. Martha Root, "A Bahai Pilgrimage to South America," *Star of the West* (Chicago), vol. 11, no. 12, (16 Oct. 1920): 206.
16. Procès-verbal de l'Assemblée Spirituelle de Paris (Spiritual Assembly of Paris, Meeting minutes, Nov. 1934). National Bahá'í Archives of France, Folder: Communauté bahá'íe de Paris (1AC).
17. Hippolyte Dreyfus, *Essai sur le Béhaïsme. Son histoire, sa portée sociale.* Nouvelle édition comprenant *Le but d'un nouvel ordre mondial* (extraits), by Shoghi Effendi, et *L'Économie mondiale de Bahāou'llāh* (extraits), by Horace Holley.
18. Leo Tolstoy (1828–1910), was a Russian writer, best known for his novels on Russian society, such as *War and Peace* or *Anna Karenina.* Often described as a mystical anarchist, he was famous for his statements against organized religion and militarism. Many critics regard him as one of the greatest authors of all time. (https://en.wikipedia.org/wiki/Leo_Tolstoy).
19. Leo Tolstoy to Hippolyte Dreyfus, in Luigi Stendardo, *Leo Tolstoy and the Bahá'í Faith,* pp. 33–34.
20. Ibid., p. 44.
21. Bahá'u'lláh, quoted in Hippolyte Dreyfus, *Essai sur le Béhá'isme,* 4e éd., p. 76. The revised translation of this passage reads, "The most glorious fruit of the tree of knowledge is this exalted word: Of one tree are all ye the fruit, and of one bough

the leaves. Let not man glory in this that he loveth his country, let him rather glory in this that he loveth his kind." (See the sixth Ishráq in Bahá'u'lláh, *Tablets of Bahá'u'lláh revealed after the Kitab-i-Aqdas,* pp. 127–28).

22. Ivan Ivanovič Gorbunov (1864–1940), Russian writer, poet, and publisher.
23. Leo Tolstoï to Ivvan Ivanovič Gorbunov, 14 May 1909, in Luigi Stendardo, *Leo Tolstoy and the Bahá'í Faith,* p. 44.
24. *The Tampa Tribune,* 12 March 1911, p. 30.
25. Hippolyte Dreyfus-Barney to Ahmad Sohrab, 5 March 1909, National Bahá'í Archives, United States.
26. Violette Nakhjavani, *The Maxwells of Montreal: Early Years 1870–1922,* p. 254.
27. Hippolyte Dreyfus, *Le Machreqou'l-Azkār d'Achqābād.*
28. National Bahá'í Archives of France, Laura Dreyfus-Barney Folder (1AP), "Hippolyte Dreyfus, *A Baha'i Institution: The Mashriqu'l-Azkar of Ashqabad,* 1909." *The Bahá'í World* (Wilmette) vol. 8, 1938–1940 (1942): 525–32.
29. Hippolyte Dreyfus, *Le Machreqou'l-Azkār d'Achqābād,* pp. 5–13.

13 / Inspiring the Believers in North America

1. 'Abdu'l-Bahá to Hippolyte Dreyfus, 9 June 1910, National Bahá'í Archives of France (Letter-15). Provisional translation from the Persian prepared by the authors, reviewed and improved by Ms. Hoda Seioshansian and Ms. Mary Victoria, to whom we are grateful.
2. Los Angeles Bahai Assembly to Hippolyte Dreyfus, 23 June 1910, National Bahá'í Archives of France, Laura Dreyfus-Barney Folder, File: Hippolyte: "Correspondance passive" (1AP-I-D3).
3. Ibid.
4. Corinne True to Hippolyte Dreyfus, 19 June 1910, National Bahá'í Archives of France, Laura Dreyfus-Barney Folder, File: Hippolyte: "Correspondance passive" (1AP-I-D4).

5. "London, England," *Bahá'í News* (Chicago), vol. 1, no. 6 (June 24, 1910): 12.
6. Isabella D. Brittingham, "New York City," *Bahai News* (Chicago), vol. 1, no. 6 (June 24, 1910): 13.
7. "Baltimore," *Bahai News,* vol. 1, no. 6 (June 24, 1910): 12.
8. Joseph H. Hannen, "Washington, D.C.," *Bahai News* (Chicago), vol. 1, no. 7 (July 13, 1910): 15.
9. "Chicago" *Bahai News* (Chicago), vol.1, no. 7 (July 13, 1910): 11.
10. Zia Bagdadi, address on February 3rd, 1929, a memorial meeting for H. Dreyfus-Barney, at the Foundation Hall of the Bahá'í Temple (Wilmette). National Bahá'í Archives of France, Laura Dreyfus-Barney Folder, File: Hippolyte: "Documents postérieurs à Hippolyte Dreyfus-Barney" (1AP-I-F).
11. *Star of the West* was a Bahá'í periodical published in the United States of America. Located in Chicago, it was published every nineteen days. The first volume was published in March, 1910 under the title *Bahai News.* Albert R. Windust and Gertrude Buikema served as editors, and Mirza Ahmad Sohrab joined them later in the year to manage a Persian section. 'Abdu'l-Bahá praised on several occasions the publication of *Star of the West.* It has a unique role in the history of the Faith, as it was for a very long time a direct channel between the Master and the believers, and 'Abdu'l-Bahá used it as a means by which to make known the Tablets He revealed.
12. According to 'Abdu'l-Bahá, "The Mashriqu'l-Adhkár is one of the most vital institutions in the world, and it hath many subsidiary branches. Although it is a House of Worship, it is also connected with a hospital, a drug dispensary, a traveller's hospice, a school for orphans, and a university for advanced studies. Every Mashriqu'l-Adhkár is connected with these five things." (See: *Selections from the Writings of 'Abdu'l-Bahá,* no. 64.1).
13. Hippolyte Dreyfus, "The following letter from Monsieur Hippolyte Dreyfus of Paris," *Bahai News* (Chicago), vol. 1, no. 7, (July 13, 1910): 8–9.

14. 'Abdu'l-Bahá to Hippolyte Dreyfus, National Bahá'í Archives of France (Letter-13). Provisional translation from the Persian prepared by the authors, reviewed and improved by Ms. Hoda Seioshansian and Ms. Mary Victoria, to whom we are grateful.
15. Layli Maria Miron, "Laura Barney's Discipleship to 'Abdu'l-Bahá: Tracing a Theological Flow from the Middle East to the United States, 1900–1916," *The Journal of Bahá'í Studies* (28.1–2), (2018): 22–25.
16. Isabel Grinevskaya, Баб: Драматическая поэма из истории Персии в 5 действиях и 6 картинах [Báb: a dramatic account on the History of Persia]. 2nd ed., ImWerden, 2007.
17. Laura Clifford Barney, *God's Heroes,* p. viii.
18. Alfred Sugar, "In Memoriam: Florence George," *The Bahá'í World* (Wilmette) vol. 12, 1950–1954 (1956): 697.
19. Grandson of Náṣiri'd-Dín Sháh. He was, along with his father, Ẓillu's Sulṭán, responsible for the persecutions and many executions of prominent Bahá'ís in several cities in Persia. After the passing of the shah, they hastily fled from Persia.
20. 'Abdu'l-Bahá to Hippolyte Dreyfus, National Bahá'í Archives of France (Letter-10). Provisional translation from the Persian prepared by the authors, reviewed and improved by Ms. Hoda Seioshansian and Ms. Mary Victoria, to whom we are grateful.
21. Dreyfus-Barney. "Faire-part du décès de Lucien Dreyfus-Cardozo." Georges Arthur Lucien Dreyfus-Cardozo (père de Hippolyte et de Yvonne Dreyfus-Cardozo): né le 20 mai 1840 - Paris, décédé le 4 janvier 1911 à Paris. Enterré au cimetière de Montmartre," (Mr Lucien Dreyfus-Cardozo Obituary—father of Hippolyte and Yvonne Dreyfus- Cardozo—born on May 20, 1840, died on January 4, 1911 in Paris. Buried in Montmartre Cemetery). Laura Dreyfus-Barney Folder, received from National Bahá'í Archives of the United States.
22. Laura Clifford Barney, "Monsieur Lucien Dreyfus-Cardozo . . .", *Bahai News* (Chicago), vol. 1, no. 18, (Feb. 7, 1911): 9.
23. Thornton Chase to Hippolyte Dreyfus, Feb. 12, 1911, Na-

tional Bahá'í Archives, United States: Thornton Chase P, B2 - corr. D. Dreyfus.

24. Hippolyte Dreyfus to Ahmad Sohrab, Jul. 25, 1911, National Bahá'í Archives, United States: Ahmad Sohrab.

14 / Marital Union for Joint Service to the Cause

1. Now located at 7 Haparsim Street, Haifa.
2. At that time, the apartment was located at 100 rue du Bac.
3. Mona Khademi. "A Glimpse into the Life of Laura Dreyfus Barney." *Lights of Irfan: Book 10,* p. 85.
4. Agenda de voyages de Hippolyte Dreyfus en Inde. [Hippolyte's travelogue of his voyages to India]. (1906). (1AP-I-A1).
5. Ugo R. Giachery, "In Memorium: Laura Clifford Dreyfus-Barney, 1879–1974," *The Bahá'í World* (Haifa) vol. 16, 1973–1976 (1978): 536.
6. Ugo Giachery, *Laura Dreyfus Barney, Une appréciation,* pp. 17–18. National Bahá'í Archives of France, Laura Dreyfus-Barney Folder, "additional documents."
7. Jean L. Kling, *Alice Pike Barney, Her Life and Art,* p. 223.
8. Marianne Girard to Laura Dreyfus-Barney, 30 Dec. [1928], National Bahá'í Archives of France, Laura Dreyfus-Barney Folder, file: "Correspondance passive—condoléances" (1AP-II-D).
9. 'Abdu'l-Bahá to Hippolyte Dreyfus, National Bahá'í Archives of France (Letter-21).
10. Christian Hemmick (1887–1962), an American actor, who married Alice Pike Barney in 1911. They would eventually divorce in 1920.
11. "Mme Barney weds young Hemmick: Wealthy Widow of Albert Barney, Aged 61, Married to Youth of 26 in Paris: Romance of theatricals," *The New York Times* (April 16, 1911). The *New York Times* headline is incorrect; in actuality, she was fifty-three, and he was twenty-three.
12. "Laura Barney is Bride of Bahaist High Priest," *The Washington Herald,* (April 29, 1911): p. 1, col. 4. It is well-known, of

course, that there are no priests in the Bahá'í Faith, let alone "high priests."

13. "Miss Barney to wed. Said to be Engaged to Hippolyte Dreyfus—Brahma Rites at Wedding." *The New York Times* (April 23, 1911). Contrary to the quotation, Bahá'í Faith has no "leader" and is instead administered today by the nine-member bodies of Local and National Spiritual Assemblies, and the Universal House of Justice. During Hippolyte's time, of course 'Abdu'l-Bahá was the head of the Bahá'í Faith, followed by His appointment of Shoghi Effendi as Guardian of the Faith, who served in that role from 'Abdu'l-Bahá's passing in 1921 until his own passing in 1957.
14. Five years earlier, in 1906, Hippolyte and Laura went to Persia. See chapter 9.
15. "Our Persian section: Announcement of the marriage of Miss Laura C. Barney and Mons Hippolyte Dreyfus," *Star of the West,* vol. 2, no. 4 (May 17, 1911): Persian section, pp. 4–5.
16. 'Abdu'l-Bahá to Hippolyte Dreyfus, National Bahá'í Archives of France (Letter-20).
17. Roxana Mavaddat-Baghdadi, "Un oiseau parmi les oiseaux du paradis" in *Bahá'í France* (Paris) no. 167, p. 19.
18. 'Abdu'l-Bahá, *Selections from the Writings of 'Abdu'l-Bahá,* nos. 84.3 and 84.5.

15 / Welcoming 'Abdu'l-Bahá to Europe

1. The Young Turks were a nationalist political party in early twentieth century in the Ottoman Empire. They were the main leaders of a revolt against the monarchy that led to the dethronement of 'Abdu'l-Ḥamíd II and the establishment a new constitution in 1908.
2. 'Abdu'l-Ḥamíd II (1842–1918) was the thirty-fourth reigning sultan of the Ottoman Empire from 1876 until he was deposed on 27 April 1909, a few months after the Young Turks revolution.
3. 'Abdu'l-Bahá to Hippolyte Dreyfus, National Bahá'í Archives

of France (Letter-11). Provisional translation from the Persian prepared by the authors, reviewed and improved by Ms. Hoda Seioshansian and Ms. Mary Victoria, to whom we are grateful.

4. The few Persian believers designated to travel with 'Abdu'l-Bahá.
5. Hippolyte Dreyfus to Albert Windust, 27 Oct. 1910, National Bahá'í Archives, United States.
6. 'Abdu'l-Bahá to Hippolyte Dreyfus, National Bahá'í Archives of France (Letter-12).
7. W. Tudor-Pole, "The First Universal Races Congress," *Star of the West* (Chicago), vol. 2, no. 9 (Aug. 20, 1911): 3–7.
8. Robert Weinberg, *Lady Blomfield: Her Life and Times,* p. 57.
9. Horace Holley, *Bahaism: the Modern Social Religion,* pp. 211–13.
10. Laura Dreyfus-Barney, "Hippolyte Dreyfus-Barney," *Article for Bahai World,* (1AP-I-F).
11. Juliet Thompson and Marzieh Gail, *Diary of Juliet Thompson,* pp. 178–79.
12. Jan Teofil Jasion, *'Abdu'l-Bahá in France 1911 & 1913,* p. 27.
13. Juliet Thompson and Marzieh Gail, *Diary of Juliet Thompson,* p. 174.
14. Ibid., p. 180.
15. Ibid., pp. 172–73.
16. Lady Sara Louisa Blomfield, *The Chosen Highway,* p. 151.

16 / 'Abdu'l-Bahá's First Visit to Paris

1. Lady Sara Louisa Blomfield, *The Chosen Highway,* p. 179.
2. Ahang Rabbani, trans., "'Abdu'l-Bahá's Meeting with Two Prominent Iranians," *World Order Magazine,* vol. 30, no. 1 (1998): 45, https://bahai.works/World_Order/Series2/Volume_30/Issue_1.
3. Ibid., p. 180.
4. See 'Abdu'l-Bahá, *Paris Talks,* 11th edition (UK Bahá'í Publishing Trust, 1972).

5. Myrtil Airel "Le Bahaisme: Chez le Chef de la Religion Universelle," *La Liberté* (Paris) (13 Oct. 1911): 2, col. 2–3.
6. Rémy de Gourmont (1858–1915), was a French Symbolist novelist, poet, journalist, and art critic.
7. Rémy de Gourmont, "Les idées du jour: Le Béhaïsme," *La France* (Paris) no. 263 (21 Oct. 1911): 1, col. 4.
8. Louis Le Leu (born in 1865), was one of the founders of the *Alliance spiritualiste* (Spiritualist Alliance) in Paris, a monthly magazine for the independent spiritualist schools (Écoles spiritualistes autonomes). He met 'Abdu'l-Bahá several times in Paris in 1911 and 1913.
9. He is referring to Hippolyte's 1908 conference paper introducing the Bahá'í Faith.
10. Louis Le Leu, in "Alliance Spiritualiste of Paris, Reception to Abdul-Baha Abbas," *Star of the West,* vol. 2, no. 17 (Jan. 19, 1912): 2.
11. Alice Breed (1860–1929) was an American Bahá'í.
12. Alice Breed, "A Glimpse of Abdul-Baha in Paris," *Star of the West* (Chicago), vol. 2, no. 18 (February 7, 1912): 6–7.
13. Jan Teofil Jasion, *'Abdul-Bahá in France 1911 & 1913,* pp. 90–92, 119–22, 148, 177–81, 200–202, 237–40.
14. Ibid.
15. Ibid., pp. 111–16.
16. Ibid., p. 134.
17. 'Abdu'l-Bahá, *Paris Talks,* nos. 53.13–23.
18. Jan Teofil Jasion, *'Abdul-Bahá in France 1911 & 1913,* p. 246.
19. Ibid., p. 254.

17 / Traversing the United States

1. 'Abdu'l-Bahá to Hippolyte Dreyfus, National Bahá'í Archives of France (Letter-17).
2. The RMS *Titanic* was a British passenger liner that sank in the Atlantic Ocean after striking an iceberg on April 15, 1912. More than 1,500 died, making the *Titanic* tragedy one of the most fatal maritime accidents in history.

3. Hippolyte Dreyfus "Cahier des notes de voyages" [Travelogue], New York, 25 April 1912. National Bahá'í Archives of France, Laura Dreyfus-Barney Folder, File: Hippolyte "Manuscrit-œuvre" (1AP-I-B).
4. Hippolyte Dreyfus "Cahier des notes de voyages" [Travelogue], New York, 25 April 1912. (1AP-I-B).
5. The term "public Victoria" refers to a type of horse-drawn carriage, popular in the nineteenth and early twentieth centuries, used for public transportation in urban areas in the United States. Characterized by their open design and typically drawn by horses, these carriages served as taxis or personal conveyances, similar to Victorian carriages from England.
6. Marzieh Gail, *Arches of the Years,* p. 85.
7. Hippolyte Dreyfus "Cahier des notes de voyage" [Travelogue], New York, 25 April 1912. (1AP-I-B).
8. Laura Dreyfus-Barney, "Hippolyte Dreyfus-Barney." Article for *Bahai World,* (1AP-I-F).
9. Natalie Barney, "Hippolyte mon beau-frère . . ." (1AP-I-F).
10. Agnes Parsons, *'Abdu'l-Bahá in America: Agnes Parsons' Diary,* April 11, 1912–November 11, 1912, p. 61.
11. Hippolyte Dreyfus, "Cahier des notes de voyages" [Travelogue], New York, 25 April 1912. (1AP-I-B).
12. Hippolyte to Yvonne, 8 June 1912. Iowa Women's Archives.
13. Handmaiden of Bahá refers here to Laura.
14. Hassan M. Balyuzi, *'Abdu'l-Bahá: The Centre of the Covenant of Bahá'u'lláh,* p. 212.
15. Hippolyte to Paul Meyer-May, 26 June 1912. Iowa Women's Archives.
16. Mírzá Maḥmúd Zarqání, *Maḥmúd's Diary,* p. 176.
17. Annie T. Boylan, "Matrimony in the Bahai Spirit: Mr. and Mrs. Ober," *Star of the West* (Chicago) vol. 3, no. 12 (Oct. 16, 1912): 14–15.
18. Ibid, p. 14.

18 / 'Abdu'l-Bahá Returns to Europe

1. The Adelphi Hotel was built in 1826 in Liverpool City center. Before the first world war, it was regarded as one of the most luxurious hotels outside London. It is now named the Britannia Adelphi Hotel and is recorded in the National Heritage List for England.
2. Isabel Fraser, "Abdul-Baha's Arrival in England," *Star of the West,* vol. 3, no. 17 (January 19, 1913): 1–2.
3. Isabel Fraser, "The Search for Truth: Address of Abdul-Baha before the Theosophical Society, Liverpool, England, Saturday Night, December 14, 1912," *Star of the West,* vol. 3, no. 17 (January 19, 1913): 3.
4. Polow (or polo), a traditional Persian dish, is rice mixed with meat and/or vegetables, along with different herbs.
5. Most probably Siyyid Asadu'lláh-i-Qumí, one of the Persian friends who accompanied 'Abdu'l-Bahá during His travels to the West.
6. A Bahá'í from Persia who worked as consul of Persia in Port Said, Egypt.
7. A Baptist church in Liverpool that counted 1,500 followers. The building no longer exists today.
8. Ahmad Sohrab to Harriet Magee, 15 December 1912. National Bahá'í Archives of the United States.
9. Ahmad Sohrab to Harriet Magee, 16 December 1912. National Bahá'í Archives of the United States.
10. Hasan M. Balyuzi, *'Abdu'l-Bahá: The Centre of the Covenant of Bahá'u'lláh,* pp. 344–45.
11. Edward Granville Browne (1862–1925) was a British orientalist, a specialist in Iranian studies, and a scholar of the languages of India, Farsi, Arabic, and Turkish. Browne entered the presence of Bahá'u'lláh in 1890 when he was a guest at Bahjí.
12. Professor Browne's wife: Alice Caroline.

13. Albert Basil Orme Wilberforce (1841–1916) was an Anglican priest. He was the Chaplain of the Speaker of the House of Commons and became Archdeacon of Westminster in 1900.
14. Hippolyte Dreyfus-Barney to Edward Browne, 14 September 1911. National Bahá'í Archives of France, Laura Dreyfus-Barney Folder, File: Hippolyte: "Correspondance passive" (1AP-I-D4).
15. 'Abdu'l-Bahá, quoted in Robert Weinberg, *Lady Blomfield: Her Life and Times,* p. 127.
16. Hippolyte Dreyfus, quoted in Isabel Fraser, "Abdul-Baha in London," *Star of the West,* vol. 3, no. 17 (Jan. 19, 1913): p. 10.
17. It is unclear whom 'Abdu'l-Bahá meant by "the ḥákim" and "the válí." Both words refer to someone who exercises a certain kind of authority—typically a governor or chief magistrate—and given their synonymity, 'Abdu'l-Bahá may have been using both titles for the same person. The closest equivalent to these positions in Edinburgh at that time would have been the Lord Provost, also known as the Lord-lieutenant. However, such contemporaneous records as the chronicle of Mírzá Maḥmúd Zarqání and the diary letters of Mírzá Ahmad Sohrab make no mention of 'Abdu'l-Bahá meeting with anyone bearing that title, nor do they specifically name anyone who might have held that office.
18. 'Abdu'l-Bahá to Hippolyte. Original text published in *Muntakhabátí az Makátíb-i-Ḥaḍrat-i-'Abdu'l-Bahá,* vol. 5, p. 59 (selection #69), translated into English by Adib Masumian and published in *A supplement to Abdu'l-Baha in Europe, 1912–1913, Part II: Selections from Tablets of Abdu'l-Bahá Regarding His Western Journey.*
19. 'Abdu'l-Bahá to Hippolyte. Original text published in *Muntakhabátí az Makátíb-i-Ḥaḍrat-i-'Abdu'l-Bahá,* vol. 5, p. 59 (selection #68), translated into English by Adib Masumian and published in *A supplement to Abdu'l-Baha in Europe,*

1912–1913, Part II: Selections from Tablets of Abdu'l-Bahá Regarding His Western Journey.

20. Caxton Hall is a building on the corner of Caxton Street and Palmer Street in London. In the 1910s, it hosted artistic and political events.
21. The London Peace Society, or International Peace Society, was a British pacifist organization founded in 1816 for the promotion of permanent and universal peace. In 1930, the Peace Society merged with the International Christian Peace Fellowship and was renamed the International Peace Society.

19 / 'Abdu'l-Bahá's Second Stay in Paris

1. Jan Teofil Jasion, *'Abdu'l-Bahá in France 1911 & 1913,* p. 290.
2. Maḥmúd Zarqání, *Badáyiu'l-Athar,* vol. 2, p. 100.
3. Hassan M. Balyuzi, *'Abdu'l-Bahá: The Centre of the Covenant of Bahá'u'lláh,* pp. 372–74.
4. Maḥmúd Zarqání, *Badáyiu'l-Athar,* vol. 2, p. 104.
5. *Abdul Baha on Divine Philosophy,* compiled by Isabel Fraser Chamberlain, pp. 29–30.
6. Jan Teofil Jasion, *'Abdu'l-Bahá in France 1911 & 1913,* p. 314.
7. Ibid., p. 296.
8. Ahmad Sohrab to Harriet Magee, 26 May 1913. National Bahá'í Archives of the United States: Ahmad Sohrab papers. For more information on 'Abdu'l-Bahá's stay in Paris, see Jan Teofil Jasion, *'Abdu'l-Bahá in France 1911 & 1913.*
9. Ahmad Sohrab to Harriet Magee, 6 February 1913. National Bahá'í Archives of the United States.
10. Jan Teofil Jasion, *'Abdu'l-Bahá in France 1911 & 1913,* p. 351.
11. Ibid., p. 301.
12. Ibid., p. 326.
13. Ahmad Sohrab to Harriet Magee, 8 May 1913. National Bahá'í Archives of the United States.
14. Ahmad Sohrab to Harriet Magee, 13 May 1913. National Bahá'í Archives of the United States.

15. In 1913, there were many Bahá'í gatherings in Paris. Among those, two weekly meetings were particularly systematic and popular: one at the Dreyfus-Barney home every Friday evening, and one at the Scott's every Monday. Gatherings at Edith Sanderson's apartment also attracted many souls.
16. Ahmad Sohrab to Harriet Magee, 7 February 1913. National Bahá'í Archives of the United States.
17. Ahmad Sohrab to Harriet Magee, 14 March. 1913. National Bahá'í Archives of the United States.
18. Hassan M. Balyuzi, *'Abdu'l-Bahá: The Centre of the Covenant of Bahá'u'lláh,* pp. 372–74.
19. Such as the Book of Certitude, the Epistle to the Son of the Wolf, the Seven Valleys, etc. . . .
20. Maḥmúd Zarqání, *Badáyiu'l-Athar,* vol. 2, p. 163.
21. Ahmad Sohrab to Harriet Magee, 29 March 1913. National Bahá'í Archives of the United States.
22. Jan Teofil Jasion, *'Abdu'l-Bahá in France 1911 & 1913,* pp. 365–68.
23. Ibid, pp. 372–77.
24. Ibid, pp. 419–28.
25. Ahmad Sohrab to Harriet Magee, 26 March 1913. National Bahá'í Archives of the United States.
26. Ahmad Sohrab to Harriet Magee, 30 March 1913. National Bahá'í Archives of the United States.
27. The word *Bábí* here does not refer to the followers of the Báb, but to the followers of Mírzá Yaḥyá (Ṣubḥ-i-Azal), who were sometimes known as Azalis. One of the great sources of concern for the Master was that the general public, and even some of the believers, would mistakenly assume that Mírzá Yaḥyá's proponents, who maneuvered against and were trying to subvert the Qájár dynasty, as being of the same ilk as the Bahá'ís, who were earnestly engaged in spreading a message of love and unity.

28. 'Abdu'l-Bahá to Hippolyte Dreyfus, National Bahá'í Archives of France (Letter-22). Provisional translation from the Persian prepared by the authors, reviewed and improved by Ms. Hoda Seioshansian and Ms. Mary Victoria, to whom we are grateful.
29. Moojan Momen, *The Covenant and Covenant-breaker.* See http://bahai- library.com/momen_encyclopedia_covenant.
30. Ahmad Sohrab to Harriet Magee, 9 March 1913. National Bahá'í Archives of the United States.
31. Edward Browne to Hippolyte Dreyfus, 8 September 1911. National Bahá'í Archives of France (1AP-I-D4).
32. Jan Teofil Jasion, *'Abdu'l-Bahá in France 1911 & 1913,* p. 477.
33. Jack Winsor Hansen, The Sibyl Sanderson Story: Requiem for a Diva, p. 49.
34. Jan Teofil Jasion, *'Abdu'l-Bahá in France 1911 & 1913,* p. 582.
35. Ibid., p. 647.
36. Maḥmúd Zarqání, *Badáyiu'l-Athar, vol. 2,* pp. 160–63.
37. Ahmad Sohrab to Harriet Magee, 27 February 1913. National Bahá'í Archives of the United States.
38. Ahmad Sohrab to Harriet Magee, 29 February 1913. National Bahá'í Archives of the United States.
39. Ahmad Sohrab to Harriet Magee, 5 March 1913. National Bahá'í Archives of the United States.
40. Ahmad Sohrab to Harriet Magee, 8 February 1913. National Bahá'í Archives of the United States.
41. Ahmad Sohrab to Harriet Magee, 12 March 1913. National Bahá'í Archives of the United States.
42. Maḥmúd Zarqání, *Badáyiu'l-Athar,* vol. 2, p. 179.
43. Ahmad Sohrab to Harriet Magee, 19 March 1913. National Bahá'í Archives of the United States.
44. Now the Waldorf Trocadéro.
45. Ahmad Sohrab to Harriet Magee, 18 March 1913. National Bahá'í Archives of the United States.
46. Maḥmúd Zarqání, *Badáyiu'l-Athar,* vol. 2, p. 321.

47. Achraf Achraf, "Souvenir du jeune A. Achraf, étudiant bahá'í iranien à Paris," *Sur les pas d"Abdu'l-Bahá à Paris: Paris deviendra un jardin de roses,* dirigé par Paul Hakim (Paris: Librairie bahá'íe, 1998), p. 56.
48. Ahmad Sohrab to Harriet Magee, 1 April 1913. National Bahá'í Archives of the United States.
49. Ahmad Sohrab to Harriet Magee, 1 May 1913. National Bahá'í Archives of the United States.
50. Ahmad Sohrab to Harriet Magee, 2 May 1913. National Bahá'í Archives of the United States.
51. Maḥmúd Zarqání, *Badáyiu'l-Athar,* vol. 2, p. 321.
52. Ibid., p. 281.
53. An American Bahá'í.
54. *Abdul Baha on Divine Philosophy,* compiled by Isabel Fraser Chamberlain, p. 78.
55. Ahmad Sohrab to Harriet Magee, 23 May 1913. National Bahá'í Archives of the United States.
56. The Declaration of the Báb and the birth of 'Abdu'l-Bahá both happened on the same day: May 23, 1844.
57. *Abdul Baha on Divine Philosophy,* compiled by Isabel Fraser Chamberlain, pp. 47–50.
58. Ahmad Sohrab to Harriet Magee, 23 May 1913. National Bahá'í Archives of the United States.
59. Maḥmúd Zarqání, *Badáyiu'l-Athar,* vol. 2, p. 310.
60. Fanny Almine Knobloch (1859–1949), was an American Bahá'í, originally born in Germany. She served the Faith in Germany and South Africa for many years.
61. Fanny Knobloch, *Manuscript about her Baha'i history,* pp. 26-30, HKC, BAWDC, in Hannen Knobloch Collection at the Bahá'í Archives of Washington DC.
62. Mary Magdalene, or Mary of Magdala, was one of the devoted followers and a true disciple of Jesus. She traveled with Him and was a witness to His crucifixion. Bahá'í writings accord to Mary Magdalene a very high station.

63. Ahmad Sohrab to Harriet Magee, 3 June 1913. National Bahá'í Archives of the United States.
64. Ahmad Sohrab to Harriet Magee, 12 June 1913. National Bahá'í Archives of the United States.
65. Rúḥá Khánum, one of 'Abdu'l-Bahá's daughters, who was then hospitalized in Paris.
66. Ahmad Sohrab to Harriet Magee, 13 June 1913. National Bahá'í Archives of the United States.

20 / The Epistle to the Son of the Wolf

1. 'Abdu'l-Bahá, quoted in Jan Teofil Jasion, *'Abdu'l-Bahá in France 1911 & 1913,* pp. 663–64.
2. Bahá'u'lláh, L'Épître au Fils du loup, traduction française par Hippolyte Dreyfus (Paris: Honoré Champion, 1913).
3. Hippolyte Dreyfus, "Introduction," in Bahá'u'lláh, *Épître au Fils du Loup,* pp. vi–ix.
4. Clément Huart, "Comptes-rendus: Bahâol'llâh. L'Epitre au Fils du Loup, traduction française par Hippolyte Dreyfus. . . ." *Journal Asiatique* (Paris) 11 s., t. 3 (January–February 1914): 184.
5. Henri Lammens, "Bulletin oriental," *Études* (Paris) t. 137 (20 November 1913): 37.
6. M.G.D., "L'épitre au Fils du Loup par Bahaoullah, traduction française par Hippolyte Dreyfus. . . " *Revue Critique d'Histoire et de Littérature* (Paris) no. 41 (11 October 1913): 281–82.
7. *Le Figaro* is a daily French newspaper. It was founded in 1826 and is the oldest national daily newspaper in France that continues to still be published. Many prominent writers and political figures, such as Zola, Proust, Pierre de Coubertin, were regular contributors.
8. Ph.-Emmanuel, Glasser, "Petite Chronique des Lettres" *Le Figaro* (Paris) no. 38 (7 February 1913): 5, col. 3.
9. "La Religion moderne: le congrès du progrès religieux," *Les Conférences* (Paris) no. 455 (3 July 1913): 175–82.

10. Hippolyte Dreyfus, "Le mouvement Bahaï" (Appendice), *Travaux du 6 congrès international du progrès religieux (Chrétiens progressifs et libres-croyants),* (Paris : Librairie Fischbacher, 1913): 520–22.
11. "La Religion moderne: le congrès du progrès religieux," *Les Conférences,* pp. 175–82.
12. Obituary notice: Inès Dreyfus, deceased on 2 October 1913. National Bahá'í Archives, United States (Albert Windust P 1 B3 1 1910–13, 22).
13. Cimetière parisien du Nord-Montmartre: Situation de sépulture. [Montmartre Cemetery – location of sepulchre]. National Bahá'í Archives of France, Laura Dreyfus-Barney Folder, File Hippolyte: "Documents postérieurs à Hippolyte Dreyfus-Barney" (1AP- I-F).

21 / Covering the Southern United States

1. Alice Pike Barney, Laura's mother.
2. Hippolyte Dreyfus to Yvonne Meyer-May (Dreyfus), 30 November 1913. National Bahá'í Archives of France, Laura Dreyfus-Barney Folder, File: Hippolyte "Correspondance active: famille" (1AP-I-C1).
3. Hippolyte Dreyfus to Yvonne Meyer-May (Dreyfus), 23 December 1913. National Bahá'í Archives of France (1AP-I-C1).
4. "City News Notes," *The Washington Times* (10 December 1913): 3, col.1.
5. Hippolyte Dreyfus to Yvonne Meyer-May (Dreyfus), 24 January 1914. National Bahá'í Archives of France (1AP-I-C1).
6. Hippolyte Dreyfus to Yvonne Meyer-May, 02 February 1914. National Bahá'í Archives of France (1AP-I-C1).
7. Spiritual Assembly of the Bahá'ís of New York to Laura Dreyfus-Barney, 17 Jan. 1929, National Bahá'í Archives of France, Laura Dreyfus-Barney Folder, File: "Condoléances" (1AP-II-D).
8. Hippolyte Dreyfus to Yvonne Meyer-May, 08 February 1914. National Bahá'í Archives of France (1AP-I-C1).

9. Hippolyte Dreyfus to Yvonne Meyer-May, 05 February 1914. National Bahá'í Archives of France (1AP-I-C1).
10. Hippolyte Dreyfus to Yvonne Meyer-May, 08 February 1914. National Bahá'í Archives of France (1AP-I-C1).
11. Hippolyte Dreyfus to Yvonne Meyer-May, 02 October 1914. National Bahá'í Archives of France (1AP-I-C1).
12. Francisco I. Madero (1873–1913) was a Mexican revolutionary who became president of Mexico between 1911 and 1913. He was removed after a military coup in Mexico and eventually assassinated in 1913.
13. Victoriano Huerta (1850–1916) was a high-ranking officer in the Mexican army, who became president of Mexico from 1913 to 1914 after mounting a coup.
14. Emiliano Zapata (1879–1919) was one of the most iconic figures and the main leader of the revolution in Mexico until he was killed in an ambush in 1919.
15. Hippolyte Dreyfus to Yvonne Meyer-May, 02 October 1914. National Bahá'í Archives of France (1AP-I-C1).
16. Valentine's older brother, Hippolyte's nephew.
17. Hippolyte Dreyfus to Valentine Meyer-May, 13 February 1914. National Bahá'í Archives of France, Laura Dreyfus-Barney Folder, File: Hippolyte "Correspondance active: famille" (1AP-I-C1).
18. Jean L. Kling, *Alice Pike Barney, Her Life and Art,* p. 237.
19. Hippolyte Dreyfus to Yvonne Meyer-May, 17 February 1914. National Bahá'í Archives of France (1AP-I-C1).
20. Hippolyte Dreyfus to Paul Meyer-May, 21 February 1914. National Bahá'í Archives of France, Laura Dreyfus-Barney Folder, File: Hippolyte "Correspondance active: famille" (1AP-I-C1).
21. Moojan Momen, *The Covenant and Covenant-breaker* [online]. See footnote no. 431.
22. Hushang Guharriz, *Mubashirín-i-Mísáq dar Gharb [Disciples of 'Abdu'l-Bahá in the West],* pp. 43–57.

23. Talk given by M. H. Dreyfus, S.F. *[San Francisco]* Assembly, 28 February 1914, National Bahá'í Archives, United States, pp. 4–6.
24. Ibid., pp. 9–10.

22 / Exploring the Far East

1. "Personal Mention," *Honolulu Star Bulletin* (Honolulu), (March 12, 1914), p. 4, col. 5.
2. Samuel Parker (1853–1920), known as Kamuela Parker, was a businessman and a wealthy landowner in Hawaii. He also made a career in politics and was asked by the Queen Lili'uo-kalani to serve in several capacities at different ministries.
3. The Spreckels were close friends of the Dreyfus family; they were known for making a fortune with the founding of the Spreckels Sugar Company.
4. Hippolyte Dreyfus to Yvonne Meyer-May, 15 March 1914. National Bahá'í Archives of France (1AP-I-C1).
5. Laura Dreyfus-Barney, *From the Peace of the East to the War of the West,* typescript, Dec. 1916, National Bahá'í Archives of France, Laura Dreyfus-Barney Folder, File: "Manuscrits" (1AP-II-B), p. 31.
6. Mr and Mrs Philip H. Dodge, an American couple who moved to Japan as teachers.
7. Agnes Baldwin Alexander, *History of the Baha'i Faith in Japan 1914–1938,* p. 6.
8. Empress Shōken (1849–1914), was the wife and adviser of Emperor Meiji, who was the 122nd Emperor of Japan and the first monarch of the Empire of Japan.
9. Hippolyte Dreyfus to Yvonne Meyer-May, 10 April 1914. National Bahá'í Archives of France (1AP-I-C1).
10. Hippolyte Dreyfus to Yvonne Meyer-May, 25 April 1914. National Bahá'í Archives of France (1AP-I-C1).
11. As previously mentioned in chapter 1, Hippolyte's family is very well off. Hippolyte, even though he is consecrating most of his time to spreading the Cause, is also managing, in collab-

oration with his brother-in-law, Paul Meyer-May, a portfolio of financial and real estate assets. Laura's family is extremely wealthy: her father, Albert Clifford Barney, was the son of a manufacturer of railway cars, a business that he inherited and made even more prosperous. When he passed away in 1902, he left to his wife and to Laura and Natalie a massive inheritance of millions of US dollars. Moreover, Hippolyte was working with Paul Meyer-May, his brother-in-law, on finance and real estate projects. One of their closest collaborators was Arthur Spitzer (1871–1944), founder of the Bank Spitzer, now known as Finindus.

12. Hippolyte Dreyfus to Yvonne Meyer-May, 25 April 1914. National Bahá'í Archives of France (1AP-I-C1).
13. Laura Dreyfus-Barney, *From the Peace of the East to the War of the West,* pp. 42–48.
14. Known as Mount Itsukushima.
15. Hippolyte Dreyfus to Yvonne Meyer-May, 6 May 1914. National Bahá'í Archives of France (1AP-I-C1).
16. Peking was the French spelling for Beijing in the early 1900s.
17. Hippolyte Dreyfus to Paul Meyer-May, 21 February 1914. National Bahá'í Archives of France (1AP-I-C1).
18. Laura Dreyfus-Barney, *From the Peace of the East to the War of the West,* p. 60.
19. Now Shenyang in China.
20. Laura Dreyfus-Barney, *From the Peace of the East to the War of the West,* p. 69.
21. Alexandre Robert Conty (1864–1947), French diplomat, Ambassador Extraordinary and Plenipotentiary in Beijing between 1912 and 1917.
22. Mr. De Laas was working in China for the French industrial mission, particularly on railway projects.
23. Hippolyte Dreyfus to Yvonne Meyer-May, 2 June 1914. Iowa Women's Archives.
24. Alfred Sao-Ke Sze (1876–1958), prominent Chinese diplomat. First Chinese student to graduate from Cornell Univer-

sity in 1901, he returned to China 1902 to work for the Chinese government. Between 1914 and 1920, he would become China's minister to the United Kingdom a member of the Chinese delegation to the Paris Peace Conference in 1919.

25. Hippolyte Dreyfus to Yvonne Meyer-May, 6 June 1914. Iowa Women's Archives.
26. Now Zhangjiakou in Hubei Province.
27. Former name of Ulaanbaatar, currently the capital of Mongolia.
28. Hippolyte Dreyfus to Paul Meyer-May, 28 May 1914. Iowa Women's Archives.
29. Laura Dreyfus-Barney, *From the Peace of the East to the War of the West,* p. 80.
30. Ibid., pp. 80–81.
31. Ibid., pp. 81–82.
32. Now Chengde, in the Hubei province of China.
33. Hippolyte Dreyfus to Yvonne Meyer-May, 24 June 1914. Iowa Women's Archives.
34. Hippolyte Dreyfus to Yvonne Meyer-May, 30 June 1914. Iowa Women's Archives. This is the only instance we know of Hippolyte becoming angry and raising his voice, which apparently was caused by his companion being unjustly treated.
35. "Tsingtau after war started as seen by well-known people: Mr. and Mrs. H. Dreyfus-Barney Give Account of Blockaded Port," *Honolulu Star Bulletin* (Honolulu), (22 October 1914), p. 10, col. 1.
36. Hippolyte Dreyfus to Yvonne Meyer-May, 3 August 1914. Iowa Women's Archives.
37. Laura Dreyfus-Barney, "Hippolyte Dreyfus-Barney," Article for Bahai World, (1AP-I-F).
38. "Tsingtau after war started as seen by well-known people: Mr. and Mrs. H. Dreyfus-Barney Give Account of Blockaded Port," Honolulu Star Bulletin (Honolulu), (22 October 1914), p. 10, col.1.

39. Laura Dreyfus-Barney, *From the Peace of the East to the War of the West,* p. 107.
40. By visiting the French embassy in 1914, Hippolyte received official acknowledgment of his presence and compliance with military obligations. The statement of presentation served as proof that he was not avoiding his assignment. As he was traveling internationally, the embassy was the only official French institution accessible to him. Failing to show up could have been seen as evasion of his duties and would have potentially led to serious legal consequences, including martial penalties. This step was crucial for validating his position and avoiding accusations of desertion.
41. Ambassade de la République Française aux États-Unis, Washington, 28 September 1914, "Engagement d'Hippolyte à rejoindre son Corps d'affectation en France." National Bahá'í Archives of France, Laura Dreyfus-Barney Folder, File: Hippolyte "Papiers et objets personnels" (1AP-I-A).
42. Hippolyte Dreyfus to Yvonne Meyer-May, 27 September 1914. Iowa Women's Archives.

23 / First World War

1. Laura Dreyfus-Barney, *From the Peace of the East to the War of the West,* pp. 115–16.
2. Ibid., pp. 116–17.
3. Laura Dreyfus-Barney, "Hippolyte Dreyfus-Barney," *Article for Bahai World,* (1AP-I-F).
4. Laura Dreyfus-Barney, *From the Peace of the East to the War of the West,* p. 123.
5. Ibid., p. 126.
6. Hippolyte Dreyfus to George Latimer, 2 October 1918, National Bahá'í Archives, United States.
7. Hippolyte Dreyfus à George Latimer, January 1919, National Bahá'í Archives, United States.

8. Report from the Ministry of War, through a General who is its Chief of Staff, Paris, 23 December 1918. National Bahá'í Archives of France, Laura Dreyfus-Barney Folder, File Hippolyte: "Papiers et objets personnels" (1AP-I-A).
9. Laura Dreyfus-Barney, 'Hippolyte Dreyfus-Barney." *Article for Bahai World,* (1AP-I-F).
10. In 1919, Egypt is in the midst of its first modern revolution. The insurgents, mainly led by Saad Zaghloul, instigate disorder all over the country to fight against the British government which is controlling both Egypt and the Sudan. This revolution would lead to the independence of Egypt in 1922.
11. Laura Dreyfus-Barney, *The Way Reopens,* p. 4.
12. Permit to enter Palestine (April 4, 1919). National Bahá'í Archives of France, Laura Dreyfus-Barney Folder, File Hippolyte: "Papiers et objets personnels" (1AP-I-A).
13. Mona Khademi, *Some Questions Answered: The Life of Laura Barney,* p. 181.
14. A guardsman watching over the security and safety of the railroad.
15. Shoghi Effendi to Ahmad Sohrab, April 5, 1919, Hannen-Knobloch Family Papers, National Bahá'í Archives, United States.
16. Hassan M. Balyuzi, *'Abdu'l-Bahá: The Centre of the Covenant of Bahá'u'lláh,* p. 433.
17. Mona Khademi, *Some Questions Answered: The Life of Laura Barney,* pp. 181–82.
18. Shoghi Effendi to an unknown recipient, April 6, 1919, Hannen-Knobloch Family Papers, National Bahá'í Archives, United States.
19. Mona Khademi, *Some Questions Answered: The Life of Laura Barney,* p. 182.
20. Mírzá Mihdí (1848–1870) the youngest brother of 'Abdu'l-Bahá who tragically passed away at the of age of 22 after he fell through the skylight in the roof of the prison onto a crate ly-

ing on the floor below, a broken shard of which fatally pierced his body.

21. Shoghi Effendi to Ahmad, April 14, 1919, Hannen-Knobloch Family Papers, National Bahá'í Archives, United States.
22. Shoghi Effendi to Ahmad, April 15–18, 1919, Hannen-Knobloch Family Papers, National Bahá'í Archives, United States.
23. Laura Dreyfus-Barney, *The Way Reopens,* pp. 5–6.

24 / The Tablets of the Divine Plan

1. Mona Khademi, *Some Questions Answered: The Life of Laura Barney,* pp. 186–87.
2. The Tablets of the Divine Plan were officially presented in the United States during a ceremony in 1919 between April 26 and 30.
3. Shoghi Effendi quoted in 'Abdu'l-Bahá, *Tablets of the Divine Plan,* p. xv.
4. 'Abdu'l-Bahá, *Tablets of the Divine Plan,* p. xix.
5. 'Abdu'l-Bahá to Hippolyte Dreyfus, National Bahá'í Archives of France (Letter-24). Provisional translation from the Persian prepared by the authors, reviewed and improved by Ms. Hoda Seioshansian and Ms. Mary Victoria, to whom we are grateful.
6. Hippolyte Dreyfus to Elle Cooper, (March 9, 1919), National Bahá'í Archives, United States.
7. "Society," *The Evening Star,* (Washington), (20 Nov. 1919), p. 9.
8. Laura's mother is waiting for the decision from the court regarding her divorce with Christian Hemmick.
9. Alice Pike Barney, Laura's mother.
10. Yvonne's daughter, Valentine Meyer-May, is about to get married with Robert Maroni.
11. Hippolyte Dreyfus to Yvonne Meyer-May, 3 December 1920, Iowa Women's Archives.

12. The British West Indies ("BWI") were the British territories in the Caribbean. In 1919, the BWI included the Bahamas, Barbados, British Guiana, the British Honduras, Jamaica, Trinidad and Tobago, the British Leeward Islands, and the British Windward Islands.
13. The Riondas are Ellen Gouin and her husband Manuel Enrique Rionda (1877–1950).
14. Hippolyte Dreyfus to Yvonne Meyer-May, 15 January 1920, National Bahá'í Archives of France.
15. Hippolyte Dreyfus to Yvonne Meyer-May, 21 January 1920, Iowa Women's Archives.
16. "Miscellaneous," *The Brooklyn Daily Eagle,* (Brooklyn, New York), (13 March 1920), p. 16.
17. Hippolyte Dreyfus to Yvonne Meyer-May, 21 May 1920, Iowa Women's Archives.
18. Eustache de Lorey (1875–1938) was a French diplomat, archaeologist, and an expert in Islamic art history. He was in charge of the French institute of archaeology and Islamic art in Damascus from 1922 to 1930. He met 'Abdu'l-Bahá in 1911 in Paris at Herman Bemberg's home.
19. Mary M. Rabb (1872–1940) was a Bahá'í from the United States.
20. Hippolyte Dreyfus to Mary Rabb, 20 June 1923, National Bahá'í Archives of France (1AP-I-C1).
21. Hippolyte Dreyfus to de Lorey, 31 January 1913, National Bahá'í Archives of France (1AP-I-C1).
22. Laura Dreyfus-Barney, "Hippolyte Dreyfus-Barney," *Article for Bahai World,* (1AP-I-F).
23. Shoghi Effendi, "Hippolyte Dreyfus-Barney: An Appreciation," pp. 210–14.
24. Most probably Gabriel Puaux (1883–1970), French diplomat, secretary general of the Tunisian government between 1919 and 1922.

25. In Tunisia during the 1920s, "Bey" referred to a title of nobility and governance, denoting a significant political figure with authority over local affairs. Although the role of the Bey diminished after Tunisia became a French protectorate in 1881, the title retained its social prestige.
26. Hippolyte Dreyfus to Yvonne Meyer-May, [undated—Saturday evening], Iowa Women's Archives.
27. Now Essaâda Palace.
28. Hippolyte Dreyfus to Yvonne Meyer-May, 27 April 1920, Iowa Women's Archives.
29. Shaykh Muḥyí'd-Dín Ṣabri.
30. Marjorie and Mountfort Mills, an American Bahá'í couple who were very close to the Dreyfus-Barneys.
31. Hippolyte Dreyfus to Yvonne Meyer-May, 14 March 1921, Iowa Women's Archives.
32. Vicomte Odon Henri Edmond Antoine de Castillon de Saint Victor (1870–1949) was a French minister. He was secretary of several embassies in Santiago, Montevideo, Copenhagen, Athens, and Rio de Janeiro. He was first delegate at the Residence of France in Tunis between 1921 and 1925. He was named Chevalier, and a few years later, Officier of the French Légion d'Honneur.
33. Cheikh Mohieddine Sabri and Shaykh Muḥyí'd-Dín Sabri are references to the same person.
34. "Destourians" refers to the members of the Tunisian political party called "Destour," a pseudonym for al-Ḥizb al-Ḥurr al-Dustūrī al-Tūnisī, which was especially active in the 1920s and 30s in raising Tunisian national consciousness and opposition to the French protectorate.
35. De Castillon Saint-Victor, Délégué à la Résidence générale de France à Tunis au ministre des Affaires étrangères, Tunis, (4 Oct. 1923): no. Rg. 1526.
36. Hippolyte Dreyfus-Barney, "Le Bahaïsme," *La Vie Tunisienne,* (Tunis) vol. 6 (March 1923): 61–63.

25 / Adventures at the Border of Indochina

1. Shoghi Effendi, "Hippolyte Dreyfus-Barney: An Appreciation," pp. 210–14.
2. Marzieh Gail, *Arches of the Years,* p. 185.
3. 'Abdu'l-Bahá to Hippolyte Dreyfus, National Bahá'í Archives of France (Letter-25).
4. Ministère des Affaires étrangères, Paris, 26 Oct. 1913, [Letter of Recommendation introducing Hippolyte Dreyfus-Barney and his wife], National Bahá'í Archives of France, Laura Dreyfus-Barney Folder, File: Hippolyte "Papiers et objets personnels" (1AP-I-A).
5. Philippe Berthelot (1866–1934) was a French diplomat. He served in several posts in Asia, notably in China. Back in France, he became secretary to the Ministry of Foreign Affairs, with the rank of ambassador.
6. Philippe Berthelot, Ministre plénipotentiaire, Chef du Cabinet du ministre des Affaires étrangères, [Letter of Recommendation], 27 Oct. 1913. National Bahá'í Archives of France, (1AP-I-A).
7. Now El Qantara.
8. Hippolyte to Yvonne Meyer-May, 23 November 1920. Iowa Women's Archives.
9. Ibid.
10. Dutch East Indies was a Dutch colony in Southeast Asia before World War II. It was comprised of a number of islands corresponding, more or less, to what is now Indonesia, Sumatra, Java, Borneo, and Sulawesi, and others.
11. Now Sri Lanka.
12. Laura Dreyfus-Barney, "Hippolyte Dreyfus-Barney," Article for *Bahai World,* (1AP-I-F).
13. Ramona Allen Brown, *Memories of 'Abdu'l-Bahá,* pp. 97–98.
14. Now Jakarta.
15. Most probably Emil Helfferich (1878–1920) Karl Hellferich's (1872–1924) brother, a German politician and banker was living in Indonesia in the 1920s.

16. Hippolyte is saying that, since he and Laura will be on the road, they will be out of touch during this leg of their journey.
17. The "control" was a nickname used to designate the location where communications were "controlled" (checked).
18. Hippolyte to Yvonne Meyer-May, 15 December 1920. Iowa Women's Archives.
19. Laura Dreyfus-Barney, *The Way Reopens,* pp. 21–31.
20. They notably met M. Dekat Angelino, a Dutch public officer, and Dr. Schricke, assistant director at the office of indigenous affairs.
21. In his personal travel diary, Hippolyte mentions the name of H. Lenoir, owner of coffee and rubber plantations at Silosanen. See Agenda de voyages d'Hippolyte Dreyfus en Extrême Orient (1920–22). [Hippolyte's travelogue of his voyages to the Far East, 1920–22]. National Bahá'í Archives of France, (1AP-I-A1).
22. Laura Dreyfus-Barney, *The Way Reopens,* pp. 35–37.
23. Ibid, p. 45.
24. The individual assigned to enforce the regional laws regarding the use of opium, which was legal under certain conditions, such as for medical purposes.
25. Ibid, pp. 46–49.
26. The Straits Settlements were a group of British territories located in Southeast Asia and consisted of the individual settlements of Penang, Singapore, Malacca, and the Dindings, plus some islands like Christmas Island or the Cocos Islands. The Straits Settlements are mentioned in the Tablets of the Divine Plan.
27. Laura Dreyfus-Barney, *The Way Reopens,* pp. 63–65.
28. Now Ho Chi Minh City.
29. The Dreyfus-Barneys spent most of their time in Indochina with two couples: the Lasseignes and the Lochards. Lucien Lasseigne was working for the Industrial Bank of China, in Indochina. He managed offices in Haiphong, then Saigon, and eventually became the general manager of all the bank

agencies in Indochina. André Lochard (1880–1946), graduated from France's top schools, École polytechnique and École des mines (1905), and was sent by the French government to Indochina to restore the industrial and economic situation there.

30. Laura Dreyfus-Barney, *The Way Reopens,* p. 66.
31. Now Thailand.
32. Laura Dreyfus-Barney, *The Way Reopens,* pp. 76–83.
33. Ibid, pp. 85–91.
34. Now Vung Tau.
35. Agenda de voyages d'Hippolyte Dreyfus en Extrême Orient (1920–22) [Hippolyte's travelogue of his voyages to the Far East, 1920–22], National Bahá'í Archives of France, (1AP-I-A1).
36. Now Đà Năng.
37. Laura Dreyfus-Barney, *The Way Reopens,* p. 103.
38. Hải Vân Pass.
39. Laura Dreyfus-Barney, *The Way Reopens,* pp. 112–20.
40. Hippolyte to Yvonne Meyer-May, 24 May 1921. Iowa Women's Archives.
41. Hippolyte to Yvonne Meyer-May, 30 May 1921. Iowa Women's Archives.
42. Laura Dreyfus-Barney, *The Way Reopens,* p. 126.
43. Now Kunming, capital of the Yunnan province.
44. Most probably Amizhou, city located in the southern part of the Yunnan province, and now called Kaiyuan.
45. Laura Dreyfus-Barney, *The Way Reopens,* p. 142.
46. Hippolyte to Yvonne Meyer-May, 10 July 1921. Iowa Women's Archives.
47. Léon Robert (1866–1956), was a Father of the Foreign Mission Society of Paris. He came to China after his ordination in 1888, and was appointed as his Society's Procurator in Shanghai in 1891. He remained in China for twelve years and then came as Procurator to Hong Kong, where he stayed eighteen years.

48. Laura Dreyfus-Barney, *The Way Reopens,* pp. 150–53.
49. Wu Ting Fang (1842–1922) was a Chinese diplomat and politician. A lawyer by training, he served as Minister of Foreign Affairs and Premier of the Republic of China during the early years of the government of Sun Yat-sen.
50. Laura Dreyfus-Barney, *The Way Reopens,* p. 156.
51. Ibid., pp. 158–61.
52. Ibid., pp. 163–79.
53. Ibid., pp. 180–81.
54. Ibid., pp. 182–87.
55. Ibid., p. 188.
56. Ibid, pp. 188–89.
57. Mírzá Jalál, the son of Mírzá Muḥammad-Ḥasan, the King of Martyrs; and his wife Rúhá, third daughter of 'Abdu'l-Bahá.
58. Hippolyte to Yvonne Meyer-May, 5 January 1922. Iowa Women's Archives.
59. Laura Dreyfus-Barney, *The Way Reopens,* p. 189.
60. Ibid. p. 190.
61. Ibid., pp. 190–92.
62. Ibid., pp. 192–215.
63. Mohandas Karamchand Gandhi (1869–1948) was an Indian anti-colonialist politician and a spiritual guide who employed nonviolent civil resistance to achieve his aim of Indian independence from the United Kingdom.
64. It refers here to the Khilafat Movement, a Pan-Islamist protest campaign launched by Muslims in British India to restore the political authority of the Ottoman Caliphate at the end of the First World War.
65. Swaraj refers here to the concept of Indian independence from foreign domination as expounded by Gandhi.
66. Laura Dreyfus-Barney, *The Way Reopens,* pp. 220–21.
67. *Bombay Chronicle,* 24 May 1944.
68. M. V. Gandimohan, *Mahatma Gandhi and the Bahá'ís: Striving towards a Nonviolent Civilization,* (New Delhi: Bahá'í Publishing Trust of India, 2000).

69. Spiritual hermitage at which Gandhi and his followers resided.
70. Agenda de voyages d'Hippolyte Dreyfus en Extrême Orient (1920–22) [Hippolyte's travelogue of his voyages to the Far East, 1920–22], National Bahá'í Archives of France, (1AP-I-A1).

26 / The Days of the Guardian

1. Shoghi Effendi, quoted in Rúḥíyyih Rabbaní, *The Priceless Pearl,* p. 43.
2. 'Abdu'l-Bahá, *The Will and Testament of 'Abdu'l-Bahá,* Wilmette (USA): Bahá'í Publishing Trust, 1990.
3. Rúḥíyyih Rabbaní, *The Priceless Pearl,* pp. 42–43.
4. Earl Redman, *Shoghi Effendi Through the Pilgrim's Eye, Volume 1: Building the Administrative Order, 1922–1952,* pp. 30–32.
5. Ibid, p. 58.
6. Shoghi Effendi, quoted in Amatu'l-Bahá Rúḥíyyih Khánum, "The Guardian of the Faith," *The Bahá'í World* (Haifa) vol. 13, 1954–1963 (1970): 76. These "vexations" refer to the heartrending disobedience shown by his own relatives towards the Will of his beloved Grandfather.
7. Edith de Bons-McKay, "Avec le premier groupe bahá'í de Paris: Quelques souvenirs de Mme Edith de Bons-McKay," La Pensée Baha'ie, (Nyon, Suisse), no. 56, (June 1976): 27.
8. Shoghi Effendi to Laura Dreyfus-Barney, 21 Dec. 1928, National Bahá'í Archives of France, File "Gardien à la France."
9. Robert Weinberg, *Lady Blomfield: Her Life and Times,* p. 232.
10. Earl Redman, *Shoghi Effendi Through the Pilgrim's Eye, Volume 1: Building the Administrative Order, 1922–1952,* chap. 2, "1922: A Gathering of the Learned."
11. Rúḥíyyih Rabbaní, *The Priceless Pearl,* p. 56.
12. Robert Weinberg, *Lady Blomfield: Her Life and Times,* pp. 234–35.
13. Ibid., p. 237.
14. Bahiyyih Randall-Winckler, *William Henry Randall: Disciple of 'Abdu'l-Bahá,* p. 210.

15. A town in the South of Germany that 'Abdu'l-Bahá visited in 1912.
16. Hippolyte to Yvonne Meyer-May, 18 March 1922. Iowa Women's Archives.
17. Earl Redman, *Shoghi Effendi Through the Pilgrim's Eye, Volume 1: Building the Administrative Order, 1922–1952,* chap. 2, "1922: A Gathering of the Learned."
18. Robert Weinberg, *Lady Blomfield: Her Life and Times,* p. 238.
19. Ibid., pp. 238–39.
20. Ibid., pp. 238–42.
21. Mary Esther Hall (1888–1950).
22. Robert Weinberg, *Lady Blomfield: Her Life and Times,* p. 243.
23. Formative Age: see Glossary.
24. Hippolyte to Yvonne Meyer-May, April 10, 1922. Iowa Women's Archives.

27 / The Writings of Bahá'u'lláh

1. The Lawḥ-i-Aqdas, published in Bahá'u'lláh, *Tablets of Bahá'u'lláh revealed after the Kitáb-i-Aqdas.*
2. Bahá'u'lláh, *L'Œuvre de Baháou'llah,* t.1, pp. 6–7.
3. Lucien Bouvat (1872–1942) was a French orientalist, a specialist on Islam and the languages of the Ottoman Empire. He was a librarian at the *Société Asiatique* and eventually became Professor at the Collège de France. He was a very prolific contributor to *Revue du Monde Musulman.*
4. Lucien Bouvat, "Comptes rendus: L'œuvre de Bahâ'oullâh. Traduction française de Hippolyte Dreyfus . . . ," *Journal Asiatique,* (Paris) t. 203 (Oct–Dec. 1923): 343.
5. Félix Lacôte (1873–1925), was a French translator and orientalist, a specialist in Indian culture and the Sanskrit language.
6. Félix Lacôte, "Bahâou'llâh (L'œuvre de), Premier volume . . . ," *Revue critique d'histoire et de littérature* (Paris) no. 7 (1st April 1924): 143.
7. Dreyfus-Barney, H. "Le Bahaïsme," *Vers l'Unité: revue internationale* (Genève) no. 26, (March–April 1924): 24–26.

8. Ibid., p. 24.
9. Ibid., p. 25.
10. Ibid., p. 26.
11. H. Dreyfus-Barney, "Le Bahaïsme," *Vers l'Unité: revue internationale,* p. 24.
12. This complete work, *The Súriy-i-Haykal,* is titled *Súrih of the Temple* in English and is published in *Summons of the Lord of Hosts,* including the first part, which is sometimes called the Tablet of the Temple.
13. Bahá'u'lláh, *L'Œuvre de Baháou'llah,* t. 2, pp. 7–9.
14. Clément Huart. "Analyses et comptes rendus : L'Œuvre de Bahâou'llàh, traduction française de Hippolyte Dreyfus. T.2 . . . ," *Revue de l'histoire des religions* (Paris) t. 89 (1924): 262–64.

28 / Traveling on Behalf of the Guardian

1. Mona Khademi, *Some Questions Answered: The Life of Laura Barney,* pp. 216–30.
2. "News of the Cause," *Bahá'í News Letter* (New York), no. 2 (January 1925): 3.
3. "The Baha'i Assembly—Meets," *The Pasadena Post,* (Pasadena, California), 28 February 1925, p. 5.
4. Mírzá Asadu'lláh Fáḍil-i-Mázandarání (1881–1957) became a Bahá'í in Tehran in 1909. He traveled to Egypt in 1919–1911 where he met with 'Abdu'l-Bahá and was sent to India and Burma to promote the Faith. 'Abdu'l-Bahá sent him to North America for the period 1920–1921. He also visited North America again in 1923–1925 at the request of Shoghi Effendi. His work, *Ẓohur-al-Ḥaqq* (variously also called *Tārik-e Ẓohur-al-Ḥaqq* and *Ketāb-e Ẓohur-al-Ḥaqq),* is a significant historical compilation of the history of the Bábí and Bahá'í Faiths in Iran. It has not been translated into English yet, but the World Center has indicated that it will be translated at some point in the future. (https://bahai-library.com/walbridge_notes_zuhurulhaqq_haqq).

5. Nellie S. French, "A Notable Fellowship Dinner," *Star of the West: the Bahá'í Magazine,* vol. 16, No. 4 (July 1925): 504.
6. This annual Convention was an opportunity for the representatives of the many local communities in North America to gather together and consult on the development of the Faith and to elect their National Spiritual Assembly. In 1925, the Convention was held between the 4th and 9th of July.
7. "The Seventeeth Annual Convention and Baha'i Congress," *The Bahá'í News* (New York), no. 6 (July–August 1925): 1–3.
8. "Chronologie des activités d'Hippolyte par Laura," manuscrit, [Timeline of Hippolyte's activities, by Laura, manuscript] National Bahá'í Archives of France, Laura Dreyfus-Barney Folder, File: Hippolyte "Documents postérieurs à Hippolyte" (1AP-I-F).
9. 'Abdu'l-Bahá, *Tablets of the Divine Plan,* p. 43.
10. Robert Weinberg, *Ethel Jenner Rosenberg: The Life and Times of England's Outstanding Bahá'í Pioneer Worker,* p. 240.
11. "News of the Cause," *The Bahá'í News* (New York), no.15 (January 1927): 8.
12. Shoghi Effendi to Hippolyte Dreyfus, 1926, manuscript, National Bahá'í Archives of France, Letters from the Guardian to France.
13. Procès-verbal de l'Assemblée spirituelle bahá'íe de Paris, (Nov. 1925). [Meeting minutes of the Spiritual Assembly of Paris, November 1925] National Bahá'í Archives of France, folder Bahá'í Community in Paris (1AC).

29 / Legal and Diplomatic Protection of the Faith

1. Mountfort Mills to Laura Dreyfus-Barney, 9 April 1943, National Bahá'í Archives of France, Laura Dreyfus-Barney Folder, File: Hippolyte "Correspondance passive" (1AP-II-D5).
2. The three major monotheistic religions: Judaism, Christianity, and Islam.
3. Mustapha Rowshan, *The Bahá'í Faith in Egypt: A Historical Survey of the First Twelve Decades.* Published with the approval

of the NSA of Egypt (2023) and available at http://rowshan-mustapha.com, pp. 34–39.

4. Mountfort Mills à Laura Dreyfus-Barney, 9 April 1943. National Bahá'í Archives of France (1AP-II-D5).
5. Beni Suef is a city in Egypt, located on the west bank of the River Nile, 100km south of Cairo.
6. Rúḥíyyih Rabbaní, *The Priceless Pearl,* p. 319.
7. Beba is a city located in the Beni Suef governorate.
8. Following the verdict, all four men remained steadfast in their faith. One of the wives expressed that, as a Bahá'í, the judgment did not pertain to her, and she chose to remain loyal to both her faith and her husband. One wife sadly passed away during the period of conflict, while the other two divorced. One of the husbands left the village, but the others chose to stay. From a letter written by Mr. Mustapha Roshawan to the author dated November 6, 2024.
9. Shoghi Effendi, quoted in Rúḥíyyih Rabbaní, *The Priceless Pearl,* p. 319.
10. Mountfort Mills à Laura Dreyfus-Barney, 9 April 1943. National Bahá'í Archives of France (1AP-II-D5).
11. Ibid.
12. Shoghi Effendi, "Hippolyte Dreyfus-Barney: An Appreciation," *The Bahá'í World,* p. 210.
13. It seems that Hippolyte traveled at least once with Mountfort Mills to Iraq, as Laura Dreyfus-Barney mentions a journey to Iraq in the timeline she prepared of Hippolyte's activities. See National Bahá'í Archives of France, Laura Dreyfus-Barney Folder, File: Hippolyte "Documents postérieurs à Hippolyte" (1AP-I-F).
14. At that time, Iraq was administered by Great Britain and was known as The Kingdom of Iraq under British Administration, or Mandatory Iraq.
15. Faisal I bin Al-Hussein bin Ali Al-Hashemi (1885–1933), known as Faisal I of Iraq, was king of the Arab kingdom of Syria in 1920 and king of Iraq from August 23, 1921 to 1933.

16. League of Nations: Permanent Mandates Commission. Minutes of the Fourteenth Session held at Geneva. Annex 17. Petition from the Bahá'í Spiritual Assembly at Baghdad, dated September 11th, 1928. National Bahá'í Archives of France, Laura Dreyfus-Barney Folder, File: "Documents rassemblés" (1AP-II-E).
17. Rúḥíyyih Rabbaní, *The Priceless Pearl,* pp. 94–97.
18. Shoghi Effendi, "Hippolyte Dreyfus-Barney: An Appreciation," *The Bahá'í World,* p. 210.
19. Rúḥíyyih Rabbaní, *The Priceless Pearl,* p. 61.
20. The Mansion of Bahjí is the house in 'Akká where Bahá'u'lláh spent the last thirteen years of His life until His passing in 1892. Located adjacent to the Mansion, the Shrine of Bahá'u'lláh is the point of adoration to which Bahá'ís face when saying their daily obligatory prayer.
21. Shoghi Effendi, "Hippolyte Dreyfus-Barney: An Appreciation," *The Bahá'í World,* p. 210.

30 / Until the End of his Days

1. Rúḥíyyih Rabbaní, *The Priceless Pearl,* p. 92.
2. National Bahá'í Archives of France, Paris—1925_dreyfus-asn-usa.
3. Rúḥíyyih Rabbaní, *The Priceless Pearl,* p. 92.
4. Mona Khademi, *Some Questions Answered: The Life of Laura Barney,* pp. 223–24.
5. Bahá'u'lláh, *L'Œuvre de Baháou'llah,* traduction française par Hippolyte Dreyfus, t. 3, (Paris: Ernest Leroux, 1928).
6. Hippolyte Dreyfus, *Testament d''Abdu'l Baha et ma traduction,* Manuscrit, National Bahá'í Archives of France, Laura Dreyfus-Barney Folder, File: Hippolyte "Manuscrits, traductions" (1AP-I-B).
7. *Tablette révélée par Beha-Ullah pour le père de Badí, le porteur de la lettre au Chah de Perse,* traduit par Hippolyte Dreyfus, tapuscrit, National Bahá'í Archives of France, Laura Dreyfus-Barney Folder, File: Hippolyte "Manuscrits, traductions" (1AP-I-B).

8. *Traité sur la Politique par Abdu'l Baha,* traduit par Hippolyte Dreyfus, tapuscrit, National Bahá'í Archives of France, Laura Dreyfus-Barney Folder, File: Hippolyte "Manuscrits, traductions" (1AP-I-B).
9. *Prières écrites par Beha-Ullah traduites par Hippolyte Dreyfus,* tapuscrit, National Bahá'í Archives of France, Laura Dreyfus-Barney Folder, File: Hippolyte "Manuscrits, traductions" (1AP-I-B).
10. *Kitáb-i-Aqdas par Bahá'u'lláh,* traduction de Hippolyte Dreyfus, manuscrit et tapuscrit, National Bahá'í Archives of France, Laura Dreyfus-Barney Folder, File: Hippolyte "Manuscrits, traductions" (1AP-I-B).
11. Laura Dreyfus-Barney, "Hippolyte Dreyfus-Barney," Article for *Bahai World,* (1AP-I-F).
12. In mainland France and also in its colonies in Asia and Africa.
13. Jan Jasion, *A Bábí and Bahá'í Bibliography from Gallica* (2013), accessible online: https://bahai-library.com/jasion_bibliography_gallica.
14. 'Abdu'l-Bahá to Hippolyte Dreyfus, National Bahá'í Archives of France (Letter-19).
15. Thomas Linard, Bibliographie des ouvrages de langue française mentionnant les religions babie ou baha'ie (1844-1944), [Bibliography of French works mentioning the Bábí or Bahá'í Religions, 1844–1944], published in *Occasional Papers in Shaykhi, Babi and Bahá'í Studies,* Vol. 3, June 1997.
16. Procès-verbal de l'Assemblée spirituelle bahá'íe de Paris, (mars 1928). [Meeting minutes of the Spiritual Assembly of Paris, March 1928] National Bahá'í Archives of France, folder Bahá'í Community in Paris (1AC).
17. Passport, 25/06/1928. National Bahá'í Archives of France, Laura Dreyfus-Barney Folder (1AP), File: Hippolyte "Papiers et objets personnels" (1AP- I-A).
18. Natalie Barney, *Hippolyte mon beau-frère . . . ,* (1AP-I-F). The French expression "avoir un bon coup de fourchette" trans-

lates literally to "have a good fork" and means "to have a large appetite."

19. The expression *Gloire de Dijon* refers to a specific shade of rose, something vibrant and/or healthy, and that could be seen as a way of finding hope or comfort in a challenging situation.
20. Ibid.
21. We do not know clearly which illness took Hippolyte. Neither the Guardian, nor his family, nor the reports of the Spiritual Assembly of Paris give any indication on the reason of his sudden death. It is only mentioned that he had "a long and painful disease." (See meeting minutes of the Spiritual Assembly of Paris, 1929).
22. The American Hospital of Paris à Laura Dreyfus-Barney, 28 December 1928, National Bahá'í Archives of France, Laura Dreyfus-Barney Folder, File: Hippolyte "correspondance passive" (1AP-II-D).
23. Shoghi Effendi to Laura Dreyfus-Barney, 21 December 1928, National Bahá'í Archives of France, File "Gardien à la France."
24. "Deuils," *Le Matin* (Paris) no. 16347 (21 December 1928), p. 2, col. 4.
25. Published between 1883 and 1944, it was one of the big four daily newspapers in France. Prior to the First World War, its circulation reached 1 million.
26. "Nécrologie," *Le Temps* (Paris), no. 24597 (22 December 1928), p. 4, col. 5.
27. Cimetière Montmartre – Partie Nord – Division 2 – ligne 1 – n.1 – Carré des Israélites, Chapelle "Famille Meyer-Dreyfus."
28. Shoghi Effendi to Laura Dreyfus-Barney, 21 December 1928. National Bahá'í Archives of France.
29. Ibid.
30. Shoghi Effendi à Laura Dreyfus-Barney, 21 December 1928. National Bahá'í Archives of France.
31. "Deuil," *Le Figaro* (Paris), no. 305 de 1928 (3 December 1928), p. 2, col. 5.

32. "Nécrologie," *Le Temps* (Paris), no. 24606 (31 December 1928).
33. "Lettres, cartes, télégrammes reçus" [Letters, postcards, cables] National Bahá'í Archives of France, Laura Dreyfus-Barney Folder, File: Hippolyte "Correspondance passive, condoléances" (1AP-II-D).
34. Ahmed Bey Yazdí to Laura Dreyfus-Barney, 22 December 1928, National Bahá'í Archives of France (1AP-II-D).
35. Monever [Munavar] to Laura Dreyfus-Barney, 23 December 1928. (1AP-II-D).
36. Lady Sara Blomfield to Laura Dreyfus-Barney, 24 January 1929. National Bahá'í Archives of France (1AP-II-D).
37. George Townshend to Laura Dreyfus-Barney, 26 February 1929, National Bahá'í Archives of France (1AP-II-D).
38. Adrien Barthélémy to Laura Dreyfus-Barney, 3 January 1929. National Bahá'í Archives of France (1AP-II-D).
39. Edith Sanderson to Laura Dreyfus-Barney, [undated]. (1AP-II-D).
40. Laura Dreyfus-Barney, "Hippolyte Dreyfus-Barney," Article for *Bahai World,* (1AP-I-F).
41. Alice Barney, [27 December 1928], National Bahá'í Archives of France (1AP-II-D1). Cécile Brunschvicg, 26 January 1929 National Bahá'í Archives of France (1AP-I-F). George Townshend, 26 February 1929; Lord and Lady Aberdeen: cable, 30 December 1928; Zia Bagdadi, 26 December 1928; Sara Blomfield to Laura Dreyfus-Barney, 24 January 1929; Pierre Couvent (League of Nations), 28 December [1928]; Marianne Girard, 30 December [1928]; Elle Goodall Cooper, 6 January 1929; Beatrice Irwin, 20 February 1929; J. Juster, 11 January 1929 to Laura Dreyfus-Barney; May Maxwell, 31 December 1928; Martha Root, [undated] 1928; Monib Shahid, 29 December 1928; H. Schloesing, 26 January 1929; Josephine Scott, [undated]; Corinne True, 6 January 1929; The London Bahá'í Assembly, 6 January 1928 [1929]; The

Spiritual Assembly of the Bahá'ís of New York, 17 January 1929, National Bahá'í Archives of France (1AP-II-D).

42. Natalie Barney, *Hippolyte mon beau-frère . . .* , (1AP-I-F).
43. May Maxwell, "Hippolyte Dreyfus-Barney," *Star of the West,* p. 26.

Epilogue

1. Shoghi Effendi to Laura Dreyfus-Barney, 24 January 1929, National Bahá'í Archives of France, "Gardien à la France."
2. Shoghi Effendi, "Hippolyte Dreyfus-Barney: An Appreciation," *The Bahá'í World,* pp. 210–14.
3. Ibid., pp. 210–14.
4. Shoghi Effendi to Yvonne Meyer-May, 24 January 1929, National Bahá'í Archives of France, "Gardien à la France."
5. "The Disciples of 'Abdu'l-Bahá," *The Bahá'í World* (New York), vol. 3, 1928–1930 (1930): 84–85.
6. Shoghi Effendi to Laura Dreyfus-Barney, 30 November 1948, National Bahá'í Archives of France, "Gardien à la France."
7. Ugo Giachery, *Laura Dreyfus Barney, Une appréciation,* pp. 17–18. National Bahá'í Archives of France, Laura Dreyfus-Barney folder: documents ajoutés [additional materials].

Selected Bibliography

Works of Bahá'u'lláh

L'Appel du Seigneur des Armées: Tablettes de Bahá'u'lláh. Bruxelles: Maison d'Éditions Bahá'íes, 2004. For English, see *The Summons of the Lord of Hosts: Tablets of Bahá'u'lláh*. Wilmette, IL: Bahá'í Publishing Trust, 2006.

Épître au Fils du Loup. Bruxelles: Maison d'Éditions Bahá'íes, 2001. For English, see *Epistle to the Son of the Wolf*. Wilmette, IL: Bahá'í Publishing Trust, 2006. 1st pocket-size ed. Translated by Shoghi Effendi. Wilmette, IL: Bahá'í Publishing Trust, 1988.

Florilège d'écrits. Bruxelles: Maison d'Éditions Bahá'íes, 2006. For English, see *Gleanings from the Writings of Bahá'u'lláh*. 1st pocket-size ed. Translated by Shoghi Effendi. Wilmette, IL: Bahá'í Publishing Trust, 2005.

Le Livre de la certitude: Kitáb-i-Íqán. Bruxelles: Maison d'Éditions Bahá'íes, 2014. For English, see *The Kitáb-i-Íqán: The Book of Certitude*. Translated by Shoghi Effendi. Wilmette, IL: Bahá'í Publishing Trust, 2003.

Les Paroles cachées. Bruxelles: Maison d'éditions bahá'íes, 2011. For English, see *The Hidden Words*. Translated by Shoghi Effendi. Wilmette, IL: Bahá'í Publishing Trust, 2002.

Prayers and Meditations. Wilmette, IL: Bahá'í Publishing Trust, 2001.

Les Sept vallées; Les Quatre vallées. Bruxelles: Maison d'éditions Bahá'íes, 2004. For English, see *The Call of the Divine Beloved: Selected Mystical Works of Bahá'u'lláh.* Haifa: Bahá'í World Centre, 2008.

Tablettes révélées après le Kitáb-i-Aqdas. 2e éd. Bruxelles: Maison d'Éditions Bahá'íes, 2010. For English, *Tablets of Bahá'u'lláh revealed after the Kitáb-i-Aqdas.* Compiled by the Research Department of the Universal House of Justice. Translated by Habib Taherzadeh et al. Wilmette, IL: Bahá'í Publishing Trust, 1988.

Le Très-saint-livre: Kitáb-i-Aqdas. 2e éd. Bruxelles: Maison d'Éditions Bahá'íes, 2011. For English, see *The Kitáb-i-Aqdas, The Most Holy Book.* 1st pocket-size ed. Wilmette, IL: Bahá'í Publishing Trust, 1993.

Works of 'Abdu'l-Bahá

Abdul Baha on Divine Philosophy. Compiled by Isabel Fraser Chamberlain. Boston: The Tudor Press, 1918.

Causeries d''Abdu'l-Bahá données à Paris en 1911. Traduction par Madame E. Hesse. 3e éd. Bruxelles: Maison d'Éditions Bahá'íes, 1987. For English, see *Paris Talks: Addresses Given by 'Abdu'l-Bahá in Paris in 1991.* 2024 reprint. Wilmette, IL: Bahá'í Publishing, 2006.

Les Leçons de Saint-Jean-d'Acre. Recueillis par Laura Clifford Barney et traduites par Hippolyte Dreyfus. 4e éd revue. Paris: Presses Universitaires de France, 1970. For English, see *Some Answered Questions.* Compiled and translated from the Persian by Laura Clifford-Barney. Newly Revised by a Committee at the Bahá'í World Centre. Haifa: Bahá'í World Centre, 2014.

Sélections des Écrits. Compilé par le Département de recherches de la Maison universelle de justice auprès du Comité du Centre mondial Bahá'í et de Marzieh Gail; traduction française réalisée par Pierre Coulon. 2e éd. Bruxelles: Maison d'Éditions Bahá'íes, 2014. For English, see *Selections from the Writings of 'Abdu'l-Bahá.* Compiled by the Research Department of the Universal House of Justice. Translated by a Committee at the

Bahá'í World Center and Marzieh Gail. Wilmette, IL: Bahá'í Publishing Trust, 1997.
Tablets of Abdul Baha Abbas. Vol. I. Chicago: Bahai Publishing Society, 1909.
Les Tablettes du Plan Divin. 2e éd. rev. [S.l.] : Publications Bahá'í Canada (Québec: Service de distribution bahá'í—Québec), 2012. For English, see: *Tablets of the Divine Plan.* Pocket-sized ed. Wilmette, IL: Bahá'í Publishing Trust, 1993.
Le Testament d''Abdu'l-Bahá. 4e éd. Bruxelles: Maison d'Éditions Bahá'íes, 1984. For English, see *Will and Testament of 'Abdu'l-Bahá.* Wilmette, IL: Bahá'í Publishing Trust, 1944.

Works of Shoghi Effendi

Dieu passe près de nous. Bruxelles: Maison d'Éditions Bahá'íes, 1970. For English, see *God Passes By.* New ed. Wilmette, IL: Bahá'í Publishing Trust, 1974.
"Hippolyte Dreyfus-Barney: An Appreciation by Shoghi Effendi," *The Bahá'í World* (New York) vol. 3, 1928–1930 (1930).
Messages to the Bahá'í World, 1950–1957. Wilmette, IL: Bahá'í Publishing Trust, 1971.
"The Immortal Lua," published in *This Decisive Hour: Messages from Shoghi Effendi to the North American Bahá'ís, 1932–1946 (Messages to America).* Wilmette, IL: Bahá'í Publishing Trust, 2002.

Other Works

Afroukhteh, Youness. *Memories of Nine Years in 'Akká.* Translated by Riaz Masrour. Oxford: George Ronald, 2003.
Alexander, Agnes Baldwin. *History of the Baha'i Faith in Japan 1914–1938.* [Osaka?]: Baha'i Publishing Trust of Japan, 1977.
Amatu'l-Bahá Rúḥíyyih Kh͟ánum, see Rúḥíyyih Rabbaní.
Ardei-Amini, Parivash. *Edith L. Sanderson: Une figure historique de la communauté bahá'íe de France (13 décembre 1870–18 septembre 1955).* Paris: Librairie bahá'íe, 2017.

Azízí, Azíz'u'lláh. *Crown of Glory: Memoirs of Jináb-i-Azíz'u'lláh Azízí.* Translated by Christopher and Nahzy Buck, edited by Hamid and Sandra Azizi. North Vancouver, B.C.: [s.n], 1991.

Balyuzi, Hasan M. *'Abdu'l-Bahá: The Centre of the Covenant of Bahá'u'lláh.* Oxford: George Ronald, 1992.

Barney, Laura. *The Way Reopens,* unpublished manuscript, Archives Bahá'íes de France, 1922.

Barney, Laura Clifford. "News Notes." *Star of the West* (Chicago), vol. 1, no. 18 (Feb. 7, 1911): 9.

Beede, Alice R. "A Glimpse of Abdul-Baha in Paris." *Star of the West* (Chicago) vol. 2, no. 18 (Feb. 7, 1912): 14–15.

Blomfield, Sara L. *The Chosen Highway.* Wilmette, IL: Bahá'í Publishing Trust, 1940/1967.

B. M. "Les paroles caches." *Revue critique d'histoire et de littérature* (Paris) t. 61, no. 8 (26 février 1906): 124–25.

Bouvat, Lucien. "Comptes rendus: L'œuvre de Bahâ'oullâh, traduction française de Hippolyte Dreyfus . . ." *Journal Asiatique* (Paris) t. 203 (oct.–déc. 1923): 343.

Boylan, Annie T. "Matrimony in the Bahai Spirit." *Star of the West* (Chicago) vol. 3, no. 12 (Oct. 16, 1912): 14–15.

Bricout, Joseph. "Religion et églises: IV. Quelques ouvrages." *Revue du clergé français* (Paris), vol. 43 (juin, juillet, août 1905): 127–129.

Brieu, Jacques. "Revue du mois: Le Livre de la certitude." *Mercure de France* (Paris) no. 179, t. 52 (Nov. 1904): 481–82.

Brittingham, Isabella D. "New York City." *Bahai News* (Chicago) vol. 1, no. 6 (June 24, 1910): 13–14.

Brown, Ramona Allen. *Memories of 'Abdu'l-Bahá, Recollections of the Early Days of the Bahá'í Faith in California.* Wilmette: Bahá'í Publishing Trust, 1980.

Butt, Abbasali. "In Memoriam: An Account of the Services of Siyyid Muṣṭafá Rúmí." *The Bahá'í World* (Wilmette), vol. 10, 1944–1946 (1949): 517–520.

Collins, William P. and Jan T. Jasion. "Lev Tolstoy and the Bábí and Bahá'í Faiths: A Bibliography." *Journal of Bahá'í Studies* (Ottawa), vol. 3, no. 3 (1991): 1–9.

D., F. "Revue des livres: Mélange historique et littéraire: Béha-Ullah: Les Paroles cachés, en persan, traduction française par Hippolyte Dreyfus et. . . ." *Journal des débats politiques et littéraires* (Paris) no. 121 (2 mai 1905): 2, col.1–2.

D., M. "Dans le volume Religion et sociétés, leçons professées à l'école des hautes études sociale . . ." *Revue critique d'histoire et de littérature* (Paris), t. 61 no. 17, (30 avril 1906): 291.

D., M. G. "Bahaoullah, L'Epître au fils du Loup, trad. H. Dreyfus." *Revue critique d'histoire et de littérature* (Paris), no. 41, (11 octobre 1913): 281–282.

De Bons-McKay, Edith. "Avec le premier groupe bahá'í de Paris: Quelques souvenirs de Mme Edith de Bons-McKay." *La Pensée Baha'ie* (Nyon, Suisse), no. 56, (juin 1976): 27.

Delines, Michel. "La Perse et les persans de nos jours, seconde partie." *Bibliothèque universelle et revue suisse* (Lausanne) vol. 29 (1903): 345–69.

Dernbourg, Hartwig. "Livres offerts." *Comptes-rendus des séances de l'année, Académie des inscriptions & belles-lettres* (Paris), 52e année, no. 4 (1908): 217–20.

"The Disciples of 'Abdu'l-Bahá." *The Bahá'í World* (New York), vol. 3, 1928–1930 (1930): 84–85.

"Échos et propos: Deuils." *Le Matin* (Paris), no. 16347 (21 décembre 1928): 2, col. 4.

Egea, Amín. *The Apostle of Peace, volume I: 1871–1912.* Oxford: George Ronald, 2017.

Esslemont, John E. *Bahá'u'lláh and the New Era.* Wilmette: Bahá'í Publishing Trust, 2006.

"Excerpts from Bahá'í Sacred Writings: 'Abdu'l-Bahá." *The Bahá'í World* (Wilmette), vol. 4, (1930–1932): 114–130 [118–119].

Fadil-Mazandarani, Asadu'lláh. *Tárikh-i-Zuhúru'l-Haqq* [Compilation of the History of the Bahá'í Faith in Iran], vol. 8. Téhran: Muassisih matbúát-i-Amrí, 1968–1973.

Fraser, Isabel. "Abdul-Baha in London." *Star of the West* (Chicago), vol. 3, no. 17 (Jan. 19, 1913): 5–10.

———. "Abdul-Baha's Arrival in England." *Star of the West* (Chicago), vol. 3, no. 17 (Jan. 19, 1913): 2–3.

———. "The Search for Truth: Address of Abdul-Baha before the Theosophical Society, Liverpool, England, Saturday Night, December 14, 1912." *Star of the West* (Chicago), vol. 3, no. 17 (Jan. 19, 1913): 3–4.

Freeman Gilstrap, Dorothy. *From Copper to Gold: The Life of Dorothy Baker.* Wilmette: Bahá'í Publishing Trust, 1999.

French, Nellie S. "A Notable Fellowship Dinner." *Star of the West,* vol. 16, no. 4 (July 1925): 504.

Gail, Marzieh. *Arches of the Years.* Oxford: George Ronald, 1991.

Gandhimohan, M. V. *Mahatma Gandhi and the Bahá'ís: Striving towards a Non-violent Civilization.* New Delhi: Bahá'í Publishing Trust, 2000.

Garis, Mabel. *Martha Root: Lioness at the Threshold.* Wilmette: Bahá'í Publishing Trust, 1983.

Garlington, William. "The Baha'i Faith in India: A Developmental Stage Approach." Published in *Occasional Papers in Shaykhi, Babi and Bahá'í Studies,* vol. 1, no. 2, (June 1997). [Online] https://www.h-net.org/~bahai/bhpapers/india1.htm.

Giachery, Ugo R. "In Memoriam: Laura Clifford Dreyfus-Barney, 1879–1974." *The Bahá'í World* (Haifa) vol. 16, 1973–1976 (1978): 535–38.

Glasser, Ph.-Emmanuel. "Petite Chronique des Lettres." *Le Figaro* (Paris) no. 38 (7 Gév. 1913): 5, col. 3.

Gobineau, Arthur de. *Les Religions et les philosophies dans l'Asie centrale.* Paris: Didier, 1865.

Gourmont, Rémy de. "Les idées du jour: Le Béhaïsme." *La France* (Paris) no. 263 (21 Oct. 1911): 1, col. 4.

Guharriz, Hushang. *Mubashirín-i-Míssáq dar Gharb* [Disciples de 'Abdu'l-Bahá en Occident]. London: Badí' Editions, 2008.

Hakim, Paul. *Sur les pas d'Abdu'l-Bahá à Paris: Paris deviendra un jardin de roses.* Paris: Librairie bahá'íe, 1998.

Hannen, Joseph H. "Washington, D. C." *Bahai News* (Chicago) vol. 1, no. 7 (July 13, 1910): 15.

Hansen, Jack Winsor. *The Sibyl Sanderson Story: Requiem for a Diva.* Prompton Plains: Amadeus Press, 2005.

Ḥaydar 'Alí (Heider Ali). *Bahaï Martyrdoms in Persia in the Year 1903 A. D.* 2nd ed. Chicago: Bahai Publishing Society, 1917.

Hippolyte Dreyfus, Apôtre d'Abdu'l-Bahá, premier bahá'í français: Sa vie, son œuvre. Rédigé par le comité pour l'histoire de la foi bahá'íe en France. Paris: Librairie bahá'íe, 1996.

Hogenson, Kathryn Jewett. *Lighting the Western Sky: The Hearst Pilgrimage and the Establishment of the Bahá'í Faith in the West.* Oxford: George Ronald, 2010.

Holley, Horace. *Bahaism, the Modern Social Religion.* New York & London: Sidgwick & Jackson, Ltd., 1913.

Huart, Clément (1854–1926) "Analyses et comptes-rendus: Behaullah. Le Livre de la Certitude (Kitab-el-Ikan). Trad. H. Dreyfus et Mirza Habib-ullah Chirazi. Paris: E. Leroux, 1904." *Revue de l'histoire des religions* (Paris) t. 50 (1904): 116–21.

———. "Comptes rendus: Bahâol'llâh. L'Epitre au Fils du Loup, traduction française par Hippolyte Dreyfus . . ." *Journal Asiatique.* (Paris), t. 3 (janv.–fév. 1914): 184–86.

———. "Comptes rendus: Hippolyte Dreyfus. Essai sur le Béhaïsme, son histoire, sa portée sociale." *Journal Asiatique* (Paris) t. 13 (mars-avril 1909): 309–11.

———. "Revue des livres: Analyse et compte-rendu: Les préceptes du Béhaïsme." *Revue de l'histoire des religions* (Paris) vol. 53; no. 1 (1906): 392–96.

———. "Revue des livres: Analyse et compte-rendu: Essai sur le Béhaïsme, son histoire, sa portée sociale." *Revue de l'histoire des religions,* tome 59, (1909): 364.

Jasion, Jan Teofil. *'Abdu'l-Bahá in France: 1911 & 1913.* Traduction Pierre Spierckel. Paris: Éditions bahá'íes France, 2016.

Jasion-Hurvy, Annie-Joëlle. *Lua Getsinger: La Dame en bleu.* Paris: Librairie bahá'íe, 2017.

Khademi, Mona. "A Glimpse into the Life of Laura Dreyfus-Barney." *Lights of 'Irfán* (Darmstadt) book 10 (2009): 71–105.

———. *Some Questions Answered: The Life of Laura Barney*. Oxford: George Ronald Publisher, 2022.

Kling, Jean. *Alice Pike Barney, Her Life and Art*. Washington, DC and London: National Museum of American Art in cooperation with Smithsonian Institution Press, 1994.

Knobloch, Alma S. "The Call to Germany." *The Bahá'í World* (New York) vol. 7, 1936–1938 (1939): 732–45.

Lacôte, Felix. "Bahâou'llâh (L'œuvre de), Premier volume . . ." *Revue critique d'histoire et de littérature* (Paris), no. 7 (1er Avril 1924): 143.

Lammens. Henri. "Bulletin oriental." *Études* (Paris) t. 137 (20 Nov. 1913): 523–38.

Le Lou, Louis. "Alliance Spiritualiste of Paris Reception to Abdul-Baha Abbas, Nov. 9, 1911." *Star of the West* (Chicago) vol. 2, no. 7 (Jan. 19, 1912): 2–3.

———. "Les livres: Religions et Sociétés: Leçons professés à l'Ecole des hautes études sociales." *Revue Chrétienne* (Paris), vol. 1 (1er janvier 1905): 412–13.

League of Nations: Permanent Mandates Commission. *Minutes of the Fourteenth Session held at Geneva. Annex 13: Petition from the Bahá'í Spiritual Assembly at Baghdad, dated September 11th, 1928.* (Geneva).

Lee, Anthony A. "The Rise of the Bahá'í Community of 'Ishqábád." *Études Bahá'í Studies* (Thornhill, Ont.), vol. 5 (Jan. 1979): 1–13.

Lefranc, Jean. "Le Bahaïsme et son prophète." *Le Temps* (Paris), no. 18386 (3 Nov. 1911): 4.

Mavaddat-Baghdadi, Roxana. "Un Oiseau parmi les oiseaux du paradis." *Bahá'í France* (Paris), no. 167, (Hiver 2011–2012): 19–21.

Maxwell, May. "Hippolyte Dreyfus-Barney: The Passing of a Baha'i Scholar and Lecturer." *Star of the West* (Washington, DC), vol. 20, no. 1 (April 1929): 26–27.

Mazel, Henri. "Revue de la quinzaine: Science sociale." *Mercure de France* (Paris) t. 60, no. 191 (1er juin 1905): 427–31.

Metelmann, Velda Piff. *Lua Getsinger: Herald of the Covenant.* Oxford: George Ronald, 1997.

Moulet, Alfred. "Mission Laïque Française: Une religion nouvelle: Le Behaïsme." *Lyon universitaire* (Lyon), no. 286 (15 mai 1908).

Myrtil Airel. "Le Bahaisme: Chez le chef de la religion universelle." *La Liberté* (Paris) (13 Oct. 1911): 2, col. 2–3.

Nakhjavani, Violette. *The Maxwells of Montreal: Early Years 1870–1922.* With the assistance of Bahiyyih Nakhjavani. Oxford: George Ronald, 2011.

Nouveau Larousse illustré: Dictionnaire universel encyclopédique—Supplément, publié sous la dir. de Claude Augé (Paris: Larousse, 1906).

Parsons, Agnes. *'Abdu'l-Bahá in America: Agnes Parsons' Diary, April 11, 1912–November 11, 1912, Supplemented with Episodes from Maḥmúd's Diary.* Annotated and edited by Richard Hollinger; with a foreword by Sandra Hutchinson. Los Angeles: Kalimát Press, 1996.

Pole, W. Tudor. "The First Universal Races Congress." *Star of the West* (Chicago), vol. 2, no. 9 (Aug. 20, 1911): 3–7.

Rastgár, Nasrulláh. *Kitáb-i táríkh-i Hadrat-i Sadrus-Sudúr* [The book on Sadrus-Sudúr]. Téhran: [Bahá'í National Publishing Committee], 104 E. B. / 1947–48.

Redman, Earl. *Shoghi Effendi Through the Pilgrim's Eye, Volume 1: Building the Administrative Order, 1922–1952.* Oxford: George Ronald, 2015.

Réville, Jean. "Analyse et compte-rendu: Religions et sociétés. Leçons professées à l'École des Hautes études sociales. Paris: F. Alcan, 1905." *Revue de l'histoire des religions* (Paris), vol. 53, no. 1 (1906), pp. 359–64.

Root, Martha. "A Bahai Pilgrimage to South America, cont." *Star of the West* (Chicago), vol. 11, no. 12 (Oct. 16, 1920): 206.

Rowshan, Mustapha. *The Bahá'í Faith in Egypt: A Historical Survey of the First Twelve Decades.* Published with the approval of the NSA of Egypt, 2023.

Ruhe-Schoen Janet. *A Love Which Does Not Wait: The Stories of Lua Getsinger, May Maxwell, Martha Root, Keith Ransom-Kehler, Hyde Dunn, Susan Moody, Dorothy Baker, Ella Bailey, and Marion Jack.* Riviera Beach, Florida: Palabra Publications, 1998.

Rúḥíyyih Rabbaní (Amatu'l-Bahá Rúḥíyyih Khánum). "The Guardian of the Faith." *The Bahá'í World* (Haifa) vol. 13, 1954–1963 (1970): 58–206.

———. *The Priceless Pearl.* London: Bahá'í Publishing Trust, 1969.

Savi, Julio. "Mayflowers in the Ville Lumière: The Dawning of Bahá'í History in the European Continent." *Lights of Irfan* (Evanston) Book 12 (2011).

"Séance générale de l'A.S. Le 2 février 1913: Réception d'Abdoul Baha Abbas, chef du Béhaïsme: la paix du monde et la fraternité de l'Orient et de l'Occident." *L'Alliance spiritualiste* (Paris) no. 4 (avril 1913): 99–115.

Sprague, Sydney. *A Year with the Bahá'ís in India and Burma.* With notes and a new foreword by R. Jackson Armstrong-Ingram. Los Angeles: Kalimát Press, 1986. [Originally published as *A Year with the Bahais in India and Burma.* London: The Priory Press, 1908].

Stendardo, Luigi. *Léon Tolstoï et la foi bahá'ie.* Paris: Éditions bahá'íes France, 2009. For English, see Stendardo, Luigi. *Leo Tolstoy and the Bahá'í Faith.* Oxford: George Ronald, 1985.

Stockman, Robert. *The Baha'i Faith in America, Volume 2: Early Expansion 1900–1912.* Oxford: George Ronald, 1995.

Sugar, Alfred. "In Memoriam: Florence George." *The Bahá'í World* (Wilmette), vol. 12, 1950–1954 (1956): 697–98.

Sur les pas de 'Abdu'l-Bahá à Paris. Sous la direction littéraire et artistique de Paul Hakim. Paris: Librairie Bahá'íe, 1998.

Taherzadeh, Adib. *The Child of the Covenant: A Study Guide to The Will and Testament of 'Abdu'l-Bahá.* Oxford: George Ronald, 2000.

———. *The Revelation of Bahá'u'lláh, Volume Four: Mazra'ih and Bahjí, 1877–92.* Oxford, George Ronald: 1987.

Thompson, Juliet. *The Diary of Juliet Thompson.* With a preface by Marzieh Gail. Los Angeles: Kalimát Press, 1983.

Voirol, Sébastien. "Chez les Babis." *Mercure de France* (Paris), vol. 58 (nov.–déc. 1905): 5–23.

———. "Livres et Idées." *La Revue diplomatique* (Paris) no. 17 (25 avril 1909): 11–12.

Weinberg, Robert. *Ethel Jenner Rosenberg: The Life and Times of England's Outstanding Bahá'í Pioneer Worker.* Oxford: George Ronald, 1995.

———. *Lady Blomfield: Her Life and Times.* Oxford: George Ronald, 2012.

Winckler, Bahiyyih Randall. *William Henry Randall, Disciple of 'Abdu'l-Bahá.* Oxford: Oneworld Publications, 1996.

Zarqání, Maḥmúd. *Maḥmúd's Diary: The Diary of Mírzá Maḥmúd-i-Zarqání Chronicling 'Abdu-l-Bahá's Journey to America.* Translated by Mohi Sobhani with the assistance of Shirley Macias. Oxford: George Ronald, 1998.

———. *Badayiu'l-Athar.* [Maḥmúd's diary, volume 2]. India: Karimi Press, 1921.

Archives Consulted

National Bahá'í Archives, France. Private archives of Laura Dreyfus-Barney (1AP), Folder Hippolyte Dreyfus-Barney (1AP-I), files:

A Papiers et objets personnels, [Papers and personal objects]
B Manuscrits, œuvres [Manuscripts, works]
C Correspondance active [Active correspondence: letters written or sent by Hippolyte Dreyfus-Barney]
D Correspondance passive [Passive correspondence: letters received by Hippolyte Dreyfus-Barney]*
E Documents rassemblés [Gathered documents]
F Documents postérieur à Hippolyte Dreyfus-Barney [Documents to Hippolyte Dreyfus-Barney after his passing]

Bahá'í World Center Archives, Haifa, Israel.

National Bahá'í Archives, United States.

Iowa Women's Archives, The University of Iowa Libraries, Iowa City.

Claudine Harris papers—Correspondence—Dreyfus, Hippolyte (great-uncle of Claudine Harris): letters, 1903–1914, Box 3.

Claudine Harris papers—Correspondence—Dreyfus, Hippolyte (great-uncle of Claudine Harris): letters, 1919–1925, Box 4.

---

* Including Tablets and letters addressed by 'Abdu'l-Bahá to Hippolyte Dreyfus-Barney, as well as provisional translations that were cleared for publication by the Bahá'í World Center.

Main Works and Translations Published by Hippolyte Dreyfus-Barney*

1898 Hippolyte Dreyfus. *Des Droits de succession du conjoint survivant dans le droit français et dans les principales législations étrangères. Paris: Arthur Rousseau.*
[Inheritance rights of the surviving spouse under French law, as well as in the major foreign statutes]

1904 Beha-Ullah. *Le Livre de la certitude (Kitab-el-Ikan): un des livres sacrés du Behaïsme.* Traduit du persan par Hippolyte Dreyfus et Mirza Habib-Ullah Chirazí. Paris: Ernest Leroux. [Bahá'u'lláh. *The Book of Certitude (Kitáb-i-Íqan): one of the sacred scriptures of Bahaism.* Translated from the Persian by Hippolyte Dreyfus and Mirza Habib-Ullah Chirazí.]

1928 – *Volume III: L'Œuvre de Bahá'u'lláh*

1965 – 3e éd. Paris: Presses universitaires de France

1973 – 4e éd. Paris: Presses universitaires de France

Bahá'u'lláh. *Le Livre de la certitude (Kitáb-i-Íqán).* Introduction par P. Spierckel.

1987 – 5e éd. Paris: Presses universitaires de France

---

* An informal translation of the titles is offered in square brackets by the author for ease of reference by readers unfamiliar with French.

1905 *Les Paroles cachées* de Bahá'u'lláh, traduit du persan par Hippolyte Dreyfus et Mirza Habib-Ullah Chirazí. Comprenant *Paroles cachées* section en persan, Les *Sept Vallées*, la *Très Sainte Tablette* et la *Tablette de la Sagesse.* Paris: Ernest Leroux.
[*The Hidden Words* of Bahá'u'lláh, translated from the Persian by Hippolyte Dreyfus and Mirza Habib-Ullah Chirazí. Including the Persian section of the *Hidden Words,* the *Seven Valleys,* the *Most Holy Tablet* and the *Tablet of Wisdom*]
  1944 – *Les Sept vallées.* Wilmette: Bahá'í Publishing Committee
  1944 – *Les Paroles cachées.* Wilmette: Bahá'í Publishing Committee

1905 "Le Babisme et le Béhaïsme."
Théodore Reinach, et al. *Religions et sociétés: Leçons professées à l'École des hautes études sociales.* Paris: Félix Alcan, pp. 247–86.
  1909 – *Babismus und Behaismus.* Frankfurt am Main: Neuer Frankfurter Verlag.

1906 Beha-Ullah. *Les Préceptes du Béhaïsme: Les Ornements, Les Paroles du Paradis, Les Splendeurs, Les Révélations, précédés d'une Lettre au Sultan de Constantinople.* Traduits du persan par Hippolyte Dreyfus et Mirza Habib-Ullah Chirazí. Paris: Ernest Leroux.
[Bahá'u'lláh. *Precepts of Bahaism: the Ornaments, the Words of Paradise, the Splendours, the Effulgences and the Tablet to the Chief.* Translated from the Persian by Hippolyte Dreyfus and Mirza Habib-Ullah Chirazí]

1906 "Les Béhaïs et le mouvement actuel en Perse." *Revue du monde musulman* (Paris) t. 1, no. 1 (Dec. 1906): 198–206.
["The Bahá'ís and the current movement in Persia"]

1908 "Le Béhaïsme: Conférence faite au siège de la Société Théosophique." *Les Annales théosophiques* (Paris) 1er trimestre (1908), pp. 25–46.
["Bahaism: Conference delivered at the headquarters of the Theosophical Society."]

1908 "Le Béhaïsme, Conférence faite le 23 mai 1908." (Lyon), *Publications de la Mission laïque française, comité lyonnais,* (1908).
["Bahaism: Conference delivered on May 23, 1908 at Lyon."]

1908 *Les Leçons de Saint-Jean-d'Acre* par 'Abdu'l-Bahá, traduites du persan par Hippolyte Dreyfus. Paris: Ernest Leroux.
[*Some Answered Questions* by 'Abdu'l-Bahá, translated from the Persian by Hippolyte Dreyfus.]

- 1929 – 2e éd. Paris: Ernest Leroux
- 1954 – 3e éd. Paris: Presses universitaires de France
- 1970 – 4e éd. Paris: Presses universitaires de France
- 1982 – 5e éd. Paris: Presses universitaires de France
- 2007 – 6e éd. Bruxelles: Maison d'éditions bahá'íes

1909 *Essai sur le Béhaïsme : son histoire, sa portée sociale.* Paris: Ernest Leroux.
[*Essay on Bahaism: its history, its social scope.*]

- 1934 – Nouvelle éd. *Essai sur le Bahāïsme, son histoire, sa portée sociale.* Comprenant *Le But d'un Nouvel Ordre Mondial* (extraits), par Shoghi Effendi; *L'Économie Mondiale de Bahāou'llāh* (extraits), par Horace Holley. Paris: Ernest Leroux.
- 1962 – 3e éd. Paris: Presses universitaires de France
- 1973 – 4e éd. Paris: Presses universitaires de France
- 1909 – *Universal Religion.* London: Cope & Fenwick
- 1909 – *Universal Religion.* Chicago: Bahai Publishing Company

1920 – *Einhets-Religion.* Stuttgart: Verlag des deutschen Bahai Bewegung
1922 – (*Târík-e amr-e bahâ'í.*) (Egipt): Tab'Matba'a as-Sa'ada
1968 – *Ensayo sobre la fe bahá'í.* Tarrasa (Barcelona): E. Deny

1909 *Une Institution Béhaïe : Le Machreqou'l-Azkār d'Achqābād.* Paris : Ernest Leroux.
[A Bahá'í Institution: The Mashriqu'l-Adhkár of Ishqabad]
1942 – Facsimilé in *The Bahá'í World* (Wilmette) vol. 8, 1938–1940 (1942): 525–32.

1910 "The Following Letter from Monsieur Hippolyte Dreyfus, of Paris. . . ." *Bahai News* (Chicago) vol. 1, no. 7 (July 13, 1910): 8–9.

1913 *L'Épitre au Fils du Loup par Bahâou'llâh.* Traduction française par Hippolyte Dreyfus-Barney. Paris: Libraire Honore Champion.
[*Epistle to the Son of the Wolf* by Bahá'u'lláh. Translated by Hippolyte Dreyfus-Barney]

1913 "Le mouvement Bahaï," *Travaux du 6 congrès international du progrès religieux (Chrétiens progressifs et libres-croyants).* Paris: Librairie Fischbacher, 1913.
["The Bahá'í Movement," Proceedings of the 6th International Congress on Religious Progress]

1923 "Le Bahaïsme."
La Vie Tunisienne (Tunis) vol. 6 (mars 1923): 61–63.

1923 *L'Œuvre de Bahá'u'lláh—Volume I,* compilation des Écrits Saints de Bahá'u'lláh, traduits du persan et de l'arabe par Hippolyte Dreyfus, comprenant la *Très Sainte Tablette,* les *Paroles cachées* en persan et arabe, les *Sept Vallées,* la *Lettre sur le Bayan.* Paris: Ernest Leroux.
[*The Works of Bahá'u'lláh—Volume I,* compilation of the Holy Writings of Bahá'u'lláh, translated from the Persian and Arabic by Hippolyte Dreyfus, including The Most Holy Tablet, the Hidden Words Persian and Arabic sections, the Seven Valleys, the Letter on the Bayan].

1924 *L'Œuvre de Bahá'u'lláh—Volume II,* compilation des Écrits Saints de Bahá'u'lláh, traduits du persan par Hippolyte Dreyfus, comprenant le *Temple de Dieu,* les *Lettres aux Souverains.* Paris: Ernest Leroux.
[*The Works of Bahá'u'lláh – Volume II,* compilation of the Holy Writings of Bahá'u'lláh, translated from Persian by Hippolyte Dreyfus, including The Tablet of the Temple, and Tablet of the Kings]. Note: This complete work, *The* Súriy-i-Haykal, is titled Súrih of the Temple in English and is published in *Summons of the Lord of Hosts,* including the first part, which is sometimes called the Tablet of the Temple.

1928 *L'Œuvre de Bahá'u'lláh—Volume III,* compilation des Écrits Saints de Bahá'u'lláh, traduits du persan par Hippolyte Dreyfus, comprenant Le *Livre de la certitude.* Paris: Ernest Leroux.
[*The Works of Bahá'u'lláh—Volume III,* compilation of the Holy Writings of Bahá'u'lláh, translated from the Persian by Hippolyte Dreyfus, including *The Book of Certitude*].

List of Maps

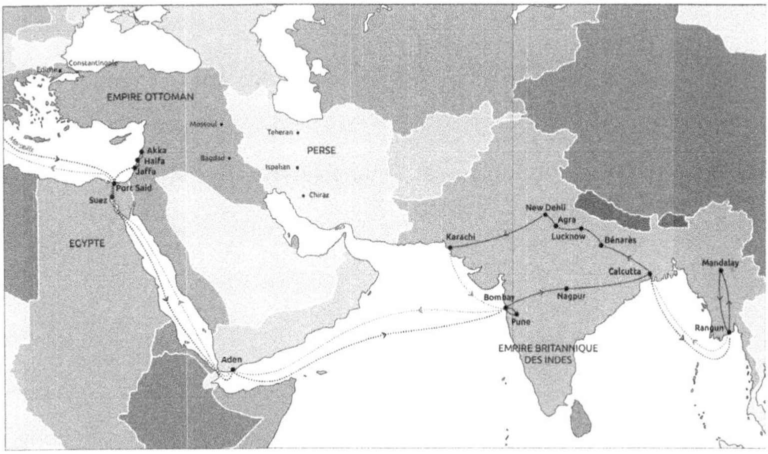

1905: Travel to India & Burma (See chapter 6)

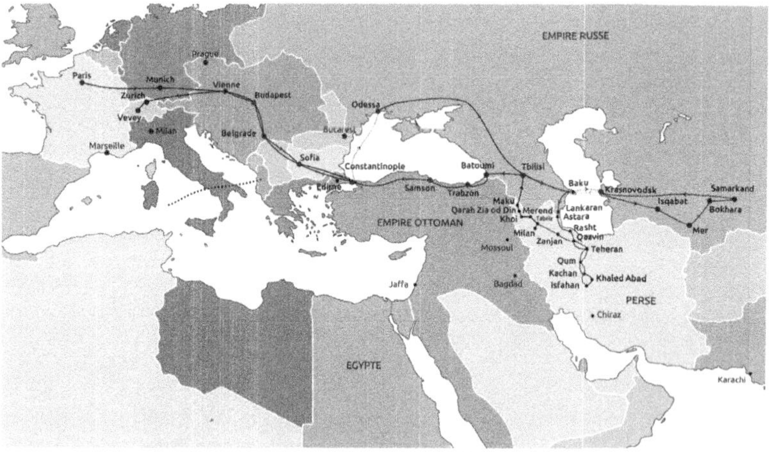

1906: Visit to the cradle of the Faith (See chapter 7)

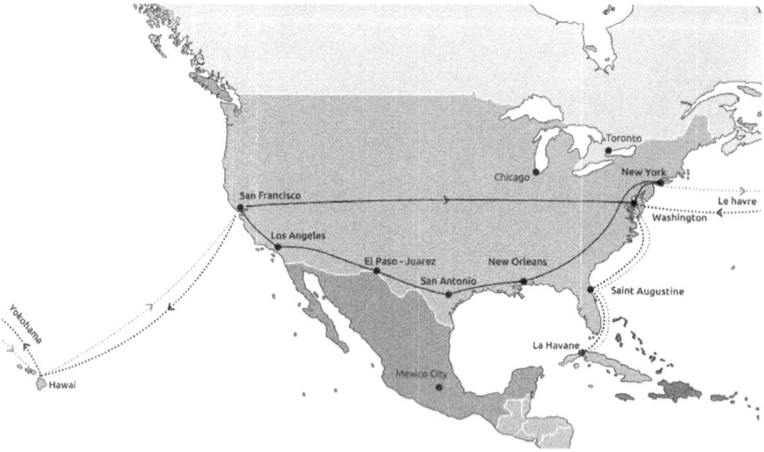

1914: Travel to the South of the United States (See chapter 21)

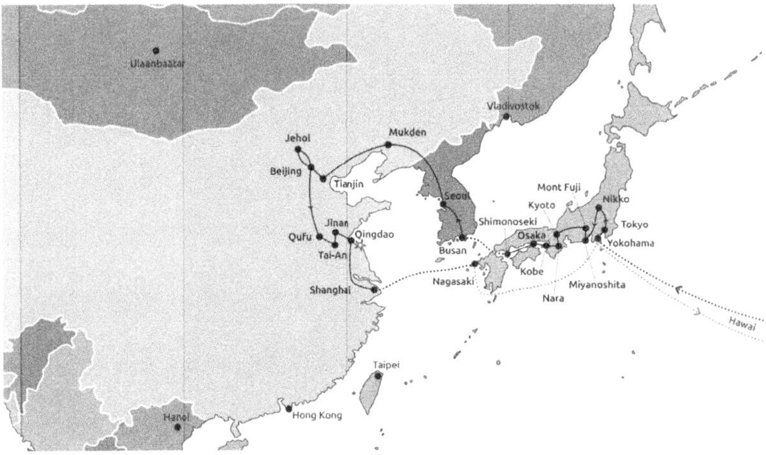

1914: First journey to the Far East (See chapter 22)

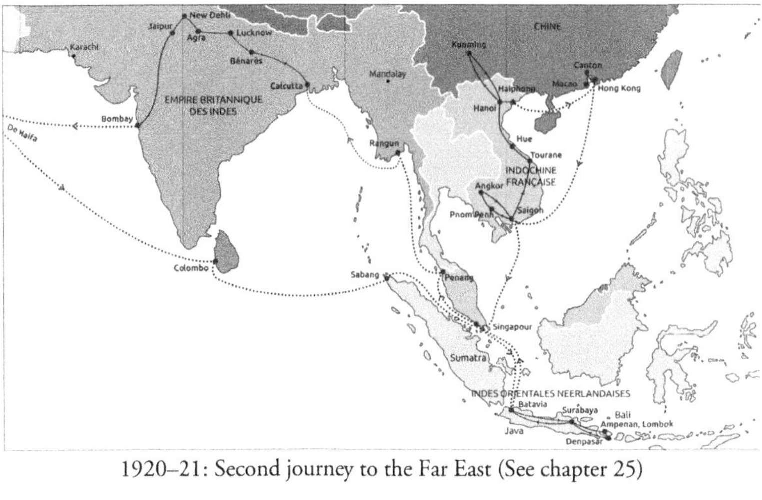

1920–21: Second journey to the Far East (See chapter 25)

Timeline

1817	*Birth of Mírzá Ḥusayn-'Alí Núrí, Bahá'u'lláh*
1819	*Birth of Siyyid 'Alí-Muḥammad, the Báb*
1844	*Declaration of the mission of the Báb*
	Birth of Abbás Effendi, 'Abdu'l-Bahá
1850	*Martyrdom of the Báb*
1873	Birth of Hippolyte Dreyfus
1892	*Ascension of Bahá'u'lláh*
1897	*Birth of Shoghi Effendi*
1901	First encounter with the Bahá'í Faith
1902	Declaration of belief in Bahá'u'lláh
	Meeting with the shah of Persia in Paris
	First visit to the Holy Land
1905	Second visit to the Holy Land
	Travel to India and Burma
1906	Travel to Ashgabat and Persia
1908	Third visit to the Holy Land
1910	First journey to the United States of America
1911	Marriage to Laura Barney
	'Abdu'l-Bahá's first visit to Europe
1912	*'Abdu'l-Bahá's visit to the United States of America*
	'Abdu'l-Bahá's second visit to Europe
1914	First journey to the Far East (Japan – Korea – China)

1914–18	*First World War*
1919	Fourth visit to the Holy Land
	Presentation of the Tablets of the Divine Plan in America
1920	Fifth visit to the Holy Land
1920–21	Second journey to the Far East (Indonesia – Indochina – China – Burma, India)
1921	*Ascension of 'Abdu'l-Bahá*
	Shoghi Effendi appointed Guardian of the Cause
1922	Sixth visit to the Holy Land
1924–26	Travels to Corsica, Denmark, Ireland, Mexico, Norway, Scotland, Switzerland, The Netherlands, United States, United Kingdom
1926	Seventh visit to the Holy Land
	Travel to Egypt to protect the interests of the Faith
1928	Passing of Hippolyte Dreyfus-Barney

Index of Photographs

Copyrights of the following photographs belong to the National Spiritual Assembly of the Bahá'ís of France.

Copyrights of the following photographs are held by the Smithsonian Institution.

Copyrights of the following photographs are held by the Bahá'í International Community.

Index

A

Y

Z